Medieval Music and the Art of Memory

The publisher gratefully acknowledges the generous contribution to this book provided by Villa I Tatti, the Harvard University Center for Italian Renaissance Studies; the Otto Kinkeldey Publication Endowment Fund of the American Musicological Society; and the University of California, Davis, Department of Music.

Medieval Music and the Art of Memory

Anna Maria Busse Berger

UNIVERSITY OF CALIFORNIA PRESS
Berkeley Los Angeles London

University of California Press
Berkeley and Los Angeles, California

University of California Press, Ltd.
London, England

Library of Congress Cataloging-in-Publication Data

Berger, Anna Maria Busse.
Medieval music and the art of memory / Anna Maria Busse Berger.
p. cm.
Includes bibliographical references (p.) and index.
ISBN 0-520-24028-6 (cloth : alk. paper)
1. Music—500–1400—History and criticism. 2. Music—15th century—History and criticism. 3. Composition (Music)—History. 4. Memory. I. Title.
ML172.B43 2005
780'.9'02—dc22 2004016542

Manufactured in the United States of America

14 13 12 11 10 09 08 07 06 05
10 9 8 7 6 5 4 3 2 1

The paper used in this publication meets the minimum requirements of ANSI/NISO Z39.48–1992 (R 1997) (*Permanence of Paper*).

For Karol, Trine, and Zuzia

CONTENTS

ILLUSTRATIONS

FIGURES

TABLES

MUSIC EXAMPLES

ACKNOWLEDGMENTS

This project was begun in 1992–93 when I was a fellow at Villa I Tatti, the Harvard Institute of Italian Renaissance Studies in Florence. I had planned to work on an entirely different topic, but within a few weeks, Jan Ziolkowski, a visiting professor at I Tatti, suggested that I look at memory texts and Mary Carruthers's new book, *The Book of Memory: A Study of Memory in Medieval Culture.* Little did I expect that it would be such a fruitful area of investigation. When I now look at the notes I made that year, I see that most of my ideas were already in place, although it took me another decade to work them out in full.

In October 1993, I read a paper on Notre Dame polyphony (chapter 5 of the present book) at the Annual Meeting of the American Musicological Society. After the talk, Edward Roesner was kind enough to tell me about an important unpublished paper by his student Stephen Immel (the paper has since been published) on the Vatican Organum Treatise, which allowed me to write another paper, on organum treatises, now incorporated in chapter 4. An earlier version of this paper was first read in March 1995 at Harvard University, and subsequently at the International Meeting of the Mediaevistenverband, Humboldt University, Berlin in February 1997. Various versions of chapter 5 were read at Music Departments at the Universities of Rome (1993), Cremona (1993), Göttingen (1998), UCLA, University of Colorado, Boulder, University of California, Berkeley, and at the Annual Meeting of the Medieval Academy of America at Boston in 1995. Chapter 1 was first read at the International Colloquium at Novacella in 1998 and at Oxford University, where I was an Astor Visiting Fellow in March 1999. Karl Kügle was kind enough to organize an afternoon's discussion on chapter 1 for the 2003 International Colloquium at Novacella. Chapter 2 was presented and discussed at the University of California Medieval Seminar, The Huntington Library, San Marino, California in March 2001. I read a portion of chapter 4, on discant and counterpoint treatises, at the Stanford Humanities Center in October 2001 and at the International Colloquium at Novacella in August 2003. Chapter 6 was given at the seminar "The Art and the Mind" at Stanford University, Center for the Advanced Study of the Behavioral Sciences, March 2002, at the University of California, Berkeley, October 2002, and at the Annual Meeting of the Medieval Academy of America at Minneapolis in March 2003. I would like to thank all of the scholars who attended these presentations for many valuable comments.

An earlier version of the section on organum treatises in chapter 4 was published in *Das Mittelalter* 3 (1998) and of chapter 5 in *Journal of Musicology* 14 (1996). I would like to thank the editors of these journals for their permission to use this material here.

In addition to the I Tatti fellowship, the research for this project was supported by a Guggenheim fellowship (1997–98), a National Endowment for the Humanities Fellowship for University Teachers (2001–2), and a fellowship at the Stanford Humanities Center (2001–2). I would like to thank all of these institutions for their generous help. The Committee on Research and the Dean of Humanities, Arts, and Cultural Studies at the University of California at Davis regularly provided me with research grants to visit libraries in Europe, order microfilms, and pay for research assistants. In addition, I received a Faculty Development Grant in 2001–2 that allowed me to finish the book.

I would like to thank Lynne Withey, Director of the University of California Press, for taking an interest in this project from the very beginning. Mary Francis, the music editor, and Rose Vekony were similarly helpful and supportive in the final stages of my work. This is my second book that Bonnie Blackburn has copyedited. As always, she has done much more than that by generously sharing her expertise with me and making substantial comments on virtually every topic. Leofranc Holford-Strevens checked and improved many translations throughout the book.

There are a great many colleagues, friends, and family members who have helped with this book. First, there is the I Tatti community, where I would like to single out Lina Bolzoni, Kathryn Bosi, Allen Grieco, Walter Kaiser, and Massimiliano Rossi. I Tatti lunches are a great way to learn new things and bounce one's ideas off colleagues. Then, at the Stanford Humanities Center I was fortunate to have feedback from John Bender, Paul Berliner, Marcel Detienne, Louise Meintjes, Marc Pearlman, and Haun Saussy. Lewis Lockwood was the first to suggest with characteristic acumen that I look at everything Ludwig and Handschin ever wrote. Little did I expect I would find such interesting material! Reinhold Brinkmann and Rudolph Stephan shared valuable papers with me and had much to say about Friedrich Ludwig and his students that would not have been available elsewhere. Reinhold Brinkmann, with typical modesty, never told me about an important article he had written on Ludwig, and I stumbled upon it more or less by accident.

My friend and colleague Christopher Reynolds was always ready to hear new theories and helped me to focus my ideas.

The following friends and colleagues either read some of the chapters or generously shared information with me: Margaret Bent, Lawrence F. Bernstein, John Butt, Hermann Danuser and Monika Schwarz Danuser, the late John Daverio, Lawrence M. Earp, Anselm Gerhard, Thomas Grey, Max Haas, Karl Kügle, Annegrit Laubenthal, Anthony Newcomb, Pierluigi Petrobelli, Alejandro E. Planchart, Anne Walters Robertson, Ursula Schaefer, Martin Staehelin, Leo Treitler, and Dorothea and Bernd Woydack. Special thanks are due to Friedrich Ludwig's grandniece, Annelotte Malik from Göttingen, who kindly shared many otherwise unavailable biographical details with me. Richard Crocker spent a lot of time on chapter 2, and I cannot begin to thank him adequately for all of the suggestions for revisions, comments, and most stimulating conversations.

The entire manuscript was read by Daniel Leech-Wilkinson, Michael P. Long, and Richard Taruskin. All three have made many useful comments and forced me to sharpen my arguments. I might add that reading the path-breaking work of these scholars has also had an impact on my thoughts. I would like to thank my students at the University of California at Davis who participated in seminars on memory, counterpoint, and notation. My warmest thanks to my research assistants Sarah Eyerly and Susanna C. Berger; to Andy Nathan, who typeset the music examples; to Anna Katharina Harboe, who was constantly available for computer problems; to Jeff Guentert, who set some of the tables; and to Patty Flowers, who has always taken care that I have the best possible working conditions at the University of California at Davis.

My father, Joseph Busse, a Lutheran theologian and anthropologist who spent much of his life in Tanzania, died when I was twenty-two. I cannot help but hope that he would have been pleased with this book. My interest in memory and orality can be traced back directly to his work on orality and to the many conversations he had with me when we lived in Africa and later in Germany. Similarly, I hope that my mother Erika Busse, who died in January 2003, would have enjoyed reading this book more than any of my previous work, which she found incomprehensible.

There are four people I would like to single out above all: Karol Berger, Edward E. Roesner, Reinhard Strohm, and Jan Ziolkowski have encouraged this project from the very beginning. They generously shared unpublished material with me, steered my work in new directions, constantly alerted me to new research that I would have missed otherwise, and reacted to the various drafts and ideas I was confronting them with. I believe I can honestly say that without their support this book would never have been finished. I feel very fortunate, indeed, to have had the support of such fine minds.

ABBREVIATIONS

MANUSCRIPT SIGLA

F	Florence, Biblioteca Medicea Laurenziana, Plut. 29.1
Mo	Montpellier, Bibliothèque Interuniversitaire, Section Médicine, H 196
MüB	Munich, Bayerische Staatsbibliothek, Musikfragmente E III 230–231
Tu	Turin, Biblioteca Reale, Vari 42
W_1	Wolfenbüttel, Herzog August Bibliothek, Guelf. 628 Helmst.
W_2	Wolfenbüttel, Herzog August Bibliothek, Guelf. 1099 Helmst.

OTHER ABBREVIATIONS

BL	London, British Library
BNF	Paris, Bibliothèque Nationale de France
CS	*Scriptorum de musica medii aevi,* ed. E. de Coussemaker, 4 vols. (Paris: A. Durand, 1864–76)
CSM	Corpus scriptorum de musica
GS	*Scriptores ecclesiastici de musica sacra,* ed. Martin Gerbert, 3 vols. (Saint-Blaise, 1784; repr. Milan: Bollettino Bibliografico Musicale, 1931)
KA	Karlsruhe, Badische Landesbibliothek
LEu	Leipzig, Universitätsbibliothek, Bibliotheca Albertina
Mbs	Munich, Bayerische Staatsbibliothek
MGG	*Die Musik in Geschichte und Gegenwart,* ed. Friedrich Blume, 16 vols. (Kassel: Bärenreiter, 1949–79)
*MGG*²	*Die Musik in Geschichte und Gegenwart,* 2nd edn, ed. Ludwig Finscher (Kassel: Bärenreiter, 1994–)
MSD	Musicological Studies and Documents
New Grove Online	*The New Grove Dictionary of Music Online,* ed. L. Macy, www.grovemusic.com
ÖNB	Vienna, Österreichische Nationalbibliothek
PL	Patrologia Latina

Introduction

While musicologists have long been aware that memorization played an important role in medieval education and that much of the music of the period was sung by heart, the role of memory in the creation and dissemination of polyphony remains to be studied. The reason for this neglect is simple. The music of the first important polyphonic collection, the Magnus liber organi, was written down in a notation that for the first time in music history attempted to specify not only pitch, but also rhythm. Consequently, the repertory has long been recognized as a milestone in the development of European art music. Thus, it was natural for scholars to approach the repertory with the same questions that were so fruitful for later European repertories, questions of authenticity and chronology. In other words, scholarship has tended to focus on the musical texts and their interrelationships, rather than on the cultural practices that produced the sources in which these texts are preserved. Underpinning this scholarship has been an unexamined assumption that the musical culture that produced the Magnus liber was literate in the same sense and to the same degree as later European music cultures.

Yet the repertory exhibits many features that are characteristic of oral transmission. The three main manuscripts of the Magnus liber organi are so different that it is impossible to arrive at a critical edition. Thus, the editor of the most recent edition, Edward Roesner, has chosen to publish the versions transmitted in each manuscript separately.[1] More than any later repertory, Notre Dame polyphony is characterized by what Fritz Reckow called "pasticciohaftigkeit," an appropriately macaronic term.[2] Scholars have generally explained the extensive interrelations among pieces as a re-

1. Roesner, ed., *Magnus liber organi.*
2. Reckow, "Das Organum," 474.

sult of the medieval habit of glossing and commenting on existing texts. Yet do we really know how and by whom the music was made and transmitted? None of the compositions is attributed to a specific composer in the manuscripts. Even though the performance of Notre Dame polyphony is attested in 1198 and 1199, all of the extant manuscripts were copied in the middle of the thirteenth century. It seems unlikely that all earlier manuscripts were lost. And finally, as Craig Wright has shown, there is every indication that the music was sung by heart; not a single manuscript is associated with Notre Dame.[3] In fact, no manuscript of polyphonic music ever appears in the lists of choirbooks or the inventories of the library, the treasury, the bishop's chapel, or the chapter house of Notre Dame. In short, there is every reason to investigate the possibility that this repertory was orally transmitted and that memory played a role in its creation.

While it seems somewhat surprising that so few scholars have explored the role of memory in Notre Dame polyphony, it makes perfect sense that no attention has been paid to a possible relationship between the art of memory and fourteenth-century isorhythmic motets. These are compositions in the modern sense of the word, attributed to specific composers. Thanks to Ars nova notation, which for the first time gave explicit relative durational value to every single note, composers were able to notate essentially every rhythm they wanted. The compositions display sophisticated structures with repetitive melodic and rhythmic patterns that would be jeopardized if a performer or scribe altered even a single note. In fourteenth-century isorhythmic motets these patterns were often applied to all parts and subjected to various manipulations such as retrograde motion and diminution.

Yet these works might also have benefited from the art of memory. First, it is generally assumed that they were sung by heart. Second, and more importantly, as Daniel Leech-Wilkinson and Jessie Ann Owens have shown in their pathbreaking studies, polyphonic pieces of the fourteenth through sixteenth centuries were not worked out in score but composed in the mind.[4] To us it seems difficult to imagine how this could be achieved. The question we would want to ask is whether the art of memory might not have provided composers with methods for creating polyphonic structures in the mind.

Just this short overview suggests that a study of the possible impact of the art of memory on music of the Middle Ages is long overdue. We would want to know how medieval singers managed to memorize and retrieve the chant. How was Notre Dame polyphony conceived? Was there such a thing as a final

3. Wright, *Music and Ceremony*, 335.

4. Leech-Wilkinson, "Machaut's *Rose, Lis*"; *Machaut's Mass*; *Compositional Techniques*; "*Le Voir Dit* and *La Messe de Nostre Dame*"; "*Le Voir Dit:* A Reconstruction"; Owens, *Composers at Work*. See also her "Milan Partbooks."

version of a composition? Can we really talk about composers? Was the composing done in writing or in the mind? If in the mind, at which point and by whom was the result transcribed into writing? Did the person who added a new text to preexistent music, or who borrowed from such music in any form, have the original text and melody written in front of him, or did he know the piece by heart? And why were thirteenth- and fourteenth-century composers so obsessed with creating tightly organized structures? (I certainly do not believe that all they wanted to do was to create a musical parallel to Gothic cathedrals.) How were isorhythmic motets conceived, in the mind or in writing? While we cannot expect to answer all of these questions, we will certainly be able to answer some if we begin to pay closer attention to the cultural context in which medieval music functioned. It is time to move beyond the vague parallels between isorhythmic motets and Gothic cathedrals, say, and look for relevant cultural contexts closer to home.

Among a number of book-length studies that have fundamentally transformed our understanding of the role of memory in composition and transmission of texts in pre-modern Europe, at least eight stand out: the precursors with particular interest in the Renaissance were Paolo Rossi, *Clavis universalis* (1960) and Frances Yates, *The Art of Memory* (1966). Jack Goody approached the problem from an anthropological background in *The Interface between the Written and the Oral* (1987). Mary Carruthers demonstrated the importance of the art of memory for the Middle Ages in her two monographs, *The Book of Memory* (1990) and *The Craft of Thought* (1998). Janet Coleman provided a survey of ancient and medieval philosophical thought on memory in *Ancient and Medieval Memories* (1992); Lina Bolzoni continued the exploration of the importance of the art of memory for the Renaissance in *La stanza della memoria* (1995), while Jocelyn Penny Small has connected the ancient art of memory to cognitive psychology in *Wax Tablets of the Mind* (1997). Of these, two authors have had a major influence on my thinking on this subject. Jack Goody has argued that it makes little sense to maintain a clear-cut distinction between oral and written culture. Instead, he suggests replacing it with a distinction between oral culture, on the one hand, and oral plus written and printed culture, on the other. The result is a considerable refinement of how formulas function in societies that have knowledge of writing, but still work out pieces in the mind. The adjustment Goody proposes might seem small, but it helps us to move away from the idea that once writing was invented, all features of an oral culture rapidly disappeared. It allows us, instead, to see in the musical culture of the Middle Ages a rich and complex interplay of oral and literate features. For me, Goody's discussion of the effects of writing on early literate societies is of particular interest: once you see something written down, you are able to analyze it, to compare texts. Writing resulted in the study of grammar, the making of lists and catalogues, the hierarchical classification of objects. Moreover, Goody shows that writing did not eliminate memorization; quite the contrary, the written page permitted different ways of memorizing material and texts. To quote Goody, "what is interesting about early schooling is that at the very moment when memory could be dispensed with for certain purposes, precise, verbatim recall came into its own."[5]

My work has also benefited tremendously from the groundbreaking books of Mary Carruthers. She too stresses that the introduction of writing resulted not in the elimination of memory, but in increased memorization. She has described this in fascinating detail and explained why the quality most admired among the learned throughout the Middle Ages was a well-developed memory. A scholar built up a memorial archive throughout his life from which he would draw in the process of composition. Thus, composition was not about creating a new, innovative work, as it has become in modern times: "Composition is not an act of writing," Carruthers says, "it is rumination, cogitation, dictation, a listening and a dialogue, a 'gathering' *(collectio)* of voices from several places in memory."[6] But perhaps most importantly, she demonstrates that the same techniques that were used to memorize existing texts were also used to create new works. An author who composed a work in his mind visualized it, usually with the aid of an imaginary architectural structure, or on a written page. These ideas are of central importance for our own understanding of the medieval compositional process in any field, music included.

The present study is an attempt to answer some of the questions posed earlier, an attempt inspired by the insights of a number of scholars of ancient and medieval culture, and guided by the desire to link our understanding of how medieval music came into being and was preserved with what we know about the creation and transmission of pre-modern texts in general. It is not a comprehensive study, but only a beginning, an exploration of several key aspects of this vast topic.

My first chapter is a historiographical study. It has become increasingly clear to me that the main reason musicologists have been applying Beethovenian art concepts to Notre Dame polyphony is connected with the fact that the field was created by the great German scholar Friedrich Ludwig, who transcribed and catalogued all medieval polyphony. In fact, he did it so well that subsequent generations of scholars have questioned almost none of his conclusions and reasoning, believing that he was doing a strict *Wissenschaft* without any presuppositions. A detailed reading of his publications made it clear

5. Goody, *Interface between the Written and the Oral,* 234.
6. Carruthers, *Book of Memory,* 197–98.

that he was full of prejudices of the evolutionary progressive kind. He judged medieval polyphony by comparing it to the music of his favorite composer, Palestrina, arrived at a chronology on the basis of Palestrina's style, and applied criteria relevant to the nineteenth-century autonomous artwork in trying to attribute compositions to composers and establish which version of a piece came first. Moreover, his work is full of blind spots, and he failed to ask some fundamental questions. He did not address the issue that medieval composers constantly reuse the same material, and he had little interest in music theory and the culture of the period.

I then contrast Ludwig with the slightly younger Swiss scholar Jacques Handschin, who brought none of these prejudices to music. However, Ludwig's hold over the discipline remains so strong to this day that subsequent scholars preferred to refine his questions rather than recognize that many of his presuppositions were wrongheaded. Ludwig's obsession with fact-finding and his exclusion of all cultural context can be blamed for the fact that to this day there are almost no studies of the impact of the art of memory on polyphonic music.[7]

The main body of the book is divided into two parts: the first explains how medieval musicians established their memorial archive; the second explains how composers used this archive in the compositional process. The memorial archive of the medieval musician had three components: chant, elementary music theory, and counterpoint. While the first two areas were important from the Carolingian times on, counterpoint acquired importance from the twelfth century on. The central question I will attempt to answer in each of the three areas is how its particular material was memorized.

In chapter 2, I suggest that music theorists and singers compiled tonaries not only, as is generally known, to choose the transition from the antiphon to the psalm verse, but also in order to memorize the chant. Tonaries classify chant first according to mode, then, within each mode, according to various differences, and then within each difference, liturgically, alphabetically, and by the distance from the final. Classification of material is generally a sign that it was intended to be memorized. Similar cataloging activity occurred in other disciplines in the Middle Ages. Elementary memory treatises recommend that if one wants to memorize long texts such as the psalms, the material needs to be divided into smaller units. More importantly, florilegia consist of excerpts and maxims from classical and biblical texts classified according to subject or alphabet. They functioned as memorial promptbooks to help in the preparation of sermons. Tonaries and florilegia were created with the same intention, to help memorize texts.

Chapter 3 concentrates on elementary theory treatises. After having mas-

7. See chap. 2 for a discussion of memorization of chant.

tered the chant, students had to learn intervals, the gamut, and, from the eleventh century on, solmization syllables and the hexachord. In this chapter, I consider not so much what they had to learn, but how they memorized the material. We encounter various short mnemonic verses to teach intervals, solmization syllables, etc. Equally important, entire treatises are often versified in order to help the student remember the material better. Finally, theorists use old mnemonic devices represented through a drawing, such as a tree, a house, and most importantly, the hand. In ancient mnemonic texts these structures were first memorized and then filled with whatever needed to be learned. Similarly, the hand was used for memorizing intervals as well as the gamut, and trees were used for memorizing modes and later the mensural system.

After having memorized the chant and elementary music theory, students from the twelfth century on (if not earlier) would learn how to perform and compose polyphonic music, the subject of chapter 4. Here too my work has benefited from the example of scholars working in neighboring disciplines. Historians of mathematics stress that arithmetic treatises of the Middle Ages and Renaissance are less interested in listing general rules than in describing individual problems for which they find solutions. Thus, the student essentially memorized the entire textbook. The same is true of counterpoint treatises: for us they make tedious reading, because the author will go through every single tone of the gamut and list all possible consonances, and then he will go through every possible interval and list all possible consonances. Again, authors and scribes will use various graphic means to help in the process of memorization. The consonances are then summarized in tables very similar to our multiplication tables that again were clearly memorized. Thus, musicians were less concerned with learning basic rules and more with memorizing various alternatives for setting melodic formulas.

The memorization of consonance tables and interval progressions brings up interesting problems about composition in the mind versus composition on paper and thus makes a smooth transition to the second part of the book. Jack Goody has pointed out that Egyptian mathematicians did their multiplications step by step and entirely in writing, while we, who have memorized multiplication tables, are able to do quite complex problems in our mind. Thus, the ability to write does not exclude composition in the mind. The situation is not much different in music: once students had memorized consonant intervals, basic progressions, and entire phrases, they were then able to plan entire compositions in their mind without having to write them down.

Part 2 is concerned with how the art of memory influenced the composition of music. In chapter 5, I explore the possibility that the rhythmic modes of Notre Dame polyphony were used as a mnemonic device. The rhythmic notation of Notre Dame polyphony is characterized by regularly recurring patterns of long and short notes. We would want to know why composers and theorists insisted on using inflexible rhythmic patterns even though separate note values that made flexible rhythms possible were already available. I would like to suggest that the invention of modal rhythmic notation might be related to the contemporary passion for didactic quantitative Latin poetry, where difficult material was put into verse form so that it could be remembered better. In both cases, the rhythmic organization depends on a regular pattern of long and short units: syllables or notes.

The last chapter attempts to answer the question of how polyphonic compositions, in particular isorhythmic motets, could have been composed in the mind. As mentioned above, we know that polyphonic pieces had been composed without the use of scores. For us it seems incomprehensible how this could have been achieved. There are three possible ways in which the art of memory could have influenced composition. First, the memorization of consonance tables and interval progressions allowed one to work out pieces in the mind. Second, I suggest that musicians were visualizing the music in their imagination rather than writing it down. Sight treatises make it clear that visualization played an important role in improvisation and composition. These treatises belong to a venerable tradition of texts describing mnemonic devices and have to be regarded as offering a first step in the compositional process. Advanced composers would be able to apply the same technique to entire polyphonic compositions. Third, mnemotechnics also provides an important background to understanding isorhythmic motets. We would want to know why thirteenth- and fourteenth-century composers were so obsessed with tightly organized sectional structures. I believe that *ars memorativa* provides a relevant background. The most common ancient and medieval technique of memorizing a text involved dividing the text into sections, devising individual "images" for each section, and locating these symbols in a reusable grid of "places." The grid of places fixed the temporal order in which the images would be recalled, and each image helped to bring to mind the section of the text with which it had been associated. Throughout the Middle Ages, it is not only the ability to retain something in memory that is admired, but also the ability to manipulate the material. If medieval writers could use mnemonic devices to construct their treatises and sermons, it should not be surprising that musicians used similar techniques when composing music. While a medieval scholar could demonstrate that he had really "learned" or "mastered" the text when he could recite it backwards, a medieval musician might be admired for applying inversions and retrograde movement to his tenors.

I hope that the results of this investigation will illuminate the intellectual and cultural world of the medieval musician. I would like to recapture the categories and images in terms of which musicians thought about their practice and imagined the materials of their art. I hope to challenge the assumption of pure literacy and replace it with a more complex picture of a world in which literacy and orality interacted. Thus, music will be placed in the larger cultural context of the period, not only within the already much studied written tradition, but also within the thus far unexplored tradition of *ars memorativa.*

1

Prologue

The First Great Dead White Male Composer

Why have musicologists been so slow to investigate the role of memory, when our sister disciplines have been thinking about these issues for more than half a century? Since the story I am trying to tell in this book is different from the one currently found in textbooks, it is important for us to understand where our notions are coming from. One of the most exhilarating musicological developments in recent years is that we have become much more conscious of our historical past. We have started to ask where, when, and why many of our views on music history originated. The best way to do this is to go back to the founding father of medieval music, Friedrich Ludwig, and the scholars dependent on him. A fresh look at Ludwig's background and achievement is needed if we are to understand his extraordinary hold on the way medieval musicology continues to be practiced.

LUDWIG'S LIFE, EDUCATION, AND WORK

Ludwig was born in Potsdam in 1872, the son of a gardener who tended the orchard of Friedrich Hiller, the Potsdam Stadtrat.[1] Since the Stadtrat had no children of his own, he decided to finance the education of the two sons of his gardener, neither of whom would have been able to study otherwise. It was a good investment, since both Ludwig boys became university professors. (Friedrich showed his gratitude by dedicating his dissertation to Hiller.) Ludwig's mother was a staunch Lutheran, his father a Catholic, and all five children received a strict Lutheran upbringing. Ludwig remained a devout Lutheran until his death. As we shall see, this religious commitment had di-

This chapter is dedicated to Reinhold Brinkmann for his seventieth birthday.

1. Communication from Ludwig's grandniece Annelotte Malik in Göttingen.

rect ramifications on his scholarship. He attended Sunday services regularly. According to his student Joseph Müller-Blattau, his favorite music was Lutheran church music of the seventeenth century, for religious reasons. Late in life, he chose to end an important university speech by reciting Luther's chorale: "Erhalt uns in der Wahrheit, gib ewigliche Freiheit, zu preisen Deinen Namen, durch Jesum Christum, Amen."[2]

Ludwig started out as a historian. He first studied in Marburg with Karl Lamprecht and Max Lehmann, and then wrote his dissertation, *Untersuchungen über die Reise- und Marschgeschwindigkeit im XII. und XIII. Jahrhundert* (1897), under Harry Breßlau in Strassburg. The dissertation won a first prize in a student competition and is an outstanding example of positivistic research. Ludwig looked at every available document, literary account, and bill to compute the average speed of troop movement during the crusades. He distinguished between trips on foot, by boat on a river, and by boat on the sea, he accounted for every night, every battle fought. He compared the speed of the troop movements to that of the messengers. Every statement is supported by detailed footnotes. There are many references to the work of other historians, and there is not a trace of the arrogance that he displayed in later musicological reviews. And yet this dissertation is very much in the same style as his later musicological work will be: he is concerned only with narrowly defined questions of fact that can be directly answered by reading the sources and he keeps speculation to an absolute minimum.

Having completed the dissertation, Ludwig continued his studies in Strassburg with the first German ordinarius in musicology, Gustav Jacobsthal, wrote his Habilitationsschrift with him, and in 1910, on Jacobsthal's retirement, became his successor. Jacobsthal was probably the most important intellectual influence on his life. Ludwig dedicated his *Repertorium* to him, had Jacobsthal's motet "Die Lehrer werden leuchten wie des Himmels Glanz; und die, so viele zur Gerechtigkeit weisen, wie die Sterne immer und ewiglich" (Daniel 12:3) sung at his "Rektoratsrede" in Göttingen in 1930, and made arrangements to have the same motet performed at his own funeral. Jacobsthal's intellectual formation was shaped by the Romantic Palestrina revival in Berlin. Several of Ludwig's students stressed that this movement also formed the most important intellectual background for Ludwig. In fact, Joseph Müller-Blattau draws a direct line from Herder via Thibaut, Winterfeld, Bellermann, and Jacobsthal to Ludwig.[3] I will examine this background later on.

Originally Ludwig wanted to write a major study of Italian trecento music that would have included a detailed discussion of fourteenth-century no-

2. Müller-Blattau, *Nachruf auf Ludwig,* 10.
3. Ibid., 7 and Besseler, "Friedrich Ludwig," 85.

tation, but the other medievalist of his generation, Johannes Wolf, managed to beat him to it and was the first to publish a study of trecento music[4] and then a *Geschichte der Mensuralnotation*.[5] The latter is a landmark in the study of medieval music. It consists of three sections: a study of mensural notation, a list of sources, and finally transcriptions of many pieces never previously available in modern edition. It is unclear whether Wolf knew that Ludwig was working on a similar notation project. When the book on mensural notation appeared, Ludwig wrote a devastating forty-four page review, concentrating mainly on small inaccuracies in the description of the sources.[6] Here is an example of a typical Ludwig put-down: "I am able to establish more or less important inaccuracies in almost all descriptions of manuscripts of the fourteenth and fifteenth centuries. Insofar as my own notes allow, the most important of these will be corrected here as briefly as possible in order to avoid further spreading of mistakes."[7] Similarly, Ludwig will start the discussion of a new section with: "The description is entirely insufficient"[8] or "the comparison with other manuscripts can only be called superficial, but we cannot go into it here."[9] (The interests of scholarship would have been much better served if Ludwig had read Wolf's book before publication and given the author the corrections, so that Wolf might have incorporated them into his manuscript.)[10]

One could argue that Wolf became the unfortunate victim of Ludwig's zeal to promote only the highest standards of scholarship in musicology. He had spent years analyzing the sources, and had all of the correct information readily available. It would certainly not have served our discipline to hold back all of this simply in order to spare Wolf. And indeed, this review and Ludwig's subsequent publications brought unprecedented standards of scholarship to our field.

Even though the review gave the impression that much of the book needed

4. Wolf, "Florenz in der Musikgeschichte des 14. Jahrhunderts."

5. Besseler, "Friedrich Ludwig," 86.

6. It is unclear to me how Ulrich Bartels, "Musikwissenschaft zwischen den Kriegen," 94, can deny that this is a negative review.

7. "Ich bin in der Lage, bei fast allen Beschreibungen von Handschriften des 14. und 15. Jahrhunderts mehr oder weniger bedeutende Ungenauigkeiten konstatieren zu müssen. Die wichtigsten sollen, soweit es mein Material erlaubt, im folgenden in möglichster Kürze berichtigt werden, um weiteren Verschleppungen der Fehler vorzubeugen." Review of Wolf, *Geschichte der Mensuralnotation*, 609.

8. "Die Beschreibung ist ganz unzureichend"; ibid., 614.

9. "Der Vergleich mit den anderen Handschriften ist nur als oberflächlich zu bezeichnen, kann aber hier nicht komplettiert werden." Ibid., 616.

10. When discussing Florence, Biblioteca Nazionale Centrale, MS Panc. 26, Ludwig admits in a footnote that Wolf told him that he himself wanted to publish a correction, but Ludwig nevertheless goes on: "ich glaube trotzdem die folgenden Zusätze und Berichtigungen nicht unterdrücken zu brauchen." Ibid., 614.

to be rewritten, Ludwig abandoned his project and turned full time to the other area that engaged his interest, the music of the thirteenth century. His work in this area culminated in the *Repertorium organorum recentioris et motetorum vetustissimi stili* of 1910,[11] to this day the most authoritative catalog of, and book on, thirteenth-century organa and motets. It was a work for which he prepared for many years, as one can see from his Nachlass in Göttingen. In the *Repertorium,* Ludwig gives the first detailed account of modal notation,[12] lists all concordances in the thirteenth-century repertory, orders them chronologically, and tries to establish which was the original and which a copy. He also includes detailed descriptions of all the sources of the period. The accuracy and ingeniousness with which the project was executed make it to this day a model for our discipline.[13]

The second part of the *Repertorium,* a catalog of thirteenth-century motets, although finished and typeset in 1911, was only published in 1961 by Ludwig's student Friedrich Gennrich. The reasons for the delay are quite characteristic of the way Ludwig worked:[14] he was a perfectionist and could not part with a work until he knew everything was correct. First, he wanted to await the publication of Jacobsthal's work on Montpellier H 196. Then, when he did manage to look at Jacobsthal's Nachlass in 1913 (Jacobsthal had died in 1912), he discovered that his teacher was still in the early stages of research. Therefore, Ludwig saw no reason to take account of Jacobsthal's work in his study. But unfortunately, he had in the meantime lost interest in the project; he was too busy with other things, and there was always the fear that new sources might be discovered, and that the *Repertorium* might not live up to his high standards. Heinrich Besseler, another Ludwig student, thought that Ludwig might have published the *Repertorium* in the 1920s, had he not been so overburdened with administrative duties.[15] In the end Gennrich published the manuscript essentially as Ludwig left it.

It is worth noting here that in his Strassburg years Ludwig became friends

11. Vol. 1: *Catalogue raisonné der Quellen,* pt. 1: *Handschriften in Quadratnotation.*

12. To this day, it is not clear who deciphered modal notation. Ludwig took credit for it and Jean Beck admitted it was Ludwig in his 1907 dissertation, *Die modale Interpretation der mittelalterlichen Melodien,* 98. See Gennrich, "Wer ist der Initiator der 'Modaltheorie.'" John Haines, however, has shown recently that there is no document to prove Ludwig's claim; see "Footnote Quarrels of the Modal Theory."

13. Let me give just one characteristic example of Ludwig's virtuosity. Since the MS La Clayette was lost at the time, Ludwig tried to reconstruct its entire contents from a copy in Paris, BNF, Coll. Moreau 1715. Unfortunately, the copy did not include the Latin motets. In spite of this, Ludwig's amazingly accurate reconstruction of the entire content of the La Clayette MS was vindicated when the mansucript was found again (Paris, BNF nouv. acq. fr. 13521). See also *Repertorium,* pt. 2, ed. Gennrich, 344.

14. Ludwig, *Repertorium organorum,* pt. 2: *Die Quellen der Motetten ältesten Stils,* ed. Gennrich, foreword.

15. Besseler, "Friedrich Ludwig," 87.

with and frequently consulted the great Romance philologist Gustav Gröber, who had a similar passion for purely philological research. Gröber's *Übersicht über die lateinische Literatur von der Mitte des VI. Jahrhunderts bis zur Mitte des XIV. Jahrhunderts* (1902) is medieval Latin's equivalent of our *Repertorium,* an overview so dense and well organized that it remains unsuperseded and indispensable nearly a century after its initial publication.[16]

After the war, Ludwig had to leave Strassburg, and after a short stay in Berlin, he was appointed to the musicology chair at Göttingen, where he remained until his death in 1930. From 1929 to 1930 he was rector of the university, the first musicologist in Germany to be so honored.[17]

In Göttingen, he returned to work on the fourteenth century. Just as he had been the first scholar to explain the system of modal rhythm, he was the first to identify a phenomenon he called isorhythm.[18] He published three volumes of the works of Guillaume de Machaut.[19] A fourth volume, the Mass of Notre Dame, although completely transcribed in the Nachlass, was published only in 1954 by Besseler.[20] The Machaut Edition too set new standards of scholarship and remains the best edition of his works, with the isorhythmic structure immediately recognizable from the layout of the page and with most variants in the different sources accounted for in the notes.

In 1924, Ludwig published a synthesis of all of his previous work in Guido Adler's *Handbuch der Musikgeschichte* (updated in 1929).[21] In addition, he published many substantial papers throughout his life.[22] Last but not least, his Nachlass, now at the Niedersächsische Staats- und Landesbibliothek in Göttingen, includes diplomatic and modern transcriptions of most known manuscripts of the thirteenth through fifteenth centuries. These transcriptions are so detailed and accurate, with extensive commentaries and musical analyses of the pieces, that Ludwig preferred them to microfilms.[23] The page layout of the transcription always reproduces the layout of the manuscript. The Nachlass has been consulted extensively by subsequent scholars, who often checked their own transcriptions against Ludwig's and found the latter to be almost always accurate.[24]

16. Ziolkowski, "Ernst Robert Curtius," 154. See also Curtius, "Gustav Gröber."

17. Jacobsthal's other student, Peter Wagner, had become a rector of the University of Fribourg in Switzerland in 1920–21. See Emerson, "Peter Wagner."

18. His first discussion of isorhythm, though, already occurs in his review of Wolf, *Geschichte der Mensuralnotation,* 622.

19. Machaut, *Musikalische Werke.*

20. Machaut, *Mass of Notre Dame.*

21. "Die geistliche nichtliturgische/weltliche einstimmige und die mehrstimmige Musik." The original edition was published in 1924.

22. For a complete list of his publications, see Besseler, "Friedrich Ludwig."

23. Gennrich, *Die Straßburger Schule,* 13.

24. Günther, "Friedrich Ludwig in Göttingen," 155–56.

Why did Ludwig publish so little of the material that is now in his Nachlass? I believe the main reason was that at the beginning of his career he was convinced that there was no interest in performing the music of the period. Ludwig wrote in 1905: "The main reason to work on and publish medieval music is not a practical but a scholarly one."[25] It seems likely that he could not really imagine that anyone would ever want to listen to any medieval music, with the exception of chant.

By 1921, his attitude had changed. In an article on Perotin, Ludwig stressed that the primary goal of musicological research was to bring music of the past back to life.[26] He regretted that so little of the Notre Dame repertory was available in modern transcription.[27] When Wilibald Gurlitt organized performances of medieval music at the Badische Kunsthalle in Karlsruhe, Ludwig wrote detailed and enthusiastic program notes with comments on the authenticity of the performances.[28] He was only too happy to provide modern transcriptions of organa, motets, and the final Kyrie from Machaut's mass. Leonin's and Perotin's organum *Alleluya Pascha* with the appropriate motets were performed for the first time, and it is clear that these performances marked the beginning of medieval music performances in Germany. They were soon followed by performances organized by Besseler.[29] Thus, by the end of Ludwig's life, the resurrection of medieval polyphony was well underway, and he can be seen as one of the people who made it happen. And if Ludwig had lived longer, he might well have published more of the material included in his Nachlass.

Ludwig taught a greater variety of courses in his Göttingen years than one would expect from his publications:[30] seventeenth-century music history (4 times), notation and paleography (4 times), Haydn and Mozart (4 times), reading of medieval writers on music (4 times), Handel and Bach (twice), medieval polyphony (only once), Beethoven (3 times), the history of older instrumental music (3 times). This shows that he was interested in composers and periods outside the scope of his published oeuvre.

Ludwig was only fifty-eight years old when he died. It is astounding that one person could achieve as much as he did in such a short life span. When Ludwig started we knew next to nothing about medieval music. By the end of his life all existing sources had been transcribed and analyzed. In the

25. "Der in erster Linie stehende Zweck von Untersuchungen und Publikationen über die mittelalterliche Mehrstimmigkeit ist kein praktischer, sondern ein wissenschaftlicher." Review of Wolf, *Geschichte der Mensuralnotation*, 620.

26. Ludwig, "Perotinus Magnus."

27. Ibid., 369.

28. "Musik des Mittelalters in der Badischen Kunsthalle Karlsruhe."

29. Besseler, "Musik des Mittelalters in der Hamburger Musikhalle."

30. The courses are listed every year in *Zeitschrift für Musikwissenschaft*, 1920–30.

process, he deciphered modal notation, discovered isorhythm, and traced the evolution of musical genres. Ludwig, then, was the first musicologist to apply the strict philological methods of classicists like Ulrich von Wilamowitz-Moellendorf and Gustav Gröber to music. This meant a conscious decision to concentrate almost exclusively on sources to the exclusion of almost everything else. It is characteristic that in his lecture *Die Aufgaben der Forschung auf dem Gebiet der mittelalterlichen Musikgeschichte* at the beginning of his career (1906), he stressed that scholars had been much too concerned with theory and that the sources should be much more central to the discipline. He praised the making of catalogs as "an extremely rewarding task."[31] Similarly, in his last lecture, *Die Erforschung der Musik des Mittelalters. Festrede im Namen der Georg August-Universität am 4. Juni 1930,* in which he summed up the achievements of the previous fifteen years, he was concerned only with the discovery of new sources and the proper evaluation of old ones.

Precisely because Ludwig concentrated narrowly on source studies and did them so well, scholars have been reluctant to question his presuppositions. The work that is interested only in "facts," which asks no more than "Who did what when," appears to be without presuppositions. And yet, we know that any scholar brings certain biases to his work. What were Ludwig's? We need to examine his background, to see what questions he asked and how he arrived at his conclusions, and we need to see to what extent we are still under his spell. In the following sections, I will show where Ludwig came from and what he brought and did not bring to the study of medieval polyphony. I will juxtapose his view of the Middle Ages with that of the other great scholar of the first half of this century, Jacques Handschin, a scholar who seems to have had much less impact. And I hope to be able to show how the overwhelming presence of Ludwig has prevented us from addressing new questions.

THE PALESTRINA REVIVAL

I mentioned earlier that several of Ludwig's students stressed his background in the Romantic Palestrina revival. The movement was a direct result of the rise of autonomous music in the eighteenth century. Vocal music became subordinated to instrumental music. The central genres were symphonies, string quartets, operas. Church music, which had taken center stage until then, was suddenly relegated to a secondary position. This was a matter of grave concern to many Christians, who therefore started looking to music of the past, in particular of ancient Italian composers, for models.

The first person to elevate Palestrina and his contemporaries to the highest realm was the Lutheran Pastor Johann Gottfried Herder. During his stud-

31. "[E]ine überaus lohnende Aufgabe," 7.

ies in Königsberg from 1762 to 1764, he started an intense exchange with Johann Georg Hamann and Johann Friedrich Reichardt on the state of true church music. Herder's starting point was the observation that church music no longer affected the congregation as it used to.[32] Gradually he came to the conclusion that, as he argued in "Cäcilia" (1793), if composers of church music would imitate great composers of the past, the congregations would be moved, "because which music of marvel and the heart did you use, holy Cecilia, to inspire your favorite composers Leo, Durante, Palestrina, Marcello, Pergolesi, Bach, and Handel?"[33] He demanded further that church music should always be performed *a cappella*,[34] and that it should not be dramatic.[35] This excluded Bach's cantatas from the service.

Herder's ideas were developed further by his old Königsberg friend Johann Friedrich Reichardt.[36] After a trip to Italy in 1783, where he heard the music of Palestrina, Reichardt founded the "Concert spiritual" in Berlin in 1784, in imitation of the Parisian concerts of the same name. His program notes for the concerts played an important role in the revival of church music. His writings are full of such expressions as "pure (*rein*) church music" and "high simplicity of the singing" (*hohe Simplizität im Gesang*).[37] He refers to Palestrina as a "saint of music" (*Musikheiliger*), as "the most important composer known to us of the elevated solemn style."[38] In 1805, Reichardt wrote that the only

32. See H. Günther, *Johann Gottfried Herders Stellung zur Musik*, 9–13.

33. "[D]enn, heilige Cäcilia, mit welchen Wunder- und Herzenstönen hast du deine Lieblinge, Leo, Durante, Palestrina, Marcello, Pergolesi, Bach, Händel begeistert?"; Herder, "Cäcilia," 260.

34. "The basis of sacred music is the choir. . . . Only by way of the choir (in the broadest meaning) does one reach that emotion and feeling which this music demands." "Die Basis der heiligen Musik ist Chor. . . . Nur auf dem Wege des Chors (im weitesten Verstande genommen) gelangt man zu jener Bewegung und Rührung, die diese Musik erfordert." Ibid., 261–62.

35. "The holy voice speaks from heaven; it is the voice of God and not of people; woe to it [the voice of God], if in order to be visible, it were to put on a theatrical gown! This invisibility, if I may call it thus, extends to the smallest arrangements and circumstances of the sacred art of music. An aria, a duet or trio, which shines on its own, each syllable in which the poet or artist speaks in order to show himself, is detrimental to the effect of the whole and will be unbearable for the pure emotion. . . . Dramatic and church music are as different from one another as eye and ear." "Die heilige Stimme spricht vom Himmel herab; sie ist Gottes Stimme und nicht der Menschen; weh ihr, wenn sie, um sich sichtbar zu machen, ein theatralisches Gewand anleget! Diese Unsichtbarkeit, wenn ich sie so nennen darf, erstreckt sich bis auf die kleinsten Anordnungen und Verhältnisse der geistlichen Tonkunst. Eine Arie, ein Duett oder Terzett, das einzeln glänzt, jede Sylbe, in welcher der Dichter oder Künstler spricht, um sich zu zeigen, schadet der Wirkung des Ganzen und wird dem reinen Gefühl unausstehlich. Dramatische und Kirchenmusik sind voneinander so unterschieden, wie Ohr und Auge." Ibid., 265.

36. Salmen, *Johann Friedrich Reichardt*, 97 and 141.

37. For the best account of Reichardt's view on Palestrina, see ibid., 284–87.

38. "[D]en größten uns bekannt gewordenen Komponisten in dem erhabenen feierlichen Stil"; *Musikalisches Kunstmagazin* 2 (1791): 55; see also Salmen, *Johann Friedrich Reichardt*, 286.

subject of music was "the inner self" (*der innere Mensch*), and "the effect on the heart is the first and highest purpose of the art of music."[39] Note the use of the adjectives "rein" and "innere," which are characteristic of the nineteenth-century attitude to classical polyphony and were still used by Ludwig. With Reichardt, the center of the movement was transferred to Berlin.

In 1789, the Singakademie in Berlin was opened by C. Fasch to stimulate the revival of choral singing. In one of the central documents of the movement, E. T. A. Hoffmann's essay on "Alte und neue Kirchenmusik" of 1814, Palestrina is elevated to a central position: "Palestrina's simple, dignified works are conceived in the highest spirit of piety and love and proclaim godliness with power and splendour."[40] He described Palestrina's music as follows:

> His music can in fact be described by words with which the Italians have designated the work of many composers who are shallow and perfunctory beside him; it really is music from the other world (musica dell'altro mondo). The movement of the individual parts recalls plainsong; rarely do they exceed the compass of a sixth, and never does an interval occur that is difficult to pitch, or as they say, does not lie in the throat. It goes without saying that Palestrina, following the practice of the time, wrote only for voices, with no instrumental accompaniment. Praise of the highest and holiest should flow straight from the human breast, without any foreign admixture or intermediary.[41]

Hoffmann differs from the others in that he does not believe it possible to resurrect the old style in modern composition. For him Palestrina has been replaced by Beethoven. Rather than composing new music in the style of Palestrina, Hoffmann demands systematic study of the history of church music and publications of early music.

In 1825, the Heidelberg law professor Anton Friedrich Justus Thibaut published a book, *Über die Reinheit der Tonkunst,* in which he argued that declining musical tastes could be refined through the reintroduction of old music into the Catholic and Lutheran service. He demanded editions of old music and considered "the editing of such a work much more glorious . . . than the eternal disagreeable self-creating."[42] He would like to see the founding of church music schools where "reine Tonkunst" would be taught. In other words, he advocated for music what the Nazarenes did for art. The Nazarenes were German artists living in Rome who practiced Catholicism by painting religious paintings inspired by art of the Middle Ages and Renaissance.

Thibaut wanted people of superior moral quality to gather in societies to

39. "[D]ie Wirkung aufs Herz ist der erste höhere Zweck der Tonkunst." *Berliner Musikzeitung* (1805): 53. See also Salmen, "Johann Friedrich Reichardt."

40. "Old and New Church Music," 357.

41. Ibid., 358.

42. "[D]ie Bearbeitung eines solchen Werkes weit ruhmvoller . . . als das ewige leidige Selbstschaffen." Thibaut, *Über die Reinheit der Tonkunst,* 15.

perform old music. "Rein," a term we will often encounter in Ludwig's writings, refers to many different things. The editor of the third edition, Ministerialrat Dr. K. Bähr, describes what the term "rein" implies for Thibaut:

> With this "purity" [*Reinheit*] he is, of course, referring not to the technical [purity], the purity of the setting or performance, but [the purity] of the art of music; for him it was a very different [purity], a higher, I would like to say moral, one, and one is fully justified in calling his book a moral act in the musical realm. He had an inborn sense for the truly ideal and sublime, for everything noble, exalted, and pure, and he combined it with an extremely fine and secure tact, to find it everywhere and call our attention to it. . . . This view of "purity" made him an irreconcilable enemy of everything soft, common, unhealthy, and light. This view guided him not only in the selection of the pieces that he had sung, but also in the selection of members for his choir.[43]

The immediate meaning of *rein* concerns the classical or classicist ideal of simplicity, but it also refers to the childlike naïveté of the Nazarenes. In music, the term *rein* implies strict counterpoint, *a cappella* style. But, in more general terms, it also expresses moral integrity and religious separation from the profane. True church music, or, as Thibaut calls it, "heilige Tonkunst" (sacred art of music) presupposes "a deep, quiet, inward-turned, pure soul."[44] It almost goes without saying that Thibaut was deeply religious.[45] He wanted to hear only choral music in large cathedrals (he approved of instrumental music for concert halls). He banned all secular music from church: "Thus, I would consider it inexcusable if even a single measure from the devout songs of Palestrina were to be included in an opera piece; on the other hand, it would be equally revolting if a mass would include even a tiny bit of the ingenious grace that distinguishes Mozart's *Figaro* in such a unique way."[46]

Thibaut set his ideas into practice: he conducted an amateur chorus that performed early music. His rehearsals were attended by Goethe, Tieck, Men-

43. "Mit dieser '*Reinheit*' meinte er natürlich nicht die technische, die Reinheit des Tonsatzes oder der Aufführung, sondern die der *Tonkunst;* es war ihm eine ganz andere, höhere, ich möchte sagen *sittliche,* und man kann mit vollem Recht seine Schrift eine sittliche Tat auf dem musikalischen Gebiete nennen. Er hatte einen angeborenen Sinn für das wahrhaft Ideale und Grossartige, für alles Edle, Erhabene und Reine und verband damit einen überaus feinen und sicheren Takt, es überall herauszufinden und darauf aufmerksam zu machen. . . . Jener Standpunkt der 'Reinheit' machte ihn zum unversöhnlichen Feind alles Seichten, Gemeinen, Ungesunden und Leichtfertigen, er leitete ihn nicht bloss bei der Wahl der Stücke, die er singen liess, sondern auch bei der Wahl der Mitglieder seines Singvereinen." Ibid., 84.

44. "[E]in tiefes, beruhigtes, in sich gekehrtes, reines Gemüt." Ibid., 41–42.

45. Ibid., 31.

46. "Ich würde es also für unverzeihlich halten, wenn aus frommen Gesängen von Palestrina nur ein einziger Takt in ein Opernstück aufgenommen werden könnte; aber abscheulich wäre es auch dagegen, wenn in einer Messe nur das Kleinste vorkäme von der genialen Leichtfertigkeit, wodurch sich Mozarts Figaro auf eine fast einzige Art auszeichnet." Ibid., 23.

delssohn, Schumann, and Hegel. Thibaut's book remained popular throughout the nineteenth and early twentieth centuries; the third edition was published in 1907.[47]

Strangely enough, another important figure in the movement was also a legal scholar, Carl von Winterfeld, the author of *Pierluigi Palestrina* (1822), *Johannes Gabrieli und sein Zeitalter* (1843), and *Der evangelische Kirchengesang* (1843).[48] In the latter book, Winterfeld proposed to see a German Palestrina in Johann Eccard. Winterfeld was an enthusiastic supporter of the Prussian monarchy and believed he found a similar attitude to his country in Johann Eccard.[49] He supervised numerous publications of Eccard's music. Another result of his book was that the Lutheran Church started to reintroduce the Lutheran chorale in the service and sing Palestrina and Lasso motets in German translation. These developments paralleled the Catholic rediscovery of Palestrina and Gregorian chant.

Yet another Berlin figure, Eduard Grell (1800–86), was the most radical advocate of *a cappella* music in the style of Palestrina.[50] Grell was both a conductor at the Berlin Singakademie and a composition teacher at the Akademie der Künste, but the only kind of composition he taught was in the style of Palestrina. He disapproved of all instrumental music and for this reason tried to boycott Joseph Joachim's appointment to the Akademie.

Grell's student Heinrich Bellermann was appointed to a professorship at Berlin University in 1867 and studied mainly sixteenth-century music history.[51] His book *Contrapunkt* was published in Berlin in 1862 and dedicated to his teacher. Like Grell, he advocated composition of music in the style of Palestrina not because he longed for a past time, but because he considered Renaissance polyphony as something eternally true and superior.[52] In his view, nineteenth-century music found itself in a state of sad decline. He wrote in the introduction to his textbook *Contrapunkt:*

> The present book is therefore written mainly for the future voice teacher, who is supposed to become acquainted through it with those times in which vocal

47. According to Professor Martin Staehelin, the music library at the University of Göttingen, where all of Ludwig's books went after his death, owned a copy of Thibaut's book with annotations by Ludwig. As of October, 2002, the book was listed in the catalogue, but could not be found anywhere. I would like to thank Christopher Reynolds for investigating this matter.

48. Other legal scholars active in the Palestrina movement were E. T. A. Hoffmann and Wilhelm Heinrich Wackenroder. See also Nowak, "Johannes Eccards Ernennung." For a new study of the topic see Garratt, *Palestrina and the German Romantic Imagination,* which appeared too late to be considered here.

49. Nowak, "Johannes Eccards Ernennung," 297.

50. Brinkmann and Wiechert, "Grell, Eduard."

51. The best account of Bellermann is in Dahlhaus, "Geschichte als Problem der Musiktheorie," 412–13; see also Sasse, "Bellermann, Heinrich."

52. Dahlhaus, "Geschichte als Problem der Musiktheorie," 412 f.

> music alone was considered artful music and was not yet spoiled through the damaging influence of instrumental music. To be sure, instrumental music too has its value and its justification, so long as it keeps to the modest boundaries of an imitator of vocal music and derives its rules from vocal music. In the course of time, as early as the beginning of the eighteenth century and earlier, this relationship has directly reversed itself.[53]

Thus, it made sense for him to make every effort to resurrect the "old true style." He published theory treatises, made an edition of the Locheimer Liederbuch, and edited many of Palestrina's motets.

Bellermann's student Gustav Jacobsthal shared with his teacher a passion for Palestrina and taught all of his students strict counterpoint in the style of Palestrina. Albert Schweitzer said of him: "Musical theory I studied under Jacobsthal, a pupil of Bellermann's, who in his one-sidedness refused to acknowledge as art any music later than Beethoven's. Pure counterpoint, however, one could learn thoroughly from him, and I have much to thank him for."[54] For him Palestrina remained the greatest composer. Jacobsthal took historical research a step further than his teachers and became one of the first scholars to occupy himself seriously with medieval music. He began with a dissertation on mensural notation of the twelfth and thirteenth centuries. He then started a long-term project on the precursors of Palestrina. He was by all accounts a perfectionist who worked slowly and systematically and published little. His most important book is *Die chromatische Alteration im liturgischen Gesang der abendländischen Kirche* (1897), considered by Ludwig and Besseler to be a model of musicological scholarship. He was beginning a project on the Montpellier Codex when he died. Even though most of his work is on medieval music, there is no doubt that the music that touched him personally and against which he measured all earlier music was Palestrina. Like some of the older scholars mentioned above, he also conducted a university choir, in Strassburg. Ludwig published a catalog of the scores the choir owned: sixteenth-century choral music is most prominent and was most often performed. In addition, the catalog lists compositions by Grell, Bellermann, and Jacobsthal himself. But the choir also sang Zelter, Gluck, Mozart, Beethoven,

53. "Das vorliegende Buch ist daher recht eigentlich für den künftigen Gesangslehrer geschrieben, der durch dasselbe mit jenen Zeiten vertraut gemacht werden soll, in denen der Gesang allein für kunstgemäße Musik gehalten wurde und noch nicht durch den schädlichen Einfluß der Instrumentalmusik verdorben war. Gewiß hat die Instrumentalmusik auch ihren Wert und ihre Berechtigung; so lange sie sich nämlich in den bescheidenen Grenzen einer Nachahmerin des Gesanges hält und von jenem ihre Gesetze ableitet. Im Laufe der Zeiten, schon seit Anfang des achtzehnten Jahrhunderts und noch früher, hat dieses Verhältnis sich aber geradezu umgekehrt." *Contrapunkt,* 8.

54. Schweitzer, *Out of My Life and Thought,* 10. See also Besseler, "Gustav Jacobsthal," 1619.

Lully, and Rameau.[55] It did not perform medieval music. It seems that Jacobsthal's interest in the Middle Ages was more theoretical than practical.

Jacobsthal stands out from the group of Lutheran Palestrina-revivalists in that he was Jewish and was never baptized. Thus, one wonders if his passion for Renaissance polyphony was combined with the religious fervor of his teachers and his student Ludwig.

In short, Ludwig's direct intellectual ancestry was in the Berlin Palestrina revival, a movement characterized by a rejection of contemporary music as religiously inappropriate and ineffective and by attempts to revive *a cappella* polyphony for use in church. The religious motivation was centrally important: the musical revival was to serve religious goals. For some this meant a rejection of all contemporary or post-Palestrina music (Grell and Bellermann), for others (Hoffmann, Winterfeld, and Jacobsthal) it went hand in hand with an admiration for Beethoven. The movement resulted in a passionate interest in music history, including the music that predated Palestrina's, and contributed more than anything else to the founding of our discipline.

LUDWIG'S INTERPRETATION OF THE MIDDLE AGES

Now, the question is: in what way did the Palestrina cult affect Ludwig's work? I think that we can safely say that he tried to follow the path of his teacher Jacobsthal to discover Palestrina's roots. From one of his earliest publications in 1902[56] to his last major publication, the 1929 version of his chapter "Die geistliche nichtliturgische/weltliche einstimmige und die mehrstimmige Musik," he saw medieval polyphony as the first step on an evolutionary ladder leading up to the great master Palestrina. We read in the 1929 text: "In the Middle Ages the lead was taken nevertheless by representatives of the polyphonic ideal, which found its highest and purest embodiment in the pure vocal music of Palestrina."[57] Notre Dame polyphony is considered important because only it will lead directly to Palestrina:

> but only from here, only from the organum, as it was called, only from this polyphonic song of the Frankish church choirs and the British choirs that learned from them, only from here did polyphony find the way to the complete artistic unfolding of unimaginably rich forces lying dormant in the organum, a way, at first, after a long difficult ascent that would only reach a first pinnacle illuminated in immortal light in the polyphony of Palestrina after

55. Ludwig, *Die älteren Musikwerke.*

56. "Die mehrstimmige Musik des 14. Jahrhunderts," 68.

57. "Die Führung blieb im Mittelalter trotzdem doch stets bei den Vertretern des polyphonen Ideals, das für die reine Vokalmusik in Palestrina seine höchste und reinste Verkörperung fand." "Die geistliche nichtliturgische . . . ," 166.

> more than half a millennium of lively development, then would reach in a faster advance the pinnacles of modern polyphonic and harmonic form in Bach's and Beethoven's creations.[58]

Note the constant use of metaphors from mountain climbing: "langwierigem, mühsamem Aufstieg" and "Gipfelpunkt." The style apart, the sentence might have come from Hoffmann's essay on old and new church music. What it implies is that all monophonic and secular music (and this is especially true of music in the fourteenth century) is considered less important than that of Notre Dame. At this point it might be worth summarizing some features for which Palestrina's motets were praised: sacred text, the same in all parts, purely vocal texture, consonant counterpoint producing fully triadic vertical harmonies, slowly moving parts, imitation and canons, or at least independent voice leading in all parts. When any of these are present, the pieces become more important and better for Ludwig. A genre like the thirteenth-century double motet, which leads nowhere, does not get high marks. He admits that motets of this kind were widespread, but he considers them only "transitional pieces (*Übergangswerke*)": "And transitional pieces they are, even though some of them were widely distributed in this form, because *before* them there exist the organic forms of the secular, purely French, and the sacred, purely Latin, double motet."[59] He continues: "It is therefore entirely wrong if in contemporary scholarship these pieces [with French triplum, Latin motetus, and tenor] are often pushed to the foreground as characteristic of the thirteenth-century motet style and serve as an example of the supposed unnaturalness not only of the motet, but above all of the polyphonic music of this period."[60] Because the tradition of double motets was not continued, they are demoted to marginal pieces.

58. "[A]ber nur von hier aus, nur vom 'Organum', wie man es nannte, nur von diesem mehrstimmigen Gesang der fränkischen und der von ihnen lernenden britischen Kirchenchöre aus, nur von hier aus fand die Mehrstimmigkeit den Weg zur vollen künstlerischen Entfaltung der ungeahnt reichen in ihr schlummernden Kräfte, einen Weg, der zunächst in langwierigem, mühsamem Aufstieg erst nach mehr als einem halben Jahrtausend lebhafterer Entwicklung einen ersten in unvergänglichem Licht erstrahlenden Gipfelpunkte in der Polyphonie Palestrina's, dann in rascherem Zuge die Gipfelpunkte modernen polyphonen und harmonischen musikalischen Gestaltens in Bach's und Beethoven's Schöpfungen erreichen sollte"; "Perotinus Magnus," 363–64. See also "Die geistliche nichtliturgische . . . ," 166.

59. "Und Übergangswerke sind es, wenn ihre Verbreitung in dieser Form teilweise auch gross ist; denn v o r ihnen existieren die durchaus organischen Formen der weltlichen rein französischen und der geistlichen rein lateinischen Doppelmotette"; *Repertorium,* pt. 2, p. 403.

60. "Es ist also völlig verkehrt, wenn in der modernen Literatur vielfach diese Werke [French triplum, Latin motetus and tenor] immer wieder als typisch für den Motettenstil des 13. Jahrhunderts in den Vordergrund gestellt werden und sie zum Beweis für die angebliche Unnatur nicht bloss der Motette, sondern auch der mehrstimmigen Musik dieser Zeit überhaupt dienen sollen." *Repertorium,* pt. 2, p. 403.

Gregorian chant and Notre Dame polyphony are elevated to high positions, because both are sung by what he believes were large choruses in alternation with soloists.[61] They are liturgical pieces that are used to enhance devotion. The fourteenth-century motet, on the other hand, receives less praise because it is sung by a small ensemble (and, even worse, with instruments) and because it is secular. In a 1925 article on the polyphonic mass of the fourteenth century we read:

> If we consider the change of repertory, it is undoubtedly based essentially on a fundamentally transformed position of the large church choirs relative to polyphonic sacred music. Moreover, the constant nurturing of polyphonic music in the service, achieved in a long-standing tradition that has made generations happy and which blossomed entirely in the service of the sacred work, which therefore does not have to be and was not inflexibly conservative in choirs such as, for example, the Notre Dame choir of Paris, had eroded possibly as early as the late thirteenth century. The period of great Proper cycles, the creation and execution of which required a continuously stable church music organization and the faithfully persevering work of an excellently trained choir, was over. It only came back as a result of the church reforms in the fifteenth century.[62]

Ludwig's view of choral music is clearly similar to that of Grell and Bellermann. Note the expression "in the service of the sacred work (*im Dienst am heiligen Werk*)," characteristic of the nineteenth-century Palestrina revival. A little later he says, when discussing isorhythmic motets, "I would say that on the whole the liturgical polyphony of this century does not count among the elevated pinnacles of sacred music."[63] He ends the article by comparing Perotin's large pieces to the motets of the fourteenth century, and praises the former for having clarity, perfection, and harmony, qualities he does not see in those of the next century, where the music has been influenced by "strong

61. On performance practice of Notre Dame Polyphony, see Ludwig, "Musik des Mittelalters," 439.

62. "Was den Repertoirewechsel angeht, so scheint er mir zweifellos im Grunde auf einer im Innersten veränderten Stellung der großen Kirchenchöre zur mehrstimmigen geistlichen Musik zu beruhen. Die stetige, in langer beharrlicher Tradition Generationen beglückende, ganz im Dienst am heiligen Werk aufgehende Pflege auch der mehrstimmigen Musik im Gottesdienst, die deshalb durchaus nicht starr konservativ gerichtet zu sein brauchte und es in Chören wie z.B. dem Notre-Dame-Chor in Paris lange auch nicht gewesen ist, war—vielleicht schon im späteren 13. Jahrhundert—in Verfall gekommen. Die Zeit für grosse Propriumzyklen, deren Schöpfung und Ausführung stets festeste kirchenmusikalische Organisation und treue anhaltende Arbeit eines auf das beste geschulten Chores zur Voraussetzung hat, war zunächst vorüber. Sie kam erst im Gefolge der Kirchenreformbestrebungen, und zwar schon des 15. Jahrhunderts, wieder." "Die mehrstimmige Messe des 14. Jahrhunderts," 431–32.

63. "Ich sage: daß im Ganzen betrachtet die liturgische Mehrstimmigkeit dieses Jahrhunderts nicht zu den ragenden Gipfeln geistlicher Musik zählt." Ibid., 434.

symptoms of the decay of the church-religious spirit, which extended all the way to the papal court of Avignon, which behaved in a disagreeably secular manner."[64] For the devout Lutheran Ludwig, religious music should be performed by a choir without instruments, should be composed in a sacred atmosphere, and should come from a deep inner religious feeling. In a 1921 paper, he praised the compositions in the Magnus liber organi: "But they all have in common that the young polyphonic art remains in the *most intimate union* with the liturgy" (my emphasis).[65] The full range of meanings inherent in the German word "innig" is not adequately captured by the English "intimate"; there are additional connotations in German. "Innige Verbindung" (intimate union) with liturgy is precisely what Herder was trying to restore when he set out to reform Lutheran church music. "Innig" goes together with "innerlich," the spiritual (often religiously tinged) world into which one escaped from everyday realities in the nineteenth century.[66]

Ludwig approved of an organum when it had features pointing in the direction of fifteenth- and sixteenth-century polyphony: voice exchange, imitation, and sequence.[67] His chronology of the various versions of the Magnus liber depends on how progressive the counterpoint is; the various versions are "enclosed in a musically ascending art of setting music."[68] Note again the mountain-climbing metaphor.

The idea of musical progress is present throughout Ludwig's writings, as one would expect from a scholar of his generation: in a paper of 1903, a two-part motet is considered more primitive than a three-part motet because he compares them to the four- or five-part motets of Palestrina.[69] Similarly, the motets in the *Roman de Fauvel* are "a weak reflection" ("ein schwacher Abglanz") of the old motets, because they are now reduced to two parts.[70] In the Magnus liber a tenor with strict rhythmic organization is always better than a tenor without such patterns and it is considered to be later.[71] And, as we have seen at the beginning of this chapter, thanks to Ludwig's research

64. "[S]tarke[n] Verfallssymptome[n] des kirchlich-religiösen Geistes bis hinauf zu dem vielfach arg weltlich sich gebahrenden Avignoneser päpstlichen Hof"; ibid., 434. See also "Die geistliche nichtliturgische . . . ," 176.

65. "Aber gemeinsam ist allen, daß die junge mehrstimmige Kunst in innigster Verbindung mit der Liturgie bleibt." "Perotinus Magnus," 364.

66. Grimm's Dictionary defines "innig" as follows: "In der neueren Sprache häufig als edles Wort für tiefe Empfindung"; it is considered the equivalent of "andächtig, im Inneren wurzelnd."

67. "Die geistliche nichtliturgische . . . ," 227.

68. "[I]n musikalisch aufsteigender Satzkunst begriffen." "Perotinus Magnus," 365.

69. "Studien über die Geschichte," 181.

70. "Die Quellen der Motetten ältesten Stils," 279.

71. *Repertorium,* pt. 1, pp. 84–85. Carl Dahlhaus was the first to recognize Ludwig's bias in 1967 in his *Foundations of Music History,* where he writes: "The evolution of thirteenth-century music was described by Friedrich Ludwig, who established the basic traits of this period, as a succession of compositional innovations, each emerging from its predecessor, rather than as,

to this day virtually every music history textbook will attribute the "earlier" organa to Leonin and the "later" ones to Perotin.

Ludwig and his contemporaries were convinced that great and original compositions had to be associated with a particular artist. Notre Dame polyphony could be taken seriously because names could be attached to it, the names of Leonin and Perotin, mentioned by the theorist Anonymous IV. (None of the Magnus liber pieces are attributed to Leonin and Perotin in the sources.) In a paper of 1902, Ludwig talks about "the individuality of the artist" ("Künstlerindividualität"), and considers Perotin's version as the "final," "definitive" one.[72] This view is repeated in a paper of 1909[73] and in the *Repertorium,* where he contrasts organum compositions of the twelfth century with earlier ones. In the twelfth century, composers succeeded "in shaping the musical creations of Western nations in a fundamentally new way and soon developed it in the richest ways; and not, as had been tried in the preceding poetry era of the learned Carolingian Renaissance, through the emulation of and dependence on old-fashioned classical models, but through the discovery and dissemination of *original* [emphasis Ludwig's] artistic talents, which had previously been almost entirely hidden, by individuals of this period; among these talents we have to count the ability to create and enjoy polyphonic music."[74] In other words, while artists in the earlier Middle Ages were emulating classical models, in the twelfth century composers become original, creative artists, and polyphony now requires a "single individual" ("Einzel-Individuum").[75] Attributing pieces to Leonin or Perotin therefore continues to be a central issue for him, although by his last publication, of 1929,[76] he has become a little more cautious in his attributions to Perotin (he realizes it might be a bit much for one person).

Ludwig himself was fully aware that thirteenth-century authors often attributed compositions to somebody in order to enhance their value. In a paper of 1905 on the Codex Calixtinus, where pieces are attributed to popes and cardinals, he mentions that these attributions were only meant to im-

---

say, a series of stages in which old and new existed side by side as integral parts of a liturgical corpus that represented a unified musical system" (p. 107).

72. See "Die mehrstimmige Musik," 19–20.

73. "Die liturgischen Organa Leonins und Perotins," 203.

74. "[D]as musikalische Schaffen der abendländlischen Völker von Grund auf neu zu gestalten und bald auf das Reichste zu entfalten; und zwar, nicht mehr, wie es die vorhergegangene Dichtungsepoche gelehrter Renaissance in der Zeit Karls des Grossen versucht hatte, im Nachbilden und Anlehnen an unzeitgemässe klassische Vorbilder, sondern im Ans-Licht-Ziehen und Ausbreiten bisher so gut wie verborgen gebliebener *origineller* [emphasis Ludwig's] künstlerischer Anlagen der Individuen dieser Zeit, Anlagen, zu denen auch die Fähigkeit des Schaffens und des Geniessens mehrstimmiger Musik gehört." *Repertorium,* pt. 1, pp. 1–2.

75. Ibid., 2.

76. "Die geistliche nichtliturgische . . . ," 56–57.

press and cannot be taken seriously.[77] Yet it never occurred to him to question the attributions of Anonymous IV, even though he commented elsewhere that the theorist's descriptions of the Notre Dame manuscripts were not accurate: Anonymous IV claims that Perotin's books were used for a long time, and Ludwig was the first one to point out that there was no evidence to support this statement.[78]

This attitude is closely related to Ludwig's wish to find the true and original version of a piece. It is characteristic for his attachment to the Palestrina cult that he chooses the words "rein" or "echt," familiar to us from Reichardt and Thibaut, to describe the original version of a piece. With the exception of the Notre Dame organa, generally for Ludwig the original version is the best one. The idea that a later composer might have improved a composition or a text is not a serious option for him. Moreover, Ludwig firmly believed that one could arrive at the correct, original version of a polyphonic piece through proper philological work. He refers with admiration to the Catholic scholars who managed to reintroduce "the true version of Gregorian Chant" ("die *echte Fassung* des Gregorianischen Gesanges").[79] This is somewhat toned down in his last lecture, "Die Erforschung der Musik des Mittelalters," when he talks about chant melodies that "have been restored as true to the historical version as possible" ("möglichst historischer Echtheit wieder hergestellt").[80] In the same lecture he regrets that the troubadour chansons are not transmitted in their original version: "that in the process this or that tune is no longer transmitted in its pure form of the true original, but has already been variously 'sung to pieces.'"[81] He assumes that there is *one* original version of the Minnelieder when he states "that also with those tunes that appear authentic we will have to attempt in each case to find out if this late transmission has not already distorted the true version of the melody."[82] He complains that it is almost impossible to achieve a "reinen Text" of the *laude*.[83]

Likewise, he simply assumes that the Notre Dame repertory goes back to one common source, and that the different versions represent different stages in the development of Notre Dame polyphony. He considers W_1 to be the earliest version of the Magnus liber, and for a scholar who is so obsessed with

77. "Ein mehrstimmiges St. Jakobs-Offizium," 12.

78. "Die liturgischen Organa Leonins und Perotins," 203 ff.

79. *Die Aufgaben der Forschung.*

80. *Die Erforschung der Musik des Mittelalters*, 7.

81. "[D]aß dabei diese oder jene Weise schon nicht mehr in der reinen Form des echten Originals, sondern schon mannigfach 'zersungen' weiter überliefert wird." Ibid., 16.

82. "[D]aß auch bei den echt erscheinenden Weisen zunächst überall der Versuch unternommen werden muß, festzustellen, ob diese späte Überlieferung nicht die echte Form der Melodie schon entstellt hat." "Die geistlichen nichtliturgischen . . . ," 202.

83. Ibid., 209.

"facts," he simply attributes fascicles 2, 3, and 4 to the "composer" Leonin.[84] The final version ("definitive Fassung") of the Magnus liber is reached with W_2 and attributed to Perotin. And in this case, for once, the "final version" is the "best," because it is least improvised, and more worked out.[85] So here the wish for an evolutionary development overrides the search for the "original" version. In his discussions of motets, however, he is mainly concerned with establishing which version was first.[86] And the original version is for him the version where the text fits best. It does not occur to him that a later poet might have added a text fitting the music better than the earlier one.

The problem of finding the original version is closely connected with the fact that music from this period constantly makes use of the same material. This begins with the use of recurrent formulas and continues with larger melodic segments, entire voice parts, two-part frames to which a new part is added, or contrafacta. Ludwig was aware of such reworkings and interrelationships and described them in great detail throughout his career, especially in the *Repertorium.* The fact that there might be a contradiction between the Romantic ideal of the original composer and the constant use of the same melodic material must have occurred to Ludwig. Perhaps this is the reason why he never asked *why* medieval composers constantly reused material they did not invent themselves. He goes on for pages listing all of the interrelationships, but never tries to come up with an explanation or even notes that an explanation is needed. Instead, he tries to excuse the practice. We can observe this as early as 1903 in a paper entitled "Studien über die Geschichte der mehrstimmigen Musik im Mittelalter,"[87] where he criticizes openly what he calls "the forcible inclusion of parts which originally did not belong together" in a new piece.[88] He concludes: "It is impossible to create an organic artwork from such a patchwork of pieces from different artistic periods."[89] As a result, he considers composers poor who reuse and borrow their materials as, for example, Adam de la Halle, because of their "constant quotations."[90] This negative view of the practice is repeated in the *Repertorium* when he discusses motets in W_2: "all of their tenors have to forgo the forming of modes, because here we have a case, rare in the history of the motet, where, as it seems, the *entire* motet [Ludwig's emphasis] consists of the adaptation

84. *Repertorium,* pt. 1, p. 15.

85. "Die geistliche nichtliturgische . . . ," 218.

86. See, for example, ibid., 236.

87. See pp. 190–91. Also here he tries to find "die reine ältere Gestalt" of a motet that has been reworked.

88. "Hineinzwängung ursprünglicher einander fremder Glieder," in "Studien über die Geschichte," 215.

89. "Aus derartigen Zusammenflickungen von Werken so verschiedener Kunstperioden ist eben kein organisches Kunstwerk zu schaffen," ibid., 216.

90. Ibid., 207–15.

and combination of previously exisiting independent melodies to a two-part setting. This is an inartistic procedure that was often considered typical of the French motet. Very unjustifiably so, as we can see from the small number of cases where it takes place and where it can be explained as a game of wit. . . . Moreover, the circulation of these pieces was not large."[91] Ludwig does not realize that the quotations employed in these pieces rely on the same principle as the use of formulas, the reemployment of tenors, two-part structures, contrafacta, etc. Admittedly, there are few motets consisting entirely of quotations, but the principle of quotation is the same as in the organa of the Magnus liber. Rather than addressing the issue, he chooses to call these motets unartistic ("unkünstlerisch") and describe quotation as a game that was never widespread.[92] They are "unkünstlerisch" because they do not correspond to the nineteenth-century idea of the original and organically unified artwork.

Since Ludwig's primary goal was the description and analysis of sources, he does not provide separate discussions of topics such as compositional process, notation, and performance practice. His views on these topics can be inferred from reading between the lines of his work. For instance, when discussing motets in the ninth fascicle of F, he makes it clear that the voices were not conceived simultaneously, but one after another.[93] More importantly, for Ludwig it goes without saying that all of medieval polyphony was composed in writing, just as the works of Beethoven were. Written composition is so self-evident for him that he does not even discuss it much. One can gather his view only indirectly when he discusses the St. Victor melismas

91. "[D]eren Tenores sämtlich auf Modus-Bildung verzichten müssen, da hier der in der Motettengeschichte selten vorkommende Fall eintritt, daß die, wie es hier den Anschein hat, *ganze* Motette aus der musikalischen Anpassung und Vereinigung verschiedener vorher unabhängig von einander existierender Melodien zu einem zweistimmigen Satz besteht. Es ist ein an sich unkünstlerisches Verfahren, das man vielfach als typisch für die französische Motette ansah; sehr mit Unrecht, wie aus der Kleinheit der Zahl der Fälle hervorgeht, in denen es in der Tat statt hat und in denen es als Spiel des Witzes zu erklären ist. . . . Auch die Verbreitung dieser Werke ist nicht gross." *Repertorium,* pt. 1, pp. 217–18.

92. In *Repertorium,* pt. 2 (p. 373) he discusses Motet no. 138 from Montpellier in a similar manner: "Verallgemeinerte Schlüsse sind indes aus dem Aufbau von Werken wie dieser Doppelmotette nicht zu ziehen, namentlich keine solchen, die die von manchen Seiten noch heute angenommene durchaus irrige Ansicht stützen könnten, eine Stileeigenart der Motette sei die Verbindung mehrerer vorher unabhängig voneinander existierender Melodien. Erstens handelt es sich auch hier in den Oberstimmen nicht um die Benutzung selbstständig existierender voller Melodien, sondern nur um solche von refrainartigen Melodie-*Abschnitten.* Und zweitens zeigt auch das nur ganz vereinzelte Vorkommen so gebauter Werke, dass auch die Vereinigung von drei derartigen ganz verschiedenartigen musikalischen Gebilden zu einer Doppelmotette, ein Paradestück musikalischer Kombinationskunst, durchaus eine Ausnahme bildet." See also Ludwig's negative evaluation of Adam de la Halle in *Repertorium,* pt. 2, p. 432, and his last publication, "Die geistliche nichtliturgische . . . ," 258.

93. *Repertorium,* pt. 1, p. 12.

that were transformed into refrains of motets. He believes that first the melismas were set polyphonically and then the text was added. And he assumes that the poet-composer of the motet and the composer of the melismas used the same sources. He does not consider the possibility that these melismas might have been transmitted orally.[94]

And yet, Ludwig is too good a scholar to ignore the evidence in the sources that points, if not to composition in the mind, at least to performance without the use of manuscripts. In his discussion of the motets in the ninth fascicle of F, he notes that the top voice begins on the recto page and is continued on the verso page. The tenor is written only on the verso page.[95] This means that the piece could not have been performed from the manuscript. But he stops the discussion at this point and does not ask himself how this motet might have been performed. In particular, he shies away from a conclusion that the piece might have been sung from memory. Similarly, he stresses that MüB is the earliest source where the music is copied in such a way that it can be performed from the manuscript.[96] In a 1905 paper he describes conductus motets that were notated without a tenor. Here Ludwig assumes that the tenors were not notated because they were so well known.[97] The conclusion that they were sung from memory seems inescapable. With all of this evidence, Ludwig might have considered the possiblity that much of the early polyphony was improvised or performed by heart. But since he consciously limited his task to a description of the sources, he asked no further questions and did not allow himself any speculation.

Ludwig's passion for source studies went hand in hand with a rejection of other evidence, in particular music theory. As we have seen, in his review of Wolf's *Geschichte der Mensuralnotation* he repeatedly criticized Wolf for paying more attention to theorists than to manuscripts (p. 602). In one of his later papers he judged theoretical treatises as follows: "Neither the rules about permitted and prohibited intervals nor the theorists' babble on voice leading gives us any idea of what the art of these masters was trying to accomplish and what was considered permissible."[98] Ludwig rejects the views from the period because he knows better what the music is all about. His rejec-

94. Ibid., 155–57.

95. Ibid., 112.

96. Ibid., 317.

97. "Über die Entstehung," 517. See also *Repertorium,* pt. 2, p. 428, where he describes a tenor in Tu where the scribe has not written out the whole text, presumably because it was so well known.

98. "Weder die Regeln über erlaubte und verbotetene Zusammenklänge noch das Theoretiker-Gestammel über die Stimmführung geben einen Begriff davon, wonach die Kunst der Meister dieser Zeit strebt und was diesen als erlaubt gilt." "Die Quellen der Motetten ältesten Stils," 288. Another writing by Ludwig criticizing the study of theory is: *Die Aufgaben der Forschung.* Ludwig's view can still be found in Wulf Arlt's recent essay in *Perotinus Magnus.* See below.

tion of theory is part and parcel of his complete lack of interest in the cultural mind of the period, of trying to find out how *they,* rather than how *he,* thought.

In his discussion of notation Ludwig is, on the one hand, remarkably free of evolutionary-progressive prejudices. Rather than lamenting the fact that modal notation is inferior to mensural notation or, for that matter, the modern notational system, he stresses repeatedly that in spite of the fact that scribes did not have a specific sign for every note value at their disposal, the modal system was more than adequate for the rhythms it was meant to indicate, and that it showed indirectly "the underlying rhythm with absolute certainty."[99] Similarly, he says about the notation of motets in the third and fourth fascicle of Montpellier: "Square notation would have been entirely sufficient also for the newly added works that are preserved only in mensural notation; this is especially true of the pieces in the third and fourth fascicle, since they are consistently dominated by modal rhythm, which remains one of the conditions for a generally unambiguous representation of works in square notation."[100] A little later he says that mensural notation only became necessary once composers had "emancipated themselves" from modal rhythm.[101]

On the other hand, once he had solved how to read modal notation in sacred polyphony, he applied modal rhythm also to the chansons of the troubadours and trouvères, which are transmitted without rhythmic notation.[102] It did not occur to him that secular music might be performed differently from sacred polyphony, because in his worldview sacred polyphony was considered vastly superior to secular monophony.[103] Again, this view can be traced back to Hoffmann and the other adherents of the Palestrina cult.

In sum, I hope to have shown that Ludwig thought (and convinced others) that he was embracing a strict, presuppositionless *Wissenschaft,* when, in fact, his work is full of prejudices of the evolutionary-progressive kind.[104] He

99. "[D]en zu Grunde liegenden Rhythmus absolut sicher." *Repertorium,* pt. 1, pp. 44–45.

100. "Auch für die hier neu hinzutretenden Werke, die uns nur in Mensural-Notation überliefert sind, speziell für die Werke des 4. und 3. Faszikels, würde die Quadrat-Notation ausreichen, da auch in ihnen durchgehends noch modaler Rhythmus herrscht, der die Voraussetzung zu einer im wesentlichen eindeutigen Aufzeichnung von Werken in Quadrat-Notation bleibt." *Repertorium,* pt. 2, p. 347.

101. Ibid., 348.

102. Ludwig, "Zur 'modalen Interpretation.'"

103. See my discussion of Handschin below. Note, though, that there is one exception to Ludwig's condescension regarding secular polyphony: he really loved trecento music. See, for example, "Die mehrstimmige Musik des 14. Jahrhunderts," 59.

104. Both Ursula Günther and Ulrich Bartels, in their recent articles on Ludwig's scholarship, have not noticed Ludwig's prejudices. They praise his objectivity. Bartels, in particular, is unable to see to what extent Ludwig was an evolutionary historian. His conclusion could not

judged medieval polyphony by comparing it with Palestrina, arrived at a chronology on the basis of Palestrina's style, and applied criteria from the nineteenth-century autonomous artwork in trying to attribute compositions to composers and to establish which version of a piece came first. Moreover, his work is full of blind spots, that is, it fails to ask fundamental questions. He did not address the issue that medieval composers constantly reuse the same material, and he had little interest in the music theory and culture of the period.[105] It might be thought that Ludwig's work and approach were necessary and had to be continued *before* any other kind of work in this area could have been attempted, the standard claim of "Let's get the music edited and available first." But there is a scholar, Jacques Handschin, who shows that this is not true.

HANDSCHIN'S LIFE, EDUCATION, AND WORK

Jacques Handschin was born in 1886 in Moscow of Swiss parents.[106] His father, a merchant, expected his exceptionally gifted son to take over the business. Therefore, he forced him to leave the German Gymnasium in St. Petersburg and attend a trade school in Neuchâtel. Handschin managed to graduate in eighteen months rather than the normal three years and was allowed to complete the Gymnasium in St. Petersburg thereafter. In 1905, he started to study history and mathematics in Basle, but already in the same year moved to Munich to read history, mathematics, philology, and economics. In addition, he took organ lessons and music theory with Max Reger. His parents were so angered by his music studies that they broke off contact with him and refused to support him any further. When Reger moved to Leipzig the following year, Handschin followed him, making the entire trip by foot. He soon took organ lessons with Karl Straube, the organist at the Thomaskirche, and attended a few lectures with Hugo Riemann. This, together with a few lectures by the ethnomusicologist Erich von Hornbostel, remains the only formal musicological training Handschin ever received.

He next traveled to Paris to study organ with Charles-Marie Widor. From 1909 to 1920 he taught organ at the St. Petersburg Conservatory, and was appointed professor there in 1916. Simultaneously, he had a successful ca-

---

be further from mine: "Gerade weil Ludwig ein guter Kenner der gesamten abendländischen Musikgeschichte und nicht allein ein Spezialist für die Musik des Mittelalters war, ging er von der unbedingten ästhetisch-qualitativen Gleichwertigkeit der Epochen und ihrer jeweiligen Musikstile aus." "Musikwissenschaften zwischen den Kriegen," 97–98.

105. Lawrence Earp has shown in an unpublished paper that Ludwig used a similar approach in his essay on Beethoven sketches, which anticipates much of the work on sketches so popular in the 1960s and 1970s. Ludwig's paper, "Beethovens Skizzen," was published in 1920.

106. See Oesch, "Handschin, Jacques Samuel" and Oesch and Kniazeva, "Handschin, Jacques."

reer as an organ virtuoso and accompanist to famous artists. He inspired several Russian composers to write for the organ: Glazunov, Lyapunov, Taneyev, and Kryzhanovsky. In 1920, he set up an acoustics laboratory together with Kovalenkov.

After the revolution Handschin decided to return to Basle, making the entire trip by foot and losing his *Habilitationsschrift* on the way. He was forced to start from scratch, was only able to get various small organist positions, and experienced serious financial hardship until he became organist at the Peterskirche in Zurich. It was only at this point that he began to concentrate on musicology, and he received his doctorate with a dissertation on thirteenth-century polyphonic music written under Karl Nef at Basle in 1921. He became a professor of musicology at the University of Basle in 1930 and an ordinarius in 1935, but continued as an organist at the Martin's Church in Basle until shortly before his death in 1955.

Handschin's eccentricity could not be further removed from the stuffy professional persona of Ludwig. There are many wonderful anecdotes in circulation about him. When it became too hot on the organ balcony, he would take off his trousers in the middle of the service and hang them over the railing, to the horror of the congregation. Similarly, many of his students remember meeting him on Basle streets in his morning robe and slippers on his way to the library.

He himself stressed repeatedly that he was an autodidact in musicology. He was probably the first musicologist to advocate a close collaboration between musicology and ethnomusicology, probably because he had a good understanding of non-European music from his years in Russia (he had an extraordinary talent for languages), and his studies with von Hornbostel. His main contributions to historical musicology are in the medieval area, including Byzantine and Syrian music. He was close to completing an edition of the polyphonic pieces of the St. Martial period when he died. Another central field of interest was the study of sound in its historical context, which resulted in *Der Toncharakter* of 1948. In the same year, he also published a survey of music history, *Musikgeschichte im Überblick,* probably the only history textbook where all periods receive equal attention. And finally, he wrote several studies on Russian music.[107]

HANDSCHIN'S INTERPRETATION OF THE MIDDLE AGES

Jacques Handschin's view of music history was very different from Ludwig's. From the beginning of his career, he was deeply opposed to an evolutionary

107. For a complete bibliography see Oesch, "Handschin, Jacques," and esp. Oesch, ed., *Gedenkschrift Jacques Handschin.*

interpretation of music history. He stressed as early as 1930: "I would like to add here the remark that when we set up stages in the development of polyphonic music we have to try to proceed gently and keep apart the different viewpoints to be considered. A monument that is 'progressive' in some way may be 'backward' in another."[108] In *Musikgeschichte im Überblick* this view is voiced on many occasions: "Objectively, we must proceed from the viewpoint that every period deserves our attention in the same way."[109] He envisions a future merging of ethnomusicology and musicology: "We might perhaps imagine that then music history will be stripped of the vulgar dynamics with which it was outfitted in the nineteenth century: the dynamics of an independent advance to something better, yes, even an advance on its own."[110]

The difference between Ludwig's and Handschin's view of history is perhaps best illuminated in their respective discussion of the famous Summer Canon. In the first part of the *Repertorium* Ludwig praises the Summer Canon because of its canonic structure and its beautiful harmonies and melodies, and calls it "the only polyphonic work of this period that, when performed in its original state, makes an immediate artistic impression even on the modern listener."[111] Handschin does not share Ludwig's enthusiasm for this work, finding it both melodically and rhythmically simplistic and repetitive: "The doubling leads, not unexpectedly, to clumsiness."[112] In an article on the Summer Canon, he contradicts Manfred Bukofzer, who had placed the piece in the fourteenth century because an earlier date would not have fit into the evolutionary scale of music history. Handschin writes:

> Modern musicians have perhaps been too impressed by the use of canonic devices in our composition, but this device is not in itself a sign of art; they have also been impressed by the "natural sweetness" of the harmony, but that only

108. "Ich möchte hier die Bemerkung einfügen, daß wir uns bemühen müssen, beim Aufstellen von Entwicklungsstadien in der Geschichte der Mehrstimmigkeit behutsam vorzugehen und die verschiedenen in Betracht kommenden Gesichtspunkte auseinanderzuhalten. Ein Denkmal, das 'fortgeschritten' in der einen Hinsicht ist, kann in der anderen 'zurückgeblieben' sein." "Der Organum Traktat von Montpellier," 52. See also his essay "Zur Biographie Hermanns des Lahmen" (originally published in 1935), where he expresses a strong dislike for the idea of progress in musicology and art.

109. "Objektiverweise müssen wir von der Annahme ausgehen, jede Epoche verdiene unsere Beachtung in gleichem Maße." *Musikgeschichte im Überblick,* 16.

110. "Dann wird, wie wir es uns vielleicht weiter ausmalen dürfen, die Musikgeschichte wohl jener vulgären 'Dynamik' entkleidet sein, mit der man sie im 19. Jahrhundert zu umkleiden liebte: der Dynamik des selbständigen Fortschreitens zum Besseren, ja auch nur des Fortschreitens als solchen." Ibid., 84.

111. "[D]as einzige mehrstimmige Werk dieser Zeit, dem bei seiner tönenden Wiedergabe in seiner Originalgestalt ein unmittelbarer künstlerischer Eindruck auch auf den modernen Hörer beschieden schien." *Repertorium,* pt. 1, p. 267.

112. "Die Verdoppelung führt, wie nicht anders zu erwarten, zur Plumpheit." *Musikgeschichte im Überblick,* 195.

> because it anticipates their cherished "perfect chord" habits. Objectively, we can only say that it exemplifies the English tendency, already mentioned, toward massive vocal sonority. . . . Under these circumstances I think we ought not to force the Summer Canon into an evolutionary-order that is not its own by maintaining that binary rhythm could not possibly appear before it was duly recognized by (French) theorists.[113]

He concludes the article by placing the Summer Canon back into the thirteenth century on the basis of paleographic evidence. Similarly, in *Musikgeschichte im Überblick,* he stresses that the use of imitation can no longer be considered a sign of "progress" because if it were, "such an important master as Ockeghem would 'disappoint' us in this respect a bit."[114]

Likewise, Handschin stresses throughout his career that simpler pieces do not necessarily have to be earlier than more complex pieces. This view allowed him to question as early as 1924 Ludwig's dating of W_1 as the oldest Notre Dame source, a dating inferred from the relative simplicity of the Magnus liber version. Similarly, Handschin questioned the chronology of the pieces found in the eleventh fascicle of W_1, which are simpler than the Magnus liber organum pieces from the other fascicles: "This shows that these pieces, when compared with the Notre Dame repertory, show a more modest taste, but neverthelesss they cannot have been composed at an early stage of the evolution."[115]

Within the Magnus liber, Ludwig attributed the organum purum and the simplest discant sections in W_1 to Leonin and the more complex discant sections in F and W_2 to Perotin. However, Helmut Schmidt, building on Handschin's ideas, pointed out in a 1931 paper that the more complex discant sections were already to be found in W_1.[116] What this implies, Schmidt thought, was that W_1 could not simply represent the earliest, that is, Leonin's, version of the Magnus liber organi. But Ludwig's authority was such that Schmidt did not dare to say directly that this overthrows much of Ludwig's chronology. It remained for Handschin to spell out this consequence of Schmidt's findings.[117] In *Musikgeschichte im Überblick,* he pointed out: "We first have to determine whether this kind of shaping in the upper voice, often found in one and the same composition, really represents subsequent peri-

113. Handschin, "Summer Canon," 79.

114. "[E]in so bedeutender Meister wie Ockeghem in dieser Hinsicht die Erwartungen etwas 'enttaüscht.'" *Musikgeschichte im Überblick,* 229.

115. "Dies zeigt, daß es sich im Vergleich zur Notre Dame-Schule um eine bescheidenere *Geschmacksrichtung* handelt, daß aber andererseits die *Entwicklungsstufe* nicht eine frühere sein kann." In "Eine wenig beachtete Stilrichtung," 57.

116. "Zur Melodiebildung Leonins und Perotins."

117. "Zur Leonin-Perotin-Frage," 319.

ods rather than aesthetically varied versions standing next to each other."[118] His conclusion on the simple pieces in the eleventh fascicle of W_1 was: "The reason for the relative 'modesty' in the makeup of these pieces is not, as F. Ludwig thought, that they had to be older than the Notre Dame compositions or that they belonged more in the context of St. Martial, but rather that they were created for a weekly special mass that does not exhibit the splendor of the Sunday and festive Mass."[119]

While Ludwig, following his evolutionary-progressive presuppositions, sought to establish the chronology among the Notre Dame sources in general, Handschin, free of such presuppositions, was able to see that the stylistic differences among various versions of the repertory did not necessarily have to be the result of an evolution. Rather, they could reflect different local preferences and practices. This is why, while Ludwig assumed that W_1, as the earliest because simplest Magnus liber source, must have originated in Paris, Handschin was able to demonstrate in 1927, mostly on the basis of liturgical peculiarities, that it was prepared in Scotland.[120] Ludwig corrected his mistake about the provenance of W_1 in a paper of 1930 and cited Handschin's work,[121] but characteristically insisted that he himself had independently come to the same conclusion concerning the provenance of W_1 on the basis of paleographic evidence.[122]

The interpretation of modal rhythm is another area where Handschin's open-mindedness led him to question the modal-rhythmic performance of troubadour and trouvère melodies advocated by Ludwig and his students. He attributed it correctly to the common prejudice that polyphonic music is superior to monophonic music and thus determines how the latter should be performed: "Is not the desire in general to interpret all monophonic mu-

118. "Es ist ja erst noch festzustellen, ob diese Art Oberstimmengestaltung, die oft in einer und derselben Komposition zu finden sind, wirklich aufeinderfolgende Epochen repräsentieren und nicht einfach im Sinne der ästhetischen Mannigfaltigkeit nebeneinander stehen." *Musikgeschichte im Überblick,* 176. See also "A Monument of English Medieval Polyphony."

119. "Die relative 'Bescheidenheit' der Faktur dieser Stücke erklärt sich also nicht, wie F. Ludwig gedacht hatte, dadurch, daß sie älter sein müssen wie die Notre-Dame Kompositionen oder daß sie in den St. Martial-Zusammenhang gehören, sondern dadurch, daß sie für eine wochentägliche Spezialmesse geschaffen wurden, die nicht den Glanz der Sonntags- oder Festmessen aufweisen." *Musikgeschichte im Überblick,* 191.

120. Handschin, "Zur Frage der melodischen Paraphrasierung."

121. "Über den Entstehungsort," 49.

122. Handschin, in turn, criticized Ludwig for not having mentioned in his last major essay "Die geistliche nichtliturgische . . . " that he had originally claimed that W_1 came from France: "Ich muß noch erwähnen, daß F. Ludwig die von mir aufgestellte These von der englischen und jüngeren Provenienz der Handschrift W_1 übernahm aber ohne es sich merken zu lassen, daß er früher das Gegenteil behauptet hatte, was eine bedauerliche Unklarheit ergibt." *Musikgeschichte im Überblick,* 214.

sic of the Middle Ages modally in reality an outgrowth of our understanding of 'polyphonic' music?"[123] Similarly, he questioned whether conductus is governed by rhythmic modes.[124] And in both cases his arguments are still valid today.[125]

Another important difference between the two scholars is that for Handschin notation and writing are not necessary to create great music. High levels of musical culture can exist without writing. He concludes: "We have to draw the conclusion that a high level of music and the use of musical notation do not necessarily have to be correlated. Yes, when we think about it more carefully, we have to admit that it could possibly be harder to do without notation and could be indicative of greater musicianship than to use it. The musician who does not use notation has to have much more in his head than the one who does."[126]

Handschin's appreciation for cultures that did not know writing may have been the result of his studies with the ethnomusicologist von Hornbostel. Not only was he open-minded with regard to musical illiteracy, he recognized that worthwhile music could have been created by composers whose names were not recorded, and he was much less obsessed with attributing anonymous compositions. When he discussed Eastern music in *Musikgeschichte im Überblick,* he concluded that "the inner value of a culture cannot be measured by the number of people who can read and write . . . "[127]

Handschin's discussion of the role of "paraphrasing" in medieval music is similarly open-minded. He was probably the first scholar to recognize the central importance of the practice of reusing the same material again and again in medieval polyphony.[128] He never tries to excuse this practice (so questionable from the standpoint of modern demands for artistic originality), but rather accepts "paraphrasing" as a legitimate aesthetic practice of composers of the period. One of the reasons he was able to come to this conclusion was that he did not treat contemporary theorists with contempt. He recognized

123. "Ist nicht die Sucht, die Monodie des Mittelalters durchweg taktisch aufzufassen, im letzten Grunde ein Ausfluß unserer 'mehrstimmigen' Musikauffassung?" See Handschin, "Die Modaltheorie und Carl Appels Ausgabe," 78.

124. "Conductus"; "Zur Frage der Conductus-Rhythmik."

125. See especially Payne, "Poetry, Politics, and Polyphony" and Page, *Latin Poetry and Conductus Rhythm*; Sanders, "Conductus and Modal Rhythm."

126. "Der Schluss, den wir ziehen müssen, ist, daß ein hoher Stand der Musik und der Besitz einer Tonschrift nicht ohne weiteres einander gleichgesetzt werden darf. Ja, wenn wir es genauer überlegen, müssen wir sagen, daß ohne Notenschrift auszukommen unter Umständen sogar in höherem Maße ein Merkmal der Musikerschaft ist, als der Gebrauch einer solchen: denn bei gleicher Leistung muß selbstverständlich der Musiker, der sich auf keine Noten stützt, viel mehr im Kopfe haben als der andere." *Musikgeschichte im Überblick,* 31.

127. "[I]st doch der innere Wert einer Kultur nicht nach der Zahl der des Lesens und Schreibens Kundigen zu bemessen"; ibid., 137.

128. "Zur Frage der melodischen Paraphrasierung."

that the melodic formulas found in Petrus dictus Palma Ociosa's treatise were not different from those encountered in compositions of the period. And, even if he did not spell it out in much detail, he realized that the entire practice of "paraphrasing" relied on memorization: "For the ancients the feeling of the existence of a melody was much more secure than for us, because it corresponded to an existing memory picture. . . . Here as well as there the composer sings by visualizing a Gregorian melody in his mind."[129]

In fact, Handschin had a good idea of the importance of *memoria* for medieval music.[130] In an article on an important treatise from Milan, Ambrosiana J 20, he does not disregard the complex and, to a modern mind, boring instructions as theory for theory's sake, but realizes that if the contents of this treatise were properly memorized, it would allow the singers to improvise polyphonically.[131]

In general, he does not consider improvisation as less valuable than composition and stresses that both are "composition," in one case oral, and in the other written: "The art of improvisation, which is finding renewed interest, is no more than composition that happens 'orally' rather than in writing. The compositional tools are the same in both cases. When improvising, you need in addition presence of mind, quick perception, and practical mastery of an instrument; when composing you have to let all of your ideas mature to such an extent that they become repeatable."[132] He is also aware that a highly developed art of composition, such as Josquin's, goes hand in hand with highly developed improvisational skills.[133] Indeed, with regard to improvisation he shows that he understands the central importance of memory. In his discussion of Tomás de Santa María's treatise *Arte de tañer fantasia*

129. "Für die Alten blieb bei alledem das Gefühl des Vorhandenseins der Melodie gesicherter als für uns, weil sie mit einem bestehenden Erinnerungsbild gleichbedeutend war. . . . Hier wie dort singt der Komponist, indem er eine gregorianische Weise im Geiste hat." In "Zur Frage der melodischen Paraphrasierung," 556.

130. Handschin's discussion of the tonaries and the hand as mnemonic tools are short, but more perceptive than those of any other musicologist of that generation. On tonaries and non-diastematic notation he says: "Unser Standpunkt ist genau der entgegengesetzte: je ungenauer die Notierung, um so mehr müssen wir die alten Sänger ästimieren, die mit einer so rudimentären Gedächtnishilfe die Melodien richtig zu singen vermochten" (*Musikgeschichte im Überblick,* 128). The hand and the solmization syllables he calls "eine Art Denkgymnastik" (ibid., 155).

131. "Aus der alten Musiktheorie," 11.

132. "Das Improvisieren, für das das Interesse neuerdings wieder zu regen beginnt, ist ein Komponieren, das statt auf dem schriftlichen auf dem 'mündlichen' Wege erfolgt. Das kompositionstechnische Rüstzeug ist also hier wie dort dasselbe. Dazu kommen als Anforderung beim Improvisieren Geistesgegenwart, behendes Erfassen und die praktische Beherrschung eines Instruments: beim Komponieren handelt es sich statt dessen darum, alles Keimende soweit ausreifen zu lassen, daß es der Wiederholung standhalte." "Über das Improvisieren," 327.

133. *Musikgeschichte im Überblick,* 271–72.

of 1565, he quotes the theorist as saying that anybody who wants to learn how to improvise must first memorize as many compositions as possible.[134]

In contrast to Ludwig, who was convinced that medieval polyphony was composed successively, Handschin argued from the beginning for simultaneous conception of all parts because of all of the motivic connections between the different voices.[135] When he discussed compositional process in Machaut's chansons, he was aware that Machaut probably started with the top part, then wrote the tenor, and ended with the countertenor, but then he continued: "even though a true composer must already have visualized the top voice together with the tenor for the most part."[136] The idea of simultaneous composition in Machaut's works was only taken up again in 1989 by Daniel Leech-Wilkinson.[137]

Most extraordinary of all is a paper Handschin wrote in 1949 on "Musicologie et musique," which anticipates some of the authenticity debates of the 1970s and 1980s.[138] He warns of the dangers of performers listening too much to musicologists,[139] and questions whether there is such a thing as a historically correct performance. He concludes by stressing the importance of imagination and "caprices" for the performance of music.

We have, then, in Handschin a scholar who brought no evolutionary prejudices to music, who tried to study medieval polyphony without comparing it to Palestrina or other later composers, and who did not impose the criteria of the nineteenth-century autonomous artwork on music of the Middle Ages. He had an independent and unconventional mind; he did not belong to any school, did not have a specific agenda, and was interested in music of all periods and cultures. He was a scholar who was constantly evolving, whose research agenda was not set once and for all, but was ever expanding, and who was not afraid to ask new questions. Of course, he could afford to ask these questions because Ludwig had done all of the ground-breaking work. This allowed him the luxury of going beyond establishing facts. He is in many ways quite similar to Gröber's student Ernst Robert Curtius, who also "faulted classical philology for its preoccupation with facts at the cost of ideas."[140]

Handschin did not leave a major book on medieval music to posterity as

134. Ibid., 262.

135. "Was brachte die Notre Dame-Schule Neues," 553; "Eine wenig beachtete Stilrichtung," 64; "Zur Frage der melodischen Paraphrasierung," 543.

136. "[O]bgleich ein wirklicher Komponist gewiß mit der Oberstimme auch den Tenor schon einigermaßen vor sich gesehen haben wird." *Musikgeschichte im Überblick,* 204.

137. Leech-Wilkinson, *Compositional Techniques.*

138. Taruskin, "On Letting the Music Speak for Itself" and *Text and Act*; Dreyfus, "Early Music Defended against its Devotees."

139. "J'ai . . . proclamé une fois que la musicologie n'est pas là pour donner des préceptes à la musique; mais cela a été assez mal accueilli." "Musicologie et musique," 17.

140. Ziolkowski, "Ernst Robert Curtius," 152.

Ludwig did, and he made no catalogs or editions. His most interesting ideas on chronology, stylistic differences, improvisation and memory, and compositional process appear almost as afterthoughts or footnotes, where they could easily be overlooked by subsequent scholars.

LUDWIG'S EFFECT ON POSTERITY

What influence did Ludwig have on musicology? Is it true that many of our views on medieval music are still influenced by his work? On the one hand, few scholars today would officially subscribe to Ludwig's evolutionary prejudices and most would support Handschin's idea that all cultures and periods are equally valid. On the other hand, there is no escaping the fact that musicological research on the Middle Ages has been dominated to a large extent by Ludwig's agenda, the discovery and analysis of musical sources. Moreover, even though Ludwig's evolutionary view is no longer considered valid, many of the questions and conclusions reached as a result of this view are still operative.[141]

Let us first discuss the study of sources. Here is what Ludwig's student Friedrich Gennrich, in a booklet on *Die Strassburger Schule der Musikwissenschaft,*[142] written on the occasion of the German reconquest of Alsace in 1940, had to say about future research in the area of medieval music: "Only [the discovery] of new source material can enlarge our knowledge. Everything else has to be considered as a gradual self-depletion through more or less unproductive combinations and speculations about material already published."[143] He made it clear that he wanted to continue the tradition of Jacobsthal and Ludwig. Within this tradition, but only within it, the idea that further knowledge depends on the discovery of new sources is believable, since knowledge consists in nothing but the description and analysis of the physical makeup and the content of the sources, as well as their neat order-

141. One of the first to recognize Ludwig's bias was Reinhold Brinkmann, in his short essay "Schwierigkeiten mit dem Mittelalter." Brinkmann's paper found no reaction in the academic community.

142. Gennrich gives the impression of being an enthusiastic Nazi in the booklet. Yet a large part is devoted to praising the contributions of Jacobsthal to musicology. Since Jacobsthal was Jewish, it must have taken some courage to write so enthusiastically about him, never mentioning that he was Jewish. In his review of the book Werner Korte promptly referred to Ludwig's teacher as "der Jude Jacobsthal." See also Brückner and Rock, *Judentum und Musik,* 132 (referring to Fritsch, *Handbuch der Judenfrage* and Stengel and Gerigk, *Lexikon der Juden in der Musik,* 121, which includes an article on Jacobsthal).

143. "Nur neues Quellenmaterial kann unser Wissen erweitern, alles andere bedeutet ein allmähliches Sich-Erschöpfen in mehr oder weniger unfruchtbaren Kombinationen und Spekulationen über das bisher veröffentlichte . . . Material." *Die Strassburger Schule,* 27. It is also possible that Gennrich was so obsessed with the study of sources because he was concerned about what Nazi idealogy could do to musicology.

ing in time and space. And the frightening prospect that the discovery of new sources might at some point come to an end is believable, because what is meant by "sources" is documents with music notation on them. Handschin called Ludwig "the scholar whose motto was the facts, the facts, and still the facts,"[144] but he forgot to add that the range of "facts" considered relevant within this tradition was exceedingly narrow.

What are the most important questions asked in recent years, and in what way do they still reflect Ludwig's evolutionary prejudices? Let us start with the question of chronology in the Magnus liber. Ludwig had attributed the organum purum and discant pieces with simple tenor patterns to Leonin, and the rhythmically and motivically more complex pieces to Perotin. Even though Handschin had raised doubts about this chronology and suggested that organum purum and discant might simply represent two different aesthetic options, twentieth-century scholars were remarkably resistant to Handschin's suggestions. Their primary concern continued to be the attribution of pieces to Leonin and Perotin.[145] In fact, Ludwig's attributions remained essentially unquestioned until Edward Roesner's 1981 article "The Problem of Chronology in the Transmission of Organum Duplum."[146] In my opinion, Roesner has fundamentally changed our understanding of Notre Dame polyphony by showing that discant sections could also be replaced by organum purum sections.[147] His conclusions essentially overthrow Ludwig's chronology through painstaking analysis of the sources. One would think that anyone who had read Roesner's work would realize that the attribution of compositions to either Leonin or Perotin is not possible on the basis of faulty chronology. And yet, the majority of Notre Dame scholars continue with Ludwig's agenda and spend much of their time trying to establish a chronology.[148] In the most recent and authoritative book on Notre Dame, *Music and Ceremony at Notre Dame of Paris* (1989), Ludwig's view is reiterated by Craig Wright: "If this was so,[149] then the great book of organum was completed by the end of the twelfth century, though his successors probably continued to modify his creations, making them rhythmically more explicit and

144. Handschin, "Monument of English Medieval Polyphony," 511.

145. Flotzinger, *Der Discantussatz*; Husmann, "Origin and Destination"; and Tischler, "Evolution of the *Magnus liber organi*."

146. See pp. 383 ff.

147. "Problem of Chronology," 371–72. For a more detailed discussion of Roesner's findings, see chap. 5.

148. See, for example, Schick, "Musik wird zum Kunstwerk"; Stenzl, ed., *Perotinus Magnus*; Flotzinger, *Perotinus musicus*.

149. Wright, *Music and Ceremony*, 258. This statement is particularly surprising because Wright has also shown that the Notre Dame repertory was performed from memory. See chap. 5.

writing substitutes for his discant sections."[150] Wright also refers to the more rhythmically structured sections as more "developed."[151] And medievalists continue to be concerned about finding out who the main composers were,[152] and how to distinguish their styles.

Scholars have also continued to analyze medieval polyphony with criteria derived from the nineteenth-century autonomous artwork. Perotin, in particular, has been hailed as the first modern "composer." In the introduction to an edition entitled *The Works of Perotin,* the editor, Ethel Thurston, writes very much in Ludwig's spirit: "he [Perotin] developed the use of unifying devices such as imitation, *Stimmtausch,* and melodic variation, which have become part of contrapuntal practice ever since. Like Bach and Mozart after him, he focussed diverse national influences into well organised large scale masterpieces which were the high point of the periods."[153]

Similarly, Fritz Reckow's discussion of Perotin reminds us of Ludwig's analysis of Notre Dame polyphony: he sees in him a great composer who has reworked Leonin's more improvisational pieces into fully worked-out compositions in the modern sense; "their singularity and finality is also expressed by the fact that . . . now composers are mentioned for the first time."[154] The organum is analyzed much like a Bach fugue, as a work of a great composer, concerned with planning every detail and integrating it within larger formal structures. When comparing different versions of a piece, Reckow, just as Ludwig, will consider the more regular version the better one.[155] Reckow admits in a footnote that his analysis is not reflected in statements by thirteenth-century music theorists: "It is difficult to say to what extent, or if at all, the attempts at a large unified form were understood and appreciated by contemporaries. Even Anonymous IV, not at all a simple mind, is mainly enthusiastic about the many *colores* and *pulchritudines*—for the most part simple stereotypical formulas—in the three-part *Alleluia Dies sanctificatus.*"[156] It never occurred to Reckow that composers might not have been interested

150. Wright is referring to the possibility that "the entire cycle of ninety-odd compositions could easily have been conceived and executed during the creative life of a single composer, Magister Leoninus" (p. 258).

151. Craig Wright, *Music and Ceremony,* 244–45.

152. See, for example, ibid., 267–94. See also Mark Everist, "From Paris to St. Andrew's," 32, and also my discussion of Schick and Arlt below.

153. Perotin, *Works of Perotin,* ed. Thurston, 1.

154. "[D]eren Einmaligkeit und Endgültigkeit auch darin zum Ausdruck kommt, dass . . . Komponisten erstmals erwähnt werden." Reckow, "Das Organum," 449.

155. Ibid., 466–74.

156. "Inwieweit die Bemühungen um grossformale Geschlossenheit von den Zeitgenossen überhaupt wahrgenommen und gewürdigt sind, ist allerdings schwer zu ergründen; selbst der gewiss nicht unbeschlagene Anonymous IV begeistert sich vor allem an dem Übermass der co-

in creating large unified forms. Why not take Anonymous IV at face value and study the use of *colores*?[157]

In a 1995 paper, Hartmut Schick sees Leonin rather than Perotin in the role of the first composer who works at his desk rather than in the church: "In the two organa by Leonin the moment of artful singing, the *ars organizandi,* has been entirely replaced by worked-out and balanced composition in the modern sense of the word, which presupposes writing and takes place at the desk and no longer in the church. And thus an important, if not the decisive, step in the evolution of music to the musical artwork has been achieved."[158]

In 2000 Jürg Stenzl published a book entitled *Perotinus Magnus* that was intended to summarize and reevaluate Notre Dame scholarship.[159] As usual, Ludwig takes center stage: his 1921 article "Perotinus Magnus" was reprinted without significant commentary. Now, considering recent developments in Notre Dame scholarship, the publication of this volume would have provided the author with an excellent opportunity to revisit Ludwig's contribution to the field, such as has been done with fascinating results for Ludwig's student Heinrich Besseler by Lawrence F. Bernstein and Laurenz Lütteken.[160] It seems thus that Stenzl subscribes to a view of the Notre Dame period that is similar to Ludwig's. Wulf Arlt, the author of an analytical article in Stenzl's volume that takes up almost half of the book, is happy to apply analytical tools honed on centuries of Beethoven research to a conductus that may or may not be by Perotin.[161] It is obvious that Arlt believes that the conductus will be fully appreciated only if he is able to demonstrate that it exhibits a complex structure similar to pieces from the canonic repertory of Western music. Ludwig had already drawn a parallel between Bach's F-major Toccata and Perotin's quadruplum *Viderunt omnes.* The only difference between Ludwig, on the one hand, and Arlt and Stenzl, on the other, is that the latter outdo even Ludwig in their zeal to canonize Perotin. For Ludwig the organa

---

lores und pulchritudines in der Hauptsache recht stereotyper Formeln in dem dreistimmigen Alleluia Dies sanctificatus." Ibid., 492.

157. See chap. 5, pp. 165–74.

158. "In den beiden Organa Leonins ist das Moment kunstfertiger (Gesangs-) Praxis, die *Ars organizandi,* vollends dem kalkulierenden und abwägenden, Schriftlichkeit vorraussetzenden (und am Schreibtisch, nicht mehr in der Kirche stattfindenden) Komponieren im modernen Sinne gewichen, und damit ein wesentlicher—wenn nicht der entscheidende Schritt—vollzogen in der Entwicklung der Musik hin zum musikalischen Kunstwerk." Schick, "Musik wird zum Kunstwerk."

159. Stenzl, ed., *Perotinus Magnus.* See also my review of the book in *Plainsong and Medieval Music* (2002): 44–54.

160. Bernstein, "Ockeghem" and Lütteken, "Heinrich Besselers musikhistoriographischer Ansatz."

161. Arlt, "Denken in Tönen und Strukturen."

were not yet as complex as the works of Palestrina and Bach; Stenzl seems not to share this opinion when he says: "After Ludwig's death in 1930 it took almost half a century until music historians were able to understand Notre-Dame organa . . . from an analytical point of view as artworks."[162] In other words, we have only recently developed the analytical tools capable of doing justice to these pieces.

Arlt concentrates in particular on one motive of a descending fourth (F–G–G–E–D, or simply G–F–E–D), which he discovers on various other scale degrees and in inversion and augmentation throughout the piece. He is so eager to discover the descending fourths and their various transformations that on occasion he will pick tones that fit his scheme, overlooking others that seem (to me) to be no less important. This is not to say that all of his examples are unconvincing; some certainly work. But a descending tetrachord is a rather basic melodic figure, which can be found throughout the Western repertory. Roesner and Immel have shown that it is a typical *coniunctura* formula with which to ornament note-against-note counterpoint (see also my discussion of this issue on p. 170).[163]

In contrast to Ludwig, Arlt is aware of his aesthetic biases. He admits that he uses analytical tools from later periods. But he does not think this is a problem because he believes that even though the compositional techniques under discussion were only described in later centuries, they were already in operation in the Middle Ages. The theorists and composers did not yet fully understand what they were doing. In short, it would seem that like Ludwig, he knows better. Even though he says explicitly that his analysis treats medieval theory just as seriously as, say, scholars of the classical style treat Heinrich Christoph Koch, this is not the case. Rather, his goal is to show that the structure of this composition is as complex as that of later periods, and he hopes that his analysis will revive interest in the Middle Ages. The difference between Ludwig and Arlt is that Arlt knows he is prejudiced, while Ludwig believed in his own objectivity. One regrets that Arlt's superior self-knowledge has had no practical consequences.

These few examples show that Ludwig's spirit is alive and well. There can be no doubt that Ludwig completed a necessary and tremendously impressive body of work. In fact, it was so impressive that subsequent scholars preferred to refine his answers rather than recognize that some of his questions were wrong-headed and other questions went unasked. Why did it take musicology so long to go beyond Ludwig? I think there are several reasons why Ludwig's influence was so strong: first, he published a book rather than a series of articles, as Handschin did. And this book, the *Repertorium,* was a cat-

162. *Perotinus Magnus,* 26.

163. Roesner, "Who 'Made' the *Magnus liber*?"; Immel, "The Vatican Organum Treatise Re-examined."

alog that simply had to be consulted by anyone who wanted to work on Notre Dame polyphony and motets, while later scholars could easily overlook Handschin's articles. Second, Ludwig left a great number of devoted students behind who continued the kind of work he started. And third, the analysis of sources is a subject that lends itself to teaching; it is a topic that anybody endowed with substantial patience and intelligence can learn.

In short, while we can state, on the one hand, that part of Ludwig's oeuvre, namely the catalog, has held up well to posterity, we have to admit, on the other hand, that Ludwig's agenda has made it possible to work in medieval music for one hundred years without ever seriously considering the role of memory in the composition and transmission of polyphony. The result is a one-sided view of medieval music that places the beginning of composition in the modern sense in the twelfth and early thirteenth centuries and simply assumes that these pieces were conceived in writing. I hope to show in the remaining chapters of this book that a study of the role of memory allows us to arrive at a new and very different picture of medieval music, a picture more in line with cultural practices of the period, where oral and written transmission interact.

PART ONE

The Construction of the Memorial Archive

The memorial archive of the medieval musician covered three areas. The first was chant, the second elementary music treatises, and the third counterpoint. While the first two areas are of importance from Carolingian times to the end of the fifteenth century, the learning of counterpoint became particularly important from the thirteenth century on. The central question I will address in all three areas is: how was the material memorized?

It is generally agreed that all music was sung from memory before the invention of the staff, and that the deterioration of performance from memory came with the advent of precise pitch notation on the staff, and even more, with precisely measured rhythmic notation. It is a common belief that once something can be written down accurately, singers no longer need to be burdened with the cumbersome process of memorization; they can sing directly from notation. My hypothesis will be exactly the opposite: the ability to write something down, to visualize it, allowed for exact memorization and opened up new ways of committing material to memory. Throughout this book my argument will be that musical notation, like writing, does not replace performance from memory, but, on the contrary, may be used to aid it. The fact that something was written down does not have to mean that it was no longer transmitted orally as well, for written texts and oral transmission may well coexist. I will examine how this argument affects each of the three areas in turn.

2

Tonaries

A Tool for Memorizing Chant

Life in early Western monasteries centered around the Divine Office. From the moment a boy entered a monastery he spent much of his time singing and memorizing chant. In 830, Agobard of Lyon described the demands made on monastic singers as follows: "Most of them have spent all the days of their life from earliest youth to gray age in the preparation and development of their singing."[1] Monks who were not particularly gifted could take from two to three years just to learn the psalms by heart.[2] Others managed to memorize all the psalms in only six months.[3]

Why did medieval students have to memorize even though they could read and write? Recent scholarship in musicology, anthropology, and literary studies has made clear that the invention of writing does not automatically put

1. "Ex quibus quam plurimi ab ineunte pueritia usque ad senectutis canitiem omnes dies vitae suae in parando et confirmando cantu expendunt"; from "De antiphonario," in *Agobardi Lugdunensis Opera omnia,* 350; see also Smits van Waesberghe, *Musikerziehung,* 25.

2. See Riché, *Education and Culture,* 115, 462–68.

3. For an entertaining, if not authentic, account of life in the monastery of Reichenau, see the "diary" compiled by a Benedictine from Einsiedeln in 1856 and published under the name of the Reichenau Abbot Walahfrid Strabo. The text derives much information from the writings of Bede, Alcuin, and Hrabanus Maurus. The description of learning and singing the psalter certainly gives an accurate impression, so much so that Smits van Waesberghe quoted it in his *Musikerziehung* as a diary entry of Walahfrid: "Every day they read a section of the psalter to us. We wrote it onto our wax tablets. Then everyone had to correct the mistakes of his neighbor. And one of them who was already studying grammar in the fourth year had to look through all the work. Then one went through it word by word, everything was explained, and the next morning we had to memorize the whole passage. This way we learned the entire psalter by heart in the course of the winter and following summer. From now on, just as the other students, we were allowed to participate in singing in the choir with the other brothers" (p. 23). For a translation into German of the entire "diary," see Messer, *Geschichte der Pädagogik,* 67–83.

an end to memorization. Quite the opposite, writing is normally used at first as a mnemonic tool.[4] Thus, we should no longer assume that the invention of the staff by Guido of Arezzo (ca. 1030), which made possible unambiguous pitch notation, eliminated or reduced performance from memory. Craig Wright has demonstrated that at Notre Dame of Paris singers were expected to memorize chant throughout the seventeenth century.[5] He quotes from the *Caeremoniale Parisiense* from 1662, which specifies: "Things should be sung by memory following the example of the metropolitan church of Paris and other cathedral churches of the realm; in which church of Paris the singers always sing by memory whatever they have to sing both at Mass and at the hours including all Invitatory psalms *Venite,* all responsories, graduals with verses, Alleluias also with verses, and certain other things."[6] Since the general trend in medieval and early modern music was toward increasing reliance on notation, it seems likely that this statement can be applied to the earlier period as well. Moreover, Wright points out that Notre Dame is a dark church, where the use of candles is required if one wants to read, and his survey of records of payments leaves no doubt that candles were only used for major festivals. At all other occasions the singers must have sung by heart. In short, even though some liturgical manuscripts existed,[7] the evidence points toward performance from memory.

What exactly did one memorize? Students learned to read by reciting the Psalter, first combining letters into syllables, syllables into words, and words into sentences. Since they did not know Latin, at first they did not know what they were reciting.[8] The term *psalteratus* referred to somebody who knew how to read. But even monks who did not learn how to read eventually memorized the Psalter by rote.[9] Benedict required the entire Psalter of 150 psalms to be sung every week.[10]

When a psalm was performed in the Divine Office, it was framed by an antiphon, of which there existed three thousand or more by the end of the Middle Ages.[11] Note, though, that these antiphons were relatively easy to memo-

4. For musicology see in particular Wright, *Music and Ceremony*; for anthropology, see Goody, *Interface between the Written and the Oral*; and for literary studies, see Carruthers, *Book of Memory*.

5. *Music and Ceremony,* 325–29.

6. Ibid., 328.

7. See ibid., 333–34.

8. Riché, "Apprendre à lire et à écrire." See also his *Education and Culture,* 115, 461–68, and S. Reynolds, *Medieval Reading*.

9. Riché, "Rôle de la mémoire," 136.

10. See especially Coleman, *Ancient and Medieval Memories,* 117–54.

11. See Hiley, *Western Plainchant,* 329. Regino of Prüm already listed over 1,000 by 900, when he wrote his tonary. His *Epistola de harmonica institutione* has been newly edited by Michael Bernhard.

rize because they used the same stock formulas again and again.[12] As for the Mass, Michel Huglo has computed that the eighth- and ninth-century Gradual contained about 560 chants: 70 introits, 118 graduals, 100 alleluias, 18 tracts, 107 offertories, and 150 communions.[13] Kenneth Levy has calculated that if one adds to this the Office Propers, we "might come to seventy-five or eighty hours of memorized matter. This would correspond to the selection of Beethoven's instrumental works plus the full Wagnerian canon."[14]

All in all, the singing in Benedictine monasteries lasted at least six hours each day. In late eleventh-century Cluny, where monks did not have to work and could concentrate fully on meditation and singing, they could easily spend the entire day in church. The number of psalms sung there every day had increased to 215. Monks attended two or three conventual Masses, in addition to offices, processions, litanies, and other public prayers.[15] Not surprisingly, this led to the overburdening of the monastic memory. Various attempts were made to drastically shorten the liturgy, most importantly by the Cistercians. Yet even in the Cistercian *Ecclesiastica Officia* (before 1154) "silence was imposed, *except* for those learning antiphons, hymns and the content of the Gradual. For such monks it was permitted that they ask other brethren to hear them as they practised reciting what they had memorized. They were forbidden to ask questions, except concerning the length of the syllables and accentuation in reciting."[16] To us it seems unimaginable how the monks could have memorized all of these pieces. How could they possibly achieve such a feat? And how would they have known which chant to sing at which occasion? What role did writing play in all of this?

The texts of the Proper chants for the entire liturgical year were written down after 800 without musical notation. Frankish graduals with neumes were notated after 900.[17] From our perspective, neumes are an ambiguous notational tool because they do not specify pitch. We can only read those neumed pieces which have been transmitted in later manuscripts in diastematic notation (that is, a notation that shows the pitch of the note vertically on the page). And yet they seem to have been adequate for medieval monks, at least for the time.[18] The function of non-diastematic neumes, then,

12. François Gevaert analyzed more than 1,000 opening formulas of Office antiphons mentioned by Regino of Prüm and classified them into forty-seven "themes" in *Mélopée antique*. For other attempts at organization, see Hiley, *Western Plainchant*, 89–90.

13. Huglo, *Livres de chant liturgique*, 102.

14. Levy, *Gregorian Chant*, 175–76.

15. Coleman, *Ancient and Medieval Memories*, 152.

16. Ibid., 175.

17. See Hiley, *Western Plainchant*, 345–73.

18. David Hughes has argued that the transmission of Gregorian chant from the ninth through the thirteenth centuries is remarkably uniform, which makes a purely oral transmis-

was not to indicate exact pitch; rather, the neumes helped singers to perform chants that they already knew very well.[19]

Even after the music was notated on the staff monks continued to memorize the chant. Probably much of the material was simply memorized by rote; the singers would repeat what their teacher sang, and gradually learn the chant.[20] First and foremost, the text would recall the melodies. Then the neumes and later the music notated on the staff would help singers in performances of pieces they already knew. But the earliest neumes were so small that singers could not have used them in the choir.[21] Kenneth Levy has suggested that the books were used only by the choirmasters,[22] and these visual aids were rarely used in performances. And since the repertory of chant was rapidly increasing, the cantor must have used other mnemonic tools that enabled him not only to memorize, but, more importantly, to retrieve the right chant for the occasion. If a cantor had memorized some 3,000 antiphons, how would he know which one to choose?

Let me stress at the outset that we will never be able to show with certainty how the chant was memorized. All we can do is look at the available sources and develop a hypothesis that seems likely and which is in accord with the general culture of the period. In the following, I first propose to explain how verbal texts were memorized and retrieved, and then to explore whether similar methods might also have been applied to musical texts.

I stated earlier that chant was memorized throughout the Middle Ages and Renaissance, even after music was notated. One could argue that the level of literacy was a very different one around 900 than around 1200. Yet I have found that the invention of diastematic notation resulted in no radical change in the procedures used to commit the chant to memory. Thus, I hope to show that the basic techniques for memorizing and retrieving the pieces remained similar from ca. 800 to 1500.

---

sion unlikely. See his "Evidence for the Traditional View." Similarly, Levy has argued that an archetype of chant must have existed around 800; see his *Gregorian Chant.* These hypotheses stand in contradiction to Leo Treitler and Helmut Hucke, who believe that the chant was reconstructed in every performance. See Treitler, "Homer and Gregory"; "Centonate Chant"; "Oral, Written, and Literate Process"; "Early History of Music Writing"; "'Unwritten' and 'Written Transmission'"; Hucke, "Toward a New Historical View." For a recent reprint of Treitler's articles see *With Voice and Pen.*

19. For an excellent summary of the function of neumes see Crocker, "Chants of the Roman Office," 166–67.

20. Smits van Waesberghe, *Musikerziehung,* 25. For the most recent discussion of memorization by rote see Crocker, *Introduction to Gregorian Chant,* 150.

21. Levy, *Gregorian Chant,* 88.

22. Ibid., 192.

MNEMONIC TECHNIQUES

Divisio in Elementary Memory Treatises

The most basic and widespread mnemonic technique consists of dividing and classifying material. Quintilian, whose *Institutio oratoria* remained standard throughout the Middle Ages, advised using *divisio* to help memorize long speeches.[23] Likewise he recommended placing *notae* in the margins to help remember particularly difficult material. In the fourth century Fortunatianus said: "What best helps the memory? Division and composition; for order most secures the memory."[24] He too recommends the addition of *notae* (in the margins or on top) for those passages which are hard to commit to memory.

The most detailed discussion of *divisio* is in Hugh of St. Victor's "De tribus maximis circumstantiis gestorum," addressed to very young students in the school of St. Victor in 1130.[25] Mary Carruthers points out that the text must have been considered basic knowledge, which, of course, makes it particularly interesting to us.[26] In fact, it was so elementary that most writers did not even bother to discuss it. According to Hugh, knowledge *(sapientia)* is acquired throughout life. It is considered a treasure *(thesaurus)* and "your heart is its strongbox *(archa)*" (p. 261). A little later he states, "a classifying-system for material makes it palpable and visible to the mind [discretio rerum evidentiam facit]. Truly such a visual scheme for one's learning both illuminates the soul when it perceives and knows things, and confirms them in memory" (ibid.). He instructs his students how to memorize the psalms as follows:

> Suppose for example that I wish to learn the psalter word for word by heart. I proceed thus: first I consider how many psalms there are. There are 150. I learn them all in order so that I know which is first, which second, which third, and so on. I then place them all by order in my heart along my [mental] numerical grid, and one at a time I designate them to the seats where they are disposed in the grid, while at the same time, accompanied by voicing [prolatio] of cogitation, I listen and observe closely [attendo] until each becomes to me of a size equivalent to one glance of my memory . . . Having learned the [whole order of] psalms, I then devise the same sort of scheme for each separate psalm, starting with the beginning [words] of the verses just as I did for the whole psalter starting with the first words of the psalms, and I can thereafter easily

23. Quintilian, *Institutio oratoria* 11.2, pp. 227–33. See also Mary Carruthers's discussion of elementary memory designs and *divisio* throughout her *Book of Memory,* but especially pp. 88–121.

24. "Quid vel maxime memoriam adiuvat? Divisio et compositio: nam memoriam vehementer ordo servat." Fortunatianus, *Artis rhetoricae libri III,* ed. Halm, 129, trans. Carruthers in *Book of Memory,* 86.

25. The text is translated by Carruthers in *Book of Memory,* 261–66.

26. Ibid., 8, 95. Further references in text are to Carruthers's translation.

> retain in my heart the whole series one verse at a time; first by dividing and marking off the book by [whole] psalms and then each psalm by verses, I have reduced a large amount of material to such conciseness and brevity. And this [method] in fact can readily be seen in the psalms or in other books containing inherent divisions. When however the reading is in an unbroken series, it is necessary to do this artificially . . . (262–63)

Hugh advises further always to use the same copy of a text when memorizing something, because one memorizes not "only the number and order of verses or ideas, but at the same time the color, shape, position, and placement of the letters, where we have seen this or that written, in what part, in what location (at the top, the middle, or the bottom) we saw it positioned, in what color we observed the trace of the letter" (264).

Hugh's advice is not different from that of modern psychologists, as Carruthers has pointed out. Most people are unable to memorize more than between five and nine units, but once the subject matter is subdivided, the amount of material that can be memorized seems infinite.[27] Similarly, Hugh arranges the pages in his *Chronica* in four columns, "with headings in red introducing groups of ten (sometimes fewer) items."[28]

The alphabetizing of chapters, units, etc. was an equally popular device, already mentioned by Aristotle in *De memoria.* He recommends using the alphabet to organize memorized material, and if there is too much to memorize, one should use several sets of alphabets.[29]

Florilegia

The most important item to which these systems of classification have been applied are florilegia. Literary historians have recognized their importance in recent years, and much has been published on their origins, functions, and classification systems.[30] As Henri-Jean Martin has recently shown, in the Middle Ages, students had a very different approach to "reading" than we do today. They "struggled with every word and every phrase until they had totally assimilated it."[31] "Reading" meant memorizing. Often it was enough

27. Ibid., 84.

28. Ibid., 93. See also her pl. 3 for a facsimile of the page layout.

29. Aristotle, *On Memory,* trans. Sorabji, 31–34; Carruthers, *Book of Memory,* 29–30, 109–10.

30. The best study on florilegia before the 13th c. is Munk Olsen's "Classiques latins dans les florilèges médiévaux." He lists twenty-six florilegia in thirty-eight manuscripts. The most important are the *Florilegium Gallicum* and *Florilegium Angelicum.* On the *Florilegium Angelicum* see Rouse and Rouse, "*Florilegium Angelicum*"; another excellent article is Taylor, "Medieval Proverb Collections." For the later Middle Ages the most important article is Rouse and Rouse, "*Statim invenire.*"

31. Martin, *History and Power of Writing,* 154.

to remember the gist of the matter rather than a word-for-word memorization.[32] The fourteenth-century English Dominican Thomas of Waleys advises that "[in] many authoritative texts of the saints . . . it is better and more useful to speak according to their sense alone than to recite word for word."[33] Waleys uses the verbs *retinere* and *dicere* for memory *ad res,* and *recitare* for memory *ad verbum.*

Florilegia came into existence because students were expected to memorize more and more texts, and it became increasingly difficult to keep track of what was committed to memory. What was needed were tools to help retrieve material from the memorial archive.

What was memorized? After having mastered reading, writing, and grammar, a student went on to memorize the *Disticha Catonis,* the Bible, and texts by Vergil, Ovid, Lucan, Statius, Boethius, and many others. William of Ockham recommended that his students extract passages from sacred learning, moral philosophy, history, and law.[34] A florilegium, then, consists of excerpts and maxims from classical and biblical texts. The original works on which later collections were modeled are the *Disticha Catonis* and the biblical Wisdom books. Later collections often attempted to harmonize biblical and classical material.

Florilegia can be divided into several groups, depending on the classification system employed. In the first group the material is preserved under the name of the author and copied in the order in which it appears in the original.[35] A typical example of this is the *Florilegium Angelicum,* which consists of extracts from ancient and patristic orations and letters. It includes maxims, aphorisms, and sententious statements of universal truth. Compiled in France during the second half of the twelfth century, it was used by Gerald of Wales in his last years.[36] Richard and Mary Rouse argue that it was not only the contents that were attractive to readers, but also the "memorable words."[37] It was extremely popular, surviving in more than seventeen manuscripts. Moreover, it had an extensive subject index. Its principal function was to aid in the composition of sermons. This florilegium was twice rearranged by subject in the middle of the thirteenth century, and then Thomas of Ireland reorganized it again in the early fourteenth century according to topic and alphabet in his *Manipulus florum.*[38]

32. Carruthers, *Book of Memory,* 161–62.

33. "[multae] sunt auctoritates sanctorum . . . melius est utilius solum sententialiter dicere quam verbaliter recitare." "De modo componendi sermones," ed. Charland, in *Artes praedicandi;* trans. Carruthers, *Book of Memory,* 90.

34. Carruthers, *Book of Memory,* 176.

35. Taylor, "Medieval Proverb Collections," 22–23 and 26.

36. Rouse and Rouse, "*Florilegium Angelicum,*" 66.

37. Ibid., 88.

38. Ibid., 93.

The second category consists of alphabetically arranged epitomes. Examples from ancient sources are the *Sententiae* of Publilius Syrus, and the very popular ninth-century *Proverbia Senecae,* which was imitated by Othlo of St. Emmeram in his *Libellus proverbiorum.*[39] The latter is derived from Christian sources, but the emulation is shown by the use of prose and the alphabetical arrangement. Important also is Papias's dictionary, *Elementarium doctrinae erudimentum,* from the middle of the eleventh century, which uses three different sizes of letters, a large letter, a middle-sized letter, and a small marginal letter, to catalog material.[40] Late twelfth-century *Distinctiones,* biblical excerpts used for preaching, were increasingly arranged alphabetically too. Examples are Peter the Chanter's *Summa seu distinctiones Abel* (about 1190) and Alain of Lille's *Distinctiones dictionum theologicarum* (before 1195).[41] But the alphabetic arrangement was by no means universal.[42] The Rouses stress that the alphabetization of theological material represented a new attitude:

> Prior to this time, alphabetization had been largely restricted to lists of things which had no known or discernible rational relationship: one alphabetized lapidaries, for instance, because no classification of stones existed. For alphabetized distinction collections, such a rule did not hold: one was in no sense compelled to use alphabetical order, as witness those collections organized according to the order of the Scriptures or some other rational order. Rather, the use of alphabetical order was a tacit recognition of the fact that each user of a work will bring to it his own preconceived rational order, which may differ from those of other users and from that of the writer himself.[43]

The most famous description of alphabetical indexing is from the late fifteenth century. Peter of Ravenna (Petrus Tommai) boasts in his *Foenix domini Petri Raven[n]atis memoriae magistri* (1491) that he has memorized 20,000 legal extracts, 1,000 texts from Ovid, 200 from Cicero, 300 sayings of the philosophers, 700 passages from the Bible, and more, and has classified it all in nineteen letters of the alphabet. It goes without saying that he needed many subdivisions: he organized his collection on the first level according to the alphabet, then the word beginnings, and finally according to subject.[44]

39. Taylor, "Medieval Proverb Collections," 26.

40. Rouse and Rouse, "*Statim invenire,*" 203. See also Daly and Daly, "Some Techniques in Mediaeval Latin Lexiography" and Daly, *Contributions to a History of Alphabetization,* 71–72.

41. PL 210: 685–1012. See also Alain de Lille, *Textes inédits,* ed. d'Alverny, 242–25, 270, 276–77.

42. Peter of Poitiers and Prepositinus arranged their *Distinctiones* in the order of the Psalter, while Peter of Cornwall (ca. 1189–1200) and Peter of Capua (ca. 1220) preferred a combination of alphabetical order with rational order. See Rouse and Rouse, "*Statim invenire,*" 211.

43. Ibid., 212.

44. See also Carruthers, *Book of Memory,* 114–15.

The third group consists of sayings by philosophers organized according to subject. One of the earliest examples is a florilegium compiled by Hadoardus, a monk from Corbie, in the early ninth century.[45] Some were organized according to moral topics.[46] Eventually *distinctiones* were made of writings of the Church Fathers and Aristotle.

What was the purpose of all of this cataloging activity? The florilegia and *distinctiones* allowed one to compose and produce new texts. They also made it easier to prepare speeches. It was now possible to retrieve material quickly, whether one checked under an author, under a subject, or under the first letter of the word, while previously it was necessary to go through entire books to find a specific passage. The passage in the florilegium could bring to mind the entire text. Jean Leclercq already showed in 1957 that simple words (he calls them hooks) could evoke the whole passage. And this passage might, in turn, provide other associations, so the result was a chain reaction.[47] We know that it was especially useful for the composition of letters *(ars dictamen)* (the *Florilegium Angelicum* was supposed to help letter-writers in episcopal chanceries) and for preaching.

The florilegia also functioned as textbooks. Barry Taylor has pointed out that Othlo's *Libellus proverbium* was intended to be read by schoolboys.[48] In fact, it was considered so basic and important that it was read, and probably memorized, immediately after the Psalms. Additionally, it had the advantage of being Christian, in contrast to Cato's *Distichs*. There are florilegia that teach versification, the most famous of which is the *Florilegium Treverense*,[49] while Mico of Riquier's florilegium was intended to instruct students in the writing of prosody.

From the very beginning the collection of these passages was considered a tool for memorization. Quintilian says that "this will train their memory, form their style in imitation of the best authors by an unconscious process of absorption, provide an abundant treasure house of vocabulary, patterns of sentence structure, and figurative expressions, and enable them to acquire a happy knack with quotations."[50] Macrobius intended originally to jot down notes while reading Vergil to help his memory; instead of a shapeless mass

45. Taylor, "Medieval Proverb Collections," 27.

46. Munk Olsen, "Classiques latins," 47–57.

47. Leclercq, *Love of Learning*, 91.

48. Taylor, "Medieval Proverb Collections," 32. Othlo, ed. Korfmacher. Othlo is also in PL 146: 299–338.

49. Ed. Brunhölzl.

50. "Nam et exercebitur memoria . . . et adsuescent optimis semperque habebunt inter se, quod imitentur; et iam non sentientes formam orationis illam, quam mente penitus acceperint, expriment. Abundabunt autem copia verborum optimorum et compositione et figuris iam non quaesitis sed sponte et ex reposito velut thesauro se offerentibus. Accedit his et iucunda in sermone bene a quoque dictorum relatio." Quintilian, *Institutio oratoria* 2.7.2–4.

it became an "ordered and manageable body of retrievable information."[51] A later florilegium, also intended to be memorized, is Gasparinus Barzizza's (1360–1430) *De imitatione.*[52] Petrarch alluded to the fact that his compilation was memorized by entitling his florilegium *Rerum memorandum libri.*[53] In short, to quote Ann Moss, "the *florilegium* remained the vehicle for committing particularly interesting passages from one's reading to writing, and thence to memory."[54] That is not to say that all of the technical scholastic florilegia were memorized, but they were used by people who had already absorbed the material cited in them earlier; thus they reminded the reader of something he already knew; they are, to use Mary Carruthers's words, "memorial promptbooks."[55] In short, the florilegium served two purposes: it helped retrieve texts already memorized, and it was also memorized in its own right.

The increasing sophistication of the florilegia also had an impact on the physical appearance of the page. In the twelfth century, for example with Gratian, running titles were common.[56] In the thirteenth and fourteenth centuries, to quote Henri-Jean Martin, "the copyists took care to punctuate such texts, not just to guide the inflection of the voice but to aid comprehension. The same led to concentrating the greatest possible amount of text on one page and to a search for a density that expressed more than a simple desire to save parchment. Hence the systematic use of conventional abbreviations, which, like ideograms, permit the reader to grasp a notion at a glance."[57]

The script, the paragraphs, the chapters, the marginal notes, the glosses, the running titles, the colors—all of this was intended to reinforce the divisions of the text, to make it easier to understand and easier to memorize.

TONARIES

We have seen that medieval singers had to memorize an enormous quantity of liturgical texts and music. From our perspective the most obvious question is why singers did not make use of musical notation earlier, and more systematically once it was invented. Were perhaps some of the techniques described above applied to the memorization of liturgical music, in spite of the differences between memorizing melodies and letters? More specifically, was there was a similar cataloging activity going on in music?

51. *Saturnalia,* ed. Willis, I Praef., 2–3; Moss, *Printed Commonplace-Books,* 13.
52. Ed. Pigman. See also Moss, *Printed Commonplace-Books,* 52–53.
53. Ed. Billanovich.
54. Moss, *Printed Commonplace-Books,* 53.
55. Carruthers, *Book of Memory,* 176.
56. See especially Parkes, "Influence of the Concepts of *Ordinatio* and *Compilatio.*"
57. Martin, *History and Power of Writing,* 151.

TABLE 1. The Carolingian Modes and Psalm Tones

			Range (nominal)	*Mode final*	*Psalm tone reciting tone*
Protus	Authentic	Mode 1	D–d	D	a
	Plagal	Mode 2	A–a	D	F
Deuterus	Authentic	Mode 3	E–e	E	(b) c
	Plagal	Mode 4	B–b	E	a
Tritus	Authentic	Mode 5	F–f	F	c
	Plagal	Mode 6	C–c	F	a
Tetrardus	Authentic	Mode 7	G–g	G	d
	Plagal	Mode 8	D–d	G	c

Tonaries may suggest an answer. In the course of the eighth century, Carolingian theorists cataloged an already existing body of liturgical chant according to the eight psalm tones of Gregorian chant. The terminology of the tonaries was transferred from the *oktoechos,* which probably came from the Jerusalem.[58] It is important to distinguish between modes and psalm tones. At this stage modes were nothing other than an abstract classifying device, while the eight psalm tones were melody types characterized by a reciting tone, a range of pitches employed, and an intonation formula (Table 1). About one hundred years later the treatise called *Alia musica* introduced the species of fourth and fifth and the Greek names to the modal system.

The tonaries typically classify antiphons for the Office, but also for the Mass; in addition there are Mass responsories, graduals, tracts, alleluias, and even sequences. Each item is identified by the textual incipit of the psalm tone (*noeane* syllables), with or without musical notation. The earliest tonary dates from the late eighth or early ninth century;[59] the last ones were printed in the early sixteenth century.[60] Tonaries were used wherever one sang chant.

The usual order of listing chants in the gradual and antiphoner followed the sequence of the liturgical calendar, starting with the First Sunday of Advent. Thus, an antiphoner would simply answer the question, What do we sing today? If one wanted to determine the mode of a piece written in diastematic notation, it was necessary to consider the last tone, the final, as well

58. The best surveys of the topic are Jeffery, "Earliest Oktoechoi"; Atkinson, "Modus"; and Powers, "Mode." Atkinson untangles the initial confusion between the terms *tonus, modus,* and *tropus.* See also Falconer, "Modes before the Modes."

59. Huglo, *Tonaires,* 26–27.

60. See, for example, Wollick, *Enchiridion musices* (1512) and Burchard, *Hortulus musices* (1514). See also Huglo, *Tonaires,* 440–41.

as the other pitch features of the melody.[61] In neumatic notation, it was impossible to recognize the mode of the piece unless it was known by heart. The most important point about the tonaries is that their compilers fundamentally reorganized the order of the antiphoners (and often graduals as well), replacing the liturgical order with a classification into eight modes.

Various systems of classification are encountered in the tonaries. Since chant was memorized throughout the entire Middle Ages and Renaissance, I have looked at tonaries between ca. 800 (the earliest is St. Riquier, which was copied in the last years of the eighth century)[62] and ca. 1500. In each case I have looked for methods of classification. I have chosen to discuss tonaries from different periods and geographic areas together because the systems of classification remained very similar, whether they were compiled with neumes or with diastematic notation.

The most distinctive feature of the tonaries is that the chant is classified hierarchically. On the first level it is always arranged by mode, and it is noteworthy that there are no exceptions to this. Then within each mode, there are a number of possibilities: the antiphons may, in turn, be arranged (a) liturgically, (b) alphabetically, (c) according to the proximity of the first note to the final, (d) according to similarities of antiphon beginnings, (e) according to the level of complexity.

Why did theorists classify by mode? It should be remembered that the modal system was not yet fully developed. In fact, in early tonaries, classification by final defines what mode is all about. It is not hard to understand why theorists began grouping the chant in this way. They noticed that many antiphons share similar designs, ranges, and beginnings and simply arranged them accordingly. In the late nineteenth century, François-Auguste Gevaert did something similar when he organized some 1,000 antiphons into forty-seven *thèmes*.[63]

In order to explain how the classification into modes might have helped cantors in the performance of antiphons, it would be useful to summarize how these were performed. In the Office each antiphon was sung with a complete psalm, in which each verse was sung to a formula, the "psalm tone," consisting of two halves. After a short intonation (usually three to four pitches) the psalm tone settled on a reciting pitch, then continued with an internal cadence (the "mediant cadence"). The second half resumed the reciting pitch, and ended with a different cadence ("termination"). To most psalms was appended the short Doxology,

61. Note, though, that one theorist, Regino of Prüm, classified the antiphons according to their first note. See his *De harmonica institutione,* ed. Bernhard. See also Boncella, "Regino Prumiensis and the Tones."

62. Huglo, *Tonaires,* 26. The tonary is in Paris, BNF lat. 13159.

63. Gevaert, *Melopée antique.*

Gloria Patri et Filio: et Spiritui sancto.
Sicut erat in principio, et nunc et semper: et in saecula saeculorum. Amen.

This was usually treated as two verses, that is, twice through the psalm tone. Each psalm was framed by an antiphon:

Antiphon, Psalm verse 1, 2, 3 . . . Gloria Patri, Antiphon.

(In alternative use, perhaps more frequently at an earlier time, the antiphon might be repeated after groups of verses, or even after every verse.) Each antiphon had its own independent set of words with its own short melody. But since, even in the early stages, there were between 1,000 and 2,000 antiphons, much reuse was made of melodic idioms, and in some cases more or less the same melody was used for a hundred or more texts (in which case the melody is known as a "model melody" or "melody type"). Each antiphon was classed in one of eight modes, according to the last pitch of the melody. The mode of the antiphon determined the choice of psalm tone to be used in singing the accompanying psalm.

There were in principle eight psalm tones, one for each modal class of antiphon. Each of these eight psalm tones had its own intonation, reciting pitch, mediant, and final cadences. The final cadence, the termination, had to lead back to the beginning of the antiphon. Since antiphons could start on one of several pitches other than their final, however, a choice of terminations was provided; the singer selected the termination that made the best retransition to the antiphon. In the ninth century, the termination was designated by the vowels EVOVAE, these being the vowels of the words *seculorum amen* that concluded the second verse of the Gloria Patri. (But if the antiphon was repeated more than just at the end, the indicated termination would be used in each verse that preceded the repetition of the antiphon.) The termination was called variously *differentia, varietas, diffinitio, divisio, figura, modus, formula.*[64]

Now, let us return to our question concerning the purpose of modal classification in the tonaries. The singer had to sing an antiphon before and after the psalm and therefore needed to know the reciting pitch and the rule of the final. Scholars have generally explained the purpose of modal classification as a tool for matching the antiphon with the correct psalm tone. Or to put it differently, the cantor needed to know the mode of the antiphon he was to sing on a specific occasion in order to select the right psalm tone. And yet if a cantor was using the tonary to find the correct psalm tone, he had to know the rule of the reciting pitches. Moreover, in order to find his antiphon in the tonary, he either had to scan the entire tonary, or else look in the right class because he already knew to which mode the antiphon was

64. Huglo, *Tonaires,* 55.

assigned. Thus, only if the cantor had previously memorized the melody would he have known the reciting pitch from previous performances and the mode of the antiphon. In other words, it seems that the purpose of the tonary was simply to organize the repertory for memorization.

The second step in the hierarchical classification of the tonaries is concerned with the question of how to match the reciting pitch with the antiphon melody. The singer would know the psalm tone from practice and remember that it consists of an intonation, a reciting pitch, a mediant cadence, reciting tone, and termination. He was confronted with two tasks: first, he needed to get from the antiphon to the psalm tone, and second, he needed to get from the psalm tone back to the beginning of the antiphon. The first of these presents no problem, since the antiphon always ends on the final. The second, however, is more difficult, because the antiphon can begin on a number of different pitches. Thus, the cantor will have to select a termination that will make a smooth transition to the beginning of the antiphon. This selection calls for judgment, since there is no simple rule. Various classifications are encountered in tonaries.

Classification Schemes

The earliest comprehensive tonary is the Metz tonary, written around 875, but probably copied from an exemplar made around 830.[65] The tonary does not use neumes. Walther Lipphardt observes, however, that the 830 original must have included neumes, because it would not have made sense to write the SECULORUM AMEN formulas (which give the termination of the psalm tone, here called *diffinitio)*[66] without neumes for every single antiphon. And indeed, the closely related Reichenau tonary,[67] which agrees in almost all *diffinitiones* with Metz, has non-diastematic neumes on the SECULORUM AMEN formulas.[68] The antiphons are arranged in three columns.

The compiler first lists the Mass antiphons (introits and communions), giving two differences for mode 1 *(Autenticus protus),* and listing under the first difference four introits in the order of the liturgical calendar, under the second difference twenty-four introits, again in liturgical order. Then he writes thirty communions for the second difference of mode 1. Other Mass antiphons are cataloged in the same way.

The classification of Office antiphons is more complicated, mainly because there are many more of them (see Figure 1a). After the intonation formula follows *Diffinitio* I, reconstructed by Lipphard as aa aG GF Ga GG from the

65. For a transcription and detailed discussion see Lipphardt, *Der karolingische Tonar.*

66. Aurelian and Regino of Prüm call the termination *divisio.* See below.

67. Bamberg, Staatsbibliothek, ms. lit. 5, fols. 1–27.

68. Lipphardt, *Der karolingische Tonar,* 9. Later somebody added neumes to fol. 67r–v.

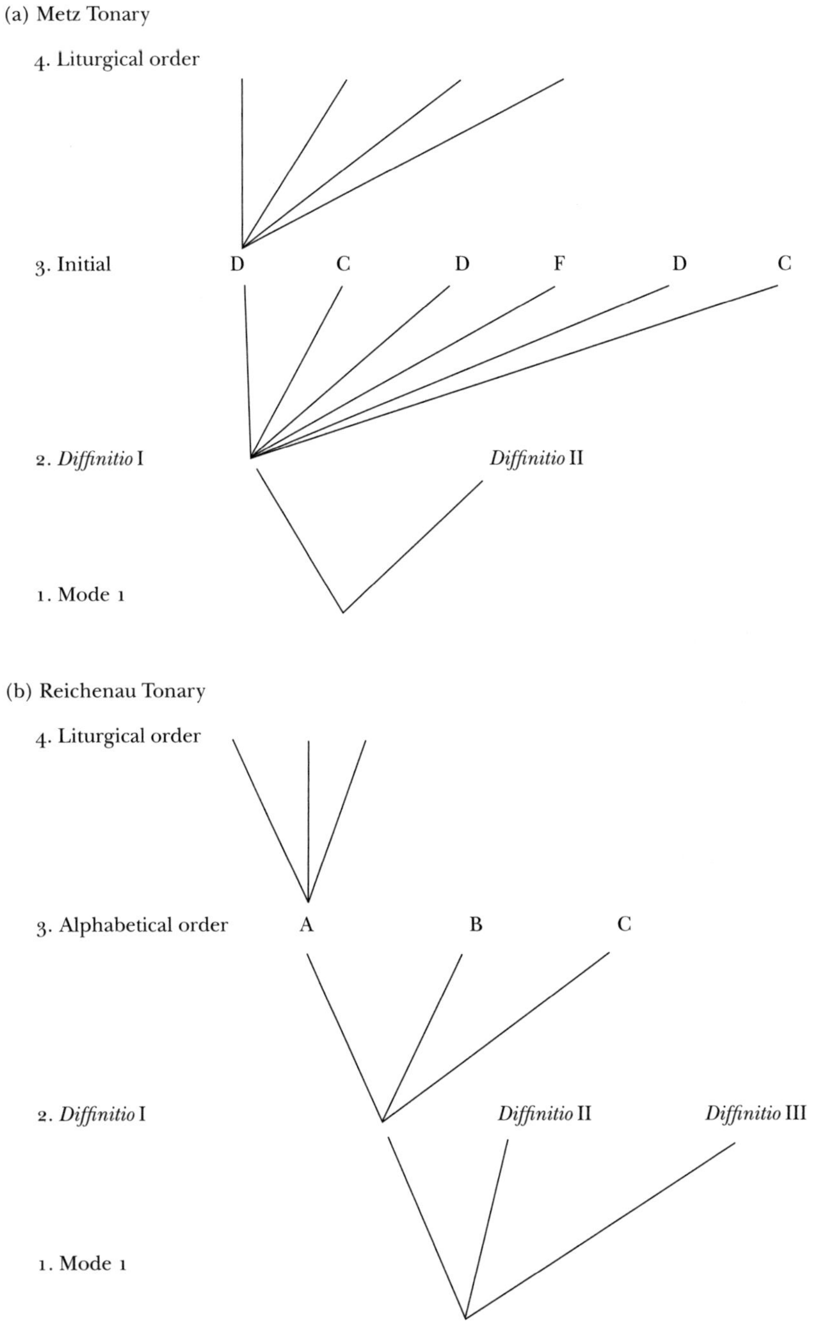

Figure 1. Hierarchies of Office antiphons

Reichenau tonary.[69] Again, the antiphons are, in general, organized liturgically (we sometimes find more than one sequence), but in addition, since there are 189, the compiler classifies them according to their starting note: the first 151 begin with a few exceptions on D, the next six on C, then again three on D (he starts a new liturgical order), then twenty-three on F (new order), and finally another six on D and C. The subdivisions within each *diffinitio* are called *varietates*. Then he moves on to *Diffinitio* II (a a aG GF Ga GFD), which is identical with the first except for the last two notes, and lists eighty-one antiphons. In the first *varietas* most antiphons begin on C, then the scribe begins a new liturgical order, which mixes antiphons beginning on D, C, F, and finally a single one on E. All of the antiphons that begin with D are followed by an ascending quilisma.[70] *Diffinitio* III lists forty-one antiphons of which eleven begin on D and the rest on C. Again, it is striking that the compiler must have studied and analyzed the antiphons carefully before classifying them, since all, even those that begin with C, have a leap from D to a at or near the beginning. Altogether he has eleven *diffinitiones (Diffinitio* XI is missing in the Bamberg MS and could therefore not be reconstructed):[71]

I	a a aG GF Ga GG
II	a a aG GF Ga GFD
III	a a aG GF Ga Ga
IV	a a a G a G
V	a a aG GF Ga a
VI	a a aG GF G a
VII	a a aG GF G Ga
VIII	a a aG GF G G aG
IX	a a a F a G
X	a a a F a G

The compiler goes through every single mode in a similar way. In sum, the 1,294 antiphons are classified not only according to their modal patterns, but also according to their beginning note and initial formulas. The result is what Hartmut Möller has called a "thematic catalogue of all antiphon beginnings."[72]

The Reichenau tonary was copied in 1001 and 1006 in Reichenau and

69. Ibid., 21. In chapters 2 and 3 I am using the medieval pitch system, while in the last three chapters I have switched to the modern one.

70. Ibid., 223–24.

71. See ibid., 32. In *Diffinitio* I Lipphardt, *Der karolingische Tonar*, has a misprint; the two first *a*s should be separated, since they are different neumes.

72. "Die Metzer Schola Cantorum," 176.

includes 1,318 antiphons, twenty-four more than Metz.[73] The scribe added non-diastematic St. Gall neumes to the *diffinitiones*. The most important difference compared with the Metz tonary is that the Office antiphons now appear in alphabetical order (see Figure 1b). For example, on fol. 6r all antiphons for *Diffinitio* I starting with the letter A are listed. However, within each letter the scribe organizes the antiphons liturgically, starting with Advent. This results in a new subdivision. Thus, the singer does not need to memorize 184 antiphons all at once, but begins with a group of seventeen starting with the letter A, then with five with the letter B, and so on. Within each letter they can be recalled easily because they are in liturgical order. Note that the alphabetical classification is not adopted for the Mass antiphons, probably because there were far fewer of those to catalog.[74]

Later tonaries and theorists follow the same system of classification as the Metz tonary with some minor differences, of which I will describe the most important ones. The anonymous early tenth-century treatise *Alia musica* is the work of at least three different theorists.[75] The terminations of the psalm tones are called *differentiae*, and the subdivisions of the terminations are called by the mnemonic term *loca*.[76]

What, exactly, were the criteria for modal classification? Ninth-century writers are vague as to how a specific mode is defined.[77] Aurelian of Réôme's *Musica disciplina*, written between 840 and 849, but very likely copied from earlier sources, never states clearly which elements determine the mode. Regino of Prüm, abbot of the monastery of Prüm from 882 to 899, wrote his *Epistola de harmonica institutione* in Trier in the form of a letter to Archbishop Rathbod.[78] Regino gave a lot of thought to modal classifications, and complained repeatedly that the antiphons of his time had "degenerated," that they no longer followed musical rules, starting in one mode and ending in another. There has been some confusion as to how Regino arrived at his modal classifications. Willi Apel has interpreted Regino to say that the mode is determined by the beginning rather than the end, "because the prudent singer

73. Huglo, *Tonaires*, 37–41. Lipphardt, *Der karolingische Tonar*, 292–309.

74. Other tonaries that are closely related to the Metz and the Reichenau tonaries are (1) Wolfenbüttel, Herzog August Bibliothek, Helmstedt 1050, 11th–12th c., which gives a longer and shorter termination indicated by *maior* and *minor* on the margin and includes only Office antiphons; the pieces are classified as in Metz; (2) Rome, Biblioteca Casanatense 54, probably written for Nonantola, early 11th c.; Office pieces are also cataloged alphabetically. Huglo, *Tonaires*, 33–45.

75. *Alia musica*, ed. Chailley; trans. Heard, "'Alia Musica.'"

76. The term *locum* is used in memory treatises to refer to a place. See chap. 3.

77. See in particular Powers, "Mode," and Hiley, *Western Plainchant*, 454–77.

78. *Epistola de armonica institutione*, 37–73; also GS 1:230–47; CS 2:3–73. See also Boncella, "Regino Prumiensis and the Tones"; Huglo, *Tonaires*, 71–88; and Hiley, *Western Plainchant*, 458–59.

has to devote a lot of work to paying attention to the tone relations at the beginning of the antiphon, introit, or communion rather than the end."[79] On the other hand, in his responsories the mode is determined by the final note. It is likely, as Huglo has suggested,[80] that what Regino had in mind was the transition from the end of the *differentiae* to the beginning of the antiphon.

The first treatise to say explicitly that the last note of the antiphon determines the mode is the early tenth-century *Commemoratio brevis de tonis et psalmis modulandi.*[81] In fact, the author seems to warn readers not to decide on the mode after having looked at the beginning only: "A word of caution: certain antiphons not belonging to the same mode have such similar beginnings that to continue one with the melody of the other would seem quite natural; special attention must be paid to the ending of each chant, where the indication of its mode appears most clearly."[82]

The music examples of this treatise are written in daseian notation,[83] which allowed accurate representation of pitch, in contrast to neumes. One wonders if emphasis on the final of the mode was not related to the ability of the singer to visualize the entire melody in front of his eyes. All later theorists echo the views encountered in *Commemoratio.*[84]

A number of theorists stress the importance of dividing up the chant into various phrases, which they call *distinctiones* (the name can also refer to the break between two phrases),[85] and list characteristic initial and medial phrases that help to define the mode. Pseudo-Odo stresses the importance of the final of the mode also for the *distinctiones:* "The *distinctiones,* too, that is, the places at which we pause in a chant and at which we divide it, ought obviously to end in each mode on the same notes on which a chant in that mode may begin. And where each mode best and most often begins, there, as a rule, it best and most suitably begins and ends its *distinctiones.* Several *distinctiones* ought to end on the note which concludes the mode."[86]

79. "Illud autem summopere prudens cantor observare debet, ut semper magis principium antyphonae, introitus vel communionis attendat in toni sonoritate, quam finem." *Epistola,* 42. Apel, *Gregorian Chant,* 18–19.

80. Huglo, "Grundlagen und Ansätze."

81. Ed. and trans. Bailey.

82. *Commemoratio brevis,* 99. For a description of modal ambiguities depending on whether the beginning or ending is taken into consideration, see also Powers, "Mode."

83. In daseian notation a set of eighteen signs is used to indicate the intervals unambiguously. See the late 9th- or early 10th-c. treatises *Musica enchiriadis* and *Commemoratio brevis.*

84. See, for example, Pseudo-Odo of Cluny, *Dialogus in musica,* trans. Strunk and McKinnon, 207; Guido of Arezzo, *Micrologus,* trans. in *Hucbald, Guido, and John on Music,* chap. 11.

85. For an excellent overview of the term *distinctio* in medieval music theory see Desmond, "*Sicut in grammatica.*"

86. *Dialogus in musica,* 207. See also *Commemoratio brevis,* 61–99; and Berno of Reichenau, *Prologus in tonarium,* ed. Rausch; *Bern Augiensis Tonarius,* ed. Rausch, 31–68.

All of these writers leave no doubt that they not only took the beginning and ending into consideration, but the melody as a whole before assigning it to a mode. Even though they did not have diastematic notation, they had a clear notion of how their melodies went. As Karen Desmond has pointed out, the division of the chant into *distinctiones* allowed the cantor "to understand, and thus to internalize and remember the segments,"[87] so that it could be performed correctly.

Let us now return to the subdivisions within each mode found in tonaries. We have seen that the Metz tonary classifies the antiphons within each difference in liturgical order, while the later Reichenau tonary prefers alphabetic organization. The alphabetic classifications were particularly popular in Germany. They allowed singers to find antiphons quickly. Alphabetic organization was adopted by Berno of Reichenau, whose *Tonarius* was written in the first quarter of the eleventh century.[88] Note, though, that not all singers seem to have preferred the alphabetic system. There is a version of Berno's *Tonarius* in Vienna, ÖNB 1836, copied in Austria ca. 1100, that returns to the liturgical sequence.[89]

Another important alphabetically organized tonary is the anonymous treatise *Libellus tonarius* copied ca. 1075.[90] The author uses a new notational system developed by Hermannus Contractus, with a special sign for every interval. The tonary usually lists only the beginnings of the texts of the antiphons in two columns, with the interval notation right next to the text. More specifically, this interval notation indicates the ambitus first below the final, and then above the final. But we also encounter neumes on top of the *differentiae*. As to the classification of the *differentiae*, the scribe starts with *differentiae* that have the fewest number of notes, and proceeds gradually to longer and longer ones.[91]

An alphabetic classification was also followed by Frutolf in the versified tonary in his *Breviarium de musica*.[92] The verse made it easy to memorize the pieces and contributed immensely to the popularity of the treatise. Frutolf was a monk in the Benedictine abbey of Michelsberg in Bamberg and died in 1103. The treatise is heavily indebted to both Regino and Berno and was one of the most successful tonaries.[93]

I have already mentioned that theorists created additional subgroups

87. "*Sicut in grammatica*," 488.

88. Ed. Rausch, 75–115.

89. See Huglo, *Tonaires*, 272. For an edition, see *Bern Augiensis Tonarius*, ed. Rausch, 225–56.

90. Ed. Sowa. The treatise survives only in a 15th-c. copy.

91. Ibid., 17 f.

92. Ed. Vivell. Michael Bernhard believes that Frutolf himself was not the author, but only copied the treatise. He argues that "Pilgrimus," mentioned in Vienna, ÖNB Cod. 1367, fol. 139v, is the author of the treatise; "Didaktische Verse," 232.

93. Huglo, *Tonaires*, 184–85.

within the liturgical and alphabetical classifications. The Metz tonary, for example, classified all pieces starting with the tone D together, then those beginning on C, etc. Similarly, Regino of Prüm classified the *differentiae* of the antiphoner according to similar beginnings, but he took his analysis a step further and reduced the fifty-four or fifty-five Carolingian differences to only thirty.[94] (For a page from Regino's tonary, see below, Figure 3.) He did, though, include the rejected differences in the margins. It seems that he eliminated them because they were melodically and rhythmically not that different from the ones he included. He arrived at his modal classifications after a careful analysis of the written antiphoner: "Since often in the church of your diocese the choir singing the psalms sang the melody with disorderly voices because of a discrepancy of the tone, and since I had often seen your worship unsettled on account of this, *I seized an antiphonary and conscientiously read it through from beginning to end in order, and divided the antiphons that I found notated in it, according to what I think are the rightful tones* [italics mine]."[95] It seems unlikely that Regino only read through the text of the antiphons; his statement shows clearly that at least for him notation was a condition for the ability to classify the pieces.

The early eleventh-century treatise *Commentum super tonos,* copied in Auvergne, takes this classification a step further and lists together all antiphons within a *differentia* that have similar beginnings.[96] Likewise, the *Libellus tonarius* and Frutolf organize the antiphons according to similar beginnings.

Finally, there are a number of theorists who classify the *differentiae* according to the distance of the first note of the antiphon to the final. The most important of these is the late tenth- or early eleventh-century Italian treatise by Odo of Arezzo, of which twenty manuscripts survive. *Differentiae* are notated in alphabetic notation. A late eleventh-century version with some interpolated texts has been published as *De modorum formulis et tonarius* (Paris, BNF lat. 10508).[97] Note that this very popular treatise was used by Guido,

94. Ibid., 85–86.

95. "Cum frequenter in ecclesie vestrae diocesibus chorus psallentium psalmorum melodiam confusis resonaret vocibus, propter dissonantiam toni, & pro huiuscemodi re vestram venerationem saepe commotam vidissem; arripui Antiphonarium, & eum a principio usque in finem per ordinem diligenter revolvens, antiphonas, quas in illo adnotatas reperi, propriis, ut reor distribui tonis." Trans. Bower in "Natural and Artificial Music," 18–19.

96. Ed. Smits van Waesberghe. See also Huglo, *Tonaires,* 129–31.

97. Ed. Brockett. In one text it is attributed to Abbot Odo. According to Huglo, it was probably compiled in the Arezzo area, and then copied in central and northern Italy. Huglo has untangled the authorship of the various treatises associated with Odo. Note that this Odo is not the author of the *Dialogus de musica.* Michel Huglo, "L'auteur du 'Dialogue sur la musique'" and *Tonaires,* 182–224. Berno, on the other hand, arranges his *differentiae* (he calls them *diffinitiones*) according to the distance of their last note from the final. See *Bern Augiensis Tonarius,* ed. Rausch, 138 and Merkley, *Italian Tonaries,* 58.

who never bothered to write his own tonary, for the instruction of his students. The *differentiae* are divided into three groups:

1. *praeposita* (*differentia* ends above the first note of the antiphon);
2. *apposita* (the *differentia* ends in unison with the first note of the antiphon);
3. *supposita* (the *differentia* ends below the first note of the antiphon).

Also here the number of antiphons that must be memorized becomes manageable once they are divided into these smaller categories.[98]

Thus we see in a great majority of treatises hierarchical subdivisions: first by mode; then within each mode by *differentiae;* then within each *differentia* variously, for instance, by letters of the alphabet, or by the liturgical calendar (the last two can also be hierarchically related), or by proximity of the initial tone of the antiphon to the final of the mode. It is this hierarchical classification that helped singers.

Consider the following example: The *Libellus tonarius* lists 226 antiphons for the principal *differentia* of mode 1.[99] This is a large number of melodies to remember. But on closer inspection one notices that even though most begin on the final D (a fourth below the last tone of the *differentia*), there are some clearly marked exceptions: a group of fourteen begin with a guttural quilisma,[100] sixteen start with the formula F–D–a, either reached stepwise or by leap, and a group of fourteen start with the formula G–C–D–D–a. Thus, by dividing a long list into smaller chunks that share the same characteristics, the list suddenly becomes manageable. Note that the classification depends both on an analysis of the music (mode, starting tone, proximity to final, and initial formulas), and on the text (liturgical and alphabetical order).

Mmemonic Aids

Thus far we have discussed how chant was classified in order to retrieve it. Now we turn to various tools that made it much easier to memorize the items listed in the tonaries. The first of these concerns mnemonic aids devised by theorists to help singers memorize the characteristic pitch set for every mode. Virtually all tonaries place at the top of each modal list of antiphons a formula of intonation, a pattern of intervals that can remind the singer of the pitch set. The earliest versions of these formulas were supplied with *echema* or *noeane* syllables derived from the Byzantine *oktoechos*.[101] For example, mode 1 is usually preceded by a formula outlining the fifth a–d (Ex-

98. The same terms are encountered in one of the commentaries on the Micrologus, the *Liber argumentorum*, ed. Smits van Waesberghe, chap. 39.

99. Ed. Sowa, 16.

100. Ibid., 16–17.

101. For a detailed discussion of these formulas see Bailey, *Intonation Formulas.*

Example 1. Intonation formulas for mode 1 from Bailey, *Commemoratio brevis,* 48

ample 1). It is generally accepted that the function of the intonation formulas was to remind the singer of where the half- and whole-steps above the final of every mode were located.[102] The singers might have quietly sung the formulas to themselves to recall how a melody in a certain mode would sound.[103]

Some time after 900, formulas with Latin texts begin to appear (Example 2). The Latin texts always allude to the number of the mode:[104]

102. Bailey has pointed out, though, that they were often ambiguous. See ibid., 32.

103. Ibid., 15. Crocker suggests that these formulas are conclusions that "help identify the class of memorized antiphons"; "Chants of the Roman Office," 169.

104. Another set from later German sources is in Huglo, *Tonaires,* 421. For more on these formulas, see ibid., 386–90.

Example 2. Latin intonation formulas from Reichenau (Bamberg, Staatsbibliothek, Ms. lit. 5; Bailey, *Commemoratio brevis,* 81–90)

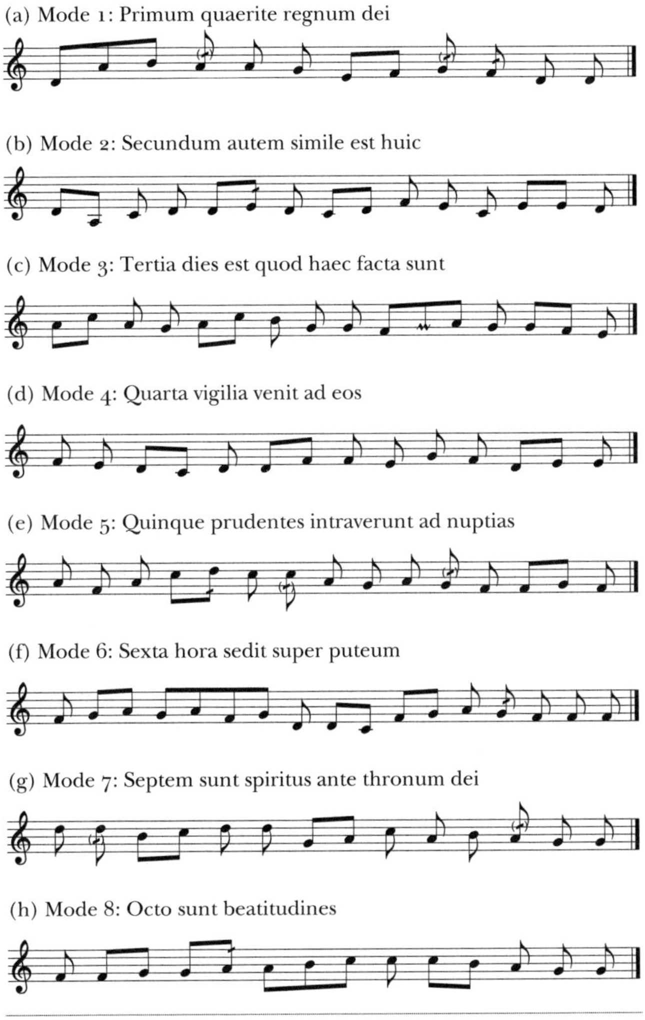
(a) Mode 1: Primum quaerite regnum dei
(b) Mode 2: Secundum autem simile est huic
(c) Mode 3: Tertia dies est quod haec facta sunt
(d) Mode 4: Quarta vigilia venit ad eos
(e) Mode 5: Quinque prudentes intraverunt ad nuptias
(f) Mode 6: Sexta hora sedit super puteum
(g) Mode 7: Septem sunt spiritus ante thronum dei
(h) Mode 8: Octo sunt beatitudines

Mode 1: "Primum quaerite regnum Dei" ("First seek ye the kingdom of God"; Matt. 6:36)

Mode 2: "Secundum autem simile est huic" ("And the second is like unto it"; Matt. 22:39)

Mode 3: "Tertia dies est quo(d) haec facta sunt" ("Today is the third day since these things were done"; Luke 24:21)

Mode 4: "Quarta vigilia venit ad eos" ("And in the fourth watch of the night Jesus went unto them"; Matt. 14:25)
Mode 5: "Quinque prudentes intraverunt ad nuptias" ("And the five wise [virgins] went to the wedding"; Matt. 25:10)
Mode 6: "Sexta hora sedit super puteum" (communal version) ("It was the sixth hour he sat on the well"; John 4:6)
Mode 7: "Septem sunt spiritus ante thronum Dei" ("There were seven spirits before the throne of God"; Rev. 4:5)
Mode 8: "Octo sunt beatitudines" ("There are eight blessings"; Matt. 5:3–11)

Huglo points out that these formulas were so popular that they are found in miniatures and sculptures in the capitals of Cluny and Autun.[105] Both Greek and Latin intonation formulas were used side by side until the twelfth century. The earliest theorists to reject Byzantine formulas in favor of the Latin ones were the author of *Dialogus in musica* and Guido of Arezzo.[106]

Since many of the *noeane* and Latin formulas fall short of specifying the modal patterns and remain ambiguous, musicians soon added a *neuma* or melisma as a continuation to both that would leave no doubt as to the mode intended.[107] In contrast to the *noeane* and Latin formulas, the *neumas* made their way into music. They are still found in tenors of thirteenth- and fourteenth-century motets.[108]

Many theorists tried to develop or even make up etymological derivations that helped singers remember the number of the mode. Aurelian, for example, says in his *Musica disciplina,* written in the 840s, but probably copied from an early ninth-century source: "The first of them is called *protus,* a term that in our language means first: hence we call the first martyrs, Abel in the old law and Stephen in the new law, the protomartyrs. The second is *deuterus,* that is, the second; for in the same Greek language a repetition or summary is called *deuterosis;* whence also Deuteronomy, second law or legislation, receives its name . . . " Aurelian has nothing for *tritus,* but comes up with this for *tetrardus:* "For four is *tetra* to the Greeks; whence also the name of God is called a *tetragrammaton,* because it is said to be written with four letters . . . All four of those that are joined to them are called plagal, a name that is said to mean side or part, or their inferiors . . . "[109] Etymologies were often used

105. Ibid., 137–38 and 387.

106. Huglo, "Auteur du 'Dialogue sur la musique,'" 168.

107. Bailey, *Intonation Formulas,* 32 and 60–77.

108. Huglo, *Tonaires,* 388–89.

109. "Primus autem eorum protus vocatur, quod nomen apud nos primum significat. Unde et protomartyrem Abel in lege veteri, in nova autem Stephanum dicimus primos martyres. Secundus autem deuteros, id est secundum. Deuterosis enim eadem Greca lingua secundatio sive recapitulatio vocatur. Inde et deuteronomium, id est secunda lex vel legislatio, nominatur. . . .

for mnemonic purposes.[110] A student who heard or read this passage would always remember the Greek names for the modes, and would know in addition that four are authentic and four are plagal.

There seems to be general agreement among theorists that basic theory training is necessary in order to memorize tonaries. Berno of Reichenau has many pious invocations in his "Epistola de tonis," written shortly after 1008.[111] Usually they make an allusion to the number of the mode and thus help students learn the theory behind the chant:

> First, O Lord, we ask that according to the heights of your justice you would have us seek the true and supreme light so that we may always rejoice with you in heaven. Amen.
>
> According [*Secundum*] to what you, O Christ, have commanded us to keep in the word of law of the mutual love of God and neighbor, whereby we may fulfill the commandments of this twofold observance.
>
> We believe, O Christ, that on the third day you rose and brought light to the world. O gracious Lord, have us always praise your name, and looking upon you seated in the domain of the eternal fatherland, Amen.
>
> Humbly proclaiming, O Christ, that in the fourth vigil of the night you gave heavenly solace to your disciples; singing to you and praising the name of your power, give us to know the strength of the fourfold voice of your gospel.
>
> You deigned, O Lord, that the five virgins receive you in heaven [Matt. 25], to reveal yourself to your people in words and show yourself in signs, and to dispose these our senses as we beseech you, O Lord.
>
> The sixth hour, O Christ, shone forth with the presence of your bodily form; grant to your church a fountain springing forth living water [John 4], and always enkindle in it the fervor of the abundance of grace.
>
> Now we also ask that you come to our aid sevenfold [refers to the seven gifts of the Holy Ghost], O gracious Paraclete [Consoler, i.e. the Holy Ghost], that our minds may always overflow with the perfect gift of your grace, and by the fire of your love enkindle whatever may redound to our benefit.[112]

Tetra enim apud Grecos quattuor dicuntur. Unde et nomen dei tetragrammaton eoquod quattuor litteris asscribi dicitur. . . . Plagi autem eis coniuncti dicuntur omnes iiii, quod nomen significare dicitur latus vel pars, sive inferiores eorum." Aurelian of Réôme, *Musica disciplina,* 79; trans. Ponte, *Discipline of Music,* 21.

110. For an excellent discussion of etymological mnemonics, see Carruthers, *Craft of Thought,* 155–60.

111. See Rausch, *Die Musiktraktate des Abtes Bern von Reichenau,* 129–30. Rausch thinks the text was written shortly after Berno became abbot.

112. This refers to an antiphon to the Holy Ghost: "Veni, Sancte Spiritus, reple tuorum corda fidelium, et tui amoris in eis ignem accende." I would like to thank Peter Schaeffer for this observation.

In the eighth place, O faithful Christ, our King, grant to your people the evangelical beatitudes [Matt. 5:3–10] of shining grace and in your kindness refresh those believing in you forever with eternal rest.[113]

In the ninth and tenth centuries, singers did not always agree on the modal classifications of the chant. As we have seen above, Regino of Prüm wrote his tonary because singers were confused about modal assignments of Office antiphons. As Susan Boynton has recently pointed out, he advocates a combination of practical and theoretical knowledge, and "exhorts singers to study *musica* as well as *cantus*."[114] He criticizes lute and lyre players for not knowing where the whole steps and half steps lie and glosses a passage from Boethius with these words: "Now, it should be known that he is not called a musician who performs only with his hands, but he is truly a musician who knows naturally how to discuss music and to elucidate its meaning with sure reasons."[115]

A combination of knowledge and memorization results in well-trained singers. Aurelian surely implies the same when he writes: "And unless my opinion is wrong, although anyone may be called by the name of singer, nevertheless he cannot be perfect unless he has implanted by memory in the sheath of his heart the melody of all the lines of text through all the modes, and the difference both of the modes and of the lines of text of the antiphons, introits, and of the responses."[116] In another passage Aurelian states that mu-

113. *Epistola de tonis,* ed. Rausch, 14–16. "Primo pro culmine tuae querere justiciae, Domine, veri summi quoque lumen fac nos, petimus, ut in caelo semper tibi jubilemus. amen. . . . Secundumque legis verbum mutua quo dilectione et Dei et proximi, Christe mandasti colere, quo per haec geminae observantiae praecepta reddamus amen. . . . Tercia te die Christe, te resurgere mundo ferre lumen credimus; o alme fac nos et tuum semper laudare nomen, et in patriae te aeterne regione cernentes sedere amen. . . . Quarta te noctis, Christe, vigilia discipulis dare caeleste solamen nos humiles fatentes, te canentes, laudantes tuaeque nomen potentiae nos quaternae tuae evangelicae vocis da cognoscere munimen. . . . Quinque tu, Domine, in caelum virgines te recipere dignatus es, plebi tuae verbis revelare, signis et ostendere, sensus ecce nostros ut te precamur, Domine, te disponere. . . . Sexta tuae, Christe, praesentiae corporalis hora resplendet, fontem aecclesiae vitam tribue salientem aquae vivae, fervore quoque plenae graciae hanc semper accende. . . . Septemplicem te nunc quoque nobis adesse deposcimus, alme paraclyte, nostrae mentes ut tuae gratiae semper exuberent perfecto munere, quaeque nocent extingue, et cuncta, quae proficiunt, accende semper amoris igne. . . . Octo, pie Christe, rex lucide, beatitudines evangelicae gratiae plebi tuae prebe benignus, et clemens sempiterna requie refove sine fine credentes in te." I would like to thank Peter Schaeffer for help with the translation.

114. Boynton, "Sources and Significance," 67.

115. "Interea sciendum est, quod non ille dicitur musicus, qui eam manibus tantummodo operatur, sed ille veraciter musicus est, qui de musica naturaliter novit disputare, et certis rationibus eius sensum enodare." Regino of Prüm, *Epistola,* XVIII, 14, ed. Bernhard, 71; trans. Boynton, "Sources and Significance," 69.

116. "Porro autem, et si opinio me non fefellit, liceat quispiam cantoris censeatur vocabulo, minime tamen perfectus esse poterit nisi modulationem omnium versuum per omnes tonos

sic took its name from the muses, who "were said to minister to the memory, because this art, unless it is imprinted in the memory, is not retained."[117]

After the modal system and the intonation formulas were firmly entrenched in the mind, students could memorize the lists of antiphons. The most common method was simply learning them by rote. Odo (of Arezzo) recommended that singers who prepare the choir for the service should study the tonary every day:

> He who wants to hold the highest position in the teaching of chant in the church, must endeavor to study with the greatest attention the formulas, which I have organized in writing for you to be sung, how every singer of the church ought to maintain the tone of the antiphons, introits, or communions, or whatever kind of chant he is able to approach. I admonish also all singers, in particular those who appear to be in charge in the church, that they provide those under them every day with these examples in a very exact manner, so that when they begin the antiphons in church, they will not create uncertainty in the beginning of the psalm and begin to wander in various directions.[118]

He goes on to criticize severely those singers who sing their songs without sufficient knowledge of the tonary, for they must "improvise."[119] This shows that for Odo there was one correct version of the chant that should be sung everywhere.

Guido has a number of important references to committing chant to memory, starting with the memorization of all the intervals.[120] In the *Prologue* to his Antiphoner, written about 1030, he stresses that memorization has to be combined with understanding: "Finally, know that, that if you wish to make progress with these notes, it is necessary that you learn by heart a considerable number of chants so that, by individual neumes, you may perceive from memory which or of which kind all intervals and sounds are. Because it is

---

discretione[m] que tam tonorum quamque versuum antiphonarum seu introituum necne responsoriorum in teca cordis memoriter insitum habuerit." *Musica disciplina,* ed. Gushee, chap. 19, p. 118; trans. (slightly altered) from Ponte, *Discipline of Music,* 46.

117. "[Q]uae ferebantur memoriam ministrare, eoquod haec ars, nisi memoria infigatur, non retineatur." *Musica disciplina,* ed. Gushee, 61; trans. Ponte, 7.

118. "Formulas, quas vobis ad cantandum scribere procuravi, qualiter omnis cantor ecclesiae tenere debeat tonum antiphonarum, officiorum seu communionum, vel qualemcumque cantum adire poterit, summo cum studio legere studeat, qui arcem magisterii in ecclesia tenere voluerit in cantu. Admoneo autem omnes cantores, praecipue tamen eos, qui in ecclesia maiores praeesse videntur, ut quotidie subditis suis haec exempla subtilius subministrent, ne quando antiphonae in ecclesia inceperint, scrupulum generent in incipientia psalmi, & per diversa incipiant evagari." GS 1:248. For more on Odo, see Huglo, *Tonaires,* 185–205, 214, and 222.

119. See also Huglo, *Tonaires,* 214.

120. *Micrologus,* trans. Babb, in *Hucbald, Guido, and John on Music,* 61.

very much different to know something by heart than to sing it from memory, since only the wise may do the former, but fools often do the latter."[121]

Similar references to the importance of memorization built on complete understanding of the system of the modes are found in the *Libellus tonarius*[122] and in a very popular fourteenth-century treatise written in leonine hexameter entitled *Flores musicae* by the German theorist Hugo Spechtshart von Reutlingen.[123]

All of the items that students had to learn were represented graphically, and it seems likely that this was done to help commit the material to memory. I give a few examples. Concerning the classification of antiphons, Berno says explicitly in the preface to his tonary that writing the antiphons down assists greatly in the process of memorizing them: "We will take care to explain it in this book (of the tones with their differences), because whatever we have in front of our eyes is committed more firmly to memory."[124]

Pseudo-Odo and Guido place the following chart in their treatises to visualize the affinities between the finals:[125]

VII	I	III	V	I	III	V	VII	I	III	V	I	III	V	VII	I
Γ	A	B	C	D	E	F	G	a	b	c	d	e	f	g	aa
VIII	II	IV	VI	II	IV	VI	VIII	II	IV	VI	II	IV	VI	VIII	II

Very likely a student will visualize the graph whenever he thinks of modal relationships. He will see that modes 7 and 8 share the same final, G, that A is a co-final of mode 1, etc.

A manuscript from twelfth-century Aquitaine (Paris, BNF lat. 7211; Figure 2) illustrates the modes with their finals by transferring them to the hand, and also includes the Byzantine *noeane* formula and the Latin formula "Octo sunt beatitudines."

Memorization is also reinforced by the page layout of tonaries: all are notated in two, three, four, or five columns. Initials are highlighted in red or blue. A new difference will be recognizable through a new paragraph, a change of letters, and color (see Regino of Prüm, Figure 3). The left column of Regino's tonary begins with the Latin invocation "Primum quaerite regnum Dei," followed by the *noeane* formula. Then comes the first *differentia,*

121. "Illud tandem cognosce, quia si vis in his notis proficere, necesse est ut aliquantos cantus ita memoriter discas, ut per singulas neumas modos vel sonos omnes, qui vel quales sint, memoriter sentias. Quoniam quidem longe aliud este memoriter sapere quam memoriter canere, cum illud soli habeant sapientes, hoc vero sepe faciant imprudentes." In *Regule rithmice,* trans. Pesce, 432–35. See also a similar quotation from the *Regule rithmice,* ibid., 383.

122. Ed. Sowa, 87.

123. Ed. Gümpel, 152.

124. "[C]um in ipso tonorum libello suis in locis id explicare curabimus, quia arctius memoriae commendatur, quicquid pre oculis habetur." *Prologus in tonarium,* ed. Rausch, 61.

125. *Dialogus de musica,* 210; *Regule rithmice,* trans. Pesce, 365.

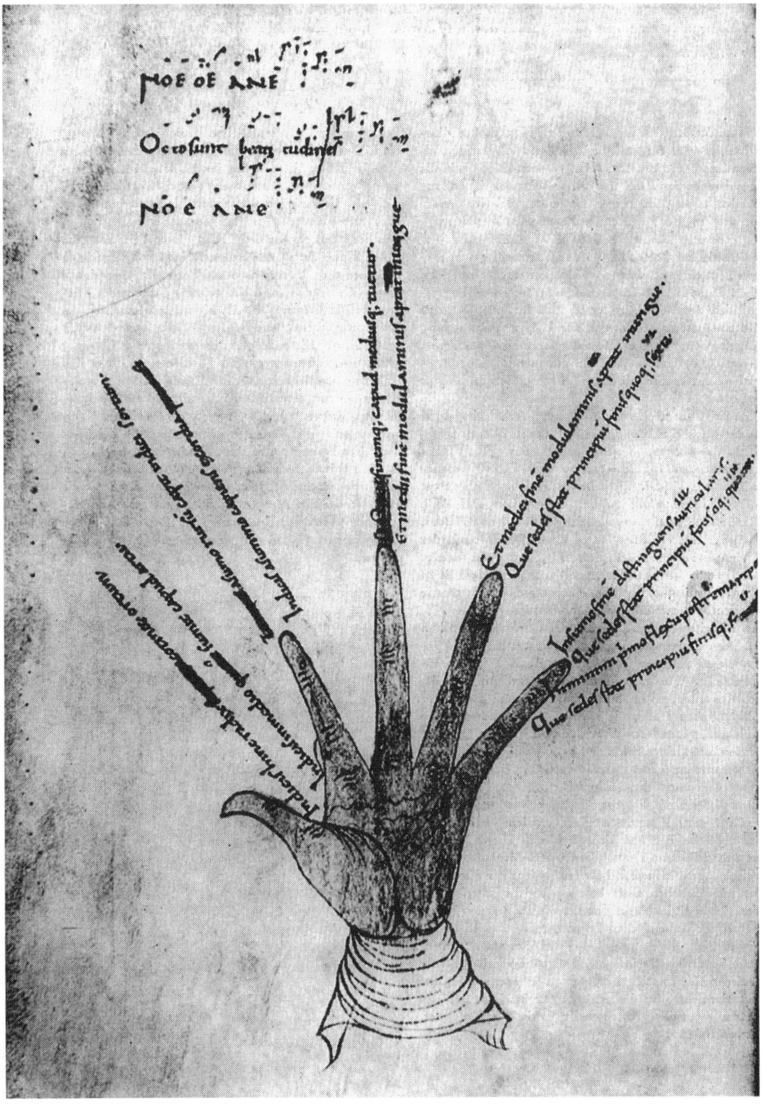

Figure 2. Hand from Aquitaine, Paris, Bibliothèque Nationale de France, MS lat. 7211, fol. 149v, published by permission of the Bibliothèque Nationale de France

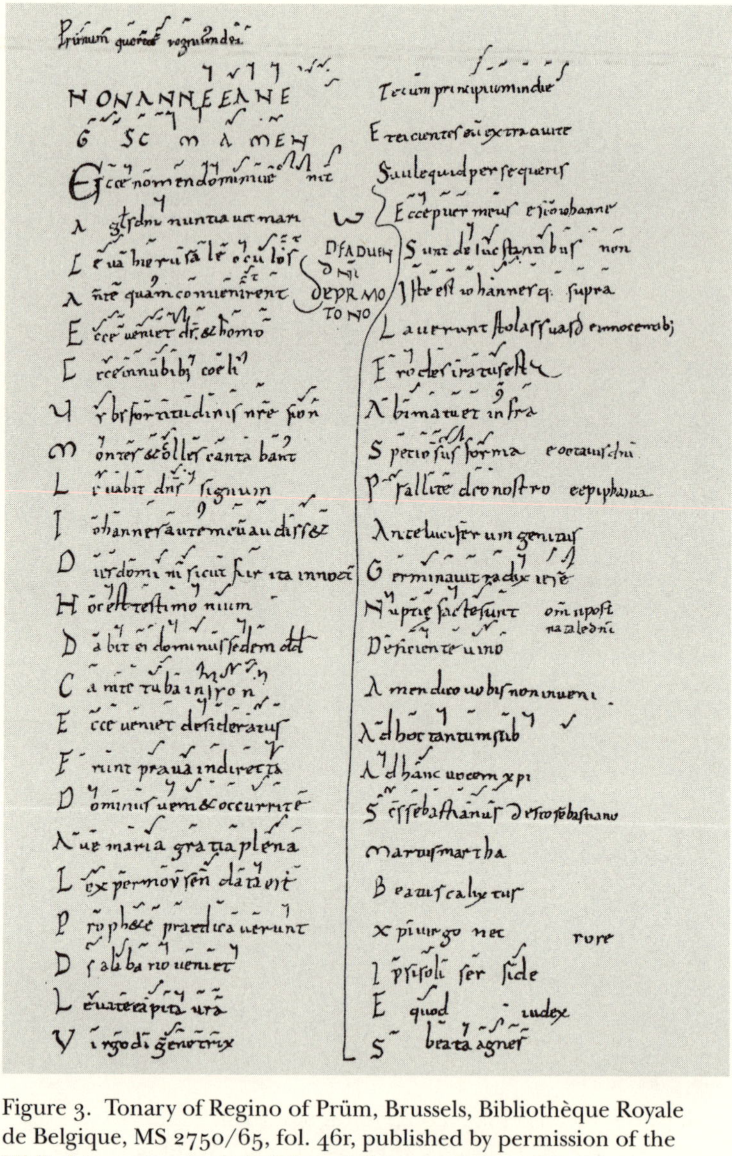

Figure 3. Tonary of Regino of Prüm, Brussels, Bibliothèque Royale de Belgique, MS 2750/65, fol. 46r, published by permission of the Bibliothèque Royale de Belgique (photograph from CS 2:5)

followed by all the antiphons. We have seen throughout that margins are used to highlight important points, for example the ambitus of an antiphon,[126] or the mode, or the *differentia*,[127] etc. In Regino's tonary there is a marginal addition after the incipit of "Angelus Domini nuntiavit Marie" that reads "De Adventu Domini, de primo tono."

Finally, a tonary may be ornamented with illuminations, and these may also have had a mnemonic function. One of the most famous manuscripts is the eleventh-century Aquitanian tonary, Paris, BNF lat. 1118 (Figure 4).[128] The first picture, which accompanies mode 1, is a representation of King David with a cythara; mode 2 has a liturgist with a trumpet (Asaph); mode 3 a liturgist with a panflute (Eman); mode 4 a jongleur with a shawm (Ethan); mode five a dancer; mode 6 David with a psaltery; mode 7 a liturgist with a psaltery (Idithun); mode 8 a jongleur with a shawm. While I was not able to discover any particular association of the figures with the modes, the link with biblical figures would help the reader of the manuscript to recall the modal formulas, *differentia*, and antiphons.

In short, we have clear references in tonaries that lists of antiphons were meant to be memorized, but only after modal theory was understood. I believe that the incipits, the *noeane* and Latin formulas, and the page layout brought the entire antiphon, which one already knew, back to mind just as a short passage in a florilegium would help recall the entire paragraph. The practice of recalling entire pieces through keywords was so common that it did not even require explanation.

The Relationship between Tonaries and Florilegia

How does the concept of *divisio* and the florilegia relate to our tonaries? There are two possible parallels. The first concerns retrieval. Chant was at first memorized by rote just as biblical passages were memorized, by constantly repeating them. But if a singer wanted to retrieve a particular chant, he needed additional tools to help him organize the archived chant. Both florilegia and tonaries classify previously memorized texts used on a daily basis. Both employ several hierarchical classification systems, and in both cases the subdivisions, especially the alphabetical one, helped find items quickly. It seems possible that they were both created in order to retrieve a lengthy passage through a short one, and that they were both promptbooks.

Second, the process of making a florilegium and a tonary might have

126. See, for example, the Dijon tonary, which gives the range and also indicates whether B or B♭ is used in the margins. See also Sowa, *Quellen zur Transformation.*

127. See, for example, Spechtshart von Reutlingen, *Flores musicae.*

128. For a detailed description see Seebass, *Musikdarstellung und Psalterillustration.*

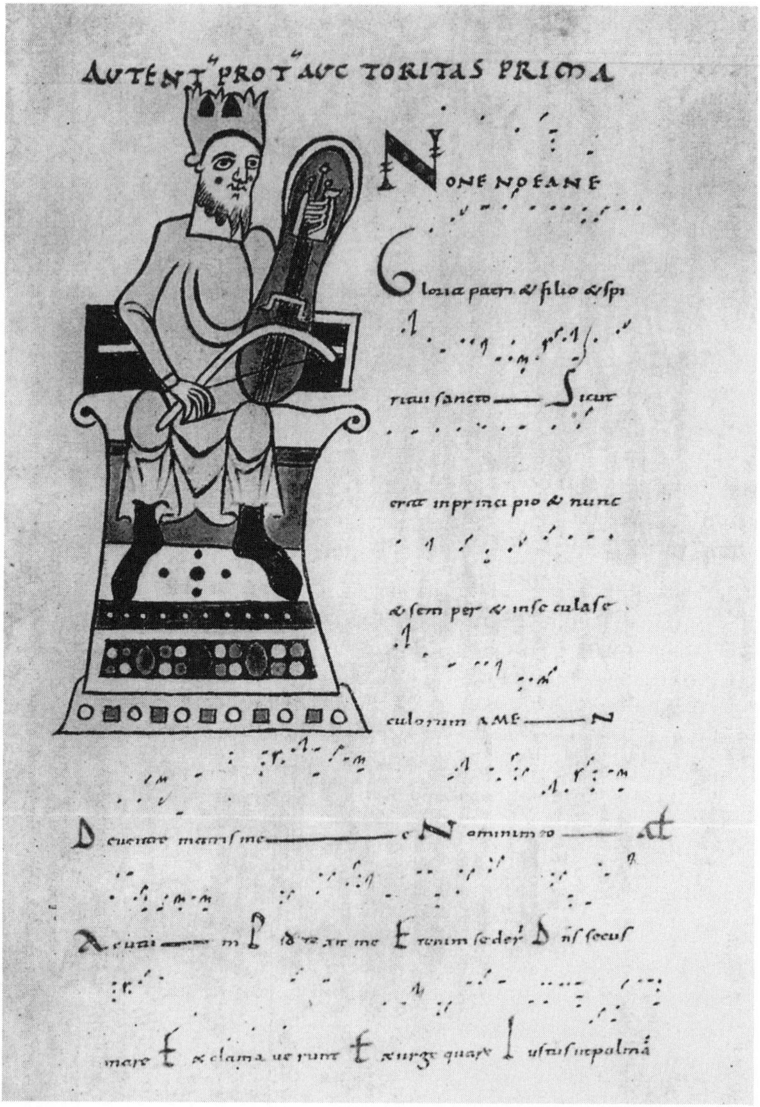

Figure 4. Tonary from Aquitaine, Paris, Bibliothèque Nationale de France, MS lat. 1118, fol. 104r, published by permission of the Bibliothèque Nationale de France

helped in the process of memorization. In fact, one can easily imagine that a cantor would want to make sure he had mastered the chant by creating a tonary.

The close relationship between tonaries and florilegia might explain the puzzling question of why, from the very beginning, so many tonaries classify pieces that have no psalm verses and thus no need for *differentiae.* The earliest preserved tonary, from the late eighth or early ninth century, for instance, Saint-Riquier, includes examples in each of the eight modes of graduals and alleluias.[129] Another is Paris, BNF lat. 780 from late twelfth-century Narbonne, which includes alleluias, offertories, invitatories, and processional antiphons. A manuscript in Montecassino, Archivio della Badia 318 from the twelfth century, lists sequences.

Most extraordinary is the Dijon tonary from the eleventh century (Montpellier, Faculté de Médecine H. 159).[130] The manuscript is very well preserved. The music notation for much of the tonary includes both adiastematic neumes and letter notation. It is significant in that it comprises not only antiphons, but a complete repertory of chants for the Proper of Mass: antiphons (introits and communions), responsories with solo verses (graduals and offertories), and alleluias and tracts. Note that in this tonary not only the incipit, but also the entire chant is notated. The chant is classified first according to mode; second, the type of chant; third, according to the starting note, from the lowest upward; and fourth, according to the top note of the melody. This is accompanied by *notae* in the margins giving the range or specifying whether there is a B or B♭ (even though these notes are incomplete). In Figure 5 we see the introit *Memento nostri, domine,* which is in mode 1. The first four introits have C as a starting tone, the next twelve begin on D. In the margins, in the middle of the right side of the page, the scribe indicated not only the range (C–c), but also the fact that the chant uses a B♮. Thus, to quote David Hiley, this manuscript was "organized not according to liturgical principles but abstract musical ones."[131]

All of this suggests that the tonaries were compiled to help the singers retrieve the individual chant melodies that they had memorized by rote,[132] according to a similar well-developed tradition of classifying and organizing

129. Huglo, *Tonaires,* 25–29, and Hiley, *Western Plainchant,* 330.

130. For the most detailed discussion of this tonary see *H 159 Montpellier,* ed. Hansen. For a facsimile see Paléographie musicale, vol. 8.

131. Hiley, *Western Plainchant,* 331.

132. Richard Crocker has suggested that tonaries might have been associated in some way with memorizing the antiphons. Crocker, "Chants for the Roman Office," 168–69. Similarly, Huglo has recently called attention to the fact that tonaries helped to memorize the chant in his "Tonary" article in the *New Grove Online.*

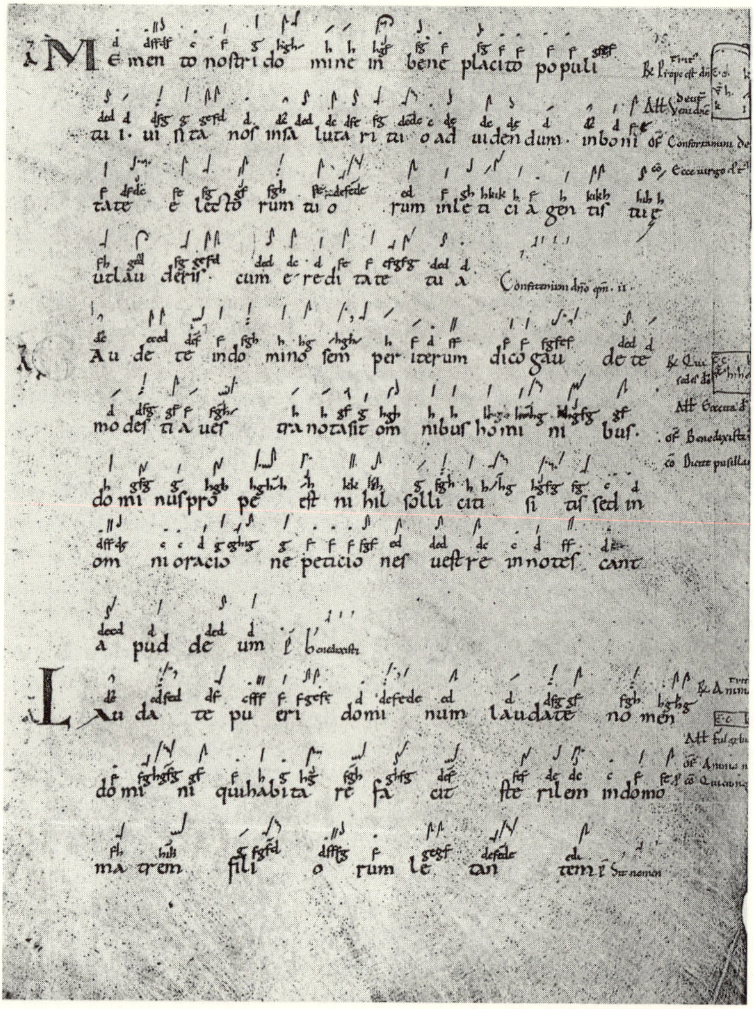

Figure 5. Dijon Tonary, Montpellier, Bibliothèque Interuniversitaire, MS H 159, fol. 15, published by permission of the Bibliothèque Interuniversitaire

literary excerpts. Florilegia allowed one to prepare sermons, to have the entire Bible at one's fingertips; similarly, tonaries allowed one to perform chant by heart. And we should not worry that there are so many types of tonaries. There are many kinds of florilegia too. In fact, one learned the material by copying, classifying, and rearranging it. Making a tonary or florilegium was part of the process of memorization.

THE IMPACT OF WRITING ON THE CONSTRUCTION OF THE MEMORIAL ARCHIVE

Throughout our discussion of tonaries, we have observed that theorists had a very exact idea of how the chant melody proceeded. To give an example, the Dijon tonary is written in non-diastematic neumes, so the neumes on their own give only a rough outline of the melody. Two antiphons in two different modes might be notated with the same neumes and yet sound very different. But neumes in combination with modal classification, especially when combined with notes in the margins concerning the range, the starting pitch, and the highest note, can give all the information needed. In other words, the compiler of the Dijon tonary mentioned above, possibly William of Dijon (d. 1031), must have undertaken a detailed analysis of the chant before classifying the music. He must have had an exact idea of every single interval, of the highest and lowest note, of the pitches on which to cadence, and he must have undertaken this analysis without the help of the staff. Similarly, we have seen that Regino could only make a tonary after reading through the entire antiphoner and analyzing the pieces. We have observed throughout this chapter that many of the compilers of the tonaries seem to have had a very definite idea of the melodic outline. In order to understand the precise relationship of writing and memorization that these facts suggest, I would like to turn now to the main ideas of the anthropologist Jack Goody. His 1987 book, *The Interface between the Written and the Oral,* is concerned with the impact of writing on oral societies.[133] I believe there is much here that can be illuminating to students of medieval music.

Goody has spent many years in Ghana, where literacy and orality co-exist, and much of his 1968 book, *Literacy in Traditional Societies,* is devoted to a description of his findings there. He tested many of his hypotheses while doing fieldwork among the LoDagaa and Gonja in Northern Ghana from 1950 (when Europeans established the first school in the town of Birifu)[134] through the 1980s, and was able to formulate important conclusions that he subsequently applied in his most recent book to other cultures and periods as well. The basic idea is very simple even though it has far-reaching implications: only if you write something down are you able to *analyze* the text. Only if you see a text inscribed on paper, parchment, or a tablet can you make a study of the grammar.[135] Writing changes the way you organize

133. See also his *Logic of Writing* and his first essay on the subject, Goody and Watt, "Consequences of Literacy"; and *Literacy in Traditional Societies.* For the most recent discussion of Goody's work see Jahandarie, *Spoken and Written Discourse.* Even though some of Goody's theories have been criticized, none of the issues raised affects this argument.

134. The local teachers had attended existing schools in other parts of the country. Goody, *Interface,* xv–xvi.

135. Ibid., 77.

your thoughts, it changes the way you memorize something.[136] According to Goody, writing "makes possible the study of grammar, of the structure of language, since it is now possible to organize auditory stimuli into a simultaneous rather than successive structure (or pattern), so that a sentence can have a synchronic character as well as a diachronic one. It does the same for argument, leading to the development of formal logic."[137]

The grammarian, Goody continues, is able to turn an "unconscious tendency into a conscious rule . . . This process is not simply one of making the implicit explicit, of an increasing awareness of what one is doing: the very formulation in writing, even where the rule was a rule and not simply a trend, gives a reflexive, feedback quality, a normative pull, that it did not previously have."[138] A written text allows one to study it, to discover inconsistencies, to rework it, to rearrange it, and to see relationships and hierarchies.

Goody lists several immediate and practical results from the graphic encounter with language. First, while in written cultures sentences are explicitly divided into words, in oral cultures there is only an implicit separation. He gives an example of the LoDagaa, who do not have a separate term for "word" but only for "a bit of speech" (p. 274). Second, written cultures develop lists, which he describes as "a single column (or a row) of linguistic, numerical or other graphemic entries which are sometimes numbered or lettered consecutively" (ibid.). And third, there are tables (lists of a binary type) and matrices (lists with many columns and rows). Finally, he believes that writing contributed to the creation of new verse forms (such as the hexameter), which helped to memorize material. "People may internalize the stanza formation of a sonnet just as they do the table (of multiplication). The one becomes a tool of 'oral arithmetic' just as the other sets the frame of an 'oral composition'" (p. 106).

Another point Goody makes that is relevant to us is that only writing made verbatim memory possible. Oral societies are less interested in exact repetition, and more in re-creation of texts (p. 85). The mnemonic feats described by Frances Yates and Mary Carruthers are characteristic of written cultures.[139] In African oral cultures something is memorized by being connected to the ritual and the ceremony itself.[140] When singers are asked to reproduce something without the ceremony, they usually make a mistake in the order of the events. Goody does not deny that there is such a thing as verbatim memo-

136. Similar observations have been made by the Russian psychologist A. R. Luria in *Working Brain,* 286.

137. Goody, *Interface,* 186. See also Goody and Watt, "Consequences of Literacy"; Havelock, *Preface to Plato* and *Muse Learns to Write.*

138. *Interface,* 266. Further references in text are to this book.

139. Yates, *Art of Memory*; Carruthers, *Book of Memory.*

140. *Interface,* 174–75.

rization of short songs and poems,[141] but finds that there is little emphasis on repetitive learning simply because there is no fixed model to which one can compare one's text. He concludes that verbatim memory is rarely called for: "Indeed, the product of exact recall may be less useful, less valuable than the product of inexact remembering."[142]

It is remarkable that the moment writing is invented and memory can be dispensed with, verbatim memory becomes significant. Similarly, the psychologist I. M. Hunter argues that lengthy verbatim recall arises only in a written context.[143] One of Goody's original contributions lies in his ability to eliminate the division between written and oral culture, instead replacing it with oral, on the one hand, and oral plus written, on the other.[144]

Finally, the invention of writing allows us to establish the right, original text. In fact, Goody argues that the wish to arrive at and distribute such an original text is intimately connected with writing, with the ability to *compare* texts.

How do Goody's conclusions affect our understanding of the compilation of tonaries? The tonaries rely on an analysis of the melodies and the texts. The former is of particular interest to us. What effect could musical notation, in particular notation combined with tonaries, have had on the transmission of chant? First, it made verbatim performances possible. Once a particular chant was categorized under, say, mode 1 and notated in neumes, the cantor when leading the singers was able to visualize the entire melody in front of his eyes. He would now know the characteristic beginning formulas, he could plan ahead in performing the chant because he had divided it into phrases *(distinctiones)* and recommended cadence pitches. This does not mean that he had to have a manuscript physically in front of him. He might also visualize a manuscript from which he had learned the music. And again, I do not mean to imply that every singer visualized the manuscript.[145]

Goody has shown that verbatim performances presuppose writing, the ability to compare texts. Thus, it makes perfect sense that Carolingians were the first to be concerned with verbatim performances, with "correct" versions of the chant. We have already mentioned Aurelian's detailed discussion above. Regino of Prüm wrote his tonary because he was upset by all of the mistakes made.[146] Similarly, Guido was concerned about disagreements among antiphoners, and wrote one (which, unfortunately, is lost), so that finally the "correct" melody would be sung everywhere.[147] As a result of no-

141. On verbatim performance of oral poetry see Finnegan, *Oral Poetry.*

142. *Interface,* 178.

143. Hunter, "Lengthy Verbatim Recall," 20.

144. *Interface,* xii.

145. See especially Levy, *Gregorian Chant,* 192.

146. *Epistola de harmonica,* ed. Bernhard, 39.

147. *Prologue to his Antiphoner,* trans. in Strunk, *Source Readings,* 212; see also a similar statement by John from the early 12th c. in *Hucbald, Guido, and John on Music,* 125.

tation, theorists could reassign chant from one mode to another, and could make sure that new melodies would conform to modal requirements.

One might even wonder, and I hasten to add that this is a pure hypothesis, if the creation of tonaries was not a direct result of neumatic notation. Until recently, scholars thought that all the chant was transmitted orally before the earliest neumed graduals were copied. However, in a 1987 paper, Kenneth Levy presented the remarkable idea that the melodies were "being cast in an authoritative neumatic edition by ca. 800 and became musically fixed at the same time and in the same process."[148] His evidence is circumstantial: only three unnotated manuscripts from ca. 800 survive, and yet we know that every church and monastery must have had at least one. This would argue for the strong possibility that others, which might have been less beautiful, got destroyed or lost. More importantly, when notated graduals did appear, they presented the same melodies with very similar neumatic configurations, even though they were written in different neumatic styles. This, according to Levy, can only be explained by a common archetype. Levy argues that the writing down must have happened in connection with the Carolingian Renaissance somewhere in the area between Aachen, Trier, and Metz. Before the invention of neumatic notation, the singers must have sung the melodies as well as they could remember.[149]

If Levy is right, and we argue with Goody that only a written text permits analysis, we can explore the hypothesis that neumatic notation might have contributed to the making of tonaries. Is it possible that music notated in neumes allowed theorists to sit down, study, and classify chant and rearrange it into tables?

Moreover, both tonaries and neumes (if we agree with Levy) came into existence around 800. It seems possible that this was not an accident. They obviously complemented one another: only when used together did they ensure accurate transmission of chant.

148. "Charlemagne's Archetype," repr. in Levy, *Gregorian Chant,* 5.

149. Levy, *Gregorian Chant,* 10. Levy's hypothesis has recently found support in a fascinating study by James Grier, who also makes a convincing case that the Carolingians must have had musical notation; "Adémar de Chabannes."

3

Basic Theory Treatises

After having mastered the chant, students had to learn intervals, the gamut, and, from the eleventh century on, solmization syllables and the hexachord. Much of the theoretical material has been described by scholars of music theory. My interest is less in *what* theorists explained than in *how* they did so. More specifically, we would want to know what methods were used to memorize the material.

THE HAND

From Carolingian times on all music theory instruction began with an explanation of the musical gamut and the memorization of intervals. Theorists employed a number of mnemonic devices to help students learn the material. Probably the most important (though not the earliest) of these is the hand. Others include simple repetition of the material, various mnemonic verses, etymological derivations, and associations with terms already known.[1]

We have seen in the previous chapter that the hand was used to memorize the basic *noeane* formulas and the eight modes. Other early uses of the hand include the calculation of the date of Easter.[2] But the most important musical usage concerns the hand as a didactic tool to memorize all the steps of the gamut. However, before embarking on a description of the hand as a mnemonic tool, I shall quickly recapitulate how the medieval gamut was constructed in its fully developed form.

1. For the most thorough discussion of music education in the Middle Ages see Smits van Waesberghe, *Musikerziehung*.

2. For a recent volume on different usages of the hand see Sherman, *Writing on Hands*; see also Smits van Waesberghe, *Musikerziehung*, 120–21.

The available steps could be represented graphically either through a *scala musicalis* or through the hand. The information included in both is the same. The figure is divided into twenty places *(loca)* (see Figure 6, drawn by Antonius van Sint Maartensdijk, Ghent, in the early sixteenth century).[3] The numbers of the *loca* from 1 through 20 are written in the right column of the graph, stretching from the lowest, Gamma, through the lowest places *(claves graves)* A to G, high places *(claves acute)* a to g, and super-high places *(claves superacute)* aa to ee, each marked by a letter called a clef *(clavis)*. The names of the *claves* can be found in the *scala* in the first column on the left, while the names of the groups of *claves* are written in half circles to the left of the letters. The *scala* bears a striking resemblance to our staff in that steps that are higher are represented visually higher in the diagram and are notated alternately on lines and spaces.

The hand (Figures 7 and 8) locates the lowest place, Γ, on the tip of the thumb; then the places move down, continue through the middle of the hand on all four fingers, then move to the top of the small finger and continue counterclockwise in spiral motion. The highest step, ee, is placed on the back of the middle finger because there is no room left on the inside.

The places are the sites of the hexachordal syllables *(voces) ut, re, mi, fa, sol, la,* which mark the interval pattern of whole tone, whole tone, semitone, whole tone, whole tone. When designating a step of the gamut, it is not enough to give the name of the place. The full name of a gamut step consists of a letter plus a syllable, so that the singer is aware of the interval pattern that surrounds it.

The seven hexachords are the hard low *(durum grave)* from Gamma *ut* to E, the natural low *(natura gravis)* from C to a, the soft low *(b molle grave)* from F to d, the hard high *(durum acutum)* from G to e, the natural high *(natura acuta)* from c to aa, the soft high *(b molle acutum)* from f to dd, and hard very high *(durum superacutum)* from g to ee. While some places have only one solmization syllable, others might contain as many as three. For example, the lowest tone will be referred to as Gamma *ut,* while the tone a sixth above has two solmization syllables, E *la mi.*

Music theorists arrived only gradually at the fully developed gamut as represented through the hand and the *scala.* The hexachord from C to a was first described by Guido in his *Epistola de ignoto cantu* as a revolutionary teaching device.[4] Why was the hexachord such a breakthrough? Students were confronted with a variety of interval patterns when learning the church modes. Take the fifth above the final in each mode:

3. For the clearest explanation of the hand and the *scala,* see Tinctoris, *Expositio manus.* For a modern study, see K. Berger, "Hand and the Art of Memory." For an updated, but shorter and less detailed summary, see K. Berger, "Guidonian Hand."

4. *Guido d'Arezzo's Regule rithmice,* ed. Pesce, "Epistola," 437–531.

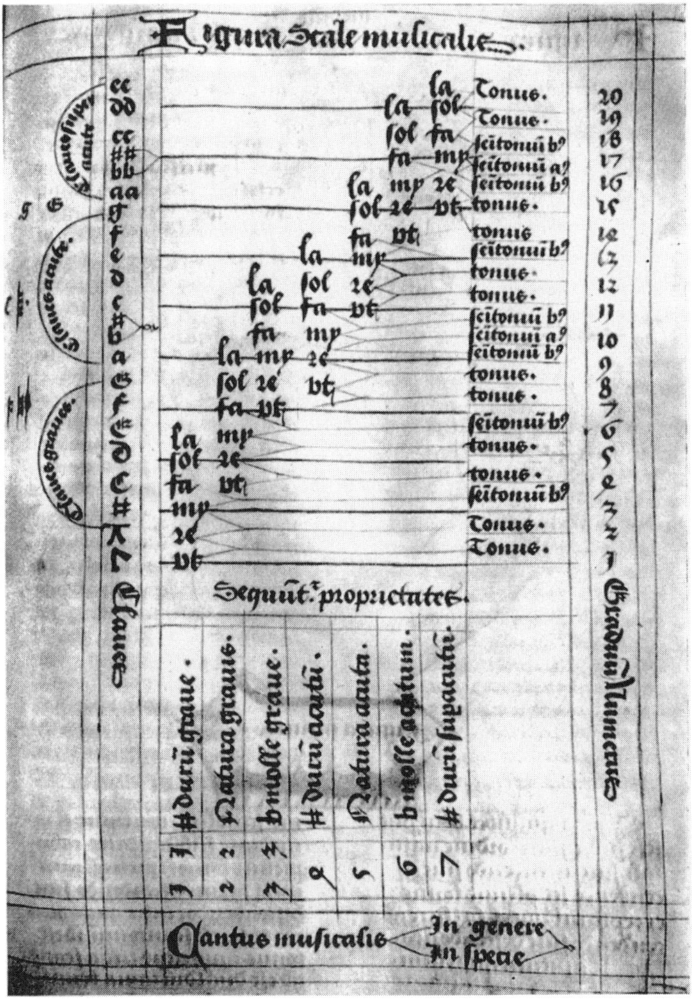

Figure 6. *Scala musicalis* from Ghent, Rijksuniversiteit, Centrale Bibliotheek, MS 70, fol. 108r, published by permission of the Rijksuniversiteit

Modes 1 and 2:	D	E	F	G	a
	t	s	t	t	
Modes 3 and 4:	E	F	G	a	b
	s	t	t	t	
Modes 5 and 6:	F	G	a	b	c
	t	t	t	s	

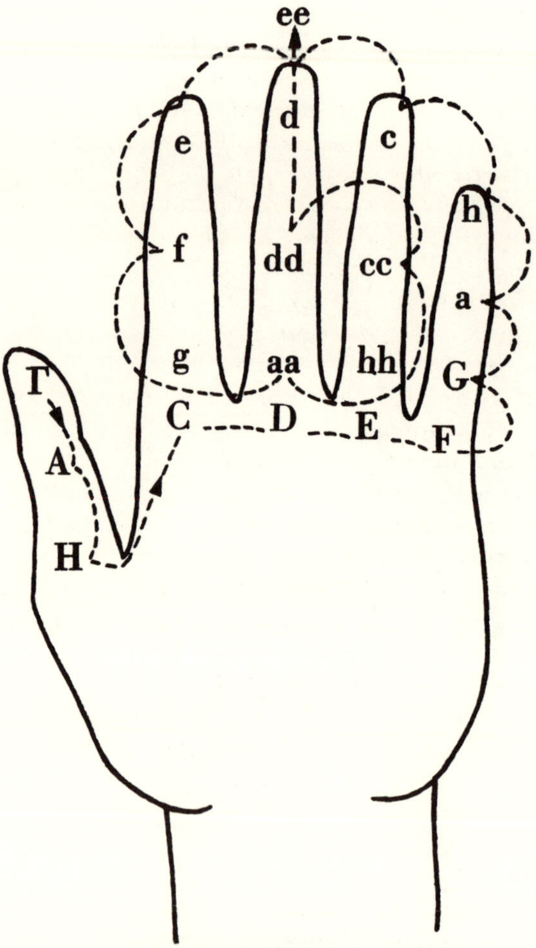

Figure 7. Diagram of the hand, from Smits van Waesberghe, *Musikerziehung*, 124

Guido first demonstrated in his *Micrologus* that modes 1 and 2 share the same interval pattern from D to a, modes 3 and 4 from E to b, and modes 5 and 6 from F to c (he calls them affinities).[5] He then proceeded to show that all modes share the same pattern tone–tone–semitone–tone–tone

5. *Micrologus,* ed. Smits van Waesberghe, 117–19. He is not able to apply this to modes 7 and 8.

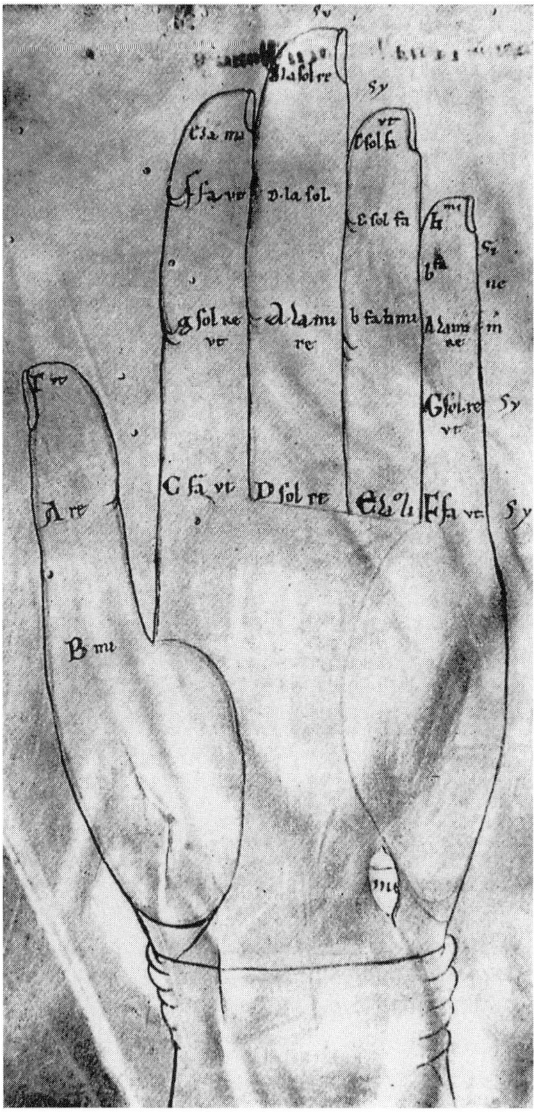

Figure 8. Twelfth-century hand from Admont, now at Rochester, Sibley Music Library, MS 92 1200, fol. 94v, courtesy of the Sibley Music Library, Eastman School of Music, University of Rochester

(TTSTT), though the final and co-final might be located at different places within the hexachord:

Modes 1 and 2: T (A or D) T S T T
Modes 3 and 4: T T (B or E) S T T
Modes 5 and 6: T T S (C or F) T T

He gives the melody *Ut queant laxis* (possibly invented by him specifically for the purpose of committing pieces to memory), where the first phrase begins with the note C and syllable *ut,* the second with D and syllable *re,* the third with E and syllable *mi,* the fourth with F and syllable *fa,* the fifth with G and syllable *sol,* and the sixth with a and syllable *la.* After the student had memorized the hexachord pattern with the solmization syllables, he could do two things: first, he could notate an unwritten melody by matching the order of the tones and semitones to the phrases of *Ut queant laxis*: "Then, when you hear any neume that has not been written down, consider carefully which of these phrases is best adapted to the last note of the neume, so that this last note and the first note of your phrase are of the same pitch."[6] And second, he could read an unknown notated melody: "And when you begin to sing an unknown melody that has been written down, take great care to end each neume so correctly that its last note joins well with the beginning of the phrase which begins with the note on which the neume ends."[7] In short, the addition of the hexachord syllables to the places permitted the singer to orient himself easily throughout the entire gamut. To quote Karol Berger: "The syllables, deductions (hexachords), and properties provide knowledge of the network of the affinities between the steps and a method of reading the steps from the notation. To know the hand means to know all the steps commonly used in music as well as their relationships and to be able to write them down and to read them."[8]

Berger and Richard Crocker have traced the gradual evolution of the gamut in the Middle Ages.[9] While Guido was the first to describe the idea behind the hexachord without writing the name, the full system of seven hexachords is found only from late thirteenth-century theorists on. The first step toward visual representation of higher and lower pitches was made in a treatise of ca. 900 entitled *Musica enchiriadis.*[10] The clefs were used for the

6. "Epistle Concerning an Unknown Chant," trans. Strunk and McKinnon, in Strunk, *Source Readings,* 217.

7. Ibid.

8. K. Berger, "Hand and the Art of Memory," 94.

9. Crocker, "Hermann's Major Sixth."

10. For a partial translation see Strunk, *Source Readings,* 189–96. For a full edition see *Musica et scolica enchiriadis,* ed. Schmid; trans. Erickson as *Musica Enchiriadis and Scolica Enchiriadis.*

first time in the anonymous treatise *Dialogus* of ca. 1000 by Pseudo-Odo.[11] Guido not only demonstrated the affinities between finals and hexachords,[12] but also described a staff with lines and spaces to which he applied Pseudo-Odo's clefs.[13] Hand diagrams with clefs and syllables are first found in the late eleventh century. Around 1100 Johannes Affligemensis advocated the use of the hand to memorize the gamut with the letters and syllables:

> So let him who strives for knowledge of music learn to sing a few songs with these syllables until he knows fully and clearly their ascents and descents and their many varieties of intervals. Also let him diligently accustom himself to measuring off his melody on the joints of his hand, so that presently he can use his hand instead of the monochord whenever he likes, and by it test, correct, or compose a song. After he has repeated these things for some time, just as we have directed, and has thoroughly memorized them, he will have an easier, unperplexed road to music.[14]

We do not know whether Guido was the first to use the hand as a mnemonic tool. A certain Sigebert of Gembloux certainly seems to have considered Guido its inventor, when he says in his *Chronica* (ca. 1105–10): "[Guido] set them [the six letters or syllables to six notes] out on the joints of the fingers of the left hand throughout the diapason so that their upward and downward ascents and descents would impress themselves on the eyes and ears."[15]

How does the musical hand relate to the art of memory? This question has been addressed in a fundamental study by Karol Berger entitled "The Hand and the Art of Memory."[16] Two concepts are central to artificial memory:[17] a background grid of what the author of *Ad Herennium* calls "places" *(loci)* and "images" *(imagines)* that one can locate within this grid. The function of the background grid of places is to determine the order in which

11. Strunk, *Source Readings,* 198–210.

12. He showed in his *Micrologus* that if the mode is placed a fourth lower, the interval pattern remains the same. *Micrologus,* ed. Smits van Waesberghe, 117–22.

13. Guido of Arezzo, *Prologus in Antiphonarium,* ed. Smits van Waesberghe, 211–14.

14. "Per has itaque syllabas is, qui de musica scire affectat, cantiones aliquot cantare discat quousque ascensiones et descensiones multimodasque earum varietates plene ac lucide pernoscat. In manus etiam articulis modulari sedulus assuescat, ut ea postmodum quotiens voluerit pro monochordo potiatur et in ea cantum probet, corrigat et componat. Haec ubi aliquandiu iuxta quod diximus frequentaverit et altae memoriae commendaverit, facilius procul dubio ad musicam iter habebit." Johannes Affligemensis, *De musica cum tonario,* ed. Smits van Waesberghe, 49 f.; trans. Babb, in *Hucbald, Guido, and John,* 103 f.

15. Sigebertus Gemblacensis, *Chronica,* PL 160:204; trans. Palisca in "Guido of Arezzo." See also Sigebertus' *Liber de scriptoribus ecclesiasticis,* PL 160:579.

16. For a thorough discussion of various uses of the hand in music theory, see Smits van Waesberghe, *Musikerziehung,* 120–43.

17. Artificial memory refers to the trained memory and is usually contrasted with the natural memory.

various parts of what we want to remember occur. A background can be provided by, for example, "a house (with many different rooms), an intercolumnar space, a recess, an arch, or the like,"[18] which, in our imagination, we walk through, always in the same order. "An image is, as it were, a figure *(forma),* mark *(nota),* or portrait *(simulacrum)* of the object we wish to remember."[19] The same set of backgrounds can be used repeatedly, but with different images: "the images, like letters, are effaced when we make no use of them, but the backgrounds, like wax tablets, should abide."[20] In other words, if the orator wants to memorize or compose a speech, he can associate a particularly memorable and striking image from each particular part of his speech in each particular room of the house (the background grid) he is accustomed to use in memorizing or composing his speeches, making sure that the order of the parts of the speech and the associated images corresponds to the order in which he normally goes through the rooms. His mind will then wander from room to room and easily recall the parts of the speech through the images. But the background does not have to be an architectural structure: any visual grid of places will do. Already in *Ad Herennium* the background grid is associated with a wax tablet on which one writes: "For the backgrounds are very much like wax tablets or papyrus, the images like the letters, the arrangement and disposition of the images like the script, and the delivery is like the reading."[21] In other words, a mnemonic system is understood to be precisely analogous to a writing system.

All authors stress the importance of remembering the background places in order, so that one can wander through them backwards and forwards. The series has to be memorized before one puts images into the places.

In his study of the origins of the so-called Guidonian hand, Berger demonstrated that the invention and perfecting of writing and reading pitches between the early ninth and early twelfth centuries involved as its fundamental presupposition the idea that pitch, an aural phenomemon, might be visually, that is, spatially, represented. In order to represent their tonal system (the system of pitches they used) visually, musicians adapted for their purposes the basic tools of the *ars memorativa.* The order of the pitches was fixed by means of the background grid of "places" provided either by the fingertips and joints of the open left hand or by the lines and spaces of the

18. "[U]t aedes, intercolumnium, angulum, fornicem, et aliae quae his similia sunt." *Ad Herennium,* ed. and trans. Caplan, 3.16.29.

19. "Imagines sunt formae quaedam et notae et simulacra eius rei quam meminisse volumus"; ibid.

20. " [N]am imagines, sicuti litterae, delentur ubi nihil utimur; loci, tamquam cera, remanere debent"; ibid., 3.17.31.

21. "Nam loci cerae aut chartae simillimi sunt, imagines litteris, dispositio et conlocatio imaginum scripturae, pronuntiatio lectioni"; ibid., 3.16.30.

scala, with each place marked by a different letter name. The specific intervals between the adjacent places, whether whole tones or semitones, were indicated by the syllables located within the places. The hand or *scala* with its clefs and syllables was the mnemonic tool for imagining the tonal system. In other words, each pitch of the tonal system could either be imagined by means of an appropriate syllable or syllables located in the appropriate place of the hand, or be notated by means of a note located on the appropriate line or space of the staff.

There can be little doubt that the staff that we use to this day is derived from the *scala.* As Berger has pointed out, the sixteenth-century theorist Sebald Heyden calls the staff *scala,* for which the most common translation is "ladder."[22] Mary Carruthers and Frances Yates have demonstrated in great detail the importance of the ladder diagram for the art of memory.[23] I would like to take the parallel to mnemotechnics a step further than Berger. The staff without clef, key signature, and notes functions as a background that can be filled with different notes. The interval pattern can sound very different if we change the key signature and add accidentals. Even if the evidence is from the sixteenth century, it is worth citing a passage by the Italian author Giovanni Battista della Porta, who interprets the staff in precisely these terms: "The places and people are fixed. The images, whether of concepts or of words, are flexible. In that exercise, the place has the same effect as does the varnished tablet or slate for music composers. The people are the lines that are there, the images are the notes that are placed on top of them, and once the composers have made use of it, rubbing on it with spit, or with a wet cloth, they get rid of what had been written (send it away), to be able to use the tablet another time."[24] The modern staff is a greatly simplified version of the medieval *scala,* and yet, as we will see in chapter 6, the imagined staff allows the singer to work out complex polyphonic compositions in the mind. The lines of the staff function as the background grid,

22. K. Berger, "Hand and the Art of Memory," 112–13.

23. Yates, *Art of Memory,* 180 f. See especially her discussion of Ramon Lull. In *Book of Memory,* Carruthers includes several references to ladder diagrams and a detailed description of Noah's Ark, which uses ladders (pp. 236–39).

24. "Stabile sono i luoghi e le persone. Mobile sono l'imagini, così de' concetti, come delle parole. Il luoco fa quell'effetto in questo essercitio che fa la carta invernicata, o pietra de' compositori di musica. Le persone sono le righe, che ivi sono, le imagini sono le note, che vi si fanno di sopra, e servito che si è il compositore di quelle, fregandole con sputo, o con un panno humido le manda via, per servirsi della carta per l'altra volta." Della Porta, *L'arte del ricordare* (1566), sig. B3v. See also a similar passage in his *Ars reminiscendi* (Naples: apud Ioan. Baptistam Subtilem, 1602), 11. I would like to thank Lina Bolzoni for calling my attention to these passages. For the use of tablets in composition see *A Correspondence of Renaissance Musicians,* ed. Blackburn, Lowinsky, and Miller, 120–23, and Owens, *Composers at Work,* 74–107. Blackburn and Owens do not mention Della Porta.

while the notes are the ever-changing images placed onto the grid. The staff perhaps is most similar to the wax tablet that can be visualized in the process of composition.

There are a number of terms that very likely derive from the art of memory. The mnemonic term *locus* is used by Tinctoris and other music theorists to denote the places or steps. To quote Berger: "The specific intervals between the places are in principle indefinite and variable and clefs are necessary in order to define them. Thus, for instance, about two adjacent places we know only which one is lower and which higher and that they are adjacent. The interval between them will be known only when specific clefs are located in the places. In other words, the function of the system of places is exactly the same in both the musical and the mnemonic theories."[25]

In *The Book of Memory,* Mary Carruthers demonstrated the importance of the term *locus.*[26] Guido used the term *ordo* instead of *locus,* an equally important term for the art of memory.[27] "Notes" (*notae,* that is, graphic signs) and hexachord "syllables" (*voces,* that is aural names) served as the mnemonic "images" that referred to the individual pitches of the tonal system. Similarly, Berger has found that the term *clavis* was used for the fixed dates for *computus,* which had to be memorized in the same way as the musical *claves.*[28]

In short, we have seen that the hand and the *scala* fit squarely into a group of mnemonic devices used throughout the Middle Ages. In chapter 6, I will explore the far-reaching consequences this finding might have for our understanding of compositional process in the late Middle Ages and Renaissance.

DIDACTIC SONGS AND VERSES

I mentioned in the previous chapter the songs used to bring the church modes to mind. Guido's *Ut queant laxis* falls in the same tradition. In the eleventh century many more didactic songs started to circulate.[29] Since most of these songs were also transmitted orally, there is often much variation between the manuscripts.

There are verses for nearly every area of music theory, and it would be beyond the scope of this book to cover them all.[30] The songs listing and simultaneously incorporating the musical intervals were very popular. The song

25. K. Berger, "Hand and the Art of Memory," 103.

26. Carruthers, *Book of Memory,* 72–73, 79, 93, 118, 125, 138–39.

27. Ibid., 81–82.

28. K. Berger, "Hand and the Art of Memory," 110 f.

29. There has recently been renewed interest in the topic. See Atkinson, "Other *Modus*"; Bernhard, "Didaktische Verse"; Bernhard, "Das musikalische Fachschrifttum"; for earlier excellent discussions of the topic see Smits van Waesberghe, *Musikerziehung* and Smits van Waesberghe, *School en Muziek,* 101–14.

30. Michael Bernhard has announced that he is preparing a detailed discussion of the topic.

E voces unisonas aequat (Example 3) goes through the unison, semitone, whole tone, minor third, major third, fourth, fifth, minor sixth, tritone, and major sixth.[31] Two of these songs have been attributed to Hermann of Reichenau. The attribution is doubtful, but they seem to come from his circle.[32] The song *Ter tria cunctorum* (Example 4), consisting of thirteen hexameters, goes through the basic nine intervals (but leaves out the tritone),[33] naming and singing them at the same time. The intervals are notated with Hermann's interval letters. This song is typically found in theoretical treatises. A simplified version of this song, *Ter terni sunt modi,* is written in Leonine hexameters and ends with the following admonition: "Since music is formed from so few intervals, it is extremely useful to commit them thoroughly to memory and not to stop doing so, until you, knowing the syllables of the intervals, understand the entire concept of music."[34] In the thirteenth century a variation of this song appears in a treatise by Lambertus: "Ter quaterni sunt species quibus omnis cantilena contexitur; Scilicet: unisonus, tonus, semitonium, ditonus, semiditonus, diatessaron, diapente, tonus cum diapente, semiditonus cum diapente, ditonus cum diapente, ad hec sonus diapason."[35] Another interval song, *Diapente et diatessaron simphonie,* was one of the most popular songs in the Middle Ages. It survives in more than thirty manuscripts from the eleventh through fifteenth centuries,[36] and appears in theoretical as well practical sources, a clear indication that it was known not only to theorists but to musicians in general. The most famous source in which this song appears is the so-called "Cambridge Songs," an eleventh-century manuscript in Cambridge, University Library, Gg. V. 35 (Cat. 1567).[37] Despite the wide

31. The song is reproduced from Smits van Waesberghe, *School en Muziek,* 87. It is transmitted in Vienna, ÖNB 51 and 2502; LEu 371; Mbs Clm. 14965 and Clm. 9921; KA 504.

32. See Hermannus Contractus, *Musica,* ed. Ellinwood; and Oesch, *Berno and Hermann von Reichenau.* Oesch believes that *Ter tria cunctorum* is by Hermann because it is consistently attributed to him and agrees with his theories, while he voices serious doubts about Hermann's authorship of *Ter terni,* which he thinks comes from a later period, when the music required a discussion of more intervals (pp. 210–11).

33. The term *limma* refers to the minor second, *limma cum tono* to the minor third, *duo toni* to the major third, *diatessaron* to the fourth, *diapente* to the fifth, *toni terni cum bino limmate* to the minor sixth, and *tonis quaternis cum lima* to the major sixth.

34. "Cumque tam paucis clausulis tota armonia formetur, utilissimum est eas alte memorie commendare nec prius ab huiusmodi studio quiescere, donec vocum intervallis agnitis armonie totius facillime queas comprehendere notitiam." For a facsimile of the song see Smits van Waesberghe, *Musikerziehung,* 77.

35. Atkinson, "Other *Modus,*" 242.

36. "Three times four are the intervals from which all songs are made. That is, unison, tone, semitone, major third, minor third, fourth, fifth, major sixth, minor sixth, major seventh, and octave." Paris, BNF lat. 6755, fol. 76r–v. The song is reproduced in facsimile in Smits van Waesberghe, *Musikerziehung,* 79. Jacques de Liège includes a variant of the *Ter terni* song, which is also reproduced in facsimile in Smits van Waesberghe's *Musikerziehung,* 78.

37. See Bernhard, "Parallelüberlieferungen," 144, for manuscripts where this song occurs.

Example 3. Interval song *E voces unisonas,* from Smits van Waesberghe, *School en muziek,* 87

dissemination of these songs, Charles Atkinson has argued that they were not much performed.[38]

Many prose treatises include one or more mnemonic poems. An early example of such a poem is "Incipiunt nunc versus de tonis Eulogia editi cum

38. For a recent discussion of musical references in the "Cambridge songs" see Atkinson, "Other *Modus,*" 245–56. For the most recent edition and translation, see Ziolkowski, *The Cambridge Songs.*

Example 4. Interval song *Ter tria cunctorum,* possibly by Hermann of Reichenau, from Frutolf, *Breviarium,* 69–70

carmine," on modes, written probably in the ninth century.[39] The poem also mentions the ethical power of the modes: authentic protus is dramatic, deuterus has something marvelous, tritus is showing off, tetrardus is very happy and jubilant. Note that the author did not write the verses underneath each other, as one usually does in poetry, probably because he did not want to waste expensive parchment. Other treatises that include short poems and songs are Goscalchus, Anonymous XI, Ugolino (see also chap. 4), and Adam of Fulda.[40] In most cases, we can assume that the author of the treatise has not composed the verse himself but is merely quoting it.[41]

Some verses are incomprehensible without an explanation:

> Pri re la, se re fa, ter mi fa, quart quoque mi la,
> Quin fa fa, sext fa la, sep ut sol, oc tenet ut fa.

The text is found in Guilielmus Monachus' treatise under the heading "There follow other verses to recognize the tones for their *seculorum.*"[42] Thus, we can conclude that the solmization syllables refer to the steps of the final and reciting tone and a translation of the verse would be as follows: "The first are d and a, the second d and f, the third e and c [on the hard hexachord], the fourth e and a, the fifth f and c [on the hard hexachord], the sixth f and a, the seventh g and d [hard hexachord], the eighth g and c [hard hexachord]."

VERSIFIED TREATISES

According to Joseph Smits van Waesberghe, half of the music theory treatises written between the ninth and the sixteenth centuries are versified.[43] We can be quite certain that theorists did not write their treatises in verse for artistic reasons. Rather, they felt that the material could be remembered better when it was versified. Anonymous of St. Emmeram makes it entirely clear that versification is done in order to help remember the material: "I propose to put [it] together in verse, because a poem put together in verse

39. "Here begin the verses on the church modes, written as a hymn of praise." Paris, BNF lat. 776, fol. 147r. The manuscript was copied in the 11th c. in Albi. See Smits van Waesberghe's discussion and a facsimile of the text in *Musikerziehung,* 98–99.

40. *Berkeley Manuscript,* ed. and trans. Ellsworth; Anonymous XI, ed. and trans. Wingell; Ugolino of Orvieto, *Declaratio musicae disciplinae,* ed. Seay, 2, bk. 2; Adam von Fulda, *Musica.*

41. Bernhard, "Didaktische Verse," 229.

42. "Sequuntur alii versus ad cognoscendum tonos per sui seculorum." Guilielmus Monachus, *De preceptis artis musicae,* ed. Seay, 58.

43. Smits van Waesberghe, "Einige Regeln." See also his *Musikerziehung* and his *School en Muziek,* 161–63. See also Bernhard, "Das musikalische Fachschrifttum," 47–48, 64, 79–80; and Gallo, "Tradizione orale."

more easily stimulates the minds of those who are hearing it to remember."[44] (See also the discussion of versification in chap. 5, pp. 180–88.) Let us look at some of these treatises in some detail.

The first versified treatise that covers all important areas of music theory is Guido's *Regule rithmice.*[45] Even though Fritz Reckow has raised doubts about the authenticity of the treatise, there now seems general agreement that the text is indeed by Guido.[46] It is significant that his *Regule* was written after the *Micrologus* and *Prologus in Antiphonarium,* because much of the material is a poetic rephrasing of the older texts. Smits van Waesberghe suggested that it was written for Guido's younger students (*puerili,* probably aged eight to thirteen) in Arezzo, while the *Micrologus* was intended for *iuvenes* (aged fourteen to eighteen).[47] The *Regule* is a long treatise, indeed—altogether 352 verses. The treatise begins with an acrostic on his name written in quantitative dactylic hexameter with leonine rhyme:

> Gliscunt corda hominum mollita meis Camenis.
> Una mihi virtus numeratos contulit ictus.
> In celi summo dulcissima cantica fundo,
> Dans aule Christi cum munera voce ministri.
> Ordine qui dixi me primo carmina scripsi.[48]

Similarly, the last section (verses 313–52), "Omnibus ecce modis," is in dactylic hexameter. Pesce suggests that it might have been added later because of the "overall rather self-consciously learned language that differs from what is found elsewhere in the *Regule* and in his other treatises."[49]

The main part of the treatise (verses 7–311) is in accentual trochaic hexa-

44. "[P]ropono metrice compilare, quia carmen metrice compilatum ad retinenda levius mentes excitat auditorum"; Anonymous of St. Emmeram, ed. Sowa, 1–2; trans. Yudkin, 4. See also Jacques de Liège, who states "memoriae commendantur metrici versus"; *Speculum musicae,* ed. Bragard, 6:147.

45. The treatise is dated ca. 1030 by Palisca in *Hucbald, Guido, and John on Music,* 51; Smits van Waesberghe, *De musico-paedagogico,* 22–23; and Dolores Pesce, in her new edition and translation of the text in *Guido d'Arezzo's Regule rithmice,* 2–3.

46. Reckow, "Diapason-diocto-octava," 8b. *Regulae,* ed. Smits van Waesberghe, 24–25; *Regule,* ed. Pesce, 3–4.

47. *Regulae,* ed. Smits van Waesberghe, 20 and Smits van Waesberghe, *Musikerziehung,* 178. Smits van Waesberghe also includes a facsimile of the Brussels MS, Bibliothèque Royale II, 784, fols. 25v and 26r.

48. "The hearts of men rejoice, made tender by my Muses. / My single talent has brought together the counted beats. / In heaven on high I pour out sweetest *cantica,* / Giving gifts to the palace of Christ with the voice of a servant. / I who have stated my name in a row at the beginning am the one who wrote the *carmina.*" *Regule rithmice,* ed. and trans. Pesce, 328–29. It is not entirely certain that the acrostichon is by Guido, but it has been appended to the treatise early on in several manuscripts. *Regule,* ed. Pesce, 3–4.

49. *Regule,* ed. Pesce, 4 and 395.

meter. The verses are easy to memorize; it is no wonder that some of them were recited in theory treatises for centuries. I cite just a few lines:

7 Musi*corum* et can*torum* magna est distanti*a*.
8 *I*sti *dicunt,* *i*ll*i* *sciunt,* que componit musi*ca*.
9 Nam qui *facit,* quod non *sapit,* diffinitur besti*a*.
. . . .
17 Not*is* ergo ill*is* spret*is* quibus vulgus u*titur*
18 qui sine ductore nusquam, ut cecus, progre*ditur*.[50]

Guido not only has rhymes at the end of the line, but in addition internal rhymes, as in lines 7, 8, 9, and 17. There are plenty of alliterations throughout the text, as in line 8. He organizes the lines in groups of three, which are then either doubled or even tripled. It can easily be imagined that students would start their theory training by memorizing the *Regule,* and then proceed to the *Micrologus* and *Prologus in Antiphonarium.* Guido covers the following material: the gamut, intervals and modes with their finals, notation through colored lines with clefs, and a section that Smits van Waesberghe has called a "method of eartraining."[51]

Aside from verses, the treatise also uses other mnemonic devices. For example, when he lists the seven pitches he reminds the student of the seven days in the week: "because there are seven pitches just as there are seven days."[52]

The main body of the poem ends with the following lines:

I made the rules accessible, and I contributed to singers an antiphoner
constructed according to the rule,
the likes of which they never had in other times.
I beg you, blessed brothers, for such great labors,
on behalf of me, miserable Guido and my helpers,
entreat holy God, that he be favorable to us.
Help the scribe of the work also by prayers.
Entreat for the teacher, whose help the author and the scribe need.
Glory be to the Lord, Amen.[53]

Note that these lines refer twice to a scribe who is clearly separated from the author. Thus, it seems likely that the treatise was composed entirely in the

50. "Great is the gap between musicians and singers, / the latter talk about what music comprises, while the former understand these things. / For he who does what he does not understand is termed a beast. / . . . Spurning therefore the notes that the common run of monks use, / (who, as if blind, advance nowhere without a guide)"; *Regule,* ed. Pesce, 330–33. I follow Pesce in underlining the rhymes. Pesce also has an excellent discussion of the verse on pp. 14–16.

51. *Regulae,* ed. Smits van Waesberghe, 28.

52. "[Q]uia vocum, ut dierum, eque fit ebdomada." *Regule,* ed. Pesce, 334–35.

53. "Feci regulas apertas, et antiphonarium / regulariter perfectum contuli cantoribus, / quale numquam habuerunt reliquis temporibus. / Precor vos beati fratres pro tantis laboribus, /

mind (or possibly partly on a wax tablet) and only then dictated to a scribe.[54] This confirms what Michael Clanchy has found in English records.[55]

Frutolf, a Benedictine monk from Michelsberg in Bamberg, who died in 1103, wrote an extremely successful treatise called *Breviarium* with verses in leonine hexameter in between prose sections. Frutolf also says that he writes in verse in order to better commit the material to memory.[56]

Christopher Page has traced the background of another important versified treatise, the *Summa musice*.[57] This text was also intended for schoolboys and probably intended to be memorized (p. 15). The material includes elementary plainchant theory, but also a chapter on polyphony. This treatise is a so-called prosimetrum, in that it alternates prose and poetry (see chap. 5). Page relates the *Summa* to a versified grammar treatise by Eberhard of Béthune and Geoffrey of Vinsauf's *Poetria nova,* both in hexameter, and to Alexander de Villa Dei's *Doctrinale.* The author explains everything twice, once in verse and once in prose. Page argues that the scribe first copied the verse; "only when he had completed this did he begin the prose, packing it around the verse in a cursive and heavily contracted script. The resulting pages look like a glossed copy of a poem in which the verse is the centre of study and the prose an ancillary aid" (p. 38). The verse is often more accomplished than the prose. The author certainly knew how to write quantitative poetry, using rhymed paired hexameters. Page has found many dactyls "to lighten the movement of the line, . . . and it is correspondingly rare to find five spondaic feet in a single hexameter" (p. 39).

Similarly, Gobelinus Person, a fifteenth-century Westphalian theorist, chose to write his treatise *Tractatus musicae scientiae* in prosimetrum.[58] He covers the use of modes in chant, as well as solmization syllables and mutations.

Hugo Spechtshart von Reutlingen's *Flores musicae* (1332–42), written in rhymed leonine hexameter and consisting of 635 verses, was extremely popular. The treatise was such a success that for centuries to come students quoted from it. He also wrote two versified grammar texts, *Speculum grammaticae* and *Forma discendi.*[59]

Finally, there are a number of versified counterpoint and mensural no-

---

pro misero Guidone, meis adiutoribus, / pium Deum exorate, nobis sit propitius. / Operis quoque scriptorum adiuvate precibus. / Pro magistro exorate, cuius adiutorio / auctor indiget et scriptor. Gloria sit Domino, Amen." *Regule,* ed. Pesce, 392–95.

54. For a detailed discussion of composition in the mind, see chaps. 4 and 6.

55. Clanchy, *From Memory to Written Record,* 125.

56. "[P]ro majoris memoriae commendatione metro etiam tradiderunt"; Frutolfus, *Breviarium,* 62–63. See also Huglo, *Tonaires,* 184–85.

57. Ed. and trans. Page, 33–40. Further references are given in the text.

58. Hamburg, Staatsbibliothek, Realkat. ND VI 4582; ed. Müller, in "Der *Tractatus musicae scientiae*"; commentary on 177–80.

59. See Gümpel's edition of the *Flores musicae,* 51–177.

tation treatises, most of which have not been published. A good example is the anonymous "Post octavam quintam si note tendunt in altum," written in hexameter and transmitted in many different sources. The author concentrates on consonance progressions.[60] Ugolino's versified section on consonance progression, discussed in chapter 4, is written in the same vein. Another is the anonymous text "Ars discantandi datur hic et dulcisonandi," found in an Erfurt manuscript (Stadtbibliothek, Amplon. Ca 8° 94, fols. 70v–71r). Verses 1–9 list the consonant and dissonant intervals; verses 10–18 give the different note values, which are drawn on the left margin; proportions are described in verses 19–28; and verses 29–45 give some basic examples of imperfection, alteration, ligatures, and rests.[61] A treatise in Cambridge, Trinity College 1441, fol. br with the incipit "Altior et prima nota que tractum dat yma,"[62] summarizes ligature rules in verse form. Coussemaker published a versified text attributed to Phillipotus Andrea entitled "De contrapuncto quaedam regulae utiles,"[63] and a versified version of Vitry's teaching was edited by Gilbert Reaney.[64] A fourteenth-century anonymous writer from the Prague area composed a treatise on mensural notation in hexameter consisting of 162 verses.[65] The text must have been quite popular as it is also found in Melk (Cod. 950), where the date 1369 has been added. In addition, fragments are transmitted in Berlin, Staatsbibliothek Preussischer Kulturbesitz, Mus. ms. theor. 1590, fol. 87r–v, Kremsmünster, Benediktinerstift, Musikarchiv, Cod. 312, fol. 207v, and Warsaw, Biblioteka Narodowa, BOZ 61, fol. 293rc.

MNEMONIC GRAPHS

Mary Carruthers has shown how important diagrams and drawings were for memorization.[66] Hugh of St. Victor, for example, used "virtually every major genre of diagram common in the twelfth century—ladders, trees, circles, columns, maps, and genealogical charts—all enclosed within the rectangular shape of the memorial page."[67] Usually there will be *tituli* added that will be associated with a figure and, in turn, provide new associations. These diagrams are frequently referred to as *archa* (ark), *thesaurus,* or *sacculus* (trea-

60. The treatise is published in CS 3:116–18. See also Sachs's discussion in *Der Contrapunctus,* 87.

61. This text is also reproduced in facsimile and explained in Smits van Waesberghe, *Musikerziehung,* 168–69.

62. For a facsimile of this text see ibid., 169.

63. CS 3:116–18.

64. Reaney, "A Postscript," 31.

65. "Versus de musica anonymi Pragensis 'Iam post has normas.'"

66. See her *Book of Memory,* 150–51, 248–57; and *Craft of Thought,* 140–42.

67. Carruthers, *Book of Memory,* 248.

sure-bag). Carruthers provides a fascinating discussion of the "wheel diagram" (*Rota Virgilis*) that might well be connected with the English expression learning "by rote."[68] All of these diagrams represent a great amount of information in little space. It was important that diagrams and *picturae* should be seen at a single glance, that is, included on one folio. Keywords or images would help recall entire passages. The drawings or diagrams could help recollect material previously memorized or they could aid in the process of composition of new texts (see chap. 6).

It is not surprising that music theorists were also very inventive in finding graphic representations for what they wanted their students to learn, ranging from simple drawings to elaborate diagrams. Again, it is beyond the scope of this book to give a thorough overview. All I can do is provide a few examples.

A beautiful lion can be found in a tenth-century manuscript in London, British Library, Harley 2637, fol. 40v, to help memorize the six consonances (Figure 9). The intervals of the fourth, fifth, octave, octave and fourth, octave and fifth, and double octave are attached to the different parts of the lion's body: the fourth to the mouth, the fifth to one front foot, the octave to the second foot, the octave and fourth to the first back foot, the octave and fifth to the second back foot, and finally the double octave to the tail.

Similarly, in the MS Brussels, Bibliothèque Royale, II 784, fol. 15r of Guido's *Micrologus*, the scribe tries to make the possible interval progressions memorable by attaching them to a human body (Figure 10). The head is entitled "Music is the movement of the notes," while the three strands of hair on each side of the head list the basic intervals whole tone, major third, and fourth on the left, and half tone, minor third, and fifth on the right. The "fingers" and "toes" give possible interval progressions.[69]

Modal theory was summarized in a diagram borrowed from Aribo (Figure 11), who wrote his text around 1080:

> The authentic and plagal modes agree and disagree as if from four bridal chambers proceeded four modest brides and their spouses and joined together in two circles of dancers . . . It works similarly with authentic and plagal modes. They have in common the five steps between the final and the fifth above the final, while the authentic modes alone have the three upper ones and the

68. Ibid., 251–52.

69. Two 15th-c. authors use the human body for mnemonic purposes. Peter of Ravenna places the various endings of the Latin noun on a naked body: "For in the body of a man I have found ymages of cases so that the head is the case of nominativa, the right hande the genityve, the left hande the datyve, the ryght foot the accusatyve, the lyfte foot the vocatyve, and the bely or stomake the ablatyve. And for the syngular nombre I set a fayre mayden naked, and for the plurell the same mayde, well arayed and rychely or her that I wolde be remembered of." The translation by Robert Coplande is from 1548. The quotation is Carruthers and Ziolkowski, *Medieval Craft of Memory*, 228. Similarly, Jacobus Publicius uses the naked human body as a mnemonic device; Carruthers, *Craft of Memory*, 226–54.

Figure 9. Lion with intervals, London, British Library, Harley 2637, fol. 40v, reproduced by permission of the British Library

plagal the three lower ones. As a result the circles of the men and women cross each other, but they also have a common space [that is, the bridal bed]; on the other hand, they each have their own space.[70]

70. "Concordant discordantque autenti cum plagis, quomodo si procederent de quatuor thalamis totidem nuptae modestae cum suis sponsis, copularentque duos chorearum circulos . . . ita autenti cum plagis. Nam quinque chordas habent communiter, tres autem singulariter: ut

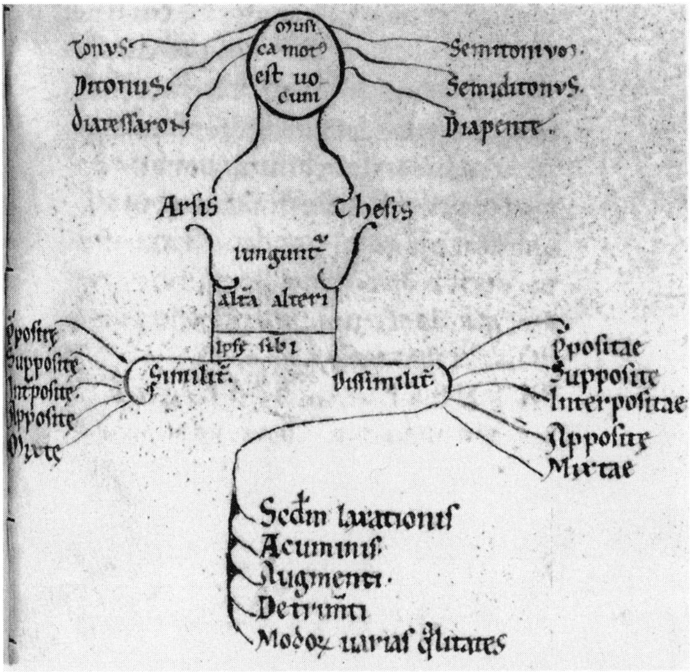

Figure 10. Human body with interval progressions in Guido's *Micrologus*, Brussels, Bibliothèque Royale de Belgique, MS II 784, fol. 15r, published by permission of the Bibliothèque Royale de Belgique

Our diagram comes from an early sixteenth-century manuscript copied by Magister Antonius de Aggere Sancti Martini (Ghent, University Library 70, fol. 56v). The small circles refer to the modes; on the upper left is the second *tonus* (plagal protus), next to it the first (authentic protus), then comes the fourth *tonus* (plagal deuterus), next the third (authentic deuterus), etc. The first large square lists the pitches of modes 1 and 2 (A through d), the two large circles are entitled *chorus matronalis* and *chorus virilis;* the final d *(finalis)* is clearly marked, as are the five common steps, and the steps below and above.[71]

A number of theorists include diagrams that summarize mensural notation

duo circuli ita sibimet sint implicati, ut utriusque extremitas centrum, id est medietatem alterius, persecet. Habent medium spacium commune, altrinsecus scilicet spacium situm sine participatione." Aribo, *De musica,* ed. Smits van Waesberghe, 17.

71. See also Smits van Waesberghe's discussion in *Musikerziehung,* 102–3.

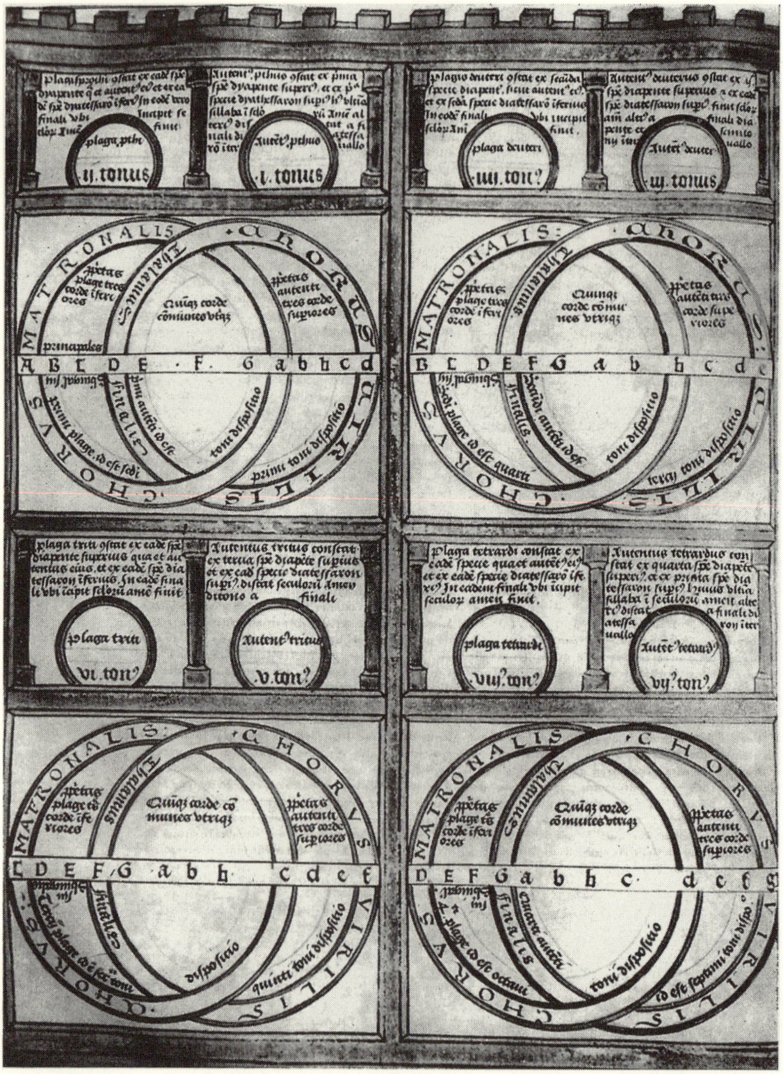

Figure 11. Diagram of modal theory, Ghent, Rijksuniversiteit, Centrale Bibliotheek, MS 70, fol. 56v, reproduced by permission of the Rijksuniversiteit

and the various subdivisions of individual notes, imperfection, and alteration. These diagrams are usually presented in addition to a detailed explanation of the basic rules. In other words, they summarize what had been learned earlier. I give two examples.

Johannes Vetulus de Anagnia's *Liber musices* was written in the middle of the fourteenth century. His main concern is the division of time. First he explains the various note values, ligatures, and mensurations. Then he demonstrates the possible mensurations on two note levels: the *larga* or *maxima* level and the *tempus* or *brevis* level. The *larga* can be *maior, minor,* or *minima,* the *tempus* can be *maius, minus,* or *minimum.* In addition, each of the subdivisions can be perfect or imperfect. The results can be summarized as follows:[72]

DIVISION OF *LARGA* INTO *BREVES*

	perfecta	*imperfecta*
maior	12	8
minor	9	6
minima	6	4

DIVISION OF *TEMPUS* INTO *MINIMAE*

	perfectum	*imperfectum*
maius	12	8
minus	9	6
minimum	6	4

The author has drawn beautiful *figurae arborum* (tree figures; Figure 12) to exemplify these divisions. The first three refer to *divisiones largae:* The *larga* is divided into twelve *breves* for *divisiones maioris largae.* In each of the divisions, there are twelve *breves,* which result from either 4 + 8, or 3 × 4, or 2 × 6. *Divisiones minoris largae* includes nine *breves,* resulting from 3 × 3, or 3 + 6. *Divisiones minimae largae* comprise six *breves,* derived from 3 × 2, 3 + 3, or 2 + 4. For all of these divisions Johannes gives additional mnemonic aids: twelve is important because there were twelve apostles, and four because there were four evangelists, three because of the Holy Trinity, to name just a few.[73]

Finally, Coussemaker's Anonymous XI and Anonymous XII, both transmitted in London, BL Add. 34200, include circles that summarize not all but most of the basic mensurations. Anonymous XI (Figure 13) includes,

72. For a detailed discussion of Johannes's mensural system see Johannes Vetulus de Anagnia, *Liber de musica,* ed. Hammond, 16–24; see also my discussion in *Mensuration and Proportion Signs,* 46–49, and Gallo, "Die Notationslehre," 322–25.

73. "The quaternary of the main *larga maioris* represents the four heads of the Trinity, that is the four evangelists, who are included in the number twelve and in the main apostles and disciples, and this same number can be reduced to the Holy Trinity." ("Quaternarius principalis largae maioris repraesentat quattuor testes trinitatis, videlicet quattuor evangelistas qui continentur in numero duodecim et principalium apostolorum et discipulorum, et ad ipsum numerum reducuntur per misterium trinitatis.") Johannes Vetulus de Anagnia, *Liber de musica,* ed. Hammond, 39.

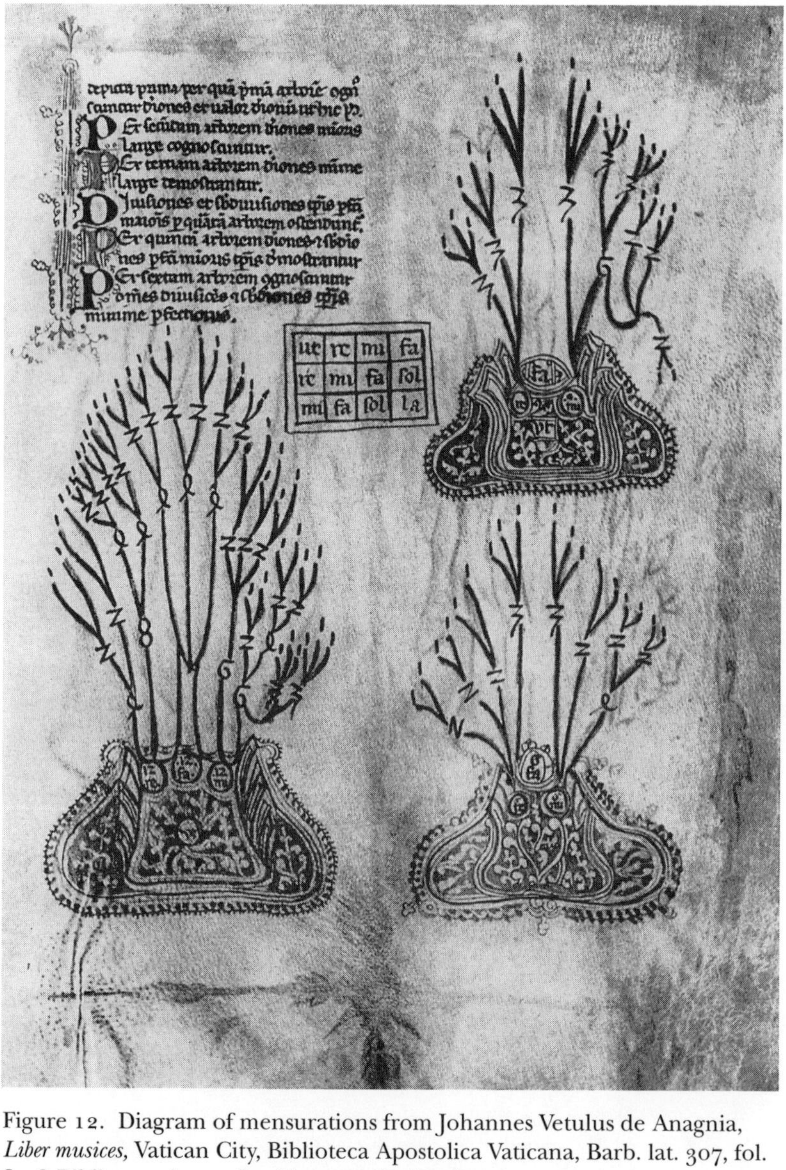

Figure 12. Diagram of mensurations from Johannes Vetulus de Anagnia, *Liber musices,* Vatican City, Biblioteca Apostolica Vaticana, Barb. lat. 307, fol. 8r, © Biblioteca Apostolica Vaticana (Vatican)

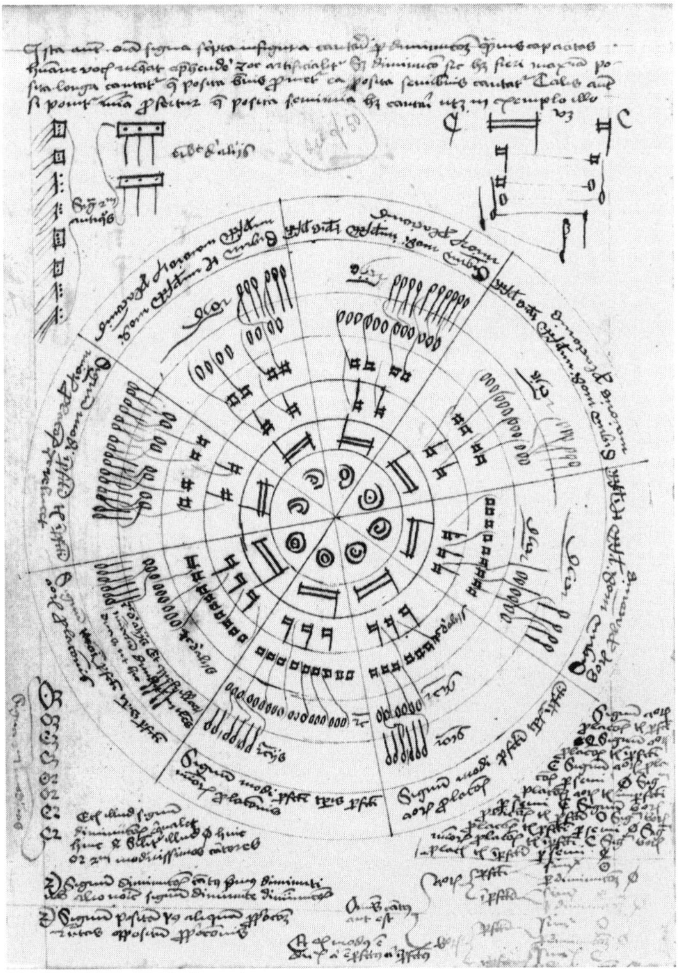

Figure 13. Anonymous XI, circle with mensural system, London, British Library, Add. MS 34200, fol. 36v, reproduced by permission of the British Library

starting in the lower left quadrant and moving counterclockwise: perfect major and minor mode, perfect time, and major prolation; perfect major and minor mode, perfect time, minor prolation; perfect major and minor mode, imperfect time, major prolation; perfect major and minor mode, imperfect time, minor prolation; imperfect major and minor mode, perfect time, major prolation; imperfect major and minor mode, perfect time, minor prolation; imperfect major and minor mode, imperfect time, major prolation; imperfect major and minor mode, imperfect time and minor prolation. Similarly, Coussemaker's Anonymous V has three diagrams summarizing imperfections and alterations.[74]

In this chapter we have seen that a variety of tools were used to help commit elementary theory to memory. These methods are not different from those used in other areas of knowledge in the Middle Ages and Renaissance. I will now consider what role the art of memory played in educating future singers and composers in polyphony.

74. *Ars cantus mensurabilis,* ed. and trans. Balensuela, 124–29.

4

The Memorization of Organum, Discant, and Counterpoint Treatises

After the choirboys had mastered chant and solmization syllables, the more talented went on to learn organum (pieces with a plainchant tenor in sustained notes against a melismatic upper voice or voices), discant, and/or counterpoint. In this chapter I use the last two terms in the most general sense as either written out or improvised pieces for two or more parts. The central questions I will address are first how organum, discant, and counterpoint were taught; and second, how this teaching influenced both performance, in particular unwritten performance, and composition. I will consider whether the answers to these questions change our image of the medieval composer. Was he the great original creator of Notre Dame organa as painted by Friedrich Ludwig at the beginning of the twentieth century (as outlined in chap. 1)? Is there any evidence that fifteenth-century polyphony was an improvisational art that had little to do with written-down composition, as claimed by Rob Wegman?[1] Neither of these claims can be investigated before we know how singing and composition of polyphony were taught.

There are two avenues of inquiry that I will follow here. First, I will gather information from various accounts and documents that describe where and how counterpoint was taught. Second, I will look at the theory treatises themselves and compare the music treatises to medieval instruction books in other fields.

HOW POLYPHONIC SINGING WAS TAUGHT

Much has been written on the performance practice of early polyphony in recent years. Our picture of the choir of Notre Dame in Paris is now very dif-

1. Wegman, "From Maker to Composer."

ferent from what it was when Friedrich Ludwig described a large choir run by Leonin and Perotin, whom he considered to be the first two composers in the modern sense (see chap. 1). Craig Wright has shown that the singing of polyphony in twelfth- and thirteenth-century Notre Dame was essentially a soloist's art.[2]

According to Wright, the choirboys at Notre Dame of Paris were supervised by a *magister cantus* by 1208 at the latest.[3] Even though we know that organum and discant were sung from the twelfth century on, most of the documents demonstrating widespread instruction in discant and counterpoint come from the fifteenth century. We do not know for sure exactly what went on earlier, but it seems likely that much of the evidence also applies to the earlier period.[4] In 1411 Jean Gerson, Notre Dame's chancellor, wrote a *Doctrina* that regulated virtually every part of the chorister's life and education. Rule 5, which concerns the instruction of discant and counterpoint, is of particular interest: "Moreover, the master of music shall teach the boys at the statutory hours primarily plainsong and counterpoint, and some honest discants, but no dissolute or ribald songs, nor should he be so insistent in these matters that the boys fail to make progress in grammar."[5]

Also elsewhere in France, in Burgundy, and in England polyphony flourished. A 1421 Bruges document stipulates that gifted choirboys should be instructed in discant and counterpoint. Four *chorales* (choirboys) had to sing Mass and vespers every day. These four would be augmented by a reserve group of boys, whose abilities to sing polyphony must also have been good. One of these boys was accepted in 1420 because he "already knew his counterpoint."[6]

While the memorization and performance of chant was generally supervised in both monasteries and cathedrals by the *cantor,* the musical training of the boys and the performance of polyphony lay in the hands of the *succentor.* Reinhard Strohm has shown that in late fourteenth-century Bruges the *succentor,* who was responsible for the performance of polyphony, had bought *libri motetorum* (books of motets).[7] Often the *succentor* was called "the

2. Wright, *Music and Ceremony,* 180 f.

3. Ibid., 166.

4. Many Dominicans, such as Thomas Aquinas and Albertus Magnus, opposed polyphony. Yet their very opposition can be taken as a sign that organum and discant thrived at Notre Dame. Wright, *Music and Ceremony,* 345–47. Wright also discusses the impact of the decree *Docta sanctorum patrum* of Pope John XXII, which was directed against hockets and motets.

5. Trans. Wright, *Music and Ceremony,* 167.

6. Strohm, *Music in Late Medieval Bruges,* 22.

7. Ibid., 14. The first *succentor* known by name in Bruges is documented from 1365, but there were others before him (p. 13). For other documents referring to the teaching of discant and counterpoint see Wright, "Performance Practices," and Wegman, "From Maker to Composer," 413–28.

master of the children." He had to teach extemporized discanting techniques, solmization, mensural notation, counterpoint, and sometimes even keyboard playing. The *succentor* was most often a "professional," but sometimes also an amateur. To quote Strohm, "He was the reader, and occasionally the author, of manuscript and printed music theory. Often he was a composer."[8] Similarly, a document from Durham Cathedral tells us that the organist John Stele had to teach the monks and eight choirboys "Pryktenote ffaburden deschaunte and counter." There is no doubt that the teaching included both unwritten and written-out music, since pricked note refers to either "notated music or, more specifically, to music written out in all parts."[9]

Strohm has also documented counterpoint instruction in Italy. The composer Matteo da Perugia is found in Milan as early as 1402 as a *biscantor* (professional singer of polyphony).[10] Furthermore, as a result of the papal bulls of Eugenius IV, singers and teachers of counterpoint were hired at the following cathedrals between 1432 and 1440: Vicenza 1432, Turin 1435, Florence 1436, Bologna (Basilica di S. Petronio) 1436, Treviso 1437, Padua 1439, Urbino 1439, and Verona 1440. The contracts are sometimes quite specific as to the duties of the *magister cantus*. For example, in 1419 Nicolò Fragerio from Liège was appointed to the cathedral of Chioggia near Venice to

> say Requiems every day in a special chapel;
>
> sing chant and polyphony *(cantar e biscantar)* in the service whenever necessary (i.e., probably on Sundays and feast days);
>
> appear in all the services, day and night;
>
> teach chant and polyphony to all those clerics who wanted to learn it.[11]

The students received free education in return for singing in the church. The choir was often enlarged with adult voices. As a result, the *succentor* would not only teach counterpoint to gifted students, but also to interested canons and other beneficiaries of the choir.[12]

A student assistant often helped the *succentor* or *magister cantus* in his instruction. In Paris he was called a *spe,* a term usually referring to a singer whose voice had broken. His main duty consisted of helping prepare the boys for the services.[13] He could be admitted to this position only if he knew

8. Strohm, *Rise of European Music,* 288.

9. Ibid., 208 This seems to contradict Wegman's claim (in "From Maker to Composer," 416, 430, 449) that the instruction of the boys was entirely oral. See also below.

10. Strohm, *Rise of European Music,* 585.

11. Ibid., 586.

12. Ibid., 289. Of course, in addition, they had to sing themselves.

13. Wright, *Music and Ceremony,* 171.

the psalter and the Commune sanctorum by heart. At St. Pharahilde in Ghent in 1423 the schoolmaster had two assistants called *submonituers.* Not only were they responsible for instructing the boys "in good manners," but they also conducted the singing of plainchant in two churches and sang contratenor parts.[14] In Bolzano "the assistants did all the day-to-day work . . . " The instruction was also done in writing because the assistants "used blackboards with music staves painted on them to teach counterpoint."[15] Thus, there can be no doubt that the instruction included both written and unwritten counterpoint.

Moreover, the teaching itself was often done with the aid of textbooks. This can be surmised from the fact that many of these choir directors left important counterpoint treatises. For whom should these treatises have been written if not for other choir directors and choirboys? The theorists who wrote treatises include Ugolino of Orvieto, Johannes Gallicus, John Hothby, Johannes Tinctoris, and Guilielmus Monachus. In fact, the *Dialogus* ascribed to Hothby was probably compiled from lecture notes taken in Lucca Cathedral, where he taught.[16]

Although we have little documentary evidence about instruction in discant and organum from the period before 1400, there is an abundance of evidence from the fifteenth century on from France, Burgundy, Italy, England, and the Tyrol. In all places written and unwritten counterpoint was taught to choirs of differing sizes, often with the help of counterpoint treatises. Obviously, we will have to study these in some detail to learn more about the pedagogical methods.

However, before turning to the treatises, I would like to make a short digression to discuss how material in other fields was learned. I will concentrate especially on instruction in grammar and arithmetic because the methods used in both have much in common with instruction in counterpoint.[17]

14. Strohm, *Rise of European Music,* 289.

15. Ibid., 289, 507 f. See also Paula Higgins, "Tracing the Career," 9 and 25, who discovered that six tablets were used in 1407/8 in the Sainte-Chapelle in Bourges "pour faire le contrepoint desdiz enffans." Thus, there seems little evidence that students did not learn how to *write,* as claimed by James Haar ("Lessons in Theory," 76, n.7) and Wegman ("From Maker to Composer," 430). Haar and Wegman base their discussion mainly on Coclico's account. And yet we do not really know how reliable Coclico's descriptions are. See also Meier, "Musica Reservata."

16. Strohm, *Rise of European Music,* 596.

17. Note that Arnoul Greban was hired in 1450 at Notre Dame de Paris "as magister grammatice" and "magister puerorum chori." In his capacity as master of the boy's choir he would certainly have taught counterpoint, and it would make sense that the methods employed to teach both subjects were the same. See D. Smith, "Arnoul Greban." I would like to thank Isabelle Ragnard for calling this fact to my attention.

ON MEDIEVAL TEACHING IN GENERAL

The Teaching of Grammar

In chapter 2, I described how students learned to read by memorizing the psalms. The next step in instruction was to learn grammar. In northern Europe, the most popular textbook was the *Ars minor* by Aelius Donatus, a fourth-century Roman grammarian, while Italians preferred a grammar entitled *Ianua,* a late medieval text of Italian origin.[18] Students began by learning nouns, adjectives, pronouns, and their declensions, followed by verbs and their conjugations. This was followed by exercises called "doing concordances," something we would now call agreement exercises. In these, adjectives were combined with nouns (for example, *homo bonus, hominis boni, homini bono*) and pronouns, and finally with verbs (for example, *bonus vir amat*). All of this was repeated again and again, until the students could recite these combinations.

The most important Renaissance grammarian, Guarino of Verona, the author of *Regulae grammaticales,* stressed the importance of memorization in a letter of 1425: "I will repeat 'and repeat again, and recommend many, many times' [a line from Vergil] that you must exercise a student's memory. Give him something to memorize, and pay more attention to repetition than to explanation."[19] Note that the drilling was both oral and in writing, in particular in Italy. The result was that students could decline, conjugate, and recite syntactic rules and entire sentences in their sleep. Next Alexander de Villa Dei's *Doctrinale*[20] and the *Disticha Catonis* were memorized,[21] followed by the Latin authors Statius, Vergil, Lucan, Juvenal, Horace, and Ovid. Finally, they would progress to the kinds of texts (florilegia, *sententiae, distinctiones,* etc.) mentioned in chapter 2. The ultimate result of all this drilling activity was that students could read and write beautiful Latin. A student was not expected to be original; rather, it was more important to have a well-stocked memory from which one could retrieve phrases and sentences.[22] To give just one example, Jan Ziolkowski has demonstrated that medieval poets systematically memorized phrases by reading and memorizing poetry, or by simply listening to somebody reading poetry, and these phrases were

18. Grendler, *Schooling in Renaissance Italy,* 175 f.

19. "Unum tibi repetam 'repetensque iterumque iterumque monebo' [Vergil, *Aeneid,* 3.345] ut puerorum memoriam exerceas; quaedam memoriae mandent, ut Virgilii versus magis frequentes quam multos." Letter to Martino di Metteo Rizzoni of October 28, 1425, cited in Grendler, *Schooling in Renaissance Italy,* 196.

20. Wright, *Music and Ceremony,* 174–75. The *Doctrinale* is versified in order to help memorize the material. See also chap. 5.

21. See also Grendler, *Schooling in Renaissance Italy,* 194–202. For an excellent summary of medieval education, see S. Reynolds, *Medieval Reading.*

22. See also Carruthers, *Book of Memory,* who makes this point throughout her book.

then incorporated into their poems.[23] We would want to know if similar instruction can be documented for performers and composers of polyphonic music.

The Teaching of Abacus

Historians of mathematics generally distinguish two kinds of "arithmetic" treatises in the Middle Ages and Renaissance.[24] The first are the so-called algorism treatises that were used in universities. Good examples are the *Algorismus vulgaris* of Sacrobosco (John of Holywood, d. 1244 or 1256) and Alexander de Villa Dei's *Carmen de algorismo* (ca. 1202).[25] Algorism treatises use Hindu-Arabic numerals to describe the basic arithmetic operations such as addition, subtraction, multiplication, division, and contain nothing more. These treatises are quite short, rarely more than ten pages, and usually do not give any examples.

The second kind were called abacus treatises, but they should not be confused with the *abacus* in use in Antiquity, a reckoning board that helped solve simple arithmetic problems. The authors of the abacus treatises are less interested in covering basic "arithmetic" operations (even though they usually do this as well) than in presenting a collection of problems with their solutions. The texts would first present a diagram called *casteluccio* (little castle), which would graphically demonstrate that one-digit numbers are smaller than two-digit numbers, two-digit numbers smaller than three-digit numbers, etc. Next they would explain finger reckoning by showing various images of the hand with fingers bent or straightened. As in the musical hand, the student would use only the left hand to signal a number that he could then write down with his right hand.[26] These numbers were used as intermediate steps in complex multiplications and divisions.

Multiplication of numbers up to 20 × 20 was memorized. For example, Pietro Cataneo entitled a chapter in his *Le practiche delle due prime matematiche* "Del multiplicar a la memoria detto vulgarmente Caselle o Librettine."[27] Like-

23. Ziolkowski, "Cultural Diglossia."

24. Note that I use the term "arithmetic" in the modern sense, namely to denote basic mathematical operations such as addition, subtraction, multiplication, division, and various commercial problems solved by "the Rule of Three." This is not the way the term was used in the Middle Ages and Renaissance.

25. The best discussions of algorism and abacus treatises are found in van Egmond, "Commercial Revolution and the Beginnings of Western Mathematics"; Grendler, *Schooling in Renaissance Italy*; Tropfke, *Geschichte der Elementarmathematik*; D. E. Smith, *History of Mathematics*; see also my *Mensuration and Proportion Signs*, chaps. 2 and 6, and my "Musical Proportions and Arithmetic."

26. See especially Grendler, *Schooling in Renaissance Italy*, 312–13.

27. *Practiche*, sig. B3v–B4r. See also Grendler, *Schooling in Renaissance Italy*, 313.

wise, students had to memorize *librettine* for monetary units. To quote the historian Warren van Egmond, "We have then a total of 10 separate tables, each containing from 50 to 100 individual entries or products. The abaci make it quite clear that all of these tables were supposed to be memorized, 'pone bene al mente' . . . , because they are a prerequisite for the study of the abacus. It is clear that the students of the abacus must have had a greater capacity for memorization than we."[28] This brings us back to Jack Goody's discussion of oral and written arithmetic (see chap. 2). Italian merchants were able to do very complex calculations in the mind because they had used the written page, or more specifically, tables, to memorize material. While Goody had only limited multiplications of probably up to 12 × 12 in mind, our merchants went much further and could multiply and divide any numbers up to 20, and transform monetary units.

After having mastered the basic operations, the abacists proceeded to solve individual problems. These problems were usually of a practical sort, for example, business problems, barter problems, interest and discount problems. To cite just one example, Paolo dell'Abbaco gave the following assignment to his students: "The distance from here to Florence is sixty miles. One man can make the trip in eight days, another takes only five days. If they both start out together, one from here and the other from Florence, after how many days will they meet?"[29] In addition, we find recreational problems that were solved as a pastime.[30]

What is striking about these problems is that each was solved individually. Even if a problem was only slightly different from an earlier one, it would be discussed separately, and special rules would be developed; consequently, rules multiplied rapidly. The result is a catalog of problems with their solutions. Note, though, that in all problems the arithmetic operations needed to solve them are few.

This is very different from our approach to arithmetic. We consider mathematics to be a symbolic and logical system where a few basic rules can be applied to a great number of problems and situations.[31] While a present-day teacher might easily present his or her students with many different word problems not very different from those in the abacus treatises, these problems would be reduced to a few basic equations and rules. While we think of specific problems as exemplifications of general rules, our medieval ancestors were not interested in the general rules; instead, they learned by memorizing a great many similar problems along with their solutions.

28. Van Egmond, "Commercial Revolution," 162.

29. Paolo dell'Abbaco, *Trattato d'aritmetica,* 89–91. See also van Egmond, "Commercial Revolution," 14.

30. See also my *Mensuration and Proportion Signs,* chap. 6.

31. Van Egmond, "Commercial Revolution," 242.

To what extent were these treatises memorized aside from the tables? In Renaissance Italy, the teacher presented the problems with their solutions to the student, who then copied everything in his own book. The process of copying would certainly help the students remember. Once the student had assembled his own book of abacus problems, he would use it to check problems he would encounter in his daily life and eventually know all the problems with their solutions by heart.

In short, the instruction in Latin grammar and abacus was fundamentally similar. To quote Grendler:

> Despite the vast difference in subject matter, abbaco pedagogy and the teaching of Latin grammar and the classics exhibited methodological similarity. Teachers and students of both focussed on individual points and problems, and seldom generalized. Latin students learned Latin grammar with textbooks that relied on a verbal, almost conversational, approach with a minimum of paradigms and rules to explain inflections and other grammatical matters. Abbaco students learned to solve individual problems by means of a step-by-step discussion of the problem. The Latin student learned a series of precise examples of usage; the abbaco student learned how to solve individual problems. The Latin student learned a variety of ways to write the same sentiments, sometimes just rearranging the words into different grammatical constructions. The abbaco student moved from problem to very similar problem. Both the Latin student and the abbaco neophyte relied heavily on memorization. The Latin student copied down *sententiae* to insert into letters and speeches; the abbaco student accumulated a book of examples for future use. The same approach and mentality underlay Latin and vernacular schooling.[32]

MUSIC TREATISES

Did the material described in organum, discant, and counterpoint treatises contribute to the creation of the musicians' memorial archive in a way that was similar to that encountered in the grammar and abacus books? And did performers and composers of polyphonic music delve into their memorial archive in the process of composition or improvisation?

How can we tell that a text and the musical examples in the text were memorized? Concerning the text, we would have to distinguish between direct and indirect evidence. In the former case, the author tells the reader directly that he should take care to memorize the entire text. But much more can be gathered by indirect evidence. First, if the text is organized in a similar way to the grammar or abacus treatises, this suggests that it was meant to be memorized. If the same or similar material is presented again and again with

32. Grendler, *Schooling in Renaissance Italy,* 319.

a multitude of rules, instead of being summarized in a few general rules that can be applied to a variety of cases, we have an organization familiar to us from the grammar and abacus texts and can assume that the text and the music examples were learned by heart. Second, we can assume that texts that are versified were meant to be learned by heart (see chap. 3). Third, the graphic layout of the material was used as a mnemonic device, as Mary Carruthers has most recently shown in her *Craft of Thought.* Concerning the music examples, first, the presence of tables similar to those encountered in abacus textbooks would also signal memorization. Second, the use of melodic formulas, especially if they are similar to formulas encountered in the music of the period, would also be a sign that they were memorized. It seems likely that texts exhibiting all or some of these characteristics were written for the choirboys and aspiring composers mentioned above.

On the other hand, treatises with few music examples, few rules, and no tables were probably not meant to be memorized, but rather written for university instruction. They were intended for academics with little or no interest in practical music. Indeed, it turns out that the vast majority of texts include music examples that were written down in order to be memorized.

Organum Treatises

Some authors say directly that the material should be memorized. A good example is an anonymous twelfth-century author of an organum treatise who states that the rules for singing discant and organum should be "retained in memory." A little later he admonishes the singer again that everything should be carefully memorized and placed in the "ark of the chest." Handschin, who edited the text, also notes the constant use of rhyme and assonance in the text for mnemonic purposes.[33]

The most important organum text is the so-called Vatican organum treatise, a Parisian theoretical text, probably copied in the first or second quarter of the thirteenth century, that is, shortly before the earliest sources of Notre Dame music.[34] The treatise consists of four sections: first, a short theoretical tract; second, melismas connected to tenor progressions; third, melismas without tenor progressions; and fourth, complete organum settings, where many of the melismas given earlier have been combined.

33. "[M]emoriter retineatur," and "quoniam si singula quaeque diligenter notata perspexeris et perfecte memoriae commendaveris, in arca pectoris veraciter conservabis omnia quae ad discantum et organum faciendum, si adsit vocis possibilitas, primus debet incipere cantum et semper finire"; in Handschin, "Aus der alten Musiktheorie," 25–26.

34. The best article on the Vatican Organum treatise is Immel, "Vatican Organum Treatise Re-Examined."

The short theoretical introduction lists the allowed consonances as octave, fourth, and fifth.[35] The second and third part of the treatise consists of thirty-one "rules," which include 343 melismas altogether. The melismas in group 2 are organized according to their tenor motion. For example, the first interval is an ascending step and the first rule says: "If the chant ascends by a second and the organum begins at the octave, let the organum descend by a third, and it will arrive at a fifth."[36] In Figure 14, partially transcribed in Example 5, we are given four possible melismas for setting against the tenor progression c–d.[37] The settings gradually become more elaborate. Most of the time the melismas for each tenor progression will be in the same hexachord. In Example 5 they are all on the hard hexachord starting on g, which is confirmed by the solmization syllables *fa–re* written underneath to designate the first and last note.[38] Next follow four melismas for the tenor progression d–e, then another four for e–f. What, then, does the word "rule" refer to? It is certainly not a rule in the modern sense of the word. Rather, the term is used as a classification device: all ascending-second tenor progressions combined with a cantus progression from octave to fifth are enclosed under this "rule." The other thirty "rules" cover other interval progressions.

The first 251 melismas can be divided into three groups, according to tenor progressions. Groups 2 and 3 repeat the same tenor progressions as group 1. The tenor progressions cover (with a few exceptions) all intervals in the natural hexachord between c and a. The first half of group 1, examples 1–44, covers ascending seconds, thirds, fourths, and fifths, always starting on c, d, e, and f. The second half, examples 45–97, gives melismas for descending seconds, thirds, fourths, and fifths, now starting with g and ending with d. For every tenor progression we are given from anywhere between two to seven alternative melodic formulas, usually arranged from simple to more elaborate. For example, Example 5 shows the first four melismas for the tenor progression c–d. Group 2, example 98 (Example 6) adds another two, which would be good if the cantus singer finds himself in a lower range, and finally in the third group c–d is combined with seven different melismas (Example 7, examples 163–69). In other words, the singer could choose between thirteen different melismas for the tenor progression c–d alone.

The next group is similarly organized, but now over a repeated tenor note. First, there are four for d–d, then two for e–e, then four for c–c (examples

35. For a more detailed discussion of the introduction see especially Immel, ibid., and "Vatican Organum Treatise," ed. Godt and Rivera, 292–98.

36. "Si cantus ascenderit duas voces et organum incipiat in dupla, descendat organum 3 voces et erit in quinta"; ibid., 264, 299.

37. From here on I am using modern designations of pitches.

38. Even though the syllables are written in the manuscript under the bottom voice, they refer to the top voice, as in the transcription.

215–23). The next six examples again give two melismas for each of the same pitches, and so on. Melismas 215–51 include "rules", while melismas 252–76 do not.

Melismas 277–343 are without tenor progressions, yet these melismas are also strictly organized. The first group (Example 8) presents all possible ascending seconds in the G hexachord between the first and the last note, followed by descending seconds (g–a, a–b, b–c , c –d , d –e , e –d , d –c , c –b, b–a, a–g). Then come thirds, fourths, fifths, fourths again, as well as sixths, sevenths, and octaves.

Two points of fundamental importance are suggested by the way the "rules" are formulated and exemplified in the treatise. First, Parisian singers of organum thought primarily in terms of an underlying note-against-note counterpoint. All the rules say something like this: if the chant ascends or descends by a given interval, and the duplum is at a given consonance above the first note, it (the duplum) should descend or ascend by a specific interval, so that it can find itself making a specific consonance with the chant. Second, the musicians thought there were alternative ways to realize the duplum from the first to the second vertical consonance. These alternative ways are, precisely, our melodic formulas. This suggests a two-stage compositional process: stage 1, where one would decide which vertical consonance to choose for the next chant note; and stage 2, where one would pick one of the suitable organal formulas to move between the two consonances. It is significant that these two stages are not treated separately in the Vatican treatise, while with most later theorists they are.

How do the formulas in the treatise relate to the Notre Dame repertory? Precisely because that repertory is considered a milestone in music history and the two composers associated with it are generally considered the first great "composers" in the modern sense, this question has received much attention (see chap. 1). Even though the music examples are not written in modal notation, scholars have long recognized their close similarity to the Notre Dame repertory. In a 1983 paper, Leo Treitler argued that the treatise represents an early version of how the Notre Dame repertory might have been before it was notated. He posited that even though the formulas were written down, they were conceived according to the principles of oral tradition, and were more improvised than composed, "ein unwiederholbares Ereignis." He contrasts the Vatican treatise with the later Notre Dame repertory, which he calls "eine fixierte Sache." Compositions are structured more economically and require consistent notation. The Magnus liber organi has to be understood "als hochkultivierte schriftgebundene Kunst."[39] Treitler

39. Treitler, "Der vatikanische Organumtraktat," 29–30. In a recent conversation, Treitler has told me that he no long subscribes to this view. See also "Vatican Organum Treatise," ed. Godt and Rivera, for a similar view, 273–74.

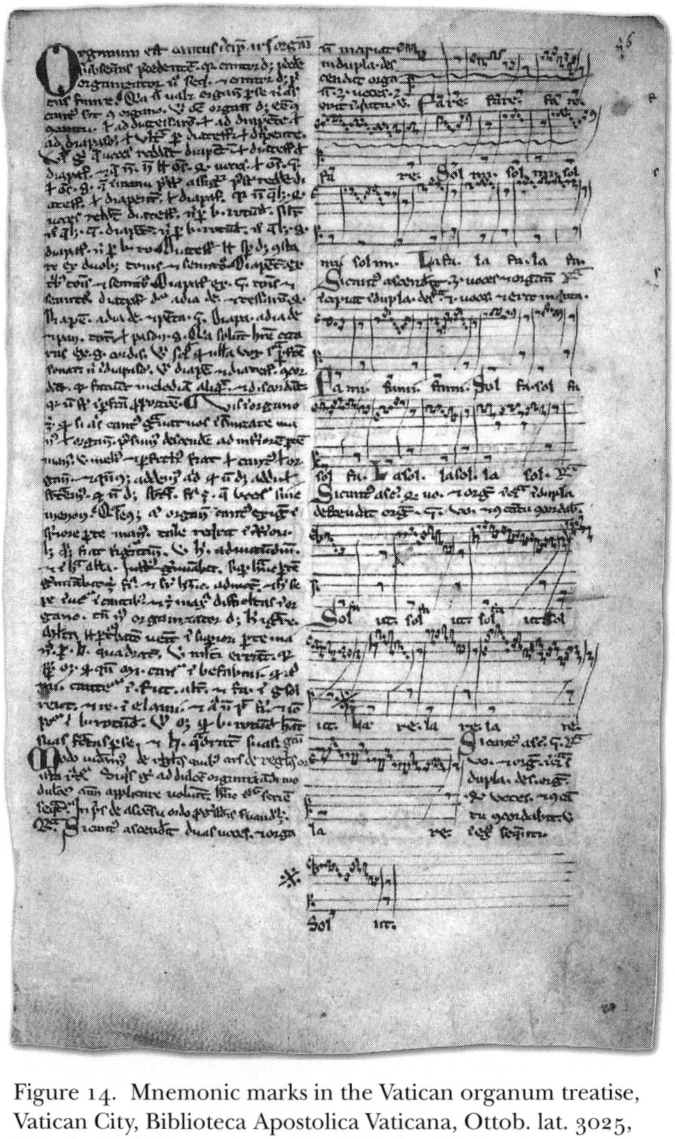

Figure 14. Mnemonic marks in the Vatican organum treatise, Vatican City, Biblioteca Apostolica Vaticana, Ottob. lat. 3025, fol. 46r, © Biblioteca Apostolica Vaticana (Vatican)

Example 5. Rule for consonances above an ascending step, Vatican organum treatise, ed. Godt and Rivera, 299

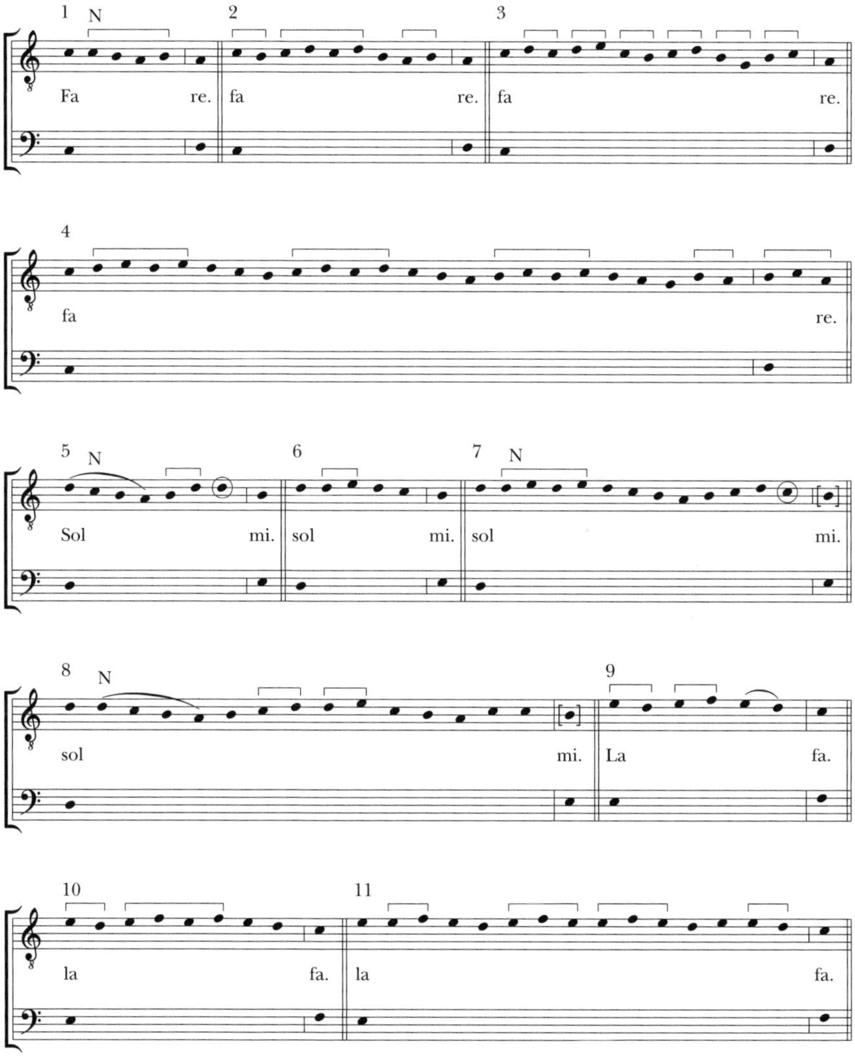

Example 6. Melismas for a tenor ascending by step, Vatican organum treatise, ed. Godt and Rivera, 311

Example 7. Melismas for a tenor ascending by step, Vatican organum treatise, ed. Godt and Rivera, 319

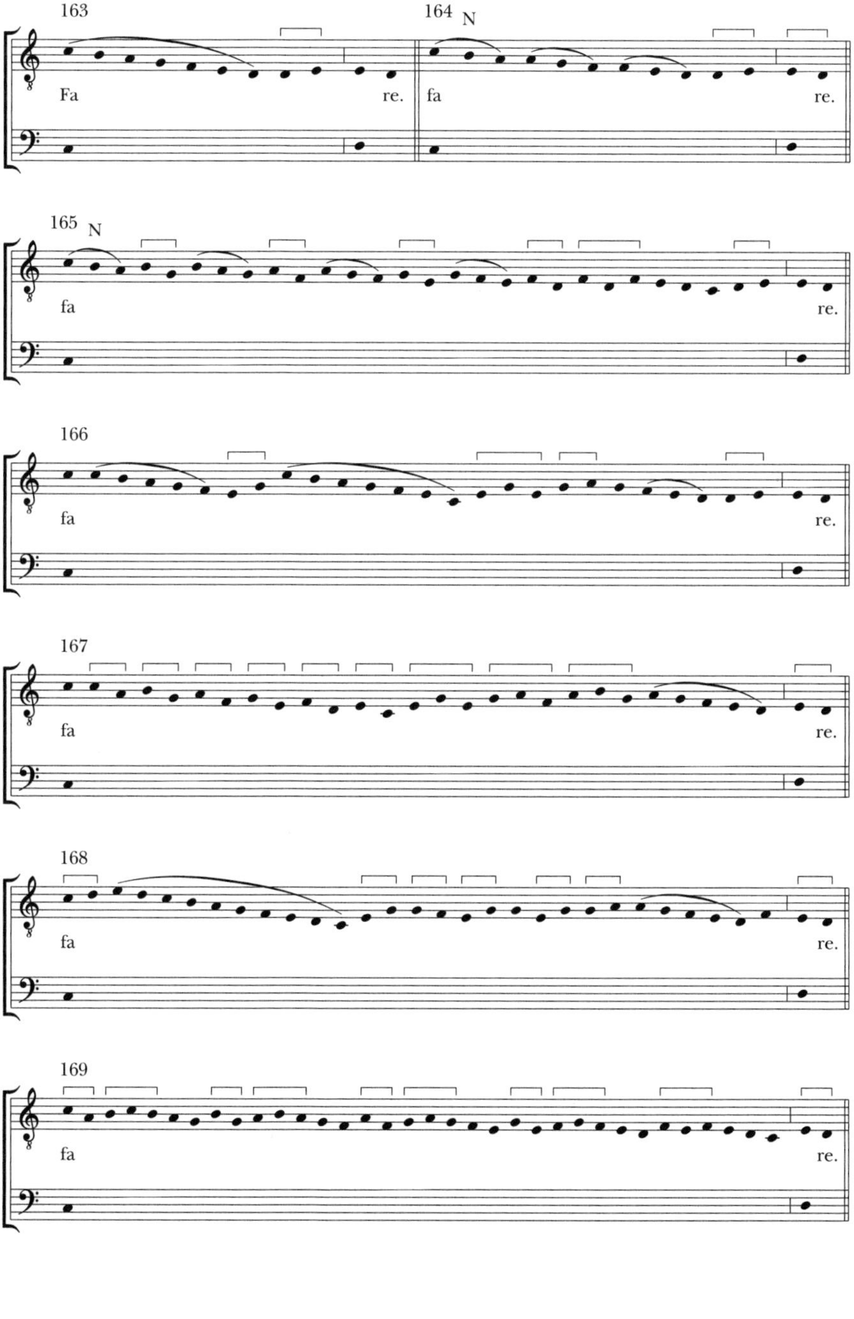

Example 8. Melismas filling in ascending steps in the G hexachord, Vatican organum treatise, ed. Godt and Rivera, 338

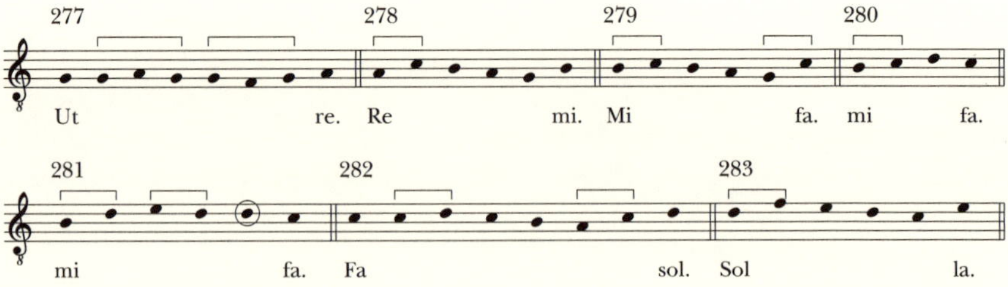

thus echoes Ludwig's view (see chap. 1) in considering Notre Dame organa as finished artworks, where every detail has been fixed in writing.

Stephen Immel compared the formulas and organa in the Vatican treatise with those in the Magnus liber organi and found that they were so similar that "the Vatican author must have had direct access to the Magnus liber in some form."[40] He provided a detailed analysis of the formulas, and classified them into a "descending repeated-note figure, a multiple echappée gesture, an expanding coniunctura gesture, an ornamented turning figure, an ascending ornamented fourth figure, and finally, a compounded figure that consists of an ornamented third coupled with a coniunctura" (pp. 130, 133). He then showed that all of these figures occur throughout the Notre Dame repertory. It would go too far to reproduce Immel's examples here. His study is an important one and his conclusion is the opposite of Treitler's: "The constant presence of Notre Dame phrases obviates the need to see an improvisational practice in this material; it seems safe to say that the true orientation of the treatise is concerned with *written* composition based on *written* models [italics added]" (pp. 164, 166). He calls the formulas *Bausteine,* building blocks that were put together in the "compositions" of Notre Dame polyphony. And he considers the treatise a grammar of Notre Dame polyphony. To quote Immel, "[The Vatican organum treatise] is concerned with the function of formulae—whether they are introductory, thematic, transitional or cadential. . . . [the Vatican] author must have hit upon questions such as: how can I work this formula in . . . or, how many times can I include this formula?" (p. 166).

I would agree with every one of Immel's conclusions except his statement that the "true orientation of the treatise is concerned with *written* composition based on *written* models (italics added)" (p. 166). While it is entirely possible that the author of the Vatican treatise had access to some manuscript version of the Magnus liber and copied his formulas from there, it is also pos-

40. Immel, "Vatican Organum Treatise," 155. Further references are given in the text.

sible that he learned the formulas from a teacher and wrote them down himself. The classification of the formulas is strikingly similar to that encountered in tonaries and grammars. Both the tonaries and the Vatican treatise rely on an analysis of the music that probably could not have happened without musical notation. To this extent, at least, Immel is right. Where I disagree with him is in the function of the treatise. We need to ask ourselves how, exactly, would a composer (or performer) have profited from such a treatise in the act of composition or performance? Was it physically in front of him whenever he conceived new pieces and copied the formulas from the treatise into his own work? Did he consult it as a "catalog" to choose from while composing on paper? There are a number of reasons why I believe that this was very unlikely. Even though it is possible that the formulas were copied from the Magnus liber organi, the only reason to copy them would have been first to classify them and then systematically to memorize them. We have seen in grammar instruction that literary composition was a "putting together" of things that had been memorized. There is no reason to think that the case of music has to be different. The Vatican treatise, then, corresponds to the grammar texts, where first words, then phrases were memorized. The phrases were assembled into sentences, which were gathered into speeches or books.

Earlier medieval theorists made an explicit connection between grammar and music: the author of the ninth-century treatise *Musica enchiriadis* and Johannes (ca. 1100) compare clauses that are combined into sentences to musical sections that are combined into whole melodies.[41] The Vatican treatise only makes sense as a text that is meant to be memorized. Otherwise it would be tedious reading, indeed. Why repeat similar "rules" and progressions again and again? The formulas in our treatise must have been easy to memorize because they are so clearly structured, both according to tenor progressions and within the melismas themselves. They cover everything from single-interval progressions to discant sections to entire organum settings. A singer who had mastered the material in this treatise would have no trouble performing or composing pieces in the style of the Magnus liber organi. In the next chapter I will try to reconstruct how a composer went about creating an organum.

The manuscript of the Vatican treatise provides a further clue that the formulas were meant to be memorized. The scribe added his personal mnemonic marks at the outer margins of all pages: For example, on the second page (see above, Figure 14), there is an *f* for *fa* and an *s* for *sol.* The marginal sign was to remind the singer/composer that the first group of formulas starts on *fa,* the second on *sol,* etc. We have seen similar graphic representations, intended to bring back entire sections, in the tonary chapter. Quintilian had already employed such marks (*notae*) in the margins and Mary Carruthers has explained that they could be either a sign or a keyword and would help recall the entire

41. Powers, "Language Models."

passage.[42] When composing a text, a writer would recall all the material stored under the keyword. Similarly, the performer of organa would recall all the possible formulas associated with each melodic progression of the tenor.

It is important to understand that the performers or composers who had memorized the formulas in the Vatican treatise were able to use them in unwritten performances as well as in written-out compositions. Thus, the evidence in the treatise allows us to conclude that there was not necessarily a difference between the performer and the composer—both relied on the same practice. One person might choose to notate their version, while another one might perform it. This is very much along the lines of the conclusions reached by Jacques Handschin, as discussed in chapter 1: "The art of improvisation, which is finding renewed interest, is no more than composition that happens in writing rather than 'orally.' The compositional tools are the same in both cases."[43] There is only one Vatican organum treatise and we must avoid drawing too far-reaching conclusions from this one text. Thus, Immel might be right to see the treatise as originally an instruction manual for written composition. Nevertheless, I believe that in view of the structure and repetitiveness of this treatise, and also of what we know about instruction methods in grammar and arithmetic, it seems more likely that the formulas in the treatise were memorized and were used for unwritten and written composition of discant and organa. We cannot assume that every Notre Dame musician memorized the formulas of this particular treatise. It seems more likely that singers would compile their own grammars of formulas excerpted from manuscripts, instruction, or performances.

Thus, the hypothesis that the formulas in the Vatican organum treatise were memorized and then applied in either oral performance or written composition is consistent with my hypothesis that the Notre Dame repertory was transmitted orally (see chap. 5). This is further supported by recent work of anthropologists and literary historians, who have argued that the use of formulas might signal oral transmission. It will be useful to briefly summarize their findings. Milman Parry and Albert Lord showed that the *Iliad* and *Odyssey* contained a large number of formulas that were combined in ever new ways. They reached this conclusion by comparing the Homeric poems with southern Slavic epics.[44] In the latter, the formulas had been learned over the years by the *guslars*. The singers were not passively repeating them, but actively participated in the process of composition by creating a new piece

42. Carruthers, *Craft of Thought*, 156 and *Book of Memory*, 107–8, 244–45, 247.

43. "Das Improvisieren, für das das Interesse neuerdings wieder zu regen beginnt, ist ein Komponieren, das statt auf dem schriftlichen auf dem 'mündlichen' Wege erfolgt. Das kompositionstechnische Rüstzeug ist also hier wie dort dasselbe." Handschin, "Über das Improvisieren," 327.

44. Lord, *Singer of Tales*.

in every performance by stitching together these standard formulas. The result was a total shift in our understanding of Homer. He was suddenly no longer an original accomplished poet, but, as Walter J. Ong put it, "an assembly-line worker. This idea was particularly threatening to far-gone literates. For literates are educated never to use clichés, in principle. How live with the fact that the Homeric poems, more and more, appeared to be made up of clichés, or elements very like clichés?"[45]

Parry and Lord were convinced that a preponderance of formulas was an indicator of oral transmission. Since then, their theories have been adapted to other languages and literatures. In a 1966 paper, "The Literary Character of Anglo-Saxon Formulaic Poetry," Larry D. Benson analyzed four metrical texts, most of which were transmitted in writing, and found that they also used formulas extensively. He concluded, therefore, that written poetry may also make use of formulas. Similiarly, J. Opland discovered that formulas are used in written *and* oral Xhosa poetry.[46] Ruth Finnegan takes this to mean that the use of formulas is by no means a sure sign of orality.[47] I believe Ong's distinction between primary and secondary orality, that is, between the orality of an oral-formulaic poet, and the academic orality of a poet operating in a society that is still to a large extent oral, is useful here. It would explain the use of formulas in written poetry. As Ong has shown, cultures that have only started to write, such as the medieval one, still use formulas and think as if they were transmitting orally rather than in writing: "Early written poetry everywhere, it seems, is at first necessarily a mimicking in script of oral performance. The mind has initially no properly chirographic resources. You scratch out on a surface words you imagine yourself saying aloud in some realizable oral setting. Only very gradually does writing become composition in writing, a kind of discourse—poetic or otherwise—that is put together without a feeling that the one writing is actually speaking aloud (as early writers may well have done in composing)."[48]

Similarly, Jan Ziolkowski has suggested that medieval poets used stock phrases that they could have acquired by reading and writing poetry, by systematic memorization, or by simple listening. These recurrent phrases would have facilitated the composition of written Latin texts. "A skillful poet could have used *repetitiones* in Latin to convey the flavor of *formulae* in the poetic system of the vernacular."[49]

What does all this mean for an analysis of music? I think the situation for medieval music is not much different from that of medieval Latin poetry. It

45. Ong, *Orality and Literacy*, 22–23.
46. Opland, *Xhosa Oral Poetry*.
47. Finnegan, *Oral Poetry*, 70–72.
48. *Orality and Literacy*, 26.
49. Ziolkowski, "Cultural Diglossia," 112.

is the situation of a musical culture that knows writing, but that still operates within a predominantly preliterate framework. Thus, we cannot take the occurrence of formulas to mean that the music was necessarily orally composed and transmitted. Yet as we have shown, it is likely that the music was transmitted orally long before it was written down. It was heard rather than read. And it was memorized. This is consistent with what we know about other cultures that are just beginning to use writing. They usually use formulas that have been previously memorized.

Discant and Counterpoint Treatises

The terms discant and counterpoint are used in a number of ways in the fourteenth and fifteenth centuries. Discant is the older term; it can refer to the part added to the tenor or to the polyphonic composition in note-against-note style in contrast to the florid organum. The term *contrapunctus* can refer first to composition for more than two parts, or to the addition of one or more parts to the tenor; and second, to the new part that is added.[50] The terms are often used interchangeably, and we will have to determine in each case how each writer uses them.

For the purposes of this chapter I am less interested in interval classification and progressions, and more in how the material was presented and learned.[51] I have looked at these texts and tried to determine whether they were memorized. I do not draw a distinction between treatises that teach improvised discant and counterpoint treatises, because the former represent only a first step to mastering the latter.

A few theorists have clear references that they expect the text to be memorized. Lyonel Power promises in the last sentence of his discant treatise that anyone who has memorized the contents of his treatise will have mastered counterpoint: "But who wil kunne this Gamme [the entire gamut] wel and ymaginacions [= counterpoint] therof and of his acordis and sette his perfite acordis with his imperfite acordis, as I have rehersid in this tretise afore, he may not faile of his Countirpoint in short tyme. Quod Lyonel Power."[52]

John Hothby reminds the reader to memorize the six rules for making counterpoint on the six solmization syllables of the hexachord, and then he proceeds to list all possible consonances.[53]

Nicolaus Burtius demands that the contents of his entire *Musices opuscu-*

50. Sachs, *Der Contrapunctus,* esp. chaps. 1 and 2.

51. Most of the discant and counterpoint treatises are discussed in Sachs's fundamental book *Der Contrapunctus.* The manuscripts are listed in the appendix.

52. Georgiades, *Englische Diskanttraktate,* 23.

53. "Item Regulae contrapuncti Johannis Octobi Carmelitae incipiunt," Florence, Biblioteca Medicea Laurenziana, Plut. XXIX.48, fols. 118–119v; ed. Reaney, 63–69.

lum be memorized when he says at the end of his preface: "I ask, therefore, that you read our work willingly. If you have read it thoroughly from beginning to end and also have memorized it, I truly expect that within three months you can be numbered not among the singers, which is less important, but among the musicians, which is most important."[54]

The German theorist Adam of Fulda, whose treatise was composed in 1490, has several references to memorization. He insists that intervals should be memorized before songs are composed.[55] More importantly, when he discusses the composition of songs he reprimands those who have not memorized properly: "I do not mention many who, although they be well imbued by teachers, so often err, since they have not entrusted a single [thing] to memory, either by fault of teachers, or of themselves."[56]

The most explicit reference to memorization is found in the latest theorist to be considered here. In his *Rerum musicarum opusculum* of 1535 Johann Frosch recommends that his readers memorize large chunks of pieces (he gives a number of four-voice segments) and incorporate them into their own compositions.[57]

Theorists Who List Consonance Tables and Interval Progressions. The first step for a student of counterpoint was to memorize the list of consonant and dissonant intervals. Most theorists do not mention explicitly that the consonant intervals and progressions are to be memorized because it was so self-evident. Yet there are some who make direct reference to memorization. The earliest discant text to do this is the Florence version of the so-called *regula del grado* treatises. Even though the manuscript was copied in the fifteenth century, the text probably came into existence in the fourteenth, because the interval classifications are typical of the earlier period.[58] The author states clearly that all the consonances and dissonances have to be memorized: "Also to remember better the consonances and dissonances on all *gradi* without

54. "Ne vos igitur pigeat: rogo: nostra legere: que si omnia a calce vsque ad finem lectitaueritis memorie quoque et commendaueritis: spero equidem trium mensium numero: nedum inter cantores quod minimum est: sed inter musicos quod est maximum posse connumerari." *Musices opusculum* (Bologna, 1487) = *Florum libellus,* ed. Massera; trans. Miller, 28.

55. *Musica,* bk. 2, chap. 11.

56. "Taceo de multis, qui licet a praeceptoribus bene imbuti sint, totiens quotiens errant, dum non sane singula memoriae commendaverint, aut praeceptorum, aut eorum culpa." Ibid., bk. II, chap. 10; trans. Slemon, 201.

57. Frosch, *Rerum musicarum opusculum,* chap. 19. For a discussion of some of Frosch's examples, see Owens, *Composers at Work,* 190–202. See also Pietro Aron's *Libri tres de institutione harmonica,* chaps. 7, 10, 11, 12, and 36; Johannes Cochlaeus, *Musica activa* (n.p., ca. 1504; 2nd ed. ca. 1505); 2nd ed. edited by Riemann, prologue; Hermann Finck, *Practica musica* (1556), sigs. Ciijr, Rrijv, Xxiiijv.

58. Scattolin, "La regola del 'grado.'"

having to list all the intervals, I am teaching you this other absolute place."[59] A more detailed discussion of the *regula del grado* treatises will follow later.

Similarly, the so-called Berkeley manuscript, most likely written by the theorist and composer Goscalchus in 1375, demands that all consonances be memorized as a prerequisite for learning discant: "I cordially admonish them that wherever there are people busy with this science, there will be people reflecting on the difference of tones and semitones, rattling off by heart the consonances of discant, so that they may be able to sing."[60]

In addition, a study of the treatises themselves leaves little doubt that consonant intervals were memorized systematically. We can observe essentially two methods that are used to make sure that every student masters the material. Both are familiar to us from grammar and arithmetic instruction. The first relies on endless drilling and repetition. When Johann Joseph Fux taught counterpoint in his *Gradus ad Parnassum* in 1725 (and most of us learned counterpoint according to his principles) he simply listed all perfect and imperfect consonances.[61] Not so theorists in the Middle Ages. When consonant and dissonant intervals are explained, they often list every single consonant interval separately as encountered within each hexachord. As a result, these treatises make very tedious reading indeed for us today. For example, in the Washington manuscript (Library of Congress, ML 171 .J6, fols. 81r–92v) of the *regula del grado* treatises, the author offers instruction on how to sing polyphony with minimal notation, using mainly the hand. When defining intervals, he is not content to give only one example of, say, the whole tone, but rather lists all possible ascending and descending whole tones on the C hexachord. Whenever the author defines discordant intervals, such as the diminished fifth and minor sixth, he not only tells us that the discordant fifth consists of two tones and two semitones, but gives a complete list of *all* diminished fifths within the gamut: B to f, e to b♭, b♮ to f , or from e to b♭ . No modern theorist would waste his time listing all possible diminished fifths and minor sixths encountered on the gamut. Most would find it sufficient to describe how a diminished fifth is composed and then expect the reader to recognize the interval in all possible places on his own. The fact that the author lists every single one is an indication that the student was expected to memorize every single diminished fifth, minor sixth, and tritone and remember once and for all where dangers could lie in the performance and composition of polyphony. Moreover, not all of the intervals of the same species are treated the same by singers. For example, a singer would certainly not miss the fact that a fifth on top of e would be flattened, while a fifth on d would not.

59. "Ancora per tenere meglio a mente le consonançe e dissonançe per tutti e gradi sança avere annoverare le voci, tinsegno questaltro absoluto posto che di sopra ti sia detto composto." *Dico che noi abbiamo nel contrapunto,* ed. Seay, 37.

60. Goscalchus, *Berkeley Manuscript,* ed. Ellsworth, 237.

61. Fux, *Steps to Parnassus,* 20–21.

Even more popular were consonance tables. Theorists as different as Ugolino of Orvieto, Lyonel Power, Guilielmus Monachus, Bartolomeus Ramis de Pareia, and Franchinus Gaffurius (Figure 15)[62] include them in their treatises for every single pitch of the hexachord or even the entire gamut. As late as 1558, Gioseffo Zarlino recommends consulting the consonance table.[63] Note that on every step the only consonances allowed are 1, 3, 5, 6, or their compound version (8, 10, 12, and 13, 15, etc.). These consonance tables bear a striking similarity to the multiplication tables (Figure 16) and, like the latter, they were probably also memorized. Later theorists such as Pietro Aaron will list consonance tables for three voices.[64]

Once the consonances and dissonances for every single pitch had been mastered, these consonances would be combined into progressions in note-against-note counterpoint. Almost all theorists present such progressions. Let us begin with a discussion of what is perhaps the most elementary kind of counterpoint treatise, the so-called *regula del grado* treatises. An in-depth discussion is in order, because the texts have not been discussed much and I believe many students, especially in Italy, started their counterpoint instruction with this method.

This family of treatises differs from the others in that the author thinks only in terms of hexachords and not in gamut steps. All intervals and progressions are given only in solmization syllables. Other theorists also thought in terms of hexachords, but they usually gave, in addition, the name of the note on the gamut.

What is a *grado*? The term is here defined by the author as "when two sing in the same hexachord making counterpoint, or one sings in one hexachord and the other in another, but neither one makes a mutation."[65] What *grado* really refers to is the relationship between the lowest note of the tenor hexachord and the lowest note of the counterpoint hexachord. They can

62. Ugolino, *Declaratio musicae disciplinae,* ed. Seay, 2:12 ff.; Lyonel Power, ed. in Bukofzer, *Geschichte des englischen Diskants,* 132–36, and Georgiades, *Englische Diskanttraktate,* 12–23 (esp. 13–15); Guilielmus Monachus, *De preceptis artis musicae,* ed. Seay, 36–37; Ramis de Pareia, *Musica practica,* ed. Wolf, 76; trans. Miller, 135; Gaffurius, *Practica musicae* (1496), sig. ddvir. See also the edition of the MS Vercelli, Biblioteca Agnesiana, cod. 11 [*Fondamenti di teoria musicale*], ed. Cornagliotti and Caraci Vela, 80–85. This list of treatises is by no means complete; there are many more.

63. *Istitutioni harmoniche* (1558), trans. Marco and Palisca, 227.

64. *Thoscanello de la musica* (1523), chap. 30. In part 3 of the *Libri tres de institutione harmonica* of 1516, chaps. 17–23, he lists consonances for three-part counterpoint, but includes no musical examples or tables, probably because the publisher Benedetto Ettore de Faellis had no music type. See Blackburn, "On Compositional Process," 218.

65. "Grado se intende quando duy cantano de una medesima chiave facendo contrapuncto, o vero l'uno cantasse per una chiave e l'altro per l'altra, né l'uno né l'altro facendo muttatione." *Dico che 'l contrapunto,* Washington, Library of Congress, ML 171 .J6 (late 15th c.), ed. Scattolin, chap. 4, p. 58.

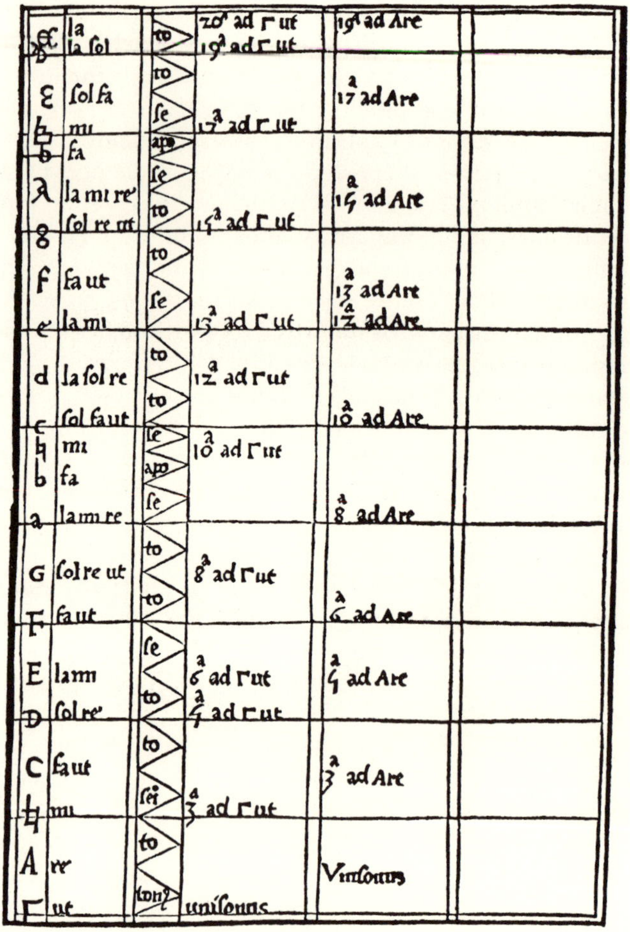

Figure 15. Consonance table from Franchinus Gaffurius, *Practica musice,* bk. 3, chap. 8

be the same (in the *grado* of the unison), or they can be different (in the *grado* of the fourth, fifth, and octave). For example, in the *grado* of the fourth the tenor sings in the hard hexachord (from Gamma *ut* to e) and the counterpoint in the natural hexachord (from c to a). The distance between the lowest note of the tenor hexachord, Gamma *ut,* and the counterpoint hexachord on c (C *fa ut*) is a fourth. Or, to give another example, in the *grado* of the octave, the tenor might sing in the natural hexachord with the lowest note on c (C *fa ut*) and the counterpoint in the natural hexachord an octave higher with the lowest note c (C *sol fa ut*).

Figure 16. Multiplication tables from Filippo Calandri, *Aritmetica,* Florence, Biblioteca Riccardiana, MS 2669, reproduced by permission of the Ministero per i Beni e le Attività Culturali

The author begins by listing every consonant and dissonant interval in every single *grado*. Here "dissonant" intervals are equivalent to our imperfect consonances (our dissonances are called "discords"). For example, when the tenor and counterpoint sing in the *grado* of the unison (and this applies to all seven hexachords), the following consonances (unisons and fifths) and dissonances (thirds and major sixths)[66] are allowed:

TENOR	NAME OF THE COUNTERPOINT NOTE THAT FORMS A CONSONANCE
ut	*ut* unis., *mi* 3, *sol* 5, *la* 6
re	*re* unis., *fa* 3, *la* 5
mi	*mi* unis., *sol* 3, *ut* 3 below
fa	*fa* unis., *la* 3, *re* 3 below
sol	*sol* unis., *mi* 3 below, *ut* 5 below
la	*la* unis., *fa* 3 below, *re* 5 below, *ut* 6 below

Two points are striking: first that the notes are given only as solmization syllables, that is, they do not refer to real notes, but rather the *ut* can be any *ut* of the seven hexachords. And second, rather than setting out a general rule permitting unisons, fifths, thirds, and the major sixth, the author lists every possible unison, fifth, third, and sixth for every tone of the hexachord. Just as before, this is an indication that the student was expected to memorize all the consonances rather than a single general rule. The consonances and dissonances for the *grado* of the fourth, fifth, and octave are similarly described in great detail.

The Washington version of the *regula del grado* treatises includes explanations on how to proceed with the singing and composing of polyphony once the consonances and dissonances have been established. We now encounter the first definition of the term *contrapuncto* as "one note going against another." Thus, it seems to refer here to the method and practice of singing or making polyphonic music. Note, though, that the author also uses the term to describe the added part.

In the next and longest section of the treatise, the author lists for every single tenor progression possible within a hexachord a suitable counterpoint progression, and he does this for every single *grado*. All of these counterpoint progressions are within the same hexachord and in contrary motion. Mutations are not explained.

Why did he choose these particular counterpoint progressions? Were they the only ones possible? And if not, what were the criteria for making the choice? The author gives a few additional rules, all of them familiar from other treatises, especially *Quilibet affectans,*[67] which helps to limit the possibilities:

66. Minor sixths are not mentioned because they are not included within the hexachord.
67. From *Ars contrapuncti secundum Johannem de Muris,* CS 3:59–68.

1. There should be contrary motion between the tenor and counterpoint (chap. 10).
2. Parallel consonances of the same type are prohibited (chap. 15), while there is no limit to the number of parallel dissonances (thirds and major sixths).
3. A consonance must open and close a piece (chap. 15).
4. A dissonance—that is, an imperfect consonance (third or major sixth)—is recommended before the final consonance (chap. 15).

The last three of these rules come at the very end of the treatise, almost as an afterthought. Clearly the author considers memorization of the consonances and dissonances and of the counterpoint progressions within the hexachords, and not of the rules, as the most crucial part of the treatise.

The great majority of progressions move from a perfect to an imperfect consonance or vice versa. The remaining interval progressions are from perfect to perfect consonance. There is not a single case of two imperfect consonances, which is surprising in view of the fact that this is not a prohibited progression and it is strongly recommended by many theorists, especially the closely related English discant and sight treatises.

Let us now try to reconstruct what choices are available. The first tenor progression is *ut re* from the *grado* of the unison: if we look back at the table of possible consonances that the student would have memorized earlier (p. 136), the possible consonances for *ut* are *ut* (1), *mi* (3), *sol* (5), and *la* (6), while the consonances for *re* are *re* (1), *fa* (3), and *la* (5). The theorist chose *sol fa* (5–3). *Ut re* can be excluded because it would result in parallel unisons. *Ut fa* (1–3) and *ut la* (1–5) do not work because there is no contrary motion between tenor and counterpoint. *Mi re* (3–1), *sol re* (5–1), and *la re* (6–1) would all be fine according to his rules. However, the only one that moves from an imperfect to a perfect consonance in contrary motion is *mi re.* (The sixth of *la re* should be going to the octave.) *La fa* (6–3) does not go from an imperfect to a perfect consonance, *la la* has the problematic interval progression 6–5, and *sol la* produces parallel fifths, which are prohibited by a number of theorists.[68] In short, there is just one alternative progression for *ut re,* namely *mi re* (3–1). This is just one example. If we were to go through all the progressions, we would discover that the performer/composer would actually have very little choice in his progressions.

The fact that the author only gives one possible interval progression does not mean that the others are unacceptable. This progression was chosen because it works well in note-against-note counterpoint. The other ones will be useful for diminished counterpoint later on. The treatise is very repetitive precisely because it was meant to be memorized. The performer/

68. Sachs, *Der Contrapunctus,* 79.

composer would have the other possible consonances at "the tip of his fingers" from the consonance tables and would easily be able to recall other options. It is therefore not surprising that Guilielmus Monachus calls these consonance tables *palma contrapunctorum.*[69] Thus it makes sense for a performer or composer to memorize every single progression. Whenever he would encounter *ut re* in the tenor, he would instinctively sing *sol fa* (and *mi re* after having eliminated the other ones).

The authors of the *regula del grado* treatises stress that the material could be learned without the use of notation. But we should not take this to mean that elementary counterpoint was always taught without notation. It seems more likely that many teachers simply used this method for beginners.[70] Even theorists whose treatises do not officially belong to the *regula del grado* group concentrated in their music examples on a tenor within one hexachord and a discant or counterpoint within the same or another hexachord.[71] For example, Ugolino of Orvieto's treatise is organized very similarly and shows that the system described in the *regula del grado* is not a separate system intended for improvisation, but simply the first step in the instruction of counterpoint.

Other texts that teach improvised counterpoint also suggest memorization of entire progressions. This is, for example, true of the sight treatises. Lyonel Power is quite typical in providing suitable counterpoint progressions for given tenor progressions. He starts with stepwise motion of two notes in the tenor, then goes on to three, four, five, and even six notes. Then he discusses leaps, leaps combined with stepwise motion, etc. Georgiades had already pointed out that these progressions might have been memorized by the student and then used for both improvisation and composition.[72] Similar instructions can be observed in Guilielmus Monachus.[73]

In sum, the *regula del grado* treatises are not about counterpoint rules. Rather, they encourage memorization of two things: first, consonances either within the same hexachord or within two hexachords a fourth, a fifth, or an octave apart; and second, tenor and counterpoint progressions for two parts, either in the same hexachord, or in two different hexachords a fourth, a fifth, or an octave apart. Note that all of the examples are for note-against-note counterpoint. Let us now see how other theorists approach counterpoint instruction.

Ugolino of Orvieto's *Declaratio musicae disciplinae* was probably written dur-

69. *De preceptis artis musicae,* 30.

70. Handschin, "Aus der alten Musiktheorie," 11.

71. See, for example, the Vatican treatise discussed above.

72. Georgiades, *Englische Diskanttraktate,* 34.

73. *De preceptis,* ed. Seay, 29–33.

ing his stay at Ferrara, in the 1430s or 1440s.[74] Book 2 is entirely devoted to counterpoint. Ugolino was a practical musician of some influence. We can assume that he used this treatise when instructing choirboys in Ferrara; but it was also used by John Hothby to teach counterpoint in Lucca, and we know that Gaffurius owned a copy. In the sixteenth century the treatise was still found among chained books in the sacristy of the cathedral in Ferrara, because it was so useful.[75] In short, it seems likely that the contents of this text reflect the teachings of a fifteenth-century choirmaster.

Ugolino discusses only note-against-note counterpoint *(stricte seu proprie contrapunctus)*. To a modern reader his treatise is exceedingly repetitive. He goes through all the intervals twice, and includes altogether nine consonance tables, as well as lists of interval progressions in the different *gradi*. The instruction is very similar to the *regula del grado* treatises: he begins with both parts in the same hexachord, then goes on to discuss a combination of hard and natural hexachords, and so on. Chapter 15 shows the hexachord combinations in four-part counterpoint, thus making it clear to the singer in which range to place each part. The next chapters present another round of consonance tables with solmization syllables, followed by seven "rules," most of which we would consider recommendations: for example, "rule" 5 allows two or three parallel thirds or sixths, provided there is a perfect consonance at the end. All of these "rules" have been discussed in some detail by Sachs and need not concern us here.[76]

Most interesting, however, is the following chapter (chap. 26), which is versified and goes systematically through all recommended interval progressions. I quote just the beginning:

> Tertia sit infra, unisonus si intenditur una. [ex.]
> Si tertia vel quarta tendit, infra diapente tenebit. [ex.]
> Si quintam ascendit, diapason cantum terminabit. [ex.][77]
>
> (If a unison rises one tone let a third be below.
> If it rises by a third or fourth, there will be a fifth below.
> If it rises by a fifth, the song will end on an octave.)

Ugolino has altogether fourteen "rules" with examples, organized in a systematic way. He begins with progression from the unison, then moves to gradually larger intervals (thirds, fifths, sixths, octaves, etc., up to twelfths going to fifteenths). In between, he also has a few examples of three-note progressions.

74. Ugolino of Orvieto, *Declaratio musicae disciplinae,* ed. Seay, 2, bk. 2.
75. See Blackburn, "Ugolino of Orvieto."
76. Sachs, *Der Contrapunctus,* 103–22.
77. *Declaratio musicae disciplinae,* 32–34.

There is, again, no doubt that the material was memorized in its entirety. The most obvious reason is, of course, that it is versified (see chaps. 3 and 5).[78] But in addition, the treatise is repetitive and moves just like the grammar treatises from small units (intervals) to larger progressions, which were repeated again and again until the student knew them by heart.[79] Finally, the methods employed to learn counterpoint bear a striking similarity to those of the abacus teacher outlined at the beginning of the chapter. Ugolino prefers to give fourteen "rules" for interval progression, which give specific suggestions for every single tenor progression. Like the theorists of the *regula del grado* group, he does not prescribe a few rules that could cover all of these progressions. It is clear that he does this because he wants students to commit these progressions firmly to memory.

I have discussed Ugolino in some detail because he is typical of many other fourteenth- and fifteenth-century theorists.[80] Like Ugolino, most of the theorists who list the individual interval progressions have a great many "rules" that elaborate these progressions, all of which have to be committed to memory.[81] The reason for all this memorization is given by an anonymous early fifteenth-century theorist who states clearly that composition

78. There is another group of versified counterpoint treatises that includes Florence, Biblioteca Medicea Laurenziana, Ashb. 1119, fols. 75v–77v and Florence, Biblioteca Medicea Laurenziana, Plut. XXIX.48, fols. 88v–89v; Milan, Biblioteca Ambrosiana, I 20 inf., fol. 36r–v; Einsiedeln, Stiftsbibliothek, MS 689, fol. 45v; Rio de Janeiro, Biblioteca Nacional, Cofre 18, fol. 619r–v; Chicago, Newberry Library, MS 54.1, fols. 6v–7r, and Vercelli, Biblioteca Agnesiana, cod. 11, fols. 182v–183r. The text of these treatises starts with "Post octavam quintam si note tendunt in altum. / Si nota unum ascendit equalis hanc iudicabis / Si stant equaliter post octavam quintam tenebis, / Et e converso si plures videbis." All the treatises were written between ca. 1390 and 1450. See also [*Fondamenti di teoria musicale*], ed. Cornagliotti and Caraci Vela, 15–31.

79. Independently, Peter Schubert has also observed that these counterpoint treatises were meant to be memorized. See his "Counterpoint Pedagogy in the Renaissance," 505–6.

80. Other theorists with similar rules are Anon., *Tractatus de discantu,* MS Saint-Dié, Bibl. Municipale, 42, ed. Reaney; see also the other discant treatises in the volume edited by Reaney; Petrus dictus Palma Ociosa, *Compendium de discantu mensurabili,* ed. Wolf; *Anonymus tractatus de contrapuncto et de musica mensurabili,* Munich, Bayerische Staatsbibliothek, Clm. 16208 et 24809, ed. Meyer; Johannes de Muris, "Quilibet affectans," from *Ars contrapuncti,* CS 3:59–68; Anon. XI, ed. and trans. Wingell, 311–34; "Tractatus de arte Contrapuncti" in Hothby, *De arte contrapuncti,* 15–49. The treatise is very close to the *regula del grado* tradition. The attribution to Hothby is doubtful (see Blackburn, "Hothby, John"); another treatise by Hothby, "Item Regulae contrapuncti Johannis Octobi Carmelitae incipiunt" *(De arte contrapuncti,* 63–69), includes the following mnemonic verse on voice-leading: "Post octavam quintam si cantus tendit in altum; si una nota ascendit, post quintam tertiam iudicabis" (p. 65); see also Hothby's "Regule di Contrapuncto," ibid., 71–79 and the anonymous *Tractatus de contrapuncto,* ed. Reaney, which is also possibly by Hothby; Burtius, *Musices opusculum,* trans. Miller, bk. 2; Guillaume Guerson, *Utilissime musicales regule* (ca. 1500). See also Ferand, "Guillaume Guerson's Rules."

81. See, for example, "Cum notum sit," which presents nine *conclusiones;* Anonymous XI has twenty rules, ed. Wingell, 319; and Guilielmus Monachus, *De preceptis artis musicae,* has eight.

consists of putting these progressions together: "Whereby the first rule must be this one: anyone who wishes to compose should proceed in all such discant in such a way that he places the progressions according to the way planned before."[82]

What is perhaps more surprising is that theorists who teach sophisticated written counterpoint also rely extensively on the memorization of interval progressions as the first step in counterpoint instruction. A good example is Johannes Tinctoris's *Liber de arte contrapuncti.* Its organization is not very different from Ugolino's *Declaratio,* with two modifications. First, Tinctoris is the most thorough music theorist of the fifteenth century. It is therefore characteristic for him to list *all* possible interval progressions just as he describes all rhythmic proportions in his *Proportionale musices.* Second, he does not transpose these progressions to all of the steps of the various hexachords. As always, the treatise is very systematic; thus the organization of the interval progressions helps the student in the process of memorization. He sets them out in the following order:[83]

Chap. 3:	1–1, 1–3, 1–5, 1–8 (concentrates on the unison)
Chap. 4:	3–1, 3–5, 3–6, 3–8, 3–10 (with the tenor starting below the counterpoint, using both minor and major thirds) 3–1, 3–3, 3–5, 3–5, 3–6, 3–8, 3–10 (with the tenor starting above the counterpoint)
Chap. 5:	4 (the fourth does not occur in two-part interval progressions)
Chap. 6:	5–3, 5–5, 5–6, 5–8, 5–10, 5–12 (tenor starting below; the whole series is then repeated with the tenor above)
Chap. 7:	6–3, 6–5, 6–6, 6–8, 6–10, 6–12 (tenor below; then repeated with the tenor above)
Chap. 8:	8–3, 8–5, 8–6, 8–8, 8–10, 8–12, 8–13, 8–15 (tenor below; then repeated with the tenor above)
Chap. 9:	10–3, 10–5, 10–6, 10–8, 10–10, 10–12, 10–13, 10–15, 10–17 (tenor below; then repeated with the tenor above)
Chap. 10:	11 (like chap. 5)
Chap. 11:	12–5, 12–6, 12–8, 12–10, 12–12, 12–13, 12–15, 12–17, 12–19 (tenor below; the repeated with tenor above)
Chap. 12:	13–10, 13–12, 13–13, 13–15, 13–17, 13–19 (tenor below, then repeated with tenor above)

82. "Quare prima regula debet esse ista: omnis volens componere faciat processum huiusmodi in omni discantu sic ut plures ponat clausulas secundum formam prenotatam." Anonymi, *Tractatus de cantu figurativo et de contrapuncto,* ed. Meyer, 105; see also p. 107.

83. The numbers refer to the interval size. Thus 1–1 is unison–unison, and 1–3 is unison–third.

Chap. 13: 15–10, 15–12, 15–13, 15–15, 15–17, 15–19, 15–20, 15–22 (tenor below, then repeated with tenor above)
Chap. 14: 17–10, 17–12, 17–13, 17–15, 17–17, 17–19, 17–20, 17–22 (tenor below, then repeated with tenor above)
Chap. 15: 18 (like chap. 4)
Chap. 16: 19–12, 19–13, 19–15, 19–17, 19–19, 19–20, 19–22 (tenor below, then repeated with tenor above)
Chap. 17: 20–17, 20–19, 20–20, 20–22 (tenor below, then repeated with tenor above)
Chap. 18: 22–17, 22–19, 22–20, 22–22 (tenor below, then repeated with tenor above)

Each of these interval progressions is described in great detail, both verbally and with numerous musical examples. For example, chapter 4 first gives a thorough definition of the third, then continues:

HOW A THIRD ABOVE DEMANDS A UNISON AFTER ITSELF

A third above demands a unison after itself when the tenor does not move, this rarely, or when it ascends one step, this more aptly, as is proven here:

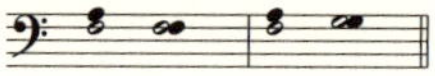

HOW ANOTHER THIRD

Another third follows a third above both above and below the tenor, if that tenor remains in the same place, or if it ascends one or two, or three or four steps; but, with the tenor descending the same number of steps, that is, one, two, three or four, this third above will have another third after itself only above that tenor, as is shown here: [84]

84. "*Quomodo tertia superior unisonum post se requirit.* Unisonum namque tertia superior post se requirit quando tenor non movetur et hoc raro, vel quando unum gradum ascendit, et hoc aptius, ut hic probatur: [ex.]. *Quomodo aliam tertiam.* Tertia alia tertiam superiorem supra et infra tenorem sequetur, si tenor ipse in eodem loco permanserit, vel si unum aut duos, tres aut quatuor gradus ascenderit. Sed tenore tot gradus, hoc est unum, duos, tres aut quatuor descendente, ipsa tertia superior aliam tertiam post se [supra] eum tantum habebit, ut hic [ex.]"; *Liber de arte contrapuncti,* 22–23; trans. Seay, 26.

Example 9. Tinctoris, example of diminished counterpoint, *Liber de arte contrapuncti*, ed. Seay, 106

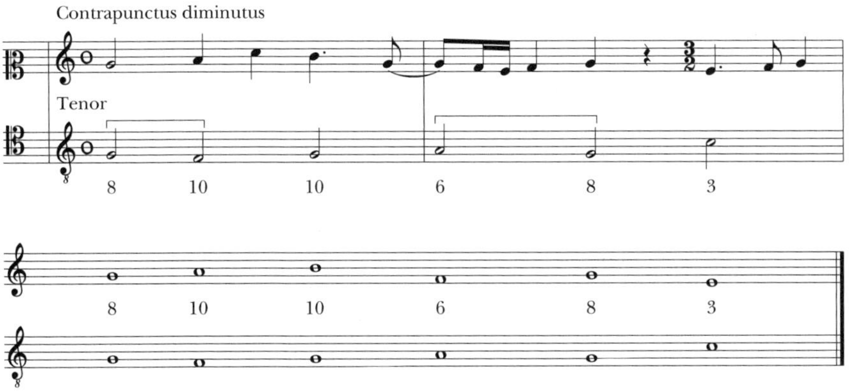

The treatise is 147 pages long in the modern edition (without the table of contents), and of these roughly eighty are listings of interval progressions; in other words, more than one-half. Most modern readers skip over these pages because they are so boring to read: we want general rules, not countless examples. And yet these specific examples were crucial. Once these progressions were memorized it was very easy to perform or compose polyphonic music.

Let us look at one of Tinctoris's own examples in Book 3 on diminished counterpoint (Example 9). Once we reduce the diminished counterpoint to a note-against-note framework, we will discover that all of the interval progressions are covered in Book 2: measure 1 moves from 8 to 10 (or 1–3), then 10 to 10 (chap. 9), 10 to 6 (chap. 4), 6–8 (chap. 7), 8–3 (chap. 8), etc. Every single interval progression one could encounter in polyphonic music would have been memorized by Tinctoris's singers.[85]

Tinctoris concludes his counterpoint book with a telling remark on the importance of learning counterpoint early: "so, in our time, I have known not even one man who has achieved eminent or noble rank among musicians, if he began to compose or sing *super librum* at or above his twentieth year of age."[86] It seems very likely that he is referring to the memorization

85. *Liber de arte contrapuncti,* 106. Note also that Tinctoris uses a ten-line staff for his counterpoint examples. Jessie Ann Owens has shown that this ten-line staff functioned as a chordal grid in her *Composers at Work,* 26–27.

86. "[S]ic et nostra tempestate neminem prorsus cognovi qui si vicesimo anno aetatis eius aut supra sive componere sive super librum canere inceperit, eminentem aut clarum inter musicos locum sibi vendicaverit." *Liber de arte contrapuncti,* 156; trans. Seay, 141. See also Christopher Reynolds, who quotes the same passage and argues that choirboys educated in the north-

of interval progressions and the facility such a training provided for both composition and improvisation.

The Spanish theorist Bartolomeo Ramis de Pareia, who taught at Bologna, addressed his treatise *Musica practica* of 1482 specifically to singers.[87] He begins the counterpoint section, after a brief discussion of intervals, with six basic "rules." We should consider some of these rules (prohibition of parallel perfect consonances), and others recommendations (two or more imperfect intervals can follow each other). For our purposes, Ramis's commentary on Ugolino's "rules" of interval progressions is the most interesting:

> In certain uncouth verses Ugolinus has written general rules about all species, both simple and composite, of which some contain truth and others have less. But just as truth enlightens and falsity shames and is confounded, I will explain these rules briefly, speaking first in this way on ascending from a unison:
>
> II-72: If a unison rises one tone let a third be below.
> II-73: If it rises a third or fourth it will have a fifth below.
> II-74: If it rises a fifth it will end only on an octave. . . .
>
> *[Quotation from Ugolino; the musical examples refer to those in Seay's edition of Ugolino's text]*
>
> The first rule is refuted in this way: If the tenor sings *f g* then the organum can say *f c* as well as *f e*. But if the tenor rises a third, as he says, it is better for the organum to remain on a third than to go to a fifth. If the tenor rises a fourth, as *g k*, the organum will correctly form *g c;* but if it rises a fifth, as *f k* , the organum will form *f f* just as correctly as *f c*.[88]

Note that he does not disapprove of memorization of the interval progressions. Quite the contrary: for Ramis Ugolino has not been thorough enough. His progressions need to be complemented.[89] Ramis concludes this section with the following sentence: "For indeed in these few rules the entire art of coun-

---

ern countries had an incomparable advantage to those from the south, because they were better trained and had memorized music and learned how to improvise; *Papal Patronage,* 136.

87. *Musica practica,* ed. Wolf, 103; trans. Miller, 170.

88. "Ugolinus quibusdam barbaris metris regulas posuit communes de omnibus speciebus tam simplicibus quam compositis, quarum aliquae verum tenent, quaedam vero minime. Sed ut veritas elucescat, falsitas autem erubescat et confundatur, easdem breviter hic explicabo, hoc modo dicendo primo de unisono ascendendo: *Tertia sit infra, unisonus si tenditur una. / Tertia vel quarta si tendit, infra diapente tenebit. / Si quintam ascendit, diapason tantum terminabit. . . .* Prima regula sic redarguitur: Si tenor psallat f g, organum ita potest dicere f c sicut f e. Quod si tertiam ascendit, ut ipse dicit, melius organum manet in tertia, quam vadat ad quintam. Quod si quartam hoc modo g k tenor, organum recte faciet g c; quod si diapente sicut f k, organum ita recte faciet f f sicut f c." *Musica practica,* ed. Wolf, 69–70; trans. Miller, 124–26.

89. All interval progressions not mentioned by Ugolino are listed by Tinctoris: f–g in the tenor with f–c in the counterpoint is found in Tinctoris on g, *Liber de arte contrapuncti,* 20 (after sentence 20); the next example is found on p. 19 (after sentence 13); the last example is found on p. 20, after sentence 20.

terpoint or organum can be contained."[90] What this implies is that anyone who has memorized these progressions has mastered the art of counterpoint.

But Ramis still goes as a step further. We have seen that with earlier theorists these formulas could be transferred from one hexachord to another. Ramis recommends transposition of these progressions into all eight modes:

> Lest anyone should consider these few examples insufficient to understand the total doctrine, we present above and below through the entire hand a more subtle procedure in them, so as to arrange the examples through lines and spaces. Then the same thing that was on the Dorian may be placed on the Phrygian, and on the Lydian, and on the Mixolydian, and the same may be done with their plagals. And when some species may not have made a good consonance let it be raised or lowered by a sign so that the first consonance may acquire its full size or may remove it if what it has is superfluous. . . . It is clear from the preceding few examples that the entire art of counterpoint is contained in the variation of examples through different positions; it is also varied by musica ficta and musica recta, and thus an excess of variation arises through the same example present with minor changes in different modes.[91]

What this then means is that once these few examples had been memorized, they could be transposed to different steps and modes and the interval could be adjusted by musica ficta accordingly.[92]

Pietro Aaron is the earliest theorist to list these interval progressions for four-part counterpoint in his *Libri tres de institutione harmonica* (1516; chaps. 17–32) and in his *Thoscanello* of 1523. Yet, Bonnie Blackburn is certainly right when she says "all this is very sketchy and cannot really be called a method of counterpoint. It is clear that Aaron has not been trained in the tradition of northern counterpoint—he never mentions with whom he studied—and that he is not interested in it."[93] Nevertheless, we have already seen that he accompanies his "rules" with constant references to memorization. Thus we can assume that both the consonance tables and the interval progressions were memorized.

90. "His etenim paucis regulis tota ars contrapuncti vel organi poterit constringi." *Musica practica,* 71; trans. Miller, 127–28.

91. "Ne quis arbitrari possit ista parva exempla non sufficere ad totam doctrinam capessendam, sub et supra per totam manum damus eis modum subtiliorem, ut per lineas et spatia ista disponant exempla. Deinde idem, quod fuit dorii, ponatur in phrygio et in lydio et in mixolydio; et de suis plagalibus similiter fiat. Et quando species aliqua bonam consonantiam non fecerit, elevetur per signum aut deprimatur, ut consonantia prima totam sui recipiat quantitatem aut dimittat, si quid superfluum habet. . . . Liquet his paucis exemplis praemissis tota ars contrapuncti concludi per variationem exemplorum per diversa loca; per fictam per rectamque musicam eadem variata sicque per idem exemplum in diversis tropis parva facta mutatione nimietas varia crescit." *Musica practica,* 72; trans. Miller, 128–29.

92. This passage might lend support to claims by 16th-c. theorists that a number of pieces can be sung in all four modes. See, in particular, Urquhart, "Calculated to Please the Ear."

93. Blackburn, "On Compositional Process," 218. See also idem, "Dispute about Harmony."

The German theorist Johannes Cochlaeus, in his treatise *Tetrachordum musices* of 1511, presents fourteen "rules" of counterpoint with musical examples. Some are more general, others very specific. For example, rule 12 says: "When a discant a third above a tenor rises one step, the tenor descends a fifth, so that together they form an octave."[94] These fourteen rules are followed by first another four "rules" for cadences in three-part counterpoint, then another five for cadences in four-part counterpoint. These verbal descriptions are also accompanied by examples. Rule 1 states: "In cadences *(clausulae),* the discant rises from a sixth with the tenor to an octave with it; the bass, a fifth below the tenor, either drops to an octave with it, or ascends to a unison, or to a fifth above the tenor" (Example 10).[95] All of these progressions would cover basic cadences in note-against-note counterpoint and must have been memorized.

Theorists Who Favor Rules over Examples. In contrast to the theorists discussed thus far, Prosdocimus de Beldemandis was not a practical musician but a teacher of music, astrology, astronomy, mathematics, and medicine at the University of Padua from at least 1422 until his death in 1428.[96] Even though he also begins by listing the most important interval progressions, he then continues:

> There are many other styles of singing different from these to be found; to write them down would be exceedingly difficult and perhaps impossible, because these different styles of singing are in a certain way infinite—and they are delightful in different and various ways, on account of which a variety of compositional practices arises. Our intellect cannot grasp the infinite, since it is not of infinite but of finite capacity (otherwise it would be equal to the divine intellect, something not to be alleged). Thus, styles of this sort are omitted from this account; nor could they even be written down, because they are infinite.[97]

Prosdocimus' treatise has many rules and few examples. Thus, one could easily argue that the text was memorized. The structure is very logical and

94. *Tetrachordum musices,* Tract 4, chap. 10; trans. Miller, 79.

95. Ibid.

96. Herlinger, "Prosdocimus de Beldemandis."

97. "Reperiuntur etiam tamen multi alii diversi modi cantandi ab istis et etiam inter se, quos scribere foret valde difficile et forte impossibile, eo quod tales diversi modi cantandi quodammodo infiniti sunt, et diversis diversimode delectabiles, qua propter insurgit diversitas componentium, et quia intellectus noster infinita capere non potest, cum non sit infinite capacitatis sed finite, eo quod aliter in hoc intellectui divino adequaretur, quod non est dicendum. Pro tanto huiusmodi modi a scriptura relinquendi sunt, nec adhuc scribi possent propter sui infinitatem." Prosdocimo de' Beldemandi, *Contrapunctus,* ed. and trans. Herlinger, 66–69. The treatise dates from 1412, but the passage cited is from the Lucca revision of 1425.

Example 10. Cochlaeus, rule for cadences in three-part counterpoint, *Tetrachordum musices* (1511), sig. E iv verso, 2

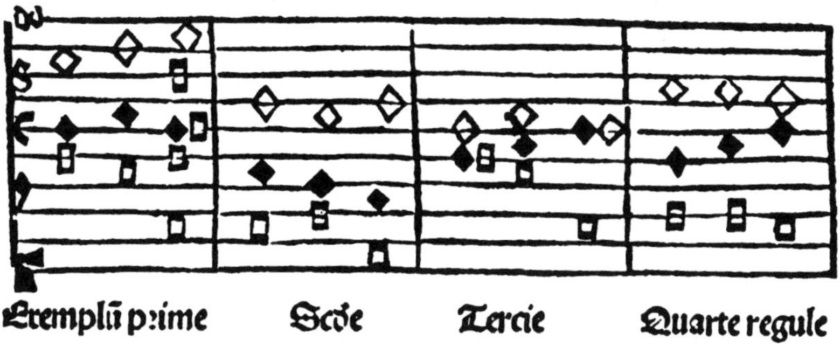

would make memorization easy: all important statements begin with "Item sciendum." On the other hand, Prosdocimus seems to have made a conscious decision to limit the number of examples. As a result, a student who memorized these rules would have an excellent knowledge of early fifteenth-century music theory, but he would not have learned how to perform or compose music. He would not have had any of the interval progressions at the tip of his fingers. He would be able to listen to music or look at manuscripts and understand what is going on in the compositions, but he would remain an outsider. Prosdocimus' treatise, therefore, belongs in the same tradition as the algorism treatise by John of Halifax. It was not intended for applied instruction, but rather for university students.[98]

The German Adam of Fulda does not list interval progressions in his *De musica* of 1490. Nevertheless, he stresses the importance of memorizing consonances (see above). In Book 2, chap. 11 he lists ten "rules," all of them without examples. He seems to be well aware that this is not a usual procedure in counterpoint texts, for he continues: "If then I had added charts to all of these, or had taken heed to elucidate more clearly, I would have introduced tedium rather than pleasure for the readers; thus I wished to omit all [that], so that the mind of the reader is not confused by greed for reading."[99] It seems that this text was more intended for "readers" than for singers, perhaps in a sim-

98. It is, of course, possible that Prosdocimus did not include music examples because he wanted the students or choirmaster to invent them on their own. For example, Burtius' treatise, discussed below, has examples added later on. I would like to thank Margaret Bent and Andrew Wathey for this observation.

99. "Si autem omnibus adiunxissem figuras, aut clarius elucidare attentassem, taedium potius legentibus quam voluptatem inferret; ideoque omnia omittere volui, ut lectoris animus aviditate legendi non confundatur." *De musica,* 353; trans. Slemon, 204.

ilar way to Prosdocimus' treatise. Yet at the time he wrote this treatise he worked as a singer for Frederick the Wise of Saxony. And he concludes his treatise by demanding that the entire treatise be "read and memorized."[100] Perhaps singers were expected to make up their own examples.

Nicolaus Burtius lists five "rules" of counterpoint followed by examples that illuminate these rules. He omits the usual interval progressions. And yet, in an appendix to the counterpoint section of the treatise in Brussels, originally intended to be part of Burtius' text,[101] all of these interval progressions are listed for the C hexachord. The examples begin with unison to third, then unison to fifth, third to fifth, fifth to octave, octave to tenth, tenth to twelfth, and twelfth to fifteenth. Then Burtius continues with three-note progressions: 1–3–5, 3–6–8, etc. It would take too long to go through all the interval progressions; what is most important is that they either were intended to be part of the original text or were added by an instructor or student later.

We have seen that the great majority of music theorists who discuss counterpoint between ca. 1300 and 1600 emphasize memorization of consonances and interval progressions. They list many "rules" that apply to specific situations. Once students had memorized these "rules," they had acquired the basics and could move on to diminished counterpoint. In other words, the counterpoint treatises are not different from the abacus books: both give separate "rules" for individual problems that were then memorized. The only theorist who is adamantly opposed to listing interval progressions is Prosdocimus de Beldemandis, a university professor whose treatise was intended for university students, who had no need to memorize the progressions.

Let us compare the medieval and Renaissance approach with that of the most famous "modern" counterpoint treatise, *Gradus ad Parnassum* by Johann Joseph Fux, first published in 1725. Of interest to us is the initial Dialogue, preceding the note-against-note section. While medieval theorists go through every pitch of the gamut and list all possible consonances, Fux lists the perfect and imperfect consonances in general. Then, he defines and gives an example for direct, contrary, and oblique motion. And finally, he gives only four rules:

> First rule: From one perfect consonance to another perfect consonance one must proceed in contrary and oblique motion.
>
> Second rule: From a perfect consonance to an imperfect consonance one may proceed in any of the three motions.

100. "Haec itaque cum lecturus es, memor eris"; *De musica,* 381.

101. Brussels, Bibliothèque Royale, MS II 785, fol. 44r–v. The appendix is included in Massera's edition, 129–33, and published in an English translation by Miller, 130–35. See also ibid., "Introduction," 9.

> Third rule: From an imperfect consonance to a perfect consonance one must proceed in contrary or oblique motion.
>
> Fourth rule: From one imperfect consonance to another imperfect consonance one may proceed in any of the three motions.[102]

Even though memorization still played an important part in music education in the eighteenth century, individual interval progressions were no longer systematically memorized, but rather subordinated to these four rules. Students memorized the rules first and then chose interval progressions that followed these rules. In contrast, the students who learned the *regula del grado* treatises or the *Liber de arte contrapuncti* first memorized the individual progressions, and only then learned the rules. In fact, Tinctoris lists these rules only toward the end of his book in a section entitled "Concerning the eight rules to be observed in all counterpoint, of which the first is that all counterpoint ought to begin and end with a perfect concord."[103] While Fux would put the rules at the top of his agenda in counterpoint instruction, Tinctoris stresses memorization of interval progressions.

Let us return for a moment to the work of Jack Goody discussed in chapter 2. While his 1987 book, *The Interface between the Written and the Oral,* deals mainly with the impact of writing on an oral society, he gives an instructive example of how memorization of a written text in a literate society allows for mental calculations. He shows how Egyptian mathematicians did their multiplications and divisions through a complicated process of addition and subtraction, which they certainly would not have been able to do without writing. We (or, at least, the older among us who were not brought up on calculators), on the other hand, are able to do quite complicated multiplications and divisions in our head. This is possible because we memorized multiplication tables, which are dependent on writing, in school.[104] What this implies, then, is that members of literate cultures are also able to work out complicated problems in their mind, and are able to do so precisely because they belong to literate cultures.

Consonance tables function in exactly the same way as multiplication tables. Not only do they look the same, they were systematically memorized. Similarly, musicians from the thirteenth through the sixteenth centuries memorized interval progressions. Thus, they had all of this musical material easily available at the tip of their fingers. Just as Renaissance merchants were able to do complex computations in their mind, Renaissance musicians

102. Fux, *Steps to Parnassus,* 22.

103. "De octo generalibus regulis circa omnem contrapunctum observandis, quarum prima est quod omnis contrapunctus per concordantiam perfectam incipere finireque debet." *Liber de arte contrapuncti,* ed. Seay, 146; trans. Seay, 132.

104. Goody, *Interface,* 82.

were able to work out entire compositions, because they had all possibilities readily available in their storehouse of memory. Additional support for this hypothesis can be found in recent research in neuroscience.

Mental Calculation in Neuroscience

Psychologists have long suspected that the central component of unusual performance in any area of expertise is hard work, that is, continuous memorization. This applies to any field from music to chess, mathematics, neurosurgery, and even basketball.[105] To give just one example, the calculating prodigy Rüdiger Gamm was not an outstanding student in mathematics as a child. At the age of twenty, he started practicing calendrical calculations for fun in order to enter a TV competition. He prepared himself by training up to four hours per day, concentrating on number facts and calculating procedures. After a few years of such drill he was able to raise two-digit numbers to powers, extract roots, calculate sines, and divide two prime numbers.[106] For example, he was able to compute the fifth root of a ten-digit numeral within a second. Gamm's achievements are well beyond what psychologists call the human working memory, which can remember 7 ± 2 unrelated items.[107] Gamm was able to do his computations because he had memorized tables of squares, cubes, and roots and in addition accumulated "an enormous store of procedures and short-cuts that allow him to solve multi-step problems. For example, to solve 68×76 takes seven steps and six intermediate results. After some practice with the task, Gamm was taking about five seconds per problem—with a high degree of accuracy. Two-digit squares, by contrast, took him just over a second because they were simply retrieved from memory."[108]

Gamm stored all of this information in what psychologists call "long-term working memory" (LTWM). In a recent study undertaken at the University of Konstanz, researchers were able to show through magnetic imaging that professional chess players have accumulated a large database of chunks (this is why neuroscientists talk about the "chunking theory of chess playing")[109] in the LTWM that allows them to work out possible scenarios for entire games in their mind very quickly.[110] Usually these prodigies and chess grandmasters have highly developed memories only in their particular field of expertise

105. Gladwell, "A Reporter at Large."

106. Butterworth, "What Makes a Prodigy"; and Pesenti *et al.*, "Mental Calculation." See also "Who Wants to be a Genius."

107. See, for example, Baddeley, *Working Memory*.

108. Butterworth, "What Makes a Prodigy," 11.

109. Elo, *Rating of Chess Players*.

110. Amidzic *et al.*, "Pattern of Focal γ-bursts."

and do not show exceptional memory in other areas. Gamm's letter span, for example, was entirely normal. The neuroscientist Mauro Pesenti and his collaborators compared Gamm's brain activity with that of six other males in their early twenties. While everyone showed activities in twelve areas of the brain, Gamm alone used an additional five areas of his brain. Of these five three had been previously linked to long-term memory.[111] Similarly, in contrast to professional chess masters, amateur players did not use their LTWM.[112]

Psychologists have thus found confirmation for something that was known to specialists of the art of memory since Antiquity: proper training and memorization, especially if done at an early age, allows one to become an expert who can work out complex calculations and planning in the mind. Thus, musicians could store chant, consonance tables, and interval progressions in their long-term memory just as a mathematician would store tables of multiplication, roots, squares, and cubes. In the next chapter I will try to reconstruct how this memorial archive could have been used in the process of composition. But before that, we must discover what role memorization played in the instruction of diminished counterpoint.

Diminished Counterpoint

From the fourteenth century on, a number of theorists distinguish between note-against-note counterpoint and diminished counterpoint. The distinction has been covered thoroughly by Claude Palisca and Klaus-Jürgen Sachs,[113] so I will concentrate here on only a few points relevant to the topic. What role did memorization play in the instruction of diminished counterpoint? Did students memorize entire phrases, as in the Vatican treatise, or were they encouraged to be "original" in their compositions?

One of the most interesting fourteenth-century texts is a treatise entitled *Compendium de discantu mensurabili,* by the Cistercian monk Petrus dictus Palma Ociosa, from Amiens.[114] After having covered intervals and their progressions in note-against-note counterpoint as well as *musica ficta,* he comes to a section entitled *flores musice mensurabilis* (flowers of mensural music), which is devoted to diminished counterpoint.[115] Petrus uses three tenor pat-

111. Pesenti et al., "Mental Calculation."

112. Amidzic, "Pattern of Focal γ-Bursts."

113. Palisca, "Kontrapunkt"; Sachs, *Der Contrapunctus.*

114. *Compendium de discantu mensurabili,* ed. Wolf; see Leech-Wilkinson "Petrus frater dictus Palma ociosa."

115. "Florid" counterpoint is one of the synonyms of "diminished" counterpoint still used today. Note that the same terminology (adding flowers) is used in the Jiangnan Sizhu Instrumental Ensemble Tradition in China to describe improvisation applied to a basic piece learned from a teacher. The piece can be melodically varied, expanded, often to such an extent that it becomes unrecognizable. See Witzleben, *"Silk and Bamboo" Music,* 71.

terns for twelve different examples. The most striking conclusion from a study of these examples is that the structural notes of the discant in the three patterns are either the same or very similar every time the tenor is repeated, and they are identical to those used in Petrus' discussion of simple counterpoint. This suggests that he conceived the compositional process in two steps: he first decided on a note-against-note framework in accordance with the previously outlined interval progressions, and then he gave various alternative ornamented versions of this note-against-note framework. Let us look at the beginning of the second example of diminished counterpoint (Example 11a). If we reduce it to its note-against-note framework (8–6–5–3–5–1), and compare it with the interval progressions previously memorized in the discant chapter, we see that they are exactly the same. 8–6 is found in Example 11b, 5–6 (the inversion of 6–5) in Example 11c, 5–3 in Example 11d.

Were the examples of diminished counterpoint also memorized? I think not. The "flowers" are intended to demonstrate diminished counterpoint in twelve different mensurations. Petrus is aware that the "flowers" of every interval progression are innumerable, so his settings serve as samples for every possible mensuration on the mode, tempus, and prolation level. Daniel Leech-Wilkinson has pointed out that Petrus did not have a vocabulary available in the fourteenth century to give rules for diminished counterpoint, so all he could do was give examples: "The student, in other words, is being told that he can only learn to write diminished counterpoint by following the practice of his master, for the possibilities are too many to define as rules. It is at precisely this point that composition ceases to be teachable (or describable) in writing and becomes oral, taught by word of mouth and by example."[116]

What the student has to learn are the note-against-note interval progressions and the mensural system; then he can either improvise or write down a composition. Thus, in contrast to note-against-note counterpoint, Petrus cannot and does not want to have detailed "rules" for diminished counterpoint: there are too many possibilities. The student is encouraged to create his own version rather than repeat memorized progressions.

Similarly Goscalchus, the first theorist to give dissonance rules for diminished counterpoint, has "verbula," examples of diminished counterpoint without a tenor in all four basic mensurations.[117] These rules are no longer specific musical examples to be memorized, but true rules that concern the prohibition of parallel consonances, the permitted length of a dissonant note against the tenor,[118] and the permitted length of syncopations. He pro-

116. Leech-Wilkinson, "Written and Improvised Polyphony," 175–76.

117. Ed. and trans. Ellsworth, 130–47. See also Bonnie Blackburn's excellent discussion of Goscalchus' dissonance rules in "On Compositional Process," 234–40.

118. See Blackburn, "On Compositional Process," 235.

Example 11. Petrus dictus Palma ociosa, counterpoint examples, *Compendium de discantu mensurabili,* ed. Wolf

(a) Wolf's example 37 (pp. 520–21)

(b) Wolf's example 13 (p. 510)

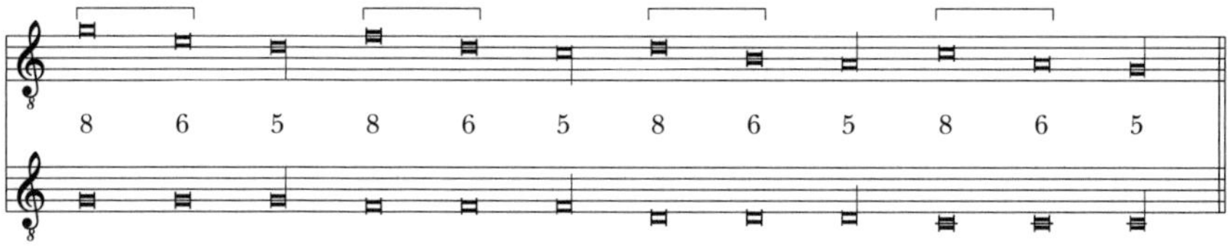

(c) Wolf's example 20 (p. 512)

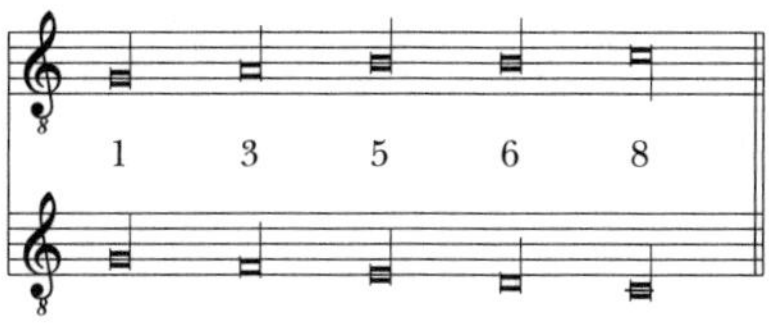

(d) Wolf's example 19 (p. 512)

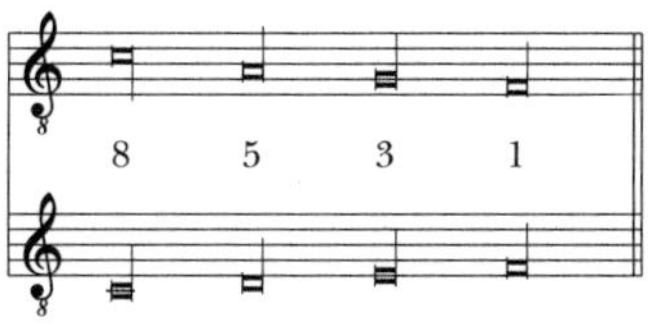

hibits parallel perfect consonances between the tenor and the added part, even when there are other notes in between (rule 1). Dissonant notes are allowed as long as the greater part or half of the note over the tenor is consonant (rule 2).[119] He does not specify the note value, but we can assume that under regular mensuration he is referring to the first part of the semibreve since his examples are in semibreves (see, however, rule 4). The term "consonance" refers "to the group of divided notes that sound together (*consonare*) with one tenor note, some of which can be dissonant."[120] The term "concordance" refers to the consonant notes, which according to some "should be named according to the larger part; others say according to the first consonant note or the first note appearing in consonance" (rule 3).[121] Consonances (in Goscalchus' nomenclature) can begin and end with a dissonant tone, as long as this dissonant tone will be less than half the value of the entire group of consonances (rule 4). Rule 4, then, is a modification of Rule 2. In other words, we are no longer dealing with musical examples that were memorized, but with rules in the modern sense of the word, general maxims that could be applied to a variety of situations. Thus, it is fitting that Goscalchus closes the counterpoint book with the following statement: "But I did not give these *verbula* simply because they are necessary or because there are not any others or more or fewer or because they could not be done in other ways. I give them, rather, so that for those studying them and their modes, the path might by chance be more beautiful; and in performing them, it might be more pleasing and refined; and in inventing them, it might be easier."[122]

A hundred years later, Tinctoris had fully developed the vocabulary in which to give detailed dissonance rules. He organized his rules like several theorists before him, according to mensuration signs. His rules apply to both written *(res facta)* and improvised *(super librum)* counterpoint.[123] Tinctoris is

119. See Sachs, *Der Contrapunctus,* 148 ff. and Blackburn, "On Compositional Process," 235–36.

120. Blackburn, "On Compositional Process," 236.

121. Ibid.

122. "Hec autem verbula non ut simpliciter necessaria sint dedi, aut quod alia vel aliter aut plura pauciorave fieri non possint. Sed ut ea speculantibus et eorum modum magis pulchra forsan, et placabiliora subtilioraque faciendi, et inveniendi facilior sit via." *Berkeley Manuscript,* 146–47.

123. *Liber de arte contrapuncti,* ed. Seay, 121; trans. Seay, 113. For this distinction before Tinctoris see in particular Prosdocimus de Beldemandis, who writes, "It must be known, too, that counterpoint taken in the proper sense is twofold, vocal and written: vocal, that which is uttered, and written, that which is notated. Everything that will be said of counterpoint below is to be understood to pertain to both. From this, it follows that counterpoint taken in the ordinary sense—which follows from that taken in the proper sense and is founded upon it—is also twofold, vocal and written: vocal, that which is uttered [*vocalem*], and written, that which is no-

the first theorist to relate the length of the permitted dissonances to what he calls *mensurae directio,* the regularly recurring beat under various mensuration signs. Thus, in major prolation the *mensurae directio* is on the minim, in minor prolation on the semibreve, and in duple proportion or *tempus diminutum* on the breve.[124] In general, the dissonance cannot be longer than half of the *mensurae directio,* so semiminim dissonances are allowed in major prolation, minims in minor prolation, and semibreves in diminished time. In addition, there are two basic rules: first, if there is a consonance at the beginning of the *mensurae directio,* a dissonance can follow of the same or smaller value introduced and left as passing tone or lower (or upper) neighbor. Sachs summarizes Tinctoris's second and third rule: "Second, where there is a penultimate note equal in value to two *mensurae directio,* consisting either of a single note or of two notes identical in pitch and length, the first part of the first *mensura* nearly always has a dissonance set against it. Third, if the penultimate is equal in value to one *mensurae directio,* then the first part can be dissonant, or when preceded by stepwise descending notes of equal value, the first part of each note can be dissonant."[125]

Tinctoris repeats these basic three rules for each *mensurae directio* of the various mensurations and proportions he discusses. Important for us is the fact that he first gives the rules and then presents the examples. Both these examples and the works of the great composers mentioned in the prologue (Ockeghem, Regis, Busnoys, Caron, Faugues, Dunstable, Binchois, and Dufay) should be studied with regard to their dissonance treatment: "And in fact I never hear, I never study them without coming away more cheerful and with a better understanding of the art; so that as Vergil in that divine work the *Aeneid* used Homer, so do I use them in my little works as models."[126] The compositions are studied and emulated, but not memorized.

Neither Goscalchus nor Tinctoris could have developed their rules without writing. Notation allowed them to arrive at a text that could be studied and from which rules could be derived. Both theorists provide a good ex-

tated [*scriptum*]." *Contrapunctus,* ed. and trans. by Herlinger, 33. The distinction has been the subject of much interpretation and controversy. See, in particular, Bent, "*Resfacta* and *Cantare Super Librum*"; Blackburn, "On Compositional Process"; and Sachs, "Arten improvisierter Mehrstimmigkeit."

124. On this topic, see my "Cut Signs in Fifteenth-Century Musical Practice."

125. Sachs, "Counterpoint."

126. "Ea quoque profecto numquam audio, numquam considero quin laetior ac doctior evadam, unde quemadmodum Virgilius in illo opere divino Eneidos Homero, ita iis Hercule, in meis opusculis utor archetypis. Praesertim autem in hoc in quo, concordantias ordinando, approbabilem eorum componendi stilum plane imitatus sum." *Liber de arte contrapuncti,* 13; trans. Holford-Strevens, "Tinctoris on the Great Composers," 193. Holford-Strevens traces the phrase "quin laetior ac doctior evadam" back to *Odyssey* 12. 186–8.

ample for Jack Goody's argument that the invention of writing allowed the study of grammar and the development of rules.[127] What was done unconsciously in an oral society became a conscious rule in the modern sense, once one was able to see it written down. It is remarkable that when Tinctoris studied the compositions of the previous generation, he must have mainly done so by putting the separate parts together in his mind, since they were not notated in score. For the most part, these were pieces worth studying, but not listening to.

What happened after Tinctoris and Aaron? It goes without saying that memorization of cadences and progressions continued. James Haar has called attention to a passage in a treatise by Giovan Tomaso Cimello from 1589 (or 1569) in a Naples manuscript: "In order to shorten and simplify the art of counterpoint so that the student will not despair of learning it after having seen so many books on plainchant, he [the student] ought to know and to reflect that everything can be found in these few but varied forms of motion over [the *canto fermo*]. Having learned these, he can go on to many graceful and masterful passages, varied and skilful; soon these will be committed to memory, and from memory pass to his lips, becoming his own interpretation."[128] As Haar has pointed out, Cimello's examples are already very similar to Fux's species counterpoint. Similarly, Gioseffo Zarlino's detailed instructions in part 3 of *Le istitutioni harmoniche* must have been memorized by many students.

Memorization played a central role in all organum, discant, and counterpoint treatises. Nevertheless, there are important differences among various types of treatises. In the Vatican organum treatise the note-against-note counterpoint is not distinguished from diminished counterpoint and thus all formulas were memorized and made their way into the Notre Dame repertory. This would support my hypothesis (see chap. 5) that the Magnus liber organi was transmitted orally since oral cultures are typically formulaic. In the discant and counterpoint treatises, consonance tables, interval progressions, and note-against-note progressions are systematically committed to memory by endless and tedious "rules" and examples, which were clearly considered the central part of learning counterpoint. We have seen that instruction in coun-

127. See my discussion of Jack Goody in chap. 2. See also his *Interface between the Written and the Oral,* 250.

128. "Per accortar et abbreviare l'arte del contraponto et che il discepolo non si sconfida d'impararlo vedendo tanti et tanti libri di canto piano deve sapere et considerare, che tutte consisteno sempre in questi pochi e varii moti sopra li quali imparsi devono molti leggiadri et maestrali passaggi varii et arteficiosi accio che poi improvisamente vengono a memoria e dalla memoria alla lingua interprete sua." Haar, "Lessons in Theory," 72–73.

terpoint is similar to that in arithmetic, where the student is given a specific "rule" for every problem rather than a few general ones. As a result, students had well-stocked memories, or what a neuroscientist would call long-term working memory, that enabled them to perform or to work out musical compositions in the mind. Thus, memorization offers another explanation for how musicians could plan pieces "in the mind" without writing them, just as we can do multiplication in our mind or a chess master can plan an entire game without recourse to paper or a chessboard. The memorization of individual note-against-note progressions continued throughout the sixteenth century. By the eighteenth century, Fux starts his treatise with a few general rules that can be applied to a variety of situations and only then gives individual examples.

Examples of diminished counterpoint, on the other hand, were not memorized. Instead, theorists taught by example and gradually developed real rules in the modern sense. And these rules were derived from a study of written-down musical compositions that were much admired. Tinctoris could not have analyzed the counterpoint without seeing the pieces in front of his eyes. This represents a significant step in the evolution from oral composition to written composition. Most of the pieces to which the dissonance rules apply are compositions that could not have come into existence without writing. This is true, in particular, of the isorhythmic motet (see chap. 6). Without notation, whether written out or visualized in front of the eyes, theorists would not have been able to formulate and apply detailed dissonance rules. Thus, while Notre Dame "composers" memorized entire pieces and quoted extensively from each other, composers of the fourteenth and fifteenth centuries memorized an enormous number of possible note-against-note progressions that would allow them to work out the frameworks of entire compositions in their minds. But there is little evidence that they memorized examples of diminished counterpoint in order to learn how to compose.[129] Rather, this is where they would have used their creativity. Tinctoris reserves his praise of great compositions for diminished counterpoint. You would never find him saying "Busnoys has better consonant interval progressions than Domarto."

And yet, even though Tinctoris formulated his rules in the belief that they would teach the student everything he needed to know about counterpoint, this view did not last long: only a generation later, the Bolognese theorist

129. Two notable exceptions are Frosch, *Rerum musicarum opusculum*, sig. E, and Tomás de Santa María in his *Libro llamado arte de tañer fantasia* (1565), 1, fol. 57r–v, who recommended memorizing phrases, cadences, or melodic progressions and incorporating them into compositions. Note, though, that both authors are much later than our theorists. Neither of them distinguishes between note-against-note and diminished counterpoint. See also Owens, *Composers at Work*, 190 ff.

Giovanni Spataro asserted that all of the treatises in the world would not make a great composer: "written rules are good for teaching the first rudiments of counterpoint to the beginner, but will not make a good composer, for good composers are born, just as are poets. The gift of heaven is almost more important than the written rules for good composers, and this is apparent every day, for learned composers (through natural instinct and a certain graceful manner, which can hardly be taught), sometimes find expressions in their counterpoint that no rules and precepts of counterpoint allow."[130]

130. "[P]erché le regole scripte possono bene insignare li primi rudimenti del contrapuncto, ma non farano el bono compositore, imperò che li compositori boni nascono così come nascono li poeti. Pertanto quasi più ci bisogna lo aiuto del celo che la regula scripta, et questo ogni giorni è apparente, perché le docti compositori (per instinto naturale et per certa gratia et modo, el quale quasi non se pò insignare) aliquando in li soi contrapuncti et concenti aducono termini, li quali da alcuna regula et precepto de contrapuncto non sono demonstrati." Giovanni Spataro to Giovanni del Lago, April 5, 1529, in *A Correspondence of Renaissance Musicians,* ed. Blackburn, Lowinsky, and Miller, 363–65. See also Lowinsky's discussion of this passage in "Musical Genius," 481–82.

PART TWO

Compositional Process in Polyphonic Music

In the last two decades, medievalists have fundamentally changed our understanding of how verbal texts were composed. Mary Carruthers, in particular, has shown that much of the composition was done in the mind, and that the final result could, but did not have to, be notated.[1] Composition consisted essentially of putting together elements or chunks that had been memorized earlier. This is a rather different understanding of compositional process than that put forward by Friedrich Ludwig and his followers. Were the techniques and tools used by composers of music similar to those used by composers of verbal texts?

In the first part of the book I have attempted to find out how musicians of the Middle Ages might have built a memorial archive. It is now time to turn our attention to the question of how this archive might have been used in the process of composition. If, as I shall argue, much of the Notre Dame repertory was transmitted orally, we would want to know how musicians could have memorized so much music and what this tells us about the compositional process. Is there such a thing as a final version of a piece? Or was the scribe or performer free to create his own interpretation? In addition, we shall see that music of the fourteenth and fifteenth centuries as well was composed in the mind and sung by heart, and, again, the art of memory must have played an important role in the creation and transmission.

The first chapter of this part is concerned with Notre Dame polyphony, which I believe was largely transmitted orally. It is a repertory that was dependent on writing in the act of performance and composition only to a limited degree. The last chapter is concerned with the fourteenth- and fifteenth-century motet repertory, which could not have come into existence without writing.

1. Carruthers, *Book of Memory.*

5

Compositional Process and the Transmission of Notre Dame Polyphony

In the middle of the twelfth century, John of Salisbury gave the following account of what must have been some kind of early Notre Dame polyphony (Leonin is considered to have been active at Notre Dame from the 1150s on):[1]

> Music sullies the Divine Service, for in the very sight of God . . . [the singers] attempt, with the lewdness of a lascivious singing voice and a singularly foppish manner, to feminize all their spellbound little fans with the girlish way they render the notes and end the phrases. Could you but hear the effete emotions of their before-singing and their after-singing, their singing and their counter-singing, their in-between-singing, and their ill-advised singing, you would think it an ensemble of sirens, not of men. . . . Indeed, such is their glibness in running up and down the scale, such their cutting apart or their conjoining of notes, such their repetition or their elision of single phrases of the text—to such an extent are the high or even the highest notes mixed together with the low or lowest ones—that the ears are almost completely divested of their critical power, and the intellect, which the pleasurableness of so much sweetness has caressed insensate, is impotent to judge the merits of the things heard. Indeed, when such practices go too far, they can more easily occasion titillation between the legs than a sense of devotion in the brain.[2]

1. Wright, "Leoninus, Poet and Musician."

2. "Ipsum quoque cultum religionis incestat quod ante conspectum Domini . . . lasciuientis uocis luxu, quadam ostentatione sui, muliebribus modis notularum articulorumque caesuris, stupentes animulas emollire nituntur. Cum praecinentium et succinentium, concinentium et decinentium, intercinentium et occinentium praemolles modulationes audieris, Sirenarum concentus credas esse, non hominum . . . Ea siquidem est ascendendi descendique facilitas, ea sectio vel geminatio notularum, ea replicatio articulorum singulorumque consolidatio, sic acuta vel acutissima grauibus et subgrauibus temperantur ut auribus sui iudicii fere subtrahatur auctoritas, et animus quem tantae suauitatis demulsit gratia, auditorum merita examinare non

Little did he know that what he was describing in such colorful language would be considered the cradle of Western polyphony 750 years later. Contrast John's view on the music with the following statement by Friedrich Ludwig written in 1902: "The greatest and most fateful moment in the entire history of music was the discovery of polyphonic music."[3] In the same essay, he refers to Leonin and Perotin as "individual artists" (*Künstlerindividuen*).[4]

We have seen in chapter 1 that for Friedrich Ludwig and his disciples these individual artists and their products were no different in kind from a Beethoven and his works. There are several reasons for this attitude. First, Ludwig thought that in the polyphony of the Magnus liber we have for the first time in European music history the names of two "composers," Leonin and Perotin, associated with a particular oeuvre. He saw great artists at work who wanted to fix every detail in writing. Thus, one of his priorities was to attribute pieces to Leonin and Perotin. Ludwig saw his role as trying to establish what these composers really intended. He wanted to come as close as possible to the "original" text. Second, Ludwig had deciphered modal notation, which represents the first systematic attempt to notate rhythm in Western music.[5] Why should theorists have invented such a complex notational system, he thought, if not in order to have the music performed and transmitted accurately as written? Third, the music is polyphonic, and many find it hard to imagine how two, three, or even four singers could anticipate each others' moves.[6] According to Ludwig, Notre Dame polyphony formed an early link in the evolutionary chain that eventually led to classical Renaissance polyphony, which could not have been conceived without notation. To question the necessity of notation for Notre Dame polyphony seems to threaten the very premise on which the whole polyphonic tradition is based.

In recent years, a growing number of scholars have begun to challenge Ludwig's picture for the following reasons.[7] First, the theorist Anonymous

---

sufficit. Cum haec quidem modum excesserint, lumborum pruriginem quam deuotionem mentis poterunt citius excitare." John of Salisbury, *Policratus*, ed. K. S. B. Keats-Rohan, 48–49, trans. Dalglish, "Origin of the Hocket," 7.

3. "Der grösste und folgenschwerste Moment der gesamten Musikgeschichte ist die Entdeckung der mehrstimmigen Musik." In Ludwig, "Die mehrstimmige Musik des 14. Jahrhunderts," 16.

4. Ibid., 20.

5. See also chap. 1, pp. 12, 25–31.

6. See, for example, Frieder Zaminer, who writes about the Vatican organum treatise: "Als Merkmal der Mehrstimmigkeit möchte ich hervorheben, daß sie auf Notenschrift angewiesen und daher ohne diese undenkbar ist." Or "Von jetzt ab konnte man Musik niederschreiben, die sich ohne Hilfe der Notenschrift nicht verwirklichen ließ." Zaminer, *Der vatikanische Organum-Traktat,* 140 and 151.

7. The first to question Ludwig's chronology was Roesner, "Problem of Chronology"; Craig Wright suggested that the Notre Dame repertory was orally transmitted in *Music and Ceremony,*

IV named two "composers," Leoninus and Perotinus, the former being responsible for creating the Magnus liber, the latter for editing it.[8] If Craig Wright is correct in identifying Leonin as the Parisian poet magister Leoninus, born around 1135, elevated to the position of canon by the 1180s, and found in records until 1201,[9] his organa dupla must have been composed in the second half of the twelfth century. Jacques Handschin had already established that most of the tripla and quadrupla were composed at the end of the twelfth and beginning of the thirteenth century, when liturgical edicts by the Bishop Eudes de Sully of 1198 and 1199 document the singing of tripla and quadrupla.[10] And yet, the oldest Notre Dame manuscripts date from the 1230s at the earliest, more likely 1240s or 1250s,[11] when we have a sudden explosion of sources. In addition to the preserved sources, Rebecca Baltzer has described seventeen lost Notre Dame manuscripts, which were listed in various collections. Again not a single manuscript was mentioned before 1240.[12] Both Baltzer and Wright note the absence of *any* polyphonic manuscripts from the lists of choirbooks, the inventories of the library, the treasury, the bishop's chapel or chapter house of Notre Dame. Of course, it cannot be excluded that all earlier manuscripts were lost, but it is also possible that much of the music before 1230 was transmitted orally.[13] Wright draws the following conclusion: "taking the absence of polyphonic sources at face value, we must conclude that much of the organum, discant, and counterpoint of the church, whether sung by memory, by improvisation, or by some combination thereof, was performed without the assistance of written notation."[14] Similarly, theoretical treatises describing modal rhythm were all writ-

325–54; for an earlier version of some of the ideas presented in this chapter, see A. M. Berger, "Mnemotechnics and Notre Dame Polyphony" and "Die Rolle der Mündlichkeit." Max Haas also believes that the repertory was orally transmitted; "Organum," 871. The most recent discussion is by Roesner, "Who 'Made' the *Magnus liber.*" But note also the following authors who follow firmly in Ludwig's footsteps: Schick, "Musik wird zum Kunstwerk"; Arlt, "Denken in Tönen und Strukturen"; and Flotzinger, *Perotinus musicus*; see also my review of Arlt's essay in *Plainsong and Medieval Music* (2002), 44–54.

8. Anon. IV, *De mensuris et discantu,* ed. Reckow, 39–40.

9. See Wright, *Music and Ceremony,* 281–88.

10. "Zur Geschichte von Notre Dame." See also Wright, *Music and Ceremony,* app. A, and *Les quadrupla et tripla de Paris,* ed. Roesner, lxiii. About the dating of the quadrupla, see also Knapp, "Polyphony at Notre Dame of Paris," 561–64.

11. Everist, "From Paris to St. Andrews"; Baltzer, "Thirteenth-Century Illuminated Miniatures"; Roesner, "Origins of W_1."

12. Baltzer, "Notre Dame Manuscripts."

13. One could argue that there are no manuscripts because the pieces were written down in *libelli,* that is, single gatherings, and then copied into a volume later. Much of medieval theory was transmitted this way. But again, there is no evidence to support this hypothesis.

14. Wright, *Music and Ceremony,* 333–34.

ten after 1230 or 1240.[15] All of this points to the possibility that the repertory up until then was, if not entirely, then to some extent transmitted orally, with little use of notation. This tradition seems to have continued in Notre Dame de Paris even after the pieces were written down elsewhere. Thus the questions arise how such a vast collection of polyphonic music could have been memorized, and why the music was notated elsewhere (that is, in churches in Paris other than Notre Dame and outside of Paris). Furthermore, what are the implications of oral transmission for the compositional process?

The second reason for the hypothesis that orality played a role in the conception and transmission of Notre Dame polyphony is that its musical texts exhibit many features similar to those found in contemporary verbal texts, and it is increasingly clear that orality played a role in their composition and transmission.[16] What orality implies in this context is that scribes might have written down pieces from memory, changing the texts they were copying either because they remembered them differently, or simply because they wanted to change them.[17] D. L. D'Avray calls this process "written improvisation."[18]

Music theorists of the Notre Dame period generally distinguish between three *species,* that is, compositional styles: organum purum, copula, and discant, of which by far the most important for the development of rhythmic notation is discant.[19] In discant both parts move in modal rhythm. The copula is placed stylistically in between organum purum and discant. It is characterized by an upper voice in modal rhythm against sustained notes in the tenor and consists of at least two phrases. Often the melody is sequential.[20] It is generally agreed that in the earliest stage organum purum had a rhythmically free melismatic upper part against a slowly moving tenor.[21] According to Fritz Reckow, the ligatures in early organum purum had no modal significance whatsoever. Accordingly, he advocated a rhythmically free performance. More recently, Edward Roesner has provided a close reading of Johannes de

15. In fact, the treatise by the theorist who provides the most information on the Notre Dame "composers," Anon. IV, might have been written as late as the early 14th c. because it mentions the *semibrevis* and *minima.* The latter were not used before this time. See Roesner, "Who 'Made' the *Magnus liber,*" 230, n. 5.

16. For a recent book on variations encountered in marriage sermons, see D'Avray, *Medieval Marriage Sermons.*

17. D'Avray has described a similar procedure for the sermons of St. Bonaventura. They were written down from notes by Marco da Montefeltro and then revised by Bonaventura. Sermons transmitted in this way are called *reportationes.* D'Avray, *Preaching of the Friars,* 97.

18. *Medieval Marriage Sermons,* 22–23. D'Avray distinguishes between scribes who simply copy the text in front of them and "scribes who feel free to paraphrase and improvise."

19. See, for example, Johannes de Garlandia, *De musica mensurabili,* ed. Reimer. See also Max Haas's overview of Notre Dame theory in "Die Musiklehre im 13. Jahrhundert."

20. See Yudkin, "*Copula* according to Johannes de Garlandia," 67.

21. See in particular Reckow, in Anon. IV, *De mensuris et discantu,* 45.

Garlandia's and Anonymous IV's statements and concluded that the interpretation of organum purum depends entirely on the context, and that it could change back and forth between measured and unmeasured rhythm.[22]

The question of differences between various versions of pieces transmitted in different sources is a complex one. According to Roesner, "In a manuscript culture, one expects to find variation, even substantial variation, among different copies of the 'same' text, but the degree of variance exhibited by the organa in particular is without parallel among ostensibly stable musical repertories."[23] The differences are most apparent in organum purum sections, whereas the transmission of the discant sections is much more stable. Roesner describes the variants in organum purum as follows:

> Taken as a whole, these variants include, among other things, (1) the addition, removal or replacement of cadential gestures that round off the phrase, of linking material that joins the phrase to the following one, and of lead-ins that direct the line to a position of melodic "weight"; (2) the ornamental reinforcement of important notes, for example emphasising the first note of a coniunctura with melodic turns, repetition and the like; (3) the filling-in of leaps in the melody with stepwise motion, or the reverse; and (4) the addition or removal of stock *colores,* the expanding or contracting of *colores,* the replacement of one *color* by a different one, and the repositioning of *colores* to different parts of the clausula. All these tactics could be used in flexible combination with one another.[24]

We have seen in the last chapter that the Vatican organum treatise consists of such *colores* or formulas. Let us now try to reconstruct how these formulas might have been used by a composer or singer of organum.

COMPOSITIONAL PROCESS ACCORDING TO THE VATICAN ORGANUM TREATISE

If, as I believe, the Vatican organum treatise was memorized, the singers had a large supply of *colores* or formulas available in their mental inventory for every note-against-note progression that they could use in the process of performance and composition (the two can hardly be distinguished in this context). They would know which *colores* would be appropriate for the beginning, the end, or the middle of a phrase. Let us look at the organum *Operibus sanctis,* copied at the end of the Vatican organum treatise, to see to what extent the piece uses the formulas of the example section (Example 12).[25]

22. "Johannes de Garlandia on *Organum in speciali.*"
23. Roesner, "Who 'Made' the *Magnus liber,*" 233.
24. Ibid., 259–60.
25. Immel has already found a number of formulas in *Operibus* that are derived from the example section; "The Vatican Organum Treatise Re-Examined," 146–48. Similarly, he has been able to trace the same formulas in various manuscripts of the Magnus liber.

Example 12. *Operibus sanctis,* Vatican organum treatise, ed. Godt and Rivera, 345₁₋₆

Steven Immel has summarized all note-against-note progressions in the Vatican treatise (Example 13). The consonances in *Operibus sanctis* between the tenor and the counterpoint in measures 1–60, and the major ones for the rest of the piece, can be summarized as follows (the top line lists the measure numbers, the lower the intervals. Cadences are shown by a double vertical, usually at the end of a phrase, and the lesser divisions by a single vertical, usually at the end of a word):

Example 13. Note-against-note progressions in the Vatican organum treatise, from Immel, "Vatican Organum Treatise," 125

Rule:
Group 1: nos. 1–97 (= 1–30)

Group 2: nos. 98–162 (= 31–56)

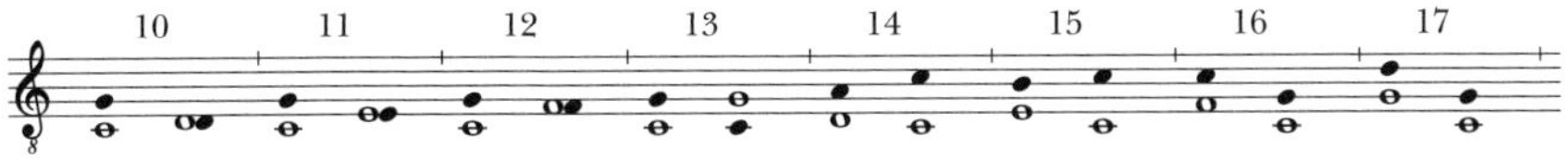

Group 3: nos. 163–214 (= 57–80)

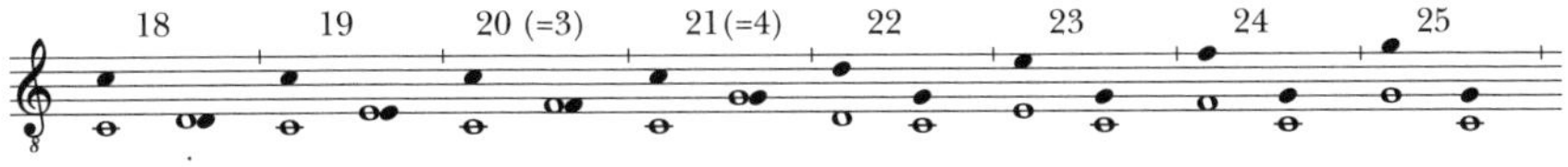

Group 4: nos. 215–251 (= 81–95)

(Supplement—no rules)
Group 5: nos. 252–276 (= 96–110)

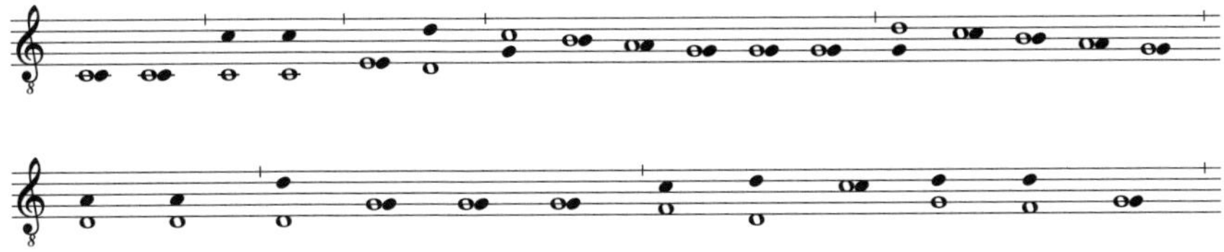

1 6 9 12 17 18 20 21 23 || 24 26 27 29 31 33 34 36 | 37 39 41 43 45 46
8 5 5 1 1 5 5 5 1 8 5 1 1 5 5 1 1 5 5 1 5 1 8

47 48 49 51 52 | 54 57 58 60 | 81 88 96 106 118 || 166
5 5 5 5 5 8 5 5 8 8 1 8 1 1 8

Throughout the composer used only three intervals: the octave, fifth, and unison. Note that only octaves and unisons are used for the major cadences (mm. 23, 118, and 166) and they are clearly preferred for the less important cadences as well. Thus, while the Vatican author does not undertake any interval classification, in practice he excludes the fourth (which Johannes de Garlandia classified together with the fifth as a medial concord) and the major and minor thirds (classified by Johannes as an imperfect concord) as possible concords.[26]

As we have seen in chapter 4, the example section in the Vatican organum treatise offers a variety of ways in which each note-against-note progression can be filled once the basic framework has been established. But before we embark on an analysis of the counterpoint, let us briefly look at the intonation. The beginning (m. 1) of *Operibus sanctis* must have served as a common intonation for beginnings not only of entire pieces, but also of sections and phrases within a piece, because we encounter it again in the same organum at the beginning of the next two sections (mm. 24 and 119) as well in measures 61 (transposed), 75, 89 (transposed), 107, 132 (transposed), and 159 (transposed). Note that the first and last organum in the treatise, *Alleluia. Hic Martinus* and *Petre amas me,* also begin with the same intonation.[27] Nevertheless, the formula is nowhere to be found in the example section. It must have been so common that the author of the treatise did not find it necessary to include it.[28]

In Example 14 measures 1–17 are reduced to a note-against-note framework. I will first compare every progression with the formula having the same tenor–counterpoint progression in the example section, and then try to find similar formulas independent of the interval progression. The first interval progression in the tenor is d–c and corresponds to rule 22: "If the chant descends by a second and the organum begins at the octave, let the organum descend by a fifth, and it will arrive at a fifth."[29] The author provides only a single formula for this tenor progression, a counterpoint moving from d-sol to g-ut, formula 198. The organum formula presents a considerably prolonged version of this formula (Example 15). While they share a similar middle section (mm. 4 and 5), the beginning and end are different. It seems, thus, that the composer chose to use formula 198 as a point of departure, extending it considerably on both ends. Which *colores* did he use to expand the basic formula?

The formula in measure 2 is very common throughout the Vatican treatise; it is what Immel calls an ornamented-third figure. For example, formula 343 ends exactly this way (Example 16). Measures 4–5 use the ornamented *coniunctura* gesture (a figure based on descending stepwise motion)[30] that has been used on different steps and in slightly altered versions in formulas

26. See also Fuller, "Organum-*discantus-contrapunctus,*" 485–89.

27. "Vatican Organum Treatise," ed. Godt and Rivera, 341 and 345.

28. On intonation formulas, see also Roesner, "Who 'Made' the *Magnus liber,*" 355–56.

29. "Si cantus descenderit duas voces et organum incipiat in dupla, descendat organum 5 voces et erit in quinta." "Vatican Organum Treatise," ed. Godt and Rivera, 324.

30. See Immel, "The Vatican Organum Treatise Re-examined," 130–32.

Example 14. *Operibus sanctis,* mm. 1–17, reduced to note-against-note counterpoint (numbers refer to measures)

Example 15. *Operibus sanctis,* mm. 1–6, compared with formula 198

Example 16. *Operibus sanctis,* m. 2, compared with formula 343

30, 44, and 178 (Example 17a–b). Example 17c–d shows that measure 5 is a shortened version of formulas 292 and 178.

The next progression corresponds to rule 23: "If the chant descends by a third and the organum begins at the octave, let the organum descend by a sixth, and it will arrive at a fifth."[31] Example 18 reproduces formula 202, which has the same *coniunctura* gestures as *Operibus sanctis,* followed by an ornamented fourth and third, but transposed a fifth down and very much shortened.

The next interval progression (mm. 10–12) follows Rule 19: "If the chant ascends by a third and the organum begins at the octave, let the organum descend by a sixth, and it will arrive at the unison."[32] Formula 182 bears a striking similarity to measures 10–12, but is, of course, a fourth higher and

31. "Si cantus descenderit 3 voces et organum incipiat in dupla, descendat organum 6 voces et erit in quinta." "Vatican Organum Treatise," ed. Godt and Rivera, 325.

32. "Si cantus ascenderit 3 voces et organum incipiat in dupla, descendat organum 6 voces et erit cum cantu." Ibid., 321.

Example 17. *Operibus sanctis* compared with formulas 44 and 292

(a) mm. 4–5 and formula 44

Formula 44

(b) mm. 5–6 and formula 292

Formula 292

Example 18. *Operibus sanctis,* mm. 8–9, compared with formula 202

Formula 202

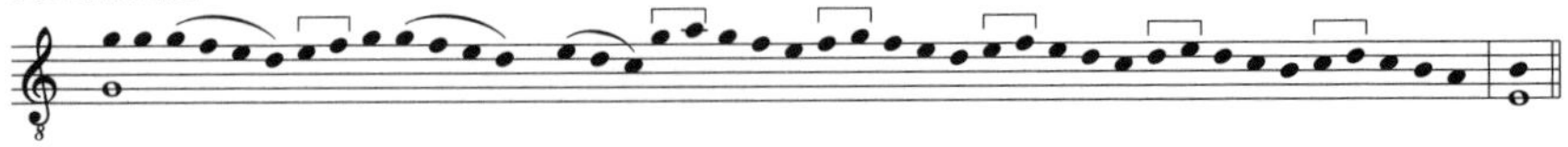

it has been expanded in measure 11 of *Operibus sanctis* (Example 19). If we look at the entire phrase independently of the tenor, measures 7–12 consist of two similar parts, both starting with two *coniunctura* gestures followed in the first phrase by an ornamented fourth, third, and neighbor, and in the second by an ornamented third alone. It has often been observed that such isoperiodicity is characteristic of the Notre Dame repertory. The ending of measure 11 is also an expanded version of formula 9 (Example 20).

The next interval progression consists of parallel unisons and is not listed in the Vatican treatise. The phrase (mm. 13–16) begins with an ascending octave. Formulas 237–241 present various possibilities for filling in an octave. The one closest to our example is formula 237 (Example 21). Measures 14–16 present the same *color* three times, a descending triad followed by an ascending ornamented fourth on c, b, and a. There are many Vatican examples that will repeat a short formula on different steps (see, for example, formulas 246 and

Example 19. *Operibus sanctis,* mm. 10–12, compared with formula 182

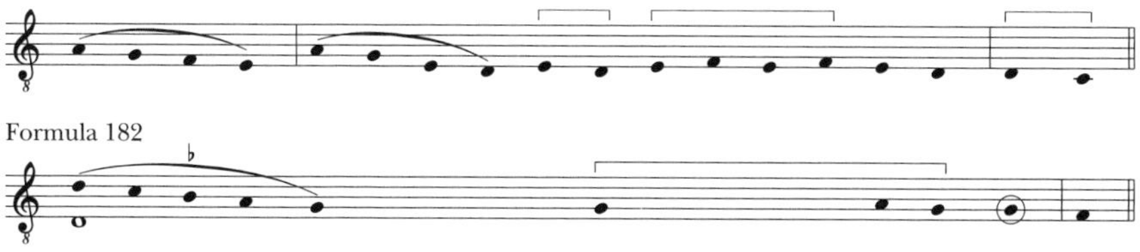

Example 20. *Operibus sanctis,* m. 11, compared with formula 9

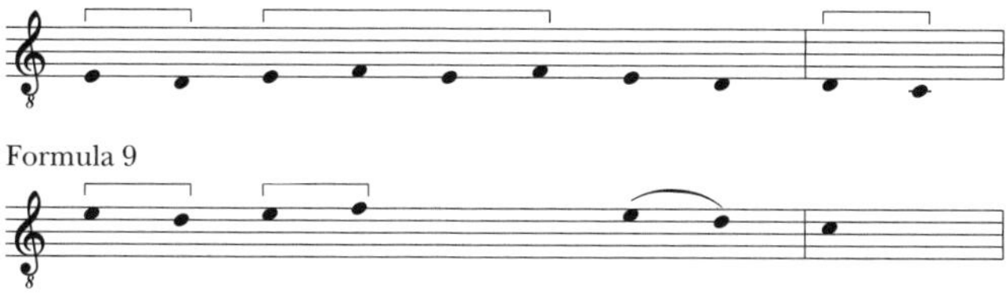

Example 21. *Operibus sanctis,* m. 13, compared with formula 237

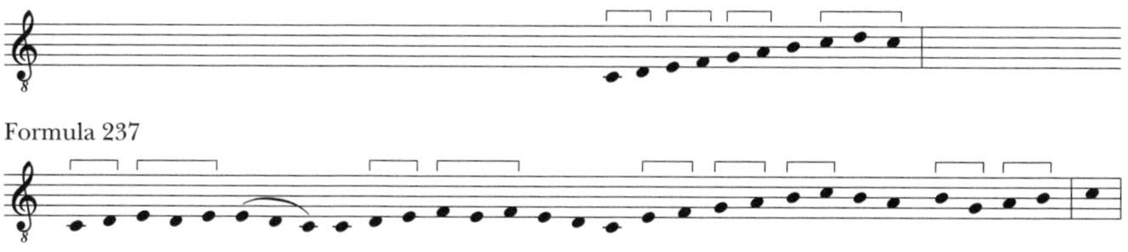

247). Formula 251 also uses the descending triad followed by an ascending fourth, but presents this sequence five rather than three times (Example 22).

Thus far we have dealt with the beginning and the middle of an organum, but do Notre Dame composers also have characteristic formulas for ending a piece or a section? We noted above that all major cadences end at the octave or unison. The first major phrase at the end of the first section marked by a double bar (mm. 22–23) ends with the *coniunctura* gesture, familiar from measures 7–8, followed by a cadential ornamented third formula (Example 23). The very same formula is used again at the end of the next major phrase, measures 117–18. In addition, we find it again at the end of a section in measures 87–88, and transposed up a third with two interpolated notes in measures 143–44. The first section of the organum *Alleluia. Hic Martinus* from the treatise also ends with this formula (mm. 21–22), as does the phrase ending in measures 42–43. In the example part of the treatise, there are many formulas similiar to our cadential gesture, such as formula

Example 22. *Operibus sanctis,* mm. 14–15, compared with formula 251

Formula 251

Example 23. *Operibus sanctis* compared with formula 244

(a) mm. 22–23

(b) m. 87

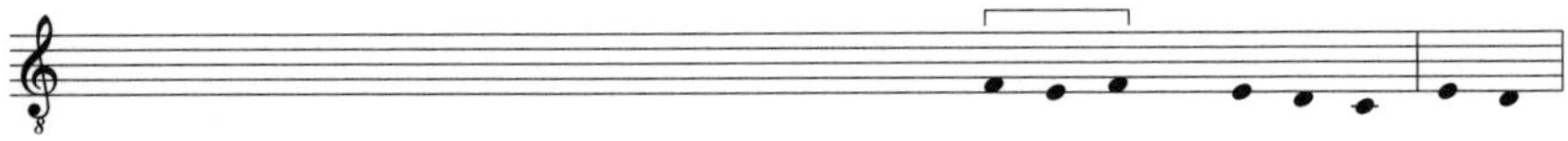

(c) m. 117

(d) Formula 244

244 (Example 23d). (Others are 131, 234, and 247.) The phrase that ends the entire organum is also derived from a formula, in this case formula 94 (Example 24).[33]

As these examples make clear, the formulas or *colores* are central to understanding the Notre Dame repertory. It should be remembered that Ludwig thought that little was to be learned from Notre Dame theorists and referred to their writings as "theorist-babble."[34] But considering how this music was put together, it makes perfect sense that Anonymous IV praises Perotin

33. For an earlier article concentrating on closing formulas in the Magnus liber, see Tischler, "Structure of Notre-Dame Organa."

34. "Die Quellen der Motetten ältesten Stils," 288.

Example 24. *Operibus sanctis*, m. 166, compared with formula 94

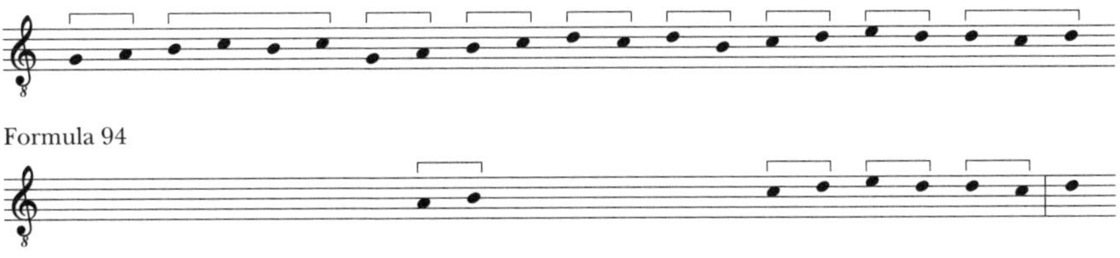

for using an "abundance of musical *colores*."[35] Thus, Fritz Reckow's and Jürg Stenzl's condescension toward Anonymous IV for not fully appreciating the musical artistry seems entirely misplaced.[36] The melismas in the treatise were not meant to be stitched together mechanically. Rather, they served as building blocks that can be shortened, lengthened, and combined with each other in ever new ways. The only restriction the composer/performer faced was that they had to be included within the note-against-note framework.

The situation we see here might be fruitfully compared with that of the sermons that have been studied in detail by D. L. D'Avray. His conclusions show a similar approach to text as that encountered in the Notre Dame sources. Some manuscripts transmit the sermons word for word, but others mingle sections from the same sermon or different sermons, expand or abbreviate certain points, or add different *exempla* and scriptural passages.[37] In addition, the oral presentation of the sermons was likely to be different from the written one. The written version served often only as a skeleton that was meant to be elaborated. This fits well with the medieval understanding of the author. As Mary Carruthers has shown, a medieval composer assembled various chunks stored in his memory, but was not interested in mechanical repetition of these chunks. Rather, in repeating another author's words, it was desirable to add something of one's own.[38]

How could the singers have performed improvised polyphony? Craig Wright has shown that there was no real choir director (as Ludwig had described it): "To see Perotinus as a *magister capellae* is not only to misconstrue the status of the composer of liturgical polyphony in the Middle Ages but also to misunderstand the workings of a medieval cathedral choir."[39] Notre

35. "cum habundantia colorum armonicae"; Anon. IV, *De mensuris et discantu*, ed. Reckow, 45–46.

36. Reckow, "Das Organum," 491.

37. D'Avray, *Preaching of the Friars*, ch. 2.

38. Carruthers, *Book of Memory*, 218.

39. Wright, *Music and Ceremony*, 219.

Dame polyphony was a soloist's art. While there might easily have been several singers on the tenor line, Wright suggests that "given the nature of the line, it is difficult to see how two singers might execute such a creation without compromising away many of the most distinctive and beautiful attributes of this music."[40] He concludes that the upper part must have been sung by a soloist. This agrees well with our findings. Only a soloist would have been able to put together the formulas.

Organum purum, even when written down, relied to a large extent on oral composition and transmission. We should abandon the idea "that this music underwent some sort of progressive linear development."[41] Rather, the sources may reflect a "regional or 'house style,' adopted by a particular cathedral or scribe."[42] As a result, there can be no such thing as a final version of a piece: a performer would make his own redaction or a scribe would recompose a piece.

THE TRANSMISSION OF DISCANT

By contrast, the transmission of discant was much more stable than that of organum purum. It is important to realize, however, that this does not mean that it could not have been transmitted orally. There is some oral poetry that is transmitted word for word, and there is oral-formulaic poetry, where the performer actively participates in the process of composition.[43] And as Treitler has shown, "neither the style of a musical or poetic item, nor the state of its text, can itself be taken as evidence that it has come down through oral transmission. For there are no universal imperatives about either style or textuality that can be associated with either written or oral transmission . . . "[44] Thus, it is the transmission of discant sections that seems to me to represent a truly new problem and one requiring an investigation.

Given that the art of memory belonged to the basic intellectual equipment of literate Europeans of the period, in particular in Paris, where Hugh of St. Victor, Johannes de Garlandia, and Albertus Magnus were active (all of whom wrote important treatises on the art of memory), it would not be surprising to find traces of its application in the music of Notre Dame. It is this idea that I want to pursue here. In the following, I will try to explain how certain aspects of the medieval culture of memory provide a context that allows us to see the function of modal rhythm in a new light.

I begin with a brief summary of the basic features of the modal rhythmic

40. Ibid., 432.
41. Roesner, "Who 'Made' the *Magnus liber,*" 234. See also his "Problem of Chronology," 398.
42. Roesner, "Problem of Chronology," 382–83.
43. For an excellent summary of these problems see Finnegan, *Oral Poetry,* 52–86.
44. See Jacobsson and Treitler, "Sketching Liturgical Archetypes," 192.

system used in discant. The system of rhythmic modes was described by a group of theorists who started to write about fifty years after Leonin's organa were first performed.[45] Their pronouncements will be the basis of the following discussion, since we do not know whether the original organa were the same as those described by the theorists. Most scholars believe that modal notation developed gradually.[46] The main idea behind the system of the rhythmic modes as described by Johannes de Garlandia is the repetition of a rhythmic pattern, constituted by one or more longs (L) and/or one or more breves (B), the long being twice or three times as long as the breve (Figure 17). In mode 1, the pattern is L B; in mode 2, B L; in mode 3, L B B; in mode 4, B B L; in mode 5, L L; and in mode 6, B B B. Modes 1, 2, and 6[47] are called *modi recti* by Johannes de Garlandia. The other three modes are called *non mensurabiles* or *ultra mensuram* (beyond measure), because the long is now one time unit longer than the original binary long, and the breve includes either one (the first of two breves) or two time units (always the second of the two breves). The music is notated in ligatures that combine several notes rather than in single notes, and the singer is able to recognize which mode is intended from the ligature pattern: for example, mode 1 will be indicated by a ternary ligature followed by one or more binary ones. Modes 1, 5, and 6 were the original modes. Mode 2 was probably developed at the same time as the concept of *ordo,* and modes 3 and 4 were most likely derived from mode 2.[48] *Ordo* is a modal phrase that counts the number of repetitions of the rhythmic pattern. For example, if a pattern occurs twice before a rest, it will be in the second *ordo.* An *ordo* is called perfect when it ends with the first element of the perfection,[49] and it is followed by a rest that fills in the re-

45. The following theorists have been considered, in approximate chronological order (see also "Notation" in *New Grove Online,* accessed October 5, 2003; for dating see Knapp, "Polyphony at Notre Dame of Paris," 567): Anonymous, *Discantus positio vulgaris* (partly from ca. 1225; the rest after 1280), in Hieronymus de Moravia, *Tractatus de musica,* ed. Cserba (trans. Knapp in "Two Thirteenth-Century Treatises"); Johannes de Garlandia, *De mensurabili musica,* ed. Reimer (ca. 1250); Amerus, *Practica artis musicae* (1271), ed. Ruini; Anonymous IV, *De mensuris et discantu* (after 1280, probably early 14th c.; see above), ed. Reckow; Dietricus, *Regula super discantum* (ca. 1275), ed. Muller; Lambertus, *Tractatus de musica* (ca. 1275), CS 1:251–81; Anonymous of St. Emmeram, *De musica mensurata* (1279), ed. and trans. Yudkin; Franco of Cologne, *Ars cantus mensurabilis* (ca. 1280), ed. Reaney and Gilles (trans. Strunk, 226–45); Anonymous VII, *De musica libellus* (postdates Franco), CS 1:378–83 (see also Pinegar, "Exploring the Margins," where she describes a second source for Anon. VII that she dates in the third decade of the 13th c.; p. 222); Walter Odington, *Summa de speculatione musicae* (ca. 1300), ed. Hammond (trans. Huff); Johannes de Grocheio, *De musica* (ca. 1275), ed. Rohloff.

46. See in particular Roesner, "Emergence of *Musica mensurabilis.*"

47. From Haas, "Die Musiklehre im 13. Jahrhundert," 138.

48. Roesner, "Emergence of *Musica mensurabilis,*" 56 ff.

49. Lambertus was the first theorist to call the *longa,* which consists of three beats or *breves,* a *perfectio:* "Longa et brevis et converso semper unam perfectionem faciunt." *Tractatus de musica,* 271. See also Frobenius, "Perfectio."

Figure 17. The rhythmic modes

maining elements of the perfection. To give an example, the second perfect *ordo* of mode 1 consists of two perfections followed by a long and a breve rest, L B L B L B-rest, and is transcribed as ♩♪♩♪♩𝄾.

Even though the system of rhythmic modes is described in similar ways in most of the treatises,[50] there exists a fundamental difference in the relationship between the perfection and the single note value in Johannes de Garlandia, the Anonymous of St. Emmeram, and Anonymous IV on the one hand, and Lambertus and Franco on the other.[51] For Johannes the two-beat long is the correct one, and the three-beat long is derived by the addition of the breve to the binary long, while Lambertus and Franco call the ternary long perfect and the binary imperfect.[52] In Johannes's system the length of the individual notes can only be gathered from the mode itself ("A figure is a representation of a sound according to its mode"),[53] while Franco attempts to present a system where the individual note or *figura* has a value independent of the mode: "A figure is a representation of a sound arranged in one

50. It should be mentioned, however, that Lambertus lists nine modes in *Tractatus de musica* (p. 279) and Franco five in *Ars* (ch. 3, sentence 4). For the most detailed summary of *modus* see Frobenius, "Modus (Rhythmuslehre)."

51. For discussions of the problem see Treitler, "Regarding Meter and Rhythm" and Haas, "Die Musiklehre von Garlandia bis Franco," 138–44.

52. *Ars,* ed. Reaney and Gilles, chap. 4.

53. "Unde figura est representatio soni secundum suum modum." *De musica mensurabili,* 44; trans. Strunk, 142.

of the modes. From this it follows that the figures ought to indicate the modes and not, as some have maintained, the contrary."[54]

The implication of Franco's way of thinking was greater rhythmic flexibility: the primacy of individual note values allowed the notation of rhythms different from the modal patterns. This went hand in hand with the emergence of the new genre of the motet. Whereas Notre Dame organa were mostly notated in ligatures, motets had to be notated in separate notes because a new text was added to a preexisting melody. As a result, their melodies could be organized in rhythms that no longer followed strictly modal patterns.[55]

Modal notation is the first system that attempts to control rhythm, but it is a highly ambiguous one: ternary ligatures can mean short–long–short or long–short–long, short–short–long, long–long–long, or short–short–short, depending on the context. Heinrich Husmann lists twelve different possible transcriptions of the *ternaria* ligature and concludes that "such an ambiguity often results in a corresponding uncertainty in the transcription of the piece."[56] That this uncertainty was also felt by late thirteenth- and early fourteenth-century theorists is attested by Walter Odington, who states:

> The first mode, according to the rules, begins with a ternary ligature without propriety and with perfection, then proceeds by binary ligatures with propriety and with perfection, thus: 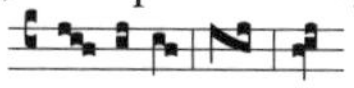
>
> Others give the ternary ligature propriety in this mode along with the binary. Consequently, in a *ternaria* the propriety indicates a long, in a *binaria*, a breve, thus: 
>
> I myself take no account of this practice because it is both improper and contrary to reason.[57]

54. "Figura est representatio vocis in aliquo modorum ordinatae, per quod patet quod figurae significare debent modos, et non converso, quemadmodum quidam posuerunt." *Ars,* chap. 4; trans. Strunk, 229.

55. See, for example, Walter Odington, *Summa de speculatione musicae,* 139–43, who describes the difference between discant and motet.

56. "Eine derartige Mehrdeutigkeit führt häufig auch zu einer entsprechenden Unsicherheit der Übertragung." Husmann, ed., *Die drei- und vierstimmigen Notre-Dame-Organa,* xix.

57. "Primus secundum regulas primo habet ternariam longam sine proprietate et cum perfectione, deinde procedit per binariam ligaturam propriam et perfectam, sic: [ex.]. Alii in isto modo faciunt ternariam ligaturam cum proprietate et binariam similiter et sic in ternaria proprietas longa, in binaria brevis, sic: [ex.] quod ego relinquo tamquam indecens et rationi dissonum." Walter Odington, *Summa de speculatione musicae,* pt. 4, p. 137; trans. Huff, 23. In the Franconian system the first ligature of the second example would be interpreted as BBL, not LBL, which corresponds to the values demanded by mode 1. See also Hammond's discussion of the issue in the "Summa de speculatione musicae of Walter Odington: A Critical Edition and Commentary" (Ph.D. diss., Yale University, 1965), 92–95. See also Anonymous IV for similar complaints about the ambiguities of ligature notation: *Anonymus IV, De musica,* 31–32; trans. Yudkin, 23–24.

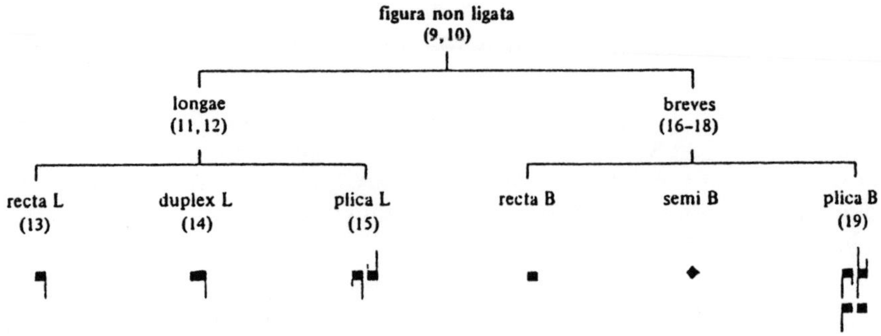

Figure 18. Note shapes in Johannes de Garlandia, *De mensurabili musica*

The interpretation of *coniuncturae* is equally unclear.[58] Similarly, the pitch indicated by the *plica* is not always specified and can, therefore, vary from performance to performance.[59] Leo Treitler describes the situation best when he states: "much of the time the notation sets up a general rhythmic type, but leaves a more or less wide range of details for the singer to settle in performance. Indeed a full description of that system must present it as functioning through the collaboration of composer, notator, and performer, with variable and uncertain boundaries for the role of each."[60]

But was an unambiguous notational system really important for Notre Dame musicians? It is striking that by the time the three main manuscripts were written down, theorists were already describing a notational system that for the first time gave explicit relative durational values to every single note. Johannes de Garlandia,[61] whose treatise was written around 1250, as well as all later theorists, clearly distinguished the individual note values (Figure 18).[62] In other words, even theorists who thought more in terms of modal patterns than individual note values include descriptions of the latter in their treatises. As has most recently been suggested by Sandra Pinegar, Johannes's treatise may have been transmitted orally and might have come directly out of the Notre Dame school.[63] Two of the three major Notre Dame manuscripts were copied in Paris. While we cannot be certain that the scribes were aware of the notational possibilities described by Johannes, it seems to me that if

58. See Apel, *Notation of Polyphonic Music,* 240–44.

59. Ibid., 235–36. The *plica* usually implied an additional eighth note in first- and second-mode ligatures. See ibid., 228–29.

60. "Regarding Meter and Rhythm in the *Ars Antiqua,*" 532.

61. *De mensurabili musica,* ed. Reimer, 1:45 ff.

62. Ibid., 2:53.

63. Pinegar, "A 'New Philology' for Medieval Theory."

a less ambiguous notational system would have been necessary for correct performance or transmission, it would have been used.[64] Ludwig himself noted, quite uncharacteristically, that modal notation was a more than adequate tool for indicating modal rhythm, and that it showed indirectly "the underlying rhythm with absolute certainty."[65] Thus, even though contemporary theorists were describing separate note values, the scribes of the Notre Dame sources preferred to use the system in which rhythmic patterns of melismatic melodies were indicated exclusively by the ambiguous means of ligature groupings. It is true that saving space might have been a factor (ligatures take less space than single notes), but this cannot have been the only reason, since very soon, and for several centuries to come, scribes were not reluctant to waste space on single notes. One wonders why Johannes and the other theorists dependent on him were not interested in developing a system based on these note shapes, which would obviously allow much greater rhythmic flexibility and be much less ambiguous, and why they concentrated instead on the modal patterns as shown through ligature formations,[66] which left so many details up to the performer.

It is significant that modal patterns provide the basis of rhythmic thinking for Johannes de Garlandia and theorists dependent on him, so much so that some theorists repeatedly stress the importance of maintaining a single modal pattern throughout a *discantus* section.[67] Thus, Anonymous of St. Emmeram says: "Also in music, according to us, there is not a mode which cannot put together and complete some melody from the beginning to the end by means of its own figures or notes arranged as it requires, and without the figures or help of other modes."[68] This is not to say, however, that all Notre Dame polyphony consists only of rigid modal patterns. The patterns are most consistently used in the tenors of *clausulae* and motets. But it is significant that until Lambertus and Franco, rhythm was imagined in terms of modal patterns rather than individual notes, which would have allowed more variety.

The question then becomes, why did the Notre Dame theorists (and, presumably, the musicians whose practice they described) insist on thinking in terms of inflexible modal patterns rather than flexible rhythms and, conse-

64. Many of the later Notre Dame sources, such as Berlin lat. 40523, transcribe organa in mensural notation. See Roesner, "Johannes de Garlandia on *Organum in speciali,*" 159, n. 85.

65. "[D]en zu Grunde liegenden Rhythmus absolut sicher." *Repertorium,* 1:44–45.

66. See Johannes de Garlandia, *De mensurabili musica,* 2:55–66.

67. See, for example, ibid. 1:35–36; Lambertus, *Tractatus de musica,* 279; Anon. VII, *De musica libellus,* ed. Knapp, 207; Anon. IV, *De musica,* 22, trans. Yudkin, 13.

68. "Item in ista musica non est modus secundum nos, qui non potest per suas figuras proprias seu voces prout exigit ordinatas a principio usque in finem cantum aliquem componere et perficere, absque figuris seu adiutorio aliorum." Anonymous of St. Emmeram, *De musica mensurata,* ed. and trans. Yudkin, 214–15.

quently, why were they satisfied with an ambiguous ligature notation even when a less ambiguous single-note notation was already conceivable?

It is important to stress that the system of rhythmic modes was used not because theorists, composers, and scribes had not yet mastered the technique of notating music in flexible rhythms; modal patterns continued to be described even after it had become common to notate motets with separate note values. This suggests that modal rhythm must have fulfilled a function that was not possible with flexible rhythms. I believe this function to have been mnemonic. I would like to suggest that the use of rhythmic modes is similar to the use of versification, which was very popular in the twelfth and thirteenth centuries; that is, that it can be related to the tradition of didactic poetry. Just as a medieval teacher would accelerate the learning process of his students by putting new and difficult material into verse, the theorists and composers would similarly help the singers memorize new pieces by applying modal patterns.

In the high Middle Ages, putting material into verse was the most common method of memorizing and was used for practically every subject. The twelfth and thirteenth centuries in particular saw an enormous growth in the use of verse for didactic purposes in such fields as grammar (Alexander de Villa Dei's *Doctrinale,* which consists of 4,000 rhymed hexameters), medicine, law, theology, arithmetic (the *Carmen de algorismo,* also by Villa Dei, which consists of 284 hexameters), *computus,* meteorology, geography, botany, zoology, pharmacy, literary history, music theory, and sermons.[69] In the eleventh century Marbod of Rennes described sixty stones in 734 hexameters in his *Liber lapidum.* According to Lynn Thorndike, "The variations in the wording and the arrangement of them as repeated by different authors suggest they had undergone a long process of use in the class-rooms, of copying and recopying, or repeating and learning, of forgetting and remembering and revising."[70]

The composer Leonin, as Craig Wright has recently discovered, fits squarely into this tradition: his *Hystorie sacre gestas ab origine mundi (Acts of Sacred History from the Origins of the World)* puts the first eight books of the Old Testament into dactylic hexameter.[71] The popularity of mnemonic verses extended into the Renaissance: in 1443 Lorenzo Valla composed a new grammar in verse to substitute Alexander de Villa Dei's now old-fashioned me-

69. The best description is by Thorndike, "*Unde versus*"; see also Klopsch, *Einführung in die Dichtungslehren,* 74–86; de Ghellinck, *L'essor de la littérature latine,* 1:235–43; Bolgar, *Classical Heritage,* 208–11; and Ziolkowski, *Alan of Lille's Grammar of Sex,* 71–72. See also Yudkin, in Anonymous of St. Emmeram, *De musica mensurata,* 4–5.

70. Thorndike, "*Unde versus,*" 193.

71. Wright, "Leoninus, Poet and Musician," 16–31.

dieval grammar.[72] Rhyming catalogs of medieval libraries were memorized by monks.[73] Frequently, the poet will state in a prologue that the material has been put into verse so that it can be remembered better. This is what Leonin says: "I strive to celebrate in song and in simple verse the acts of sacred history since the origin of the world / Which Moses and his successors thought sufficient to set down in prose and in accustomed words / But I take pleasure in bringing pleasing sound to the ear by the laws of poetry / So that the history may be no less useful to the mind, which, delighted by the brevity of the poetry and by the song, may hold it more firmly the more it enjoys it."[74] Similarly, the following verses have been placed at the beginning of the fourteenth-century *Florilegium Treverense:*

> The meters help the minds; they comprise much in little,
> recall the original, and are pleasing to the reader.
>
> Note: The meter is capable of three (things), that is, of delighting, of better memory, and of brevity.
>
> It delights, it shortens, it helps you remember better:
> it is usually done in meter because it is more pleasing.[75]

Note that it is the regularly recurring pattern of long and short syllables that helps the student retain difficult material. It is worth noting that many of these poems were written not only for didactic purposes, but to entertain the clergy.[76] Morals, fables, philosophical treatises, and even biblical passages were transmitted in verse.[77] It is remarkable that often "the need to create impressive texts that can be easily absorbed by the memory, resulted . . . also in modifications of the form and the content of the scholarly and poetic materials."[78] By the twelfth century, the command of Latin had grown to such

72. Valla, *L'arte della grammatica,* ed. Casciano. I would like to thank Dr. Robert Black for bringing this book to my attention.

73. See Thompson *et al., Medieval Library,* 613.

74. "Hystorie sacre gestas ab origine mundi / Res canere et versu facili describere conor; / Quas habuere satis moses mosenque secuti / Auctores mandare prose verbisque solutis / Lege metri sed me iuvat uti carmine gratum / Auribus ut sit opus nec sit minus utile menti / Que brevitate metri que delectata canore / Firmius id teneat quanto jocundius hausit." Trans. Wright, "Leoninus, Poet and Musician," 18–19.

75. "Metra iuvant animos, comprendunt plurima paucis, / pristina commemorant et sunt ea grata legenti. // Nota: metrum valet ad tria, scilicet ad delectionem, ad memoriam firmiorem et ad brevitatem. // Delectat, breviat, retinetur firmius: istas ob causas metrum gracius esse solet." Klopsch, *Einführung in die Dichtungslehren,* 75.

76. Manitius, *Geschichte der lateinischen Literatur des Mittelalters,* vol. 3: *Vom Ausbruch des Kirchenstreites,* 739.

77. See ibid., 762–94.

78. "Das Bedürfnis, einprägsame, dem Gedächtnis leicht einzuverleibende Texte zu schaffen, führte aber auch zur formalen und inhaltlichen Modifikation der wissenschaftlichen oder dichterischen Werke." Hajdu, *Das mnemotechnische Schrifttum des Mittelalters,* 53.

an extent that, according to J. de Ghellinck, these verses were often no longer only of didactic, but also of literary value.[79] Be that as it may, it is their widespread mnemonic use that is of importance to us.

How, then, could the principles of didactic poetry have been adapted to music? Poetry can be either quantitative (metric), or qualitative (rhythmic). Quantitative poetry depends on the length or quantity of the syllable, or, more precisely, on the distinction between a long and a short syllable, with the long syllable being twice as long as the short, and it employs a regularly repeated pattern of long and short syllables (foot). When describing the length of a line, the number of feet are counted, not the number of syllables. Qualitative poetry depends on the accent or quality of the syllable, or, more precisely, on the distinction between an accented and unaccented syllable, and it employs a regular combination of stressed and unstressed syllables. The length of the line is determined by the number of syllables. The terminology might be confusing when poetry and music are compared, since in music we distinguish between "meter," that is, a regular alternation of strong and weak beats of equal duration, which thus corresponds to rhythmic or qualitative poetry, and "rhythm," that is, patterns of values of unequal length, which thus correspond to quantitative poetry.

The possible influence of quantitative poetry on modal rhythm is a much discussed topic. Opinions range from that of William Waite, who argued that the rhythmic modes of the Notre Dame School derived from the quantitative meters of ancient poetry as decribed in St. Augustine's *De musica,*[80] to the more cautious approach of Rudolf Flotzinger and Leo Treitler, who called into question the validity of quantitative meters for the twelfth and thirteenth centuries, when, in Treitler's words, "in practice poetic meter had long since become a matter of accentual rather than durational pattern."[81] The latter scholars saw the words used to describe quantitative meters as essentially a vocabulary that was at hand to describe a music that was more accentual than quantitative. Treitler shows that quantitative poetry cannot be directly translated into modal rhythm because it does not comprise the perfections, with their upbeats and downbeats, that are so characteristic of modal rhythm. Modal rhythm is further defined by consonance and dissonance treatment, voice-leading, and phrase articulation of the melody, all of which have no relevance for quanti-

79. *L'essor de la littérature latine au XIIe siècle,* 1:8.

80. *Rhythm of Twelfth-Century Polyphony,* 29–37. One of the reasons why Waite's theory is no longer considered convincing is that Augustine's *De musica* was little known in the 13th c. See Treitler, "Regarding Rhythm and Meter," and Haas, "Die Musiklehre von Garlandia bis Franco," 145–46.

81. "Regarding Meter and Rhythm," 543; and Flotzinger, "Zur Frage der Modalrhythmik." See also Ziolkowski's *Nota Bene* on the accentual performance of classical meters in the Middle Ages. I would like to thank Professor Ziolkowski for sharing with me a manuscript of the book.

tative poetry. In other words, modal rhythm comprises what we call today rhythm and meter. Quantitative poetry, however, corresponds to rhythm only. All of this is undoubtedly correct. But it should not blind us to the fact that there is one central parameter of modal rhythm that is also found in quantitative poetry: repetitive patterns in *longae* and *breves*. And, as we have seen above, it is precisely this parameter that was used for mnemonic purposes. In considering the issue of the possible relationship between quantitative meters and rhythmic modes it is first of all important to know to what extent the meters were still known and practiced in the Middle Ages.

Even though it is no doubt correct that when Latin was *spoken* in the late Middle Ages, one no longer distinguished between short and long vowels, there can be equally little doubt that literate people of the period could understand, recite, and compose metric poetry correctly. In fact, their situation might not have been so much different from ours today: every schoolchild who memorizes Ovid will learn to distinguish between short and long vowels. It is one thing to know that Latin prose no longer differentiated between long and short vowels in the late Middle Ages, but quite another to conclude from this that therefore meters could no longer have been used.

The eleventh to thirteenth centuries witnessed an enormous revival of ancient quantitative poetry. Rudolf Flotzinger has found a passage in Alexander de Villa Dei's *Doctrinale* where the six rhythmic modes are listed in a different order: "Ancient poems distinguished a variety of feet; for us it is sufficient to make a distinction into six modes: dactyl [mode], spondee, trochee, anapest, iamb, tribrach can proceed through meter."[82] Concerning the relationship of the long to the short syllable, "the syllable that is short holds one beat in which it is pronounced; you must double the length of the long."[83] For Alexander de Villa Dei there is a clear connection, identity even, between the ancient poetic meters and modern musical modes. Alexander's reference to the poetic meters is by no means isolated. Sandra Pinegar has recently transcribed a second source for Anonymous VII, which appears on the margins of Bruges 528. The author sees a clear connection between discant, modes (which he calls *manieres*), and metrical poetry: "But, because *manieres* is present in discant or diaphony of this kind, let us first see what it is that is called *manieres*. A *manieres* is whatever runs together by means of long and breve notes of sound with the measure of *tempora* according to metrical pronunciation."[84] Similarly,

82. "Distinxere pedes antiqua poemata plures. / sex partita modis satis est divisio nobis; / dactylus et spondeus, exinde trocheus, anapestus, / iambus cum tribracho possunt praecedere metro." Flotzinger, "Zur Frage der Modalrhythmik," 205.

83. "Syllaba, quae brevis est, unum tempus tenet, in quo profertur; longae spatium debes geminare." Ibid., 207.

84. "Sed quia in huiusmodi discantu vel dyaphonia consistit manieres, videndum est primo quid appellatur manieres. Manieres est quicquid per longas et breves sonorum notulas tem-

Michel Huglo has shown that the author of the anonymous treatise in Oxford, Bodleian Library, Bodley 77 identifies the metric feet of the grammarian Donatus with ligatures indicating the rhythmic modes.[85]

But more important than these references in treatises is the fact that a widespread interest in quantitative poetry can be documented. Horace's *Carmina,* where he used many quantitative meters, are preserved in at least 132 manuscripts copied in France from the late eleventh to thirteenth centuries, many with glosses.[86] Moreover, we should by no means assume that this interest was only theoretical. There was at the same time a great interest in composing poetry in quantitative meters. To quote Dag Norberg: "Throughout the entire Middle Ages, poets continued to write quantitative verses according to the model of Vergil or Sedulius, of Horace or Prudentius. . . . But, as technical ability grew, these forms [that is, lyrical forms] gained importance; and in the eleventh century several poets, such as Alphanus of Salerno, demonstrated a remarkable talent in the art of imitating Horace, Prudence, and Boethius."[87]

Jan Ziolkowski has written a fundamental study on little-known neumed classics in the Middle Ages. He describes neumed texts from the second half of the ninth through the end of the twelfth century for "nearly two dozen of Horace's *Odes* as well as for one section of the *Carmen saeculare* and for parts of two *Epodes;* for two passages in Juvenal's eighth *Satire;* for more than a dozen in six books of Lucan's *De bello civili* (alternatively, and less properly, known as the *Pharsalia*); and in two of Vergil's *Eclogues,* two in the *Georgics,* and more than two dozen in ten books of the *Aeneid.*"[88] He believes that the manuscripts served the schoolmasters and cantors to teach the boys how to recite classical verse.

Craig Wright, in his article on "Leoninus, Poet and Musician," recognized the renewed interest of twelfth-century poets in the writers of classical antiquity and identifies Leonin as a poet "who was thoroughly versed in the laws of classical metrics."[89] He speculated that, very likely, Leonin "had studied the original works of Virgil, Ovid, and Horace, since he borrows forms as well as individual phrases."[90] Yet one of the reasons he rejects a direct relationship between quantitative meters and the use of rhythmic modes is that all of Leonin's didactic poetry is written in dactylic hexameter, while the com-

poris mensuratione sub metrica prolatione concurrit." *Tractatus de organo,* trans. Pinegar, "Exploring the Margins," 232 and 238.

85. "La notation franconienne," 127–28.

86. Munk Olsen, *L'étude des auteurs classiques latins.*

87. Norberg, *An Introduction to the Study of Medieval Latin Versification,* 180.

88. Ziolkowski, *Nota bene,* Introduction, Part A.

89. "Leoninus, Poet and Musician," 29.

90. Ibid., 28.

poser Leonin uses predominantly trochees. Admittedly, dactylic hexameter is the most common meter, but the fact that Leonin used only one meter in his poetry does not mean that he did not know the others, and that he could not have had trochees in mind when he composed pieces in mode 1, or more generally, that he, and whoever used rhythmic modes, could not have thought about a possible parallel to poetic meters.

An important and, until recently, neglected kind of writing that used many quantitative meters, in addition to dactylic hexameters, is the Latin *prosimetrum.* This was not a genre in itself, but rather a way of writing that alternated sections in prose with sections of mostly metrical poetry.[91] The two most important models from late antiquity on which medieval *prosimetra* are based are Martianus Capella's *De nuptiis Philologiae et Mercuriae* (On the Marriage of Philology and Mercury), and Boethius' *De consolatione Philosophiae* (On the Consolation of Philosophy). Martianus describes the seven liberal arts in his text. Boethius engages in a dialogue with Philosophy, which provides for him in his prison cell. Both make extensive use of meters: Martianus uses fifteen different meters and Boethius twenty-nine. Boethius' *De consolatione Philosophiae* is among the texts mentioned above that were frequently neumed throughout the Middle Ages.[92]

The *prosimetrum* could be used in all genres, such as philosophical treatises, hagiography, historiography (which includes many accounts of the crusades), grammatical and letter writing, scientific and didactic writings. The most important philosophical texts were written in the twelfth century and are connected by Peter Dronke with Tours.[93] Foremost among them are Adelard of Bath's *De eodem et diverso* (On Sameness and Difference), before 1116, Bernard Silvestris's *Cosmographia* (1147), and Alan of Lille's *De planctu Naturae* (On the Complaint of Nature), ca. 1160–70. For us, the *prosimetrum* is important for two reasons. First, it is one of the major sources of quantitative poetry from the twelfth and thirteenth centuries that uses other meters in addition to dactylic hexameter. Bernhard Pabst includes tables of meters encountered in these texts and summarizes his conclusions as follows: "In prosimetric texts from the Middle Ages one encounters altogether the impressive number of fifty different lyrical meters. Of these twenty-nine are already present in *prosimetra* from late antiquity, another seven can be derived from other ancient texts, two can have been stimulated either by ancient or medieval models. . . . No fewer than nine meters were newly formed by authors of medieval *prosimetra* (mainly from known elements) . . . also this is

91. See Dronke, *Verse with Prose from Petronius to Dante*; Pabst, *Prosimetrum*; Ziolkowski, "Prosimetrum in the Classical Tradition"; Eckhardt, "Medieval Prosimetrum Genre"; and Friis-Jensen, *Saxo Grammaticus,* 29–38.

92. Ziolkowski, "Prosimetrum in the Classical Tradition," 53.

93. Dronke, *Verse with Prose,* 46.

an indication of the lively continuation of lyrical meters within the prosimetric literature."[94]

Guibert de Nogent, for example, includes in his *Gesta Francorum et aliorum Hierosolymitanorum* "about 335 lines of his own poetry in seven different quantitative metres."[95] The vast majority of *prosimetrum* writers can be located in France. Leonin was thus living in a culture passionately interested in the use of quantitative meters.

Second, the *prosimetrum* and organum are both characterized by an alternation of rhythmically free sections (in the *prosimetrum* the prose sections, in the organum the organum purum sections) with strictly rhythmicized sections (the quantitative poetry in the *prosimetrum,* and the discant sections in modal rhythm in the organum). While it would be premature to claim that organum was modelled on the *prosimetrum,* it is certainly worth pointing out that there was a literary form that shared some essential characteristics with organum. It has long been known that the alternation of styles in an organum was governed by the distinction between the syllabic and melismatic styles of plainchant: the syllabic sections of the plainchant were set in organum purum style, while the melismatic ones were set in discant style. This way the short syllabic sections were lengthened when the organal voice was added, and the already long melismatic sections did not greatly increase in size. But why did composers and performers choose to deliver one section as rhythmically free and another in strict modal rhythm? A common explanation is that only in discant style was a strict rhythm required to coordinate the two voices. The prominence of *prosimetrum,* which musicians or composers may have known from Boethius or one of the poets mentioned above, shows that the rhythmic procedures of the organum were not new. The ultimate effect of an organum might have been very similar to that of the *prosimetrum*: rhythmically free sections alternating with sections in strict quantitative meter. This would also supply us with an additional explanation for why modal rhythm was not immediately applied to organum purum.[96] (The other is, of course, that in the organum purum sections the correlation of the two voices was not difficult.)

94. "In prosimetrischen Texten des Mittelalters trifft man insgesamt auf die beeindruckende Zahl von 50 verschiedenen lyrischen Maßen. Von diesen sind 29 bereits in den spätantiken Prosimetra präsent, weitere sieben gehen auf sonstige antike Texte zurück, zwei können entweder von antiken oder mittelalterlichen Verbildern angeregt sein. . . . Nicht weniger als neun Maße wurden (großteils aus bekannten Elementen) von den Verfassern mittelalterlicher Prosimetra neu gebildet, . . . auch dies ein Zeichen für das lebendige Fortleben der lyrischen Maße innerhalb der prosimetrischen Literatur." Pabst, *Prosimetrum,* 2:1079–1127.

95. Friis-Jensen, *Saxo Grammaticus,* 33. For an edition see Guibert of Nogent, *Memoirs,* ed. Benton.

96. In a recent study, Mark Everist has applied the same idea to conductus sections *sine littera* and *cum littera.* "Reception and Recomposition"; see also "Drying Rachel's Tears."

Another argument brought forth against a possible derivation of modal rhythm from quantitative poetry is the fact that the liturgical poetry (sequences, rhymed offices, conductus, and motets) that was set to music was accentual rather than quantitative. If the quantitative meters of poetry had been transferred to music, it is argued, it would make sense to set quantitative rather than accentual poetry to music. Leonin himself wrote four moralizing poems in quantitative meter, none of which he set to music.[97] Wright therefore concludes that the system of rhythmic modes developed for purely musical reasons: "The primacy of the musical environment in this development can be seen by the fact that the rhythmic modes are first observable in liturgical forms that were not poetic, indeed that were textless except for an initial syllable (hence *sine littera*)—in the discant sections of the Graduals, Alleluias, and Responsories of the *Magnus Liber Organi.*"[98]

But if we consider the mnemonic aspect of the composition and transmission process, we will be able to argue exactly the opposite: precisely because the discant sections were textless, a mnemonic device was useful in the place of text to help remember the music. Modal rhythm imposed on melodic lines regularly recurring patterns of *longae* and *breves*. Now, if we accept that singers performed organa from memory (and there is strong evidence for this, as we have seen), what they needed to remember insofar as discant sections were concerned were a few syllables of text (most of the discant is melismatic) and the melodies of both parts. The syllables, being so few, were of little help in memorizing the melodies. My claim is that it was the function of the regularly recurring modal patterns to help the singers to memorize the pieces, that is, that modal rhythm was used for the same purposes for which mnemonic versification was used. Of course, the modal rhythm by itself did not make the melodies memorable, rather it was the combination of repetitive rhythmic patterns with the melodies, phrases, voice-leading, and use of consonance and dissonance. Similarly, in quantitative poetry the metrical patterns are often combined with rhymes. But modal rhythm with its schematic alternation of *longae* and *breves* is the most obvious mnemonic device of all because quantity is used in a similar way in didactic poetry. This is not to say that it was necessarily invented for mnemonic purposes. Treitler might well be right when he says that the principle of modal rhythm is older than the system of rhythmic modes.[99] Quantitative poetry too was not invented in order to write didactic poetry. It was only used for didactic purposes because the main characteristic of quantitative poetry, a repeated pattern of long and short syllables, made it an ideal tool for memorization. Once the modal rhythms had been established, musicians could systematize them

97. See, in particular, Wright, "Leoninus, Poet and Musician," 29–31.
98. Ibid., 30–31.
99. See Treitler, "Regarding Meter and Rhythm," 545.

into rhythmic modes, and use these, in turn, for mnemonic purposes. It is for this reason that Johannes de Garlandia and his followers were more interested in modal patterns than in separate note values.

DIVISION IN DISCANT

So far, I have argued that modal rhythm is closely related to quantitative Latin poetry, in particular didactic poetry, in that they both use quantity as a mnemonic device. But the rhythmic organization of Notre Dame polyphony also bears traces of another tool familiar from *ars memorativa* treatises, the idea of dividing a long text into short sections in order to memorize it more easily. I mentioned in chapter 2 that Quintilian advised that "correct division will be an absolute safeguard against error in the order of our speech . . . "[100] Moreover, he advocates structure as a mnemonic device: "Again, if our structure be what it should, the artistic sequence will serve to guide the memory. For just as it is easier to learn verse than prose, so it is easier to learn prose when it is artistically constructed than when it has no such organisation. If these points receive attention, it will be possible to repeat *verbatim* even such passages as gave the impression of being delivered extempore."[101]

Carruthers has shown how the ancient ideas on *divisio* were kept alive throughout the Middle Ages.[102] I have quoted the twelfth-century Parisian writer Hugh of St. Victor, who suggests memorization of texts by classifying the text either according to the divisions that are naturally inherent in it, or, if there are none, by superimposing divisions that will help to organize the material. Similarly, D. L. D'Avray has shown that thirteenth-century sermons were easily memorized because they were based on divisions and subdivisions, often combined with rhymes.[103] He cites Guibert de Tournai, who states in his *Erudimentum doctrine* that division is "used to avoid confusion and help the memory."[104] In our century Walter Ong has given much thought to how

100. "Qui recte diviserit, numquam poterit in rerum ordine errare." Quintilian, *Institutio oratoria,* ed. and trans. by Butler, 11.2.37. See also chap. 6, where I look at the structure of motets from a mnemonic point of view.

101. "Etiam quae bene composita erunt, memoriam serie sua ducent. Nam sicut facilius versus ediscimus quam prosam orationem, ita prosa vincta quam dissoluta. Sic contingit, ut etiam quae ex tempore videbantur effusa, ad verbum repetita reddantur." Ibid., 11.2.39. See also the next chapter on Quintilian's discussion of structure.

102. Carruthers, *Book of Memory,* 80–121.

103. "The really essential features of thirteenth-century mendicant sermons transmitted in Latin would seem to have been divisions and authorities, rather than *rationes.* We have already seen that model sermons were commonly transmitted in the form of divisions and authorities and little else. These dry schemata, so apparently unpromising to the historian, can show us what was thought to be the hard core of a sermon." D'Avray, *Preaching of the Friars,* 172 and 194.

104. "[U]t cesset confusio et adiuvetur memoria." Paris, BNF lat. 15451, fol. 225rb; D'Avray, *Preaching of the Friars,* 194.

Example 25. "Dominus" melisma from *Viderunt omnes*

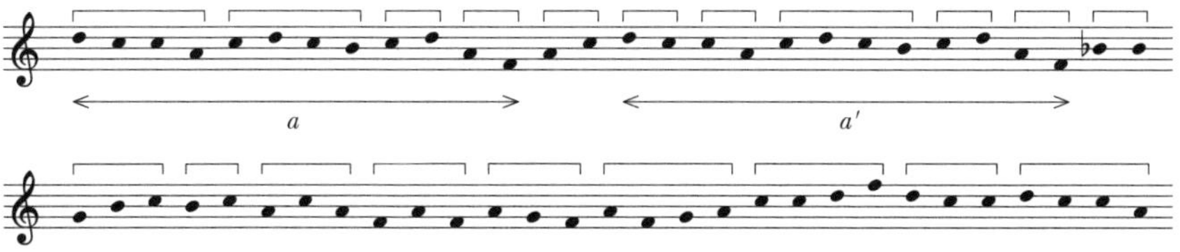

texts would have to be structured to make them memorable: "Think memorable thoughts. In a primary oral culture, to solve effectively the problem of retaining and retrieving carefully articulated thought, you have to do your thinking in mnemonic patterns, shaped for ready oral recurrence. Your thought must come into being in heavily rhythmic, balanced patterns, in repetitions or antitheses, in alliterations and assonances, in epithetic and other formulary expressions . . . "[105]

What these statements suggest, then, is the possibility that the composers imposed such a strict structure on these pieces to make them memorable, both for the composer himself in the process of composition and for the performer in the process of transmission. It is thus apparent that the rigid structure of modal rhythm and repeated patterns of *ordines* would make it easy to retain the pieces.

Let us now look at a group of settings of the "Dominus" melisma from the Christmas Day gradual *Viderunt omnes* (M1) to see how the singers might have used rigid structure and repetitive modal patterns to memorize the music. The "Dominus" melisma is fifty-seven notes long, with the first twelve notes repeated after an intervening two-note group (Example 25).[106] There are altogether fifteen settings of the "Dominus" tenor, of which I will briefly discuss three. Only one setting of the tenor (Example 26) reproduces the repetition of the first part that is naturally inherent in the tenor by ending an *ordo* in perfection 14 and repeating the duplum. In all other settings the tenor is divided artificially into *ordines* of variable length and different modal patterns. In Example 27 the tenor sings the same rhythmic pattern eleven times in mode 5. The duplum also sets up a pattern, although it is slightly modified throughout the piece (Example 28). The first two notes of the tenor *ordo* are set either against motive 1 (mm. 1–2), which occurs five times, or motive 2 (mm. 13–14), which occurs four times (Example 29).

In another *clausula* the composer chose to set the tenor in an *ordo* in mode 2

105. Ong, *Orality and Literacy*, 34.
106. The cantus firmus is taken from a thirteenth-century missal, Paris, BNF lat. 1112.

Example 26. "Dominus" tenor, W_1, fol. 21r–v, and F, fol. 99r–v

Example 27. "Dominus" tenor, W_1, no. 50, fol. 43; F, no. 26, fol. 149; and W_2, fol. 63r–v

Example 28. "Dominus" organum, W_2, fol. 63r–v, after Tischler, *Parisian Two-Part Organa,* 644–45

(continued)

Example 28 *(continued)*

Example 29. Two motives from “Dominus” organum, W_1, no. 5, fol. 43; F, no. 26, fol. 149; and W_2, fol. 63r–v

motive 1

motive 2

Example 30. "Dominus" clausula rhythm, F, no. 29, fol. 149v

Example 31. Beginning of "Dominus" clausula in mode 2, F, no. 29, fol. 149v

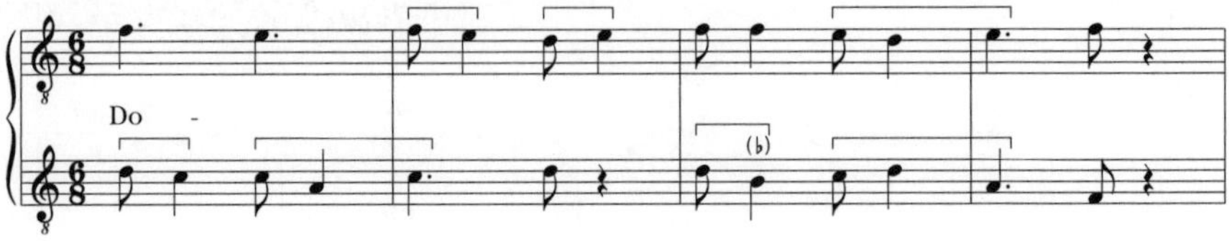

Example 32. "Dominus" clausula in mode 2, F, no. 29, fol. 149v, after Tischler, *Parisian Two-Part Organa*, 653

Example 33. "Dominus" clausula in mode 1, W_1, no. 39, fol. 47r–v, , after Tischler, *Parisian Two-Part Organa,* 653–54

that is repeated eight times (Example 30). The duplum repeats the following pattern (Example 31) with some slight variation. (For the entire *clausula* see Example 32.) Examples 33 (W_1) and 34 (F) transmit the same clausula, but in different modes: the version in W_1 is in mode 1 with *extensio modi* and the version in F in mode 2 with *extensio modi.*[107] Both versions appear equally authentic. What this, then, shows is that the modal pattern was not necessarily a fixed part of the work, but could be variable.

These examples are by no means exceptional; one could go on and on making similar comparisons. Indeed, many scholars have already commented on the use of repetitive melodic and rhythmic patterns in the Notre Dame repertory, in particular the *clausulae.* To quote Rudolf Flotzinger: "a completely unorganized, unrelated . . . upper melody is as hard to find as an unorganized tenor."[108] Just as Hugh of St. Victor organized his texts by marking off every fifth place, the composer of discant imposed a regularly

107. The term *extensio modi* refers to the interruption of the rhythmic pattern by the omission of a breve. In Example 35 we have LL at the end of the perfection instead of LBL.

108. Flotzinger, *Der Discantussatz,* 169.

Example 34. "Dominus" clausula in mode 2, F, no. 30, fol. 149v, after Tischler, *Parisian Two-Part Organa,* 653–54

recurring rhythmic pattern (mode and *ordo*)[109] on the parts. The Anonymous of St. Emmeram states: "Firstly therefore we say that mode or species is whatever runs through the requisite measure of long or short notes, and it is so named from the word regulating *(moderando),* because it divides and cuts apart, or puts together, all genera of melodies by regulating them."[110]

What we then have is a preexistent tenor that is artificially divided through

109. See, for example, Anon. IV, 22; Anon. of St. Emmeram, 197, 273; Anon. VII, 378; Johannes de Grocheio, 147.

110. "Ad primum igitur dicimus, quod modus sive species est quicquid currit per debitam mensuram longarum vel brevium notularum, et dicitur a moderando, eo quod omnia cantuum genera moderando dividat et decindat, vel componat." Anon. of St. Emmeram, ed. and trans. Yudkin, 184–85.

regular repetition of modal patterns and *ordines*. The selection of the rhythmic patterns in the tenor, in turn, determines the duplum. The singer will have placed in his mental inventory not only the chant, but also the modal patterns and *ordines* associated with that particular chant melisma. Just as the first sentence of a psalm will trigger the memory of the entire psalm for Hugh of St. Victor, the modal patterns and *ordines* will help recall the duplum, as well as the entire piece. In short, while we have no proof that Notre Dame musicians employed these methods when memorizing the music, the evidence gathered from literary history makes it likely. If they grew up using precisely these methods when learning verbal texts, it seems probable that they applied them when learning music too.

THE ROLE OF NOTATION

In this chapter, I have tried to show how organum and discant could have been transmitted orally and performed with little or no notation. And yet, Notre Dame theorists were preoccupied with developing and describing notational systems. This is what their treatises are all about. Why was writing so important to them since, clearly, oral transmission was no longer considered sufficient? The first function of writing down might have been the option of preserving the repertory. A statement by Johannes de Grocheio supports this possibility: "Just as for the grammarian the art of writing and the invention of letters were necessary to preserve the invented words given to be signed with the aid of script, so the art of writing is necessary for the musician in order to preserve the songs put together through various concords by that means."[111] Note that he does not mention the necessity of notation for either performance or composition. Preserving the music would be important for a collector. F probably falls into this category: the use of gold and azure and the presence of the fleur-de-lys on folio 1 makes it likely that it was intended for a royal patron. But preservation would also have been important for a compiler or a composer who would want to keep his particular version of a piece.[112]

The second reason for writing down the repertory is to help singers learn the new pieces. This would be particularly necessary if singers in distant centers like St. Andrews in Scotland, for which W_1 was probably copied, would want to learn the repertory. It is hard to imagine how they could have achieved this without the help of written sources or a performer trained in

111. "Sicut enim grammatico fuit ars scribendi necessaria et inventio litterarum, ut dictiones inventas et ad signandum impositas mediante scriptura reservaret, sic musico est ars scribendi necessaria, ut diversos cantus ex diversis concordantiis compositos ea mediante reservet." Ibid., 124–26.

112. For a discussion of manuscripts as collector's items see van der Werf, "Anonymous IV as Chronicler."

organum singing. On the other hand, once they had learned the repertory, they might still have sung it by heart. Or they might have used the written page to help their memory.

The written page might have triggered the memory of the melodic and rhythmic outline of the piece, a piece that the performers already knew.[113] Elias Salomonis, a French author whose treatise was written in Rome in 1274, implies this when he writes:

> [Concerning the Laity] What is more detestable, is that by scorning plainchant, which was truly ordained by angels, the holy prophets, and by blessed Gregory, [the laity] at times adopt the practices of organum, which is itself based on the practice of plainchant.
>
> And also, they scarcely deign at times to perform plainchant at its proper pace when they sing by anticipating, accelerating, retarding, and improperly phrasing the notes—from which the effect of the science of organum is achieved, because they may happen *to see the notes arranged in such a way on the page. But this [writing of notes] is done for the ornament and beauty of the notes on the page: for seeing, not for singing.* Let them know this for certain, not inquiring whether the [practices] that they see are ours, rather than God's, or proper to the art of music (of which they are ignorant). But experimenting, they sing 'meow, meow' into the air, so that a stranger may turn up and listen.[114]

The written page would simply function as a mnemonic aide for recalling both the general outline and details. In this case it is not necessarily relevant whether the performers imagined the written page or actually saw it. If they had memorized the piece once with the help of the written page, they would always use it as a mnemonic device when singing by heart. In fact, the original notation brings out the modal patterns and the division into *ordines* in a much more convincing way than modern notation. With or without the page, the singers would categorize the piece with respect to modal patterns and *ordines*.

113. Leo Treitler sketches a similar pattern for the performance of chant in Jacobsson and Treitler, "Sketching Liturgical Archetypes," 182–94.

114. "Quod execrabilius est, cantum planum, & bene ordinatum per angelos, & per sanctos prophetas, & per beatum Gregorium, deridendo, assumendo aliquoties naturam cantus scientiae organizandi, quae totaliter supra scientiam cantus plani est reperta. Et etiam vix dignantur aliquotiens pedem suum facere de cantu plano, anticipando, festinando, retardando, & male copulando punctos, ex quibus effectus scientiae organizandi completur: quia fortassis vident punctos taliter paratos. Hoc autem factum est ad decorem & honestatem positionis punctorum, & notae libri, non ad cantandum, ut videntur. Hoc sciant pro certo, non quaerentes, quae nostra sunt quae vident, nec Dei, nec debitum artis musicae, quia illam ignorant; sed speculando dicentes in aere miau minau, ut appareat & audiat hospes." Elias Salomonis, *Scientia artis musicae,* 17; trans. in McGee, *Sound of Medieval Song,* 26. I would like to thank Bruce Holsinger for connecting this passage with my hypothesis in his book *Music, Body, and Desire in Medieval Literature and Culture,* 170–71, 173.

In sum, even though Notre Dame polyphony was transmitted in writing, it was composed in a culture that was to a considerable extent still oral. Oral and written transmission coexisted and interacted. In trying to establish how oral transmission of a repertory as complex as Notre Dame polyphony could have been achieved, we have seen that organa were composed from *colores* or formulas like the ones described in the Vatican organum treatise, which elaborate a note-against-note framework. Every composer/performer/scribe made his own redaction of the piece. Thus, it makes little sense to concentrate on Leonin and Perotin as creators of polyphony. Rather, we can assume that there were many highly trained *organistae* in Paris who were able to seduce the congregation with their singing, as described by John of Salisbury.

Second, I suggest that modal theory shares a number of characteristics with mnemotechnics. We have seen that modal rhythm and didactic quantitative poetry rely on the same method for memorizing the material: repetitive patterns of *longae* and *breves*.

Third, the use of *divisio* is another trait that made its way from *ars memorativa* treatises to Notre Dame polyphony. Writing was necessary to preserve the repertory, to make it available in distant places, and to help the memory in the process of performance. And yet, modal notation was so ambiguous that it could do no more than trigger the memory of how the piece was supposed to be performed. The methods outlined in this chapter helped the singers memorize the huge repertory.

6

Visualization and the Composition of Polyphonic Music

This chapter is concerned with the impact of the art of memory on polyphonic music that was not improvised but written down, and more specifically with pieces that would not have come into existence without mensural notation. These pieces had a composer in the modern sense of the term, that is, they were put together by someone who conceived his music not only as something to be *heard,* but also as something to be *seen.*

Before we turn to a discussion of the music, it will be useful to summarize the most salient points concerning the importance of visualization for memorization and composition of texts in literature. There is general agreement among writers in antiquity and the Middle Ages that the best way to commit material to memory is by means of associating it with visual images placed in a storehouse. In Mary Carruthers's words, "there simply is no classical or Hebrew or medieval tradition regarding an 'ear of the mind' equivalent to that of the 'eye of the mind.'"[1] Cicero says this clearly in his *De oratore* when he argues that the sight is "the keenest of all of our senses."[2] This argument is further developed in the high Middle Ages by Thomas Aquinas, who states "that the sense of sight has a special dignity; it is more spiritual and more subtle than any other sense."[3] Similarly, Thomas Bradwardine reiterates the primacy of the visual image for memory: "Indeed memory is most powerfully affected by sensory impression, most

1. Carruthers, *Book of Memory,* 27.

2. *De oratore,* ed. and trans. Sutton and Rackham, 2.357.

3. Aquinas, *Commentary on Aristotle's De anima,* trans. Foster and Humphries, Lectio 14 in bk. II, par. 417.

strongly by vision; wherefore something occurs in memory as it customarily occurs in seeing."[4]

In recent years, psychologists have confirmed the efficacy of ancient and medieval memory techniques. Stephen Kosslyn has shown that the ability to visualize is central to mental planning in any field, be it chess, a game of basketball, or musical composition.[5] This ability to plan is closely linked to a highly developed visio-spatial long-term memory. A chess master is able to take one look at a chess game and then reconstruct the position of each player.[6] He is not able to do this because he has a better memory than non-chess players, but because he has played chess for hours and hours, which enables him to do what psychologists refer to as "chunking." In "chunking" one combines a number of separate items into a group.[7] For example, a four-year old child would see the letters H O U S E as separate items to be remembered, while an adult would retrieve the word "house" from long-term memory. Thus, "chunking" allows one to increase drastically the amount of information stored in long-term memory.[8]

We have seen in the previous chapter that musicians certainly were "chunking" when they memorized consonances, interval progressions, and formulas. But did they visualize as they composed? We know that they imagined the intervals on the hand or on the staff, but could they also have visualized what they were composing on the staff?

I would like to suggest that there are two areas where visualization might have played an important role. First, the ability to visualize the staff allowed composers to work out polyphonic pieces in the mind without a wax tablet or parchment. And second, polyphonic compositions were sung by heart. Thus they needed to be clearly structured so that they could be remembered. I believe that periodic articulation[9] might have been so popular because it

4. "Memoria vero maxime causatur a sensu, maxime quoque a visu, quare in memoria accidit sicut in visu accidere consuevit." Thomas Bradwardine, "De memoria artificialis," trans. Carruthers from Fitzwilliam Museum, Cambridge, MS McClean 169, in *Book of Memory,* 281.

5. Kosslyn, *Image and Mind*; *Ghosts in the Mind's Machine*; *Image and Brain*; see also his "Visual Mental Imagery." Note, however, that even though according to one study, 97% of the members of Mensa, a group of people who perform exceptionally well on IQ tests, "reported experiencing vivid imagery" (Kosslyn, *Ghosts in the Mind's Machine,* 195), there are significant differences in people's ability to visualize.

6. Stefan Zweig, in his *Schachnovelle,* describes a chess player in Nazi Austria, imprisoned over a long time period, who spent all his time practicing chess. When he left he was able to outdo every chess master thanks to visual planning.

7. See, for example, Howe, *Introduction to the Psychology of Memory,* 45.

8. See also Baddeley, *Working Memory,* 128 ff.

9. This term was suggested by Margaret Bent instead of Ludwig's term "isorhythm," which covers only some if the procedures encountered in 14th- and 15th-c. motets.

allowed one to structure and visualize long compositions in the mind. I will discuss each of these points in turn.

VISUALIZATION OF POLYPHONIC PIECES ON THE STAFF

Jacques Handschin was the first to suggest that composers conceived all parts simultaneously and that Machaut must have worked out his three-part compositions in his mind.[10] In the 1980s and 1990s these ideas were taken up again in fundamental studies by Daniel Leech-Wilkinson on compositions by Vitry and Machaut.[11] He cast doubt on the widespread idea that composers perceived "polyphony principally in a single horizontal dimension, remaining largely insensitive to vertical coincidences."[12] Most recently, Jessie Ann Owens's study on the working methods of composers leaves little doubt that sixteenth-century composers also worked out polyphonic music in their minds and did not use scores in order to compose.[13] She suggests instead that composers worked in segments: "sometimes they worked first with two 'essential' voices and added a third, while at other times the grid of essential voices added shifted from phrase to phrase."[14]

In a more extreme position, Rob Wegman has claimed that little or no writing was involved in the instruction of counterpoint, that mensural theory was taught at the university rather than in choir schools,[15] and that "notation neither represented nor embodied the 'work,' but served the purely utilitarian purpose of providing instructions for performing counterpoint."[16] He argues that "simultaneous conception must have existed, yet by definition it was heard (mentally or actually), not visualized."[17]

For us, who are totally dependent on scores, it seems hard to understand how music could have been conceived in the mind. How could composers keep track of simultaneities without actually writing the whole composition down in score? Leech-Wilkinson's hypothesis of some kind of "model-*talea*" grid that would include pitches, rhythms, and text is most appealing and would explain how the different parts were aligned correctly.[18] Owens is cer-

10. "Was brachte die Notre Dame-Schule Neues?" 553; "Eine wenig beachtete Stilrichtung," 64; "Zur Frage der melodischen Paraphrasierung," 204. See also chap. 1.

11. Leech-Wilkinson, "Machaut's *Rose, Lis*"; *Machaut's Mass*; *Compositional Techniques in the Four-Part Isorhythmic Motets*; "*Le Voir Dit* and *La Messe de Nostre Dame*"; "*Le Voir Dit:* A Reconstruction."

12. Leech-Wilkinson, "Machaut's *Rose, Lis,*" 10. Similarly, Kevin Moll argues that composers combined simultaneity and successivity in "Structural Determinants in Polyphony," 184–85.

13. Owens, *Composers at Work.* See also her "Milan Partbooks."

14. Owens, *Composers at Work,* 196.

15. See chap. 4, where I cite ample evidence that this claim is incorrect.

16. Wegman, "From Maker to Composer," 451.

17. Ibid. Unfortunately, Wegman provides little evidence in support of his claim.

18. Leech-Wilkinson, *Compositional Techniques,* 60–61, 113, 140–41, and 154. Hans Heinrich Eggebrecht makes a similar suggestion in his "Machauts Motette Nr. 9."

tainly correct in suggesting that composers were able to read polyphonic music in separate parts, and that they kept track of where they were by counting tactus units and adding lines to separate segments. Yet this seems like an impractical system for composition, and one in which the composer could easily make mistakes. Owens discovered one such mistake in Cipriano de Rore's *Miserere mei,* where the number of breves was miscounted.[19] In short, while all of this goes a long way toward explaining how composers worked, we still do not know exactly how they were able to conceive these simultaneities. I suggest that we look at the English sight treatises to see if the technique they describe of visualizing the chant with one or two added parts could have been adapted for composition.

Pseudo-Chilston

Sight treatises instruct beginning musicians how to sing polyphony with only plainchant in front of them. One of the most detailed descriptions is found in the manuscript London, British Library, Lansdowne 763, fols. 113v–116v, which was copied by John Wylde in the middle of the fifteenth century.[20] Wylde was a precentor of the monastery of the Holy Cross at Waltham, and copied the treatise together with a number of other treatises to help train "singers or makers [which refers to composers] or teachers."[21] The very tools that helped the students become good singers thus also made them good composers, an important point we shall return to later.

The first part of the treatise is devoted to English discant, and the second to faburden, which is called the "least of sights," that is, the easiest version of discant. The rules for discant are not very different from those of other counterpoint treatises. English discant is always for two voices,[22] and is only concerned with note-against-note counterpoint. The discant or counterpoint (the terms are used interchangeably here) can be either below or above the cantus firmus.

Pseudo-Chilston lists nine consonant intervals (he calls them "accords"): 1, 3, 5, 6, 8, 10, 12, 13, and 15. He prohibits parallel perfect intervals and diminished fifths and octaves. Contrary motion is recommended, especially

19. Owens, "Milan Partbooks," 292–93.

20. For an edition see Bukofzer, *Geschichte des englischen Diskants,* 53–146, and Georgiades, *Englische Diskanttraktate,* 23–27. All of my references are to sentence numbers in the Georgiades edition. There is no evidence that Chilston wrote the treatise himself. See A. Hughes, "Pseudo-Chilston." For a complete list of discant treatises see Sanders, "Discant."

21. This quotation is from Lyonel Power (see also p. 207 below). See his discant treatise, which directly precedes our treatise (fols. 105v–113) and is specifically addressed to all of the above. BL Lansdowne MS 763, fol. 105v.

22. The only theorist who mentions discant for more than two voices is Pseudo-Tunstede (CS 4:294, also 3:360b), who wrote in 1351. See below, p. 205.

Example 35. Pseudo-Chilston, mene sight

(a) as visualized

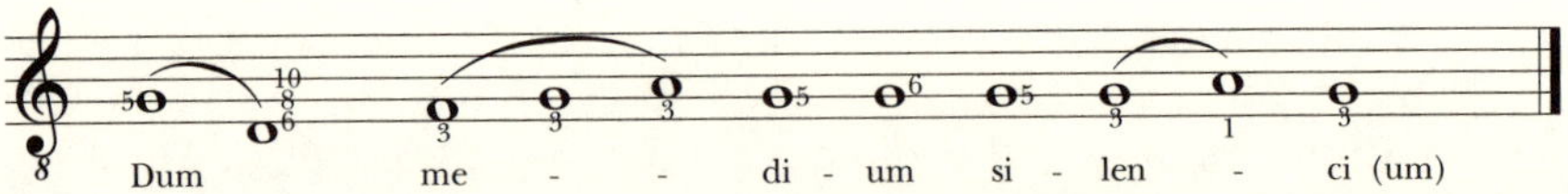

(b) in voice

when he discusses the voice-leading of the counter (the meaning of this term will be explained shortly). He recommends three, four, or five parallel imperfect consonances and alternation of perfect and imperfect consonances. So far everything is familiar.

However, in the next section he comes to two important points that distinguish English discant treatises from Continental counterpoint treatises and require detailed explanation:

1. The counterpoint can be added in any of five voice ranges or degrees: the quatreble, treble, mene, countertenor or countergymel, and counter. Depending on the range, it is either above or below the cantus firmus.

2. Discant treatises describe a system of sights where the consonant intervals of the counterpoint are visualized on the staff on which plainchant is notated. Since the intervals of the added voice are often too large to be added on the same staff as the chant without the use of ledger lines, the visualized pitch is transposed. The interval of transposition depends on the voice range. The possible voice ranges are called "sights," since they are visualized on the staff.

Let us start with a discussion of the mene sight. The mene is always transposed up a fifth. Pseudo-Chilston tells us where the mene is "in voice," that is, in real sound (Example 35b), and where it is visualized or written (Example 35a): "(5) The Mene beginneth in a fifth above the plainsong in voice and with the plainsong in Sight." Possible consonances are the unison, third, fifth, sixth, and octave. Example 35a shows that Pseudo-Chilston always writes the numbers of the intervals as they sound, that is, when he wants the singer to sing a sixth above he writes the number 6, but he puts the numbers on the spaces or lines on which they are visualized. The mene must always begin and end in voice with a fifth above the chant, which means that the singer

TABLE 2. Sights in Pseudo-Chilston

Voice and transposition	*Begins*	*Ends*	*Consonances**
Mene (up a 5th)	5 . . .	3 –5	1 3 5 6 8 (10)
Treble (up an 8va)	8 . . .	6 –8	(1) (3) 5 6 8 10 12 (13) (15)
Quatreble (up a 12th)	12	10 –12	8 10 12 13 15
Countertenor	5	(3) –5	–8 –6 –5 –3 1 3 5 6 8
Counter (down a 5th or 8va)	–8	–6 –8	–1 –3 –5 –6 –8 –10 –12 –13 –15
	1	–3 –1	
		–10 –12	
		–13 –15	

*A minus sign indicates consonances below the chant note.

visualizes a unison with the chant. And while the number 5 is put on the same line as the g of the chant, in actual performance it will become a d . When the chant descends, the last fifth should be preceded by a third above, which is notated by the number 3 a third below the chant, but, when transposed up a fifth, actually sounds in voice a third above the chant. In Example 35, the f in the chant has a 3 written on the space of the d below, but in actual sound the singer will sing the a above. Similarly, a sixth in voice is notated as a 6 a step above the chant, but sounds as a sixth. For a summary of all possible consonances in the mene, see Table 2.[23]

The treble singer always has to transpose the visualized pitch up an octave. He will begin and end with the octave, and the penultimate should be a sixth when the chant is descending. Example 36 shows that the treble singer visualizes the number 3 on the line of e, a sixth below the c . But in voice he transposes the e up an octave to e , a third above the c of the chant. The advantage of thinking in sights becomes particularly apparent in the second part of Example 36a, where no ledger lines are needed when the counterpoint is visualized, but when the counterpoint is notated as it sounds (Example 36b), four ledger lines must be added. See Table 2 for a summary of allowed consonances in the treble.[24]

The interval of transposition for the quatreble singer is a twelfth up, just as he will begin and end with a twelfth. When the chant descends, the penultimate should be a tenth. A second above in sight will become a thirteenth

23. The tenth is used in the music example, but not listed in the text.

24. The consonances in parentheses are also possible, although not mentioned in the text. Most occur in the music examples.

Example 36. Pseudo-Chilston, treble sight

(a) as visualized

(b) in voice

Example 37. Pseudo-Chilston, quatreble sight

(a) as visualized

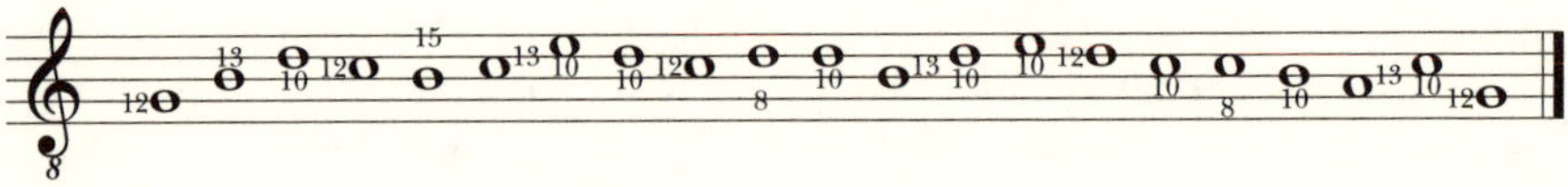

(b) in voice

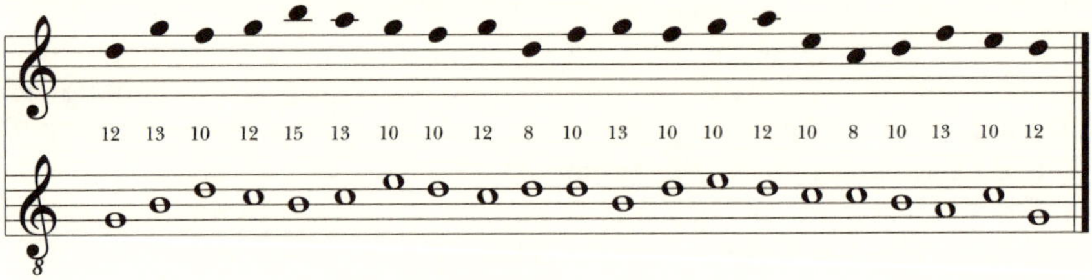

in voice, a third below in sight a tenth in voice, etc. Unfortunately, Pseudo-Chilston has not written in a counterpoint to the chant, but I have included a posssible counterpoint in Example 37a as it is visualized, and in Example 37b as it sounds. Possible consonances are summarized in Table 2. The quatreble is the highest voice and should be sung by a child, while the mene should be sung by men.

The countertenor is the only part that is not transposed, in other words, the visualized tone is the same as the one actually sung. The consonances above the chant are the same as those of the mene, but here in addition Pseudo-Chilston also lists the third, fifth, sixth, and octave below the chant. If the cantus firmus is high, the countertenor will sing below, if the cantus firmus is low, it will sing above it. The countertenor begins and ends with the fifth above the chant, as does the mene. The penultimate is not listed, but should probably be a third as it is for the mene. Since the range is the same as that of the tenor, it is sung by men. See Table 2 for a summary of possible consonances of the countertenor.[25]

In the last sentence of section 2 on the countertenor, Pseudo-Chilston mentions that the countergymel begins and ends with a unison. Georgiades suggested that countergymel refers to a countertenor that is independent of the mene in that it moves both below and above the tenor.[26] The consonances would remain the same.

The counter is the lowest part and Pseudo-Chilston stresses its similarity to the mene in that they share the same consonances. However, while the consonances of the mene are above the chant and the singer has to transpose everything up a fifth, those of the counter are below the chant and the singer has to transpose everything down a fifth. If the chant begins high, the counter will visualize a fourth below the chant, but actually sing an octave below. If the chant begins low, the counter will visualize a fifth below the chant but sing a unison in voice. Likewise, the visualized third above the chant becomes a third below, etc. The range of the counter is much larger than that of any other part. If the chant lies high, the counter may sing up to a fifteenth below. For the thirteenth and fifteenth "there is no sight beneath the plainsong within 4 rules and spaces that will serve it"; in other words, if one wants to avoid ledger lines, one has to transpose down not a fifth, but a twelfth. Pseudo-Chilston's instructions for the change of sight are as follows: the cantus firmus has c (C *sol fa ut*), the counter wants to sing the F a twelfth below in voice, so you think of c and c as unison, and then the sung thirteenth is visualized as a second, the sung fifteenth as a fourth. What our author is describing, in fact, corresponds to a quatreble below the chant. In other words, the counter is a true bass part that is essential for the harmony, while the countertenor functions only as a bass when it goes below the tenor. For allowable consonances in the counter see Table 2.

I have said earlier that English theorists, with one exception, describe only discant for two parts. Only Pseudo-Tunstede acknowledges in 1351: "Nevertheless, as long as you are discanting beneath the plainchant, no one may discant above, unless he is previously acquainted with the pitch-levels of the lower voices, because all of the upper voices must make consonance with the lowest."[27] This means that good singers, who were able to keep track of what the other two voices did, were able to sing discant for three parts almost one

25. The third is not mentioned in the text, but seems the obvious choice for the penultimate as it was in the mene.

26. *Englische Diskanttraktate,* 42.

27. "Tamen dummodo discantaveritis sub plano cantu, nullus potest discantare supra, nisi fuerit expertus de gravium vocum sedibus, quia omnes superiores voces ad graviorem vocem habent reddere concordantiam . . . " *Quatuor principalia musice,* CS, 4:194; trans. Scott, "Beginnings of Fauxbourdon," 347.

hundred years before Pseudo-Chilston's treatise was written down. Similarly, most of English discant preserved is also for three parts. Richard Crocker and Sachs both see three-part counterpoint as an extension of the two-part frame, which remains largely intact throughout the Middle Ages and Renaissance. The added voice merely functions as a filler.[28] In other words, the two-part structure described by Pseudo-Chilston could well have been a first step in the training of the singers and was later enlarged to include a third part. When singing discant for three parts, the counter singer had the most difficult job in that he had to sing not only consonant intervals with the plainchant in the middle, but also to avoid fourths, which were permitted between the top two parts.

Faburden

Let us now turn to the last section of the treatise, entitled "The sight of faburden with his accords [intervals]." As we shall see, it is nothing else but a simplified version of discant (Pseudo-Chilston calls it the "least," that is simplest, of sights) and it might well derive from discant.[29] But the instructions are difficult and have caused much controversy and misunderstanding. The faburden is the lowest part, and the only one that requires instruction, since it does not always duplicate the plainsong. Pseudo-Chilston is much less concerned with the middle part, the mene (which is the plainsong), and the treble, the top voice.

The question on which scholars have disagreed is whether the chant is transposed up a fifth and the faburden sung at the sighted pitch, as Ann Scott claims, or whether the chant is sung as written and the faburden is transposed down a fifth, as Brian Trowell claims. Example 38a (the chant is taken from Example 35, earlier in the manuscript) shows the latter solution with an untransposed chant, while in Example 38b the chant is transposed up a fifth for the mene and up an octave for the treble. Pseudo-Chilston's instructions are ambiguous and can be read either way, but the following points suggest that Scott's solution, as in Example 38b, is the correct one: first, as she has shown, the chant is usually transposed up a fifth in English music of the period. Second, in this very treatise, Pseudo-Chilston recommends that the mene be transposed up a fifth and the treble up an octave, just as in Example 38b. On the other hand, it is not common to transpose the treble up a fourth, which would be the case if the chant were sung at pitch.[30] Third, if the faburden were to be transposed down a fifth, when the plainsong lies low (see above), the faburdener would have to sing the D below G (Γ *ut*),

28. Crocker, "Discant, Counterpoint, and Harmony," and Sachs, *Der Contrapunctus,* 123.
29. See Strohm, *Rise of European Music,* 208.
30. See also ibid., 208–9.

Example 38. Faburden

(a) According to Trowell

(b) According to Scott

that is, beyond the available gamut. Trowell himself points out that these tones occur rarely in English music before the Eton manuscript of the late fifteenth century.[31] Clearly, the hexachord system did not include lower tones, because they were not thought to be part of the normal voice range. So why should they suddenly be used in faburden?

In sum, faburden is a simplified version of discant. In both the mene is transposed up a fifth and the treble up an octave. In faburden the singers of the mene and treble required no special training—they merely sing the chant at a higher pitch. In fact, when boys sang chant, they naturally transposed it up an octave as the treble singers did. The only singer who had to pay attention was the faburdener. He had to remember to begin and end in sighted unison with the chant and otherwise proceed in parallel thirds in sight a third above the chant, in voice a third below the chant.

Improvisation, Composition, and Memory

It is generally agreed that in English discant one should not draw a sharp line between performance and composition. The techniques described in these treatises could result in performance, and the result of some of these performances could be written down. This is, of course, the main reason why Lyonel Power addresses "singers or makers or techers."

What has, perhaps, not been stressed enough is that these treatises were also heavily influenced by the art of memory. This influence can be discerned in two areas: first, as we have seen in chapter 4, the examples in these treatises were also memorized by the students. We have seen that texts that are repetitive and list every single consonant interval rather than general rules were meant to be learned by heart.

31. Trowell, "Faburden and Fauxbourdon," 51.

But there is another area where the *ars memorativa* has had an impact on compositional process in music that has not been explored. In the Middle Ages, a person with a well-trained memory was able to compose complex texts entirely in the mind. The most famous example is St. Thomas Aquinas who, contemporary sources claim, seems to have composed the entire *Summa theologica* in his mind and "dictated it from memory, with the aid at most of a few written notes, and there is no reason to disbelieve them."[32] There were two qualities that allowed him to do this: first, he had a huge inventory of texts stored in his mind that functioned like a mental library. Second, he was able to structure his thoughts and arguments in his mind in such a way that he could recall or dictate them easily. The method he applied to the organization of his thoughts was the same as that used to memorize long texts.

I have discussed in chapter 3 how the ancient and medieval technique of memorizing a text involved dividing the text into sections, devising individual "images" for each section, and locating these symbols in a reusable grid of "places." The grid of places fixed the temporal order in which the images would be recalled, and each image helped to bring to mind the section of the text with which it had been associated. Now, it is important to understand that this technique was not only used for memorization, but also for the composition of texts. The writer would visualize the page while composing, just as if it were parchment. We have seen that in music the staff functioned precisely like a background grid on which the notes could be placed as "images."

Pseudo-Chilston's treatise is for beginners, yet he expects his students to visualize on the staff the consonant intervals for the entire piece. In other words, the student sees in his mind's eye his whole counterpoint with the help of sights before or while he performs it or writes it down. These visualizations often involve transpositions that appear cumbersome to us, yet they seem to have been considered easy for beginning students in the fourteenth century. Now, if beginners were able to visualize two-part counterpoint, it seems reasonable to assume that accomplished composers could visualize entire polyphonic compositions, even complex ones such as isorhythmic motets. What I am suggesting, then, is that composers of more complex polyphonic music could similarly have visualized their note-against-note structures. We have no way of knowing exactly how this visualization worked. Perhaps the composer would imagine all parts on the same staff, one after another, but always keeping track of the consonant intervals.

That there was a close connection between English discant and the system of sights can be further supported by the term Lyonel Power uses to describe counterpoint: "But who wil kunne this Gamme [the entire gamut] wel and ymaginacions [= counterpoint] therof and of his acordis and sette his

32. Carruthers, *Book of Memory*, 5. This is discussed further below.

perfite acordis with his imperfite acordis, as I have rehersid in this tretise afore, he may not faile of his Countirpoint in short tyme. Quod Lyonel Power."[33] "Ymaginacions" implies visualization and working out in the mind. In fact, the characteristic verb "imaginare" is found even earlier to describe the visualized tone in the *Compendium discantus* (ascribed to Franco, but probably later).[34] Similarly, the Italian theorist Guilielmus Monachus refers to the eyes when he says "Note, that in order to have perfect visual perception of consonances *(ad habendam perfectam perceptionem consonantiarum ocularum)*,[35] note that the unison is read as an octave, the low third is read as a high sixth, and the high sixth is read as a tenth, and the low fourth itself is read as a high fifth, and the high fifth itself is sometimes read as a twelfth, and the sixth is sometimes read as a low third and the low octave is read as a unison."[36]

Even though the most detailed descriptions of the system of sights are by English theorists, the practice was also known on the Continent. John Hothby discusses "sighted discant,"[37] as do Ramis,[38] Burtius, and Giovanni del Lago,[39] in addition to Guilielmus. I think it is entirely possible that if visualization was considered an easy tool for teaching beginners how to sing and compose, it was used by accomplished composers to work out whole compositions in the mind.[40]

33. Georgiades, *Englische Diskanttraktate,* 23.

34. Richard Crocker first called attention to this passage in "Discant, Counterpoint, and Harmony," 8: "And note that when you wish to ascend above the diapason (octave), you will imagine ('imaginabinis') yourself to be in unison with the tenor . . . " See also my discussion of "imaginare" below.

35. Manfred Bukofzer was the first to point out that this phrase refers to sights, in *Geschichte des englischen Diskants,* 63.

36. "Nota quod ad habendam perfectam perfectionem [*recte* perceptionem] consonantiarum ocularem, nota quod unisonus accipitur pro octava, tertia bassa accipitur pro sexta alta, tertia alta accipitur pro decima, et ipsa quarta bassa accipitur pro quinta alta, et ipsa quinta alta aliquotiens accipitur pro duodecima, et ipsa sexta aliquotiens accipitur pro tertia bassa, et ipsa octava bassa accipitur pro unisono." Guilielmus Monachus, *De preceptis artis musicae,* ed. Seay, 35. My thanks to Leofranc Holford-Strevens for suggesting the emendation.

37. "Sed quoniam per anglicos iste modus canendi vocatur discantus visibilis, modum infra quatuor lineas illum videre docebo"; John Hothby, *Regule . . . supra contrapunctum,* in *De arte contrapuncti,* ed. Reaney, 102.

38. "Unde si vir cum puero psallat, in unisono videntur, et tamen sunt in octava." Bartolomeus Ramis de Pareia, *Musica practica,* ed. Wolf, 63.

39. Nicolaus Burtius, *Florum libellus,* ed. Massera (Florence, 1975), bk. 2, chap. 6, "De contrapuncto practicorum qui ultramontanis et maxime gallicis est in usu"; *Musices opusculum,* trans. Miller, 87. Giovanni del Lago, *Breve introduttione di musica misurata* (Venice, 1540), [35]: "Seguita un'altra regola del contrapunto ad videndum." On p. [36] he says "Et se questo tale modo di fare il contrapunto si dimanda ad videndum, perché non potete preterire la Quarta linea del canto fermo con l'occhio, & et questo è nominato da li pratici ad videndum." Thanks to Bonnie Blackburn for this reference.

40. Even though theorists who describe singing *super librum* do not explicitly mention sights, the technique must have been similar: the singer visualizes the chant.

In the absence of scores, with their strict visual alignment, we do not really know how composers managed to create correct counterpoint. But, as I said earlier, there seems to be *no* evidence that they worked out entire compositions in writing; on the other hand, the practice of improvising polyphony above a single notated chant line gives at least some suggestion of how counterpoint might have been arrived at and controlled in the imagination, or in a combination of real and imaginary writing.

If my hypothesis is correct it means that visualized notation was part of music improvisation and composition, and it would contradict Rob Wegman's recent claim that little or no writing was involved in the instruction of counterpoint. Rather, it seems that notation, either real or imagined, was part of the most basic instruction and might have been used in pieces ranging from simple discant to complex motets with periodic articulation. This is not to say that there was no polyphonic singing without visualization. But it seems that the majority of church musicians learned notation. The question is now how these skills were applied to more complex music.

ISORHYTHMIC MOTETS AND THE ART OF MEMORY

The Problem of Isorhythmic Motets

Friedrich Ludwig discovered what he called isorhythm at the beginning of the last century.[41] He included detailed analyses of the majority of isorhythmic motets both in his editions (for example, in his Machaut edition the *color* and *talea* are always clearly indicated),[42] and in his Nachlass. But, as in other areas, he concentrated on describing what he found, rather than on addressing the question of why composers were interested in organizing their compositions in this particular fashion.

Much has been written on how these structures evolved gradually from thirteenth-century *clausulae.* First and foremost, a number of scholars have shown that the term "isorhythm," Ludwig's invention, does not really cover adequately the procedures encountered in fourteenth- and fifteenth-century motets.[43] It has been suggested that terms such as "periodic articulation" might be more appropriate. Several scholars have seen a parallel between isorhythmic motets and Gothic cathedrals,[44] and have above all done detailed analytical work, often concentrating on number symbolism.[45] For my

41. "Die 50 Beispiele Coussemakers"; and *Repertorium organorum,* 444–45.

42. Machaut, *Musikalische Werke,* ed. Ludwig, vol. 3.

43. See in particular Bent, "Isorhythm," and Kügle, "Isorhythmie," 1219.

44. See in particular Christopher Page's perceptive discussion of what he calls "cathedralism" in his *Discarding Images.*

45. The most important is Eggebrecht, "Machauts Motette Nr. 9"; see also Bent, "Deception, Exegesis and Sounding Number."

purposes, I would like to single out two studies: in an important article Hans Heinrich Eggebrecht argued that isorhythm is a structural necessity for the composer: "die Frage . . . muß lauten, ob sie (die Struktur) kompositorisch notwendig ist."[46] He went on to explain in fascinating detail how the tenor determined the structure and harmonic outline of the entire motet. More recently, Daniel Leech-Wilkinson has undertaken a fundamental study of compositional techniques in Vitry's and Machaut's four-part isorhythmic motets.[47] Through a careful analysis of the pieces he was able to demonstrate step by step how composers went about constructing these pieces. Both of these studies have not taken into consideration the art of memory.

Isorhythmic Motets as Finished Products. Isorhythmic motets are compositions in the modern sense of the word in that the composer fixes most details of pitch and rhythm in writing. Ideally, a performer cannot suddenly replace, say, two breves with three semibreves, or add a flourish at the beginning or the end without jeopardizing the intended structure of the composition.[48]

The writing down of a text has far-reaching consequences, some of which I have already addressed in chapter 2 when I discussed Jack Goody's contribution to this subject.[49] Once something has been written down, it can be reflected upon and reviewed, allowing the organization of the material in a new way, by rearranging and manipulating it. While Adam Parry had already established that writing enabled the poet "to compose a long but coherent work without immediate dependence on the vagaries of his audience,"[50] Goody went a step further and argued that "writing effectively led to a new 'tradition,' involving a new mode of transmission and possibly of creation, modifying and developing both form and content."[51] Writing is a cultural tool that allows a revolution in "relation to the internal organization of cognition and memory."[52] What this implies is that the introduction of writing will result in new and different kinds of texts.[53] In addition, Goody observed that one of the early consequences of writing was the invention of word and number

46. Eggebrecht, "Machauts Motette Nr. 9," 285.

47. Leech-Wilkinson, *Compositional Techniques.*

48. There are, however, many motets with scribal errors in the manuscript or for which various versions exist. But this need not contradict the hypothesis that the composer wished to create a piece where every pitch and note value mattered.

49. See in particular the discussion of Goody's *Logic of Writing* and *Interface between the Written and the Oral.*

50. Parry, "Have We Homer's Iliad?" 216.

51. Goody, *Interface,* 100.

52. Ibid., 186.

53. Jocelyn Penny Small gives the example of ancient historians, whose oral working methods did not allow them "to dissect in memory contradictory variants into separate elements in order to produce a single, more logical version." When one is able to access conflicting versions

games, which would have been unimaginable without writing.[54] And finally and perhaps most importantly, a composer or author who writes something wants it to be preserved intact. He will be able to distinguish the correct from the incorrect version of his piece. Many of his compositional goals will not be achieved if the text is corrupted. He will thus develop a sense of ownership.

Motets from the late thirteenth century exhibit all of the characteristics associated with written composition. While earlier motets were constantly recomposed and there was no such thing as a final version of a piece, in the later thirteenth century, to quote Ernest Sanders, "this communal aspect of art music gave way to a situation where individual compositions were no longer subject to remodeling; each composition was a finished product."[55] The most important new genre that came to dominate music of the fourteenth and early fifteenth centuries is the motet with periodic articulation, which makes use of all kinds of techniques that would have been impossible without writing, the most important of which are tenor manipulations with diminution and retrograde motion. This is a product of a written culture, if there ever was one. The invention of the isorhythmic motet goes hand in hand with the development of Ars nova notation. As Reinhard Strohm has observed: "A work in this notation could now assume an individualized and fixed structure, making it transparent how the composer had manipulated the constraints of the system. This was 'composition' proper, not just 'style'—a minstrel's performance could have style."[56]

Isorhythmic Motets as Sung by Heart. Even though these pieces were transmitted in writing, there is ample evidence from a number of different angles that strongly suggests that they were sung by heart. First, the late thirteenth-century composer Adam de la Halle wrote a motet entitled *Entre Adan et Hanikiel / Chiés bien seans / Aptatur,* where he describes four singers (Adan, [that is, Adam], Hanikiel, Hancard, and Gautelot) who sing and make hockets "tous sans livre," that is, they sing by heart.[57] Second, support for singing by heart can also be gathered from the manuscripts themselves: for example, in Machaut's motet *Tu qui gregem tuum ducis / Plange regni respublica /*

---

either written in the mind or on parchment, a new kind of argumentation is possible. See Small, *Wax Tablets of the Mind,* 185–88.

54. Goody, *Interface,* 197.

55. Sanders, "Motet." That is not to say that there may not be different versions of some motets.

56. Strohm, "Close of the Middle Ages," 270–71.

57. Adam de la Halle, *Œuvres complètes,* ed. Badel, 202–4. Of course, one could argue that he mentions singing by heart because it was so unusual. But I believe it is more likely that he mentions it because he was proud to sing the motets by heart even though they were known to be difficult and elaborate.

Tenor: Apprehende arma et scutum et exurge (M22)[58] *talea* IV and *color* 3 of the tenor are notated in two manuscripts (Paris, BNF fr. 1584, fols. ii^{c} ij.xv^{v}–vj^{r} and BNF fr. 22546, fols. 123v–124r) only by the words "Apprehende arma," surely a sign that performers knew the chant and rhythm by heart. Then there are quite a number of motets with irregular endings of the last *talea,* where the isorhythm had to be given up by the composer in order to arrive at cadences. Nevertheless, the tenor *talea* is notated only once, and the performer must make the appropriate changes himself.[59] Similarly, many motets are copied in such a way that performers could not possibly have sung from the manuscript. A good example is the motet preserved in Ivrea, Biblioteca Capitolare, MS 115, *Les l'ormel a la turelle / Mayn se leva sire gayrin / Tenor: Je n'y saindrai plus,* where the duplum ends on fol. 22v, while the triplum continues to fol. 23 and the tenor is entirely on fol. 23.

Third, there is iconographical and archival evidence: Reinhard Strohm discusses a painting of the Burgundian chapel where several people are not looking at the manuscript and therefore must either sing by heart or not at all.[60] More importantly, Strohm has unearthed evidence from Klausen (Chiusa) that reveals that the boys with their master sang by heart. Similarly, a Venetian ambassador observed that the boys in Trent had memorized their music.[61]

Fourth, through a careful study of text underlay in fifteenth-century chansons, David Fallows was able to conclude that "text underlay cannot be taken literally and that adequate singing of even the discantus demands first that the singer have a complete memory, knowledge and understanding of the vocal lines. Sight-reading—or anything approaching it—is out of the question."[62] The evidence leaves little doubt that singers did not learn music and text at the same time. And Fallows draws from this the logical conclusion that singers did not rely on the manuscript in performance and must have sung everything by heart. Similarly, Margaret Bent has shown that singers did not add to the manuscripts many of the accidentals they sang because they arrived at certain solutions during rehearsals and then memorized them.[63] Finally, John Kmetz has put forward the hypothesis that singers who wanted to perform *Tenorlieder* first learned the parts with solmization sylla-

58. Machaut, *Musikalische Werke,* ed. Ludwig, 3:79 (183)–81 (185).

59. See, for example, *Fortune, mere a doulour / Ma doulour ne cesse pas / Tenor: Doulour meus* in Ivrea 115, fol. 53; modern edition by Harrison, *Motets of French Provenance,* no. 17.

60. Strohm, *Rise of European Music,* 277.

61. Ibid., 508 and 510.

62. "Texting in the Chansonnier of Jean de Montchenu"; English version of the chapter "Placement des paroles in Chansonnier de Jean de Montchenu."

63. "Musica Recta and Musica Ficta," 74–75, 79.

bles, and then, after they had memorized them, added the text.[64] Even though the repertory Kmetz has in mind is much simpler than isorhythmic motets, it is quite possible that similar methods were used to learn these pieces.

If motets were sung by heart, they had to be constructed in such a way that they could be remembered. Walter Ong, when discussing authors who had laboriously worked out their pieces, says that the only way for them to recall their compositions would be to "think memorable thoughts."[65] "Memorable thoughts" can mean many different things. We have seen in the previous chapter that rhythmic patterns and simple structures might have triggered the musical memory. It is the latter, more specifically architectural structures, I want to explore further in the following section. But before we can discuss how these might have helped to recall complex motets, it is necessary to assemble evidence as to how architectural structures might have been applied in the transmission and composition of literary texts.

Architectural Structures

Memory Texts. Ancient writers had already stressed the importance of structure for memorization. This aspect of *ars memorativa* has been vividly brought back to life by Frances Yates in her *Art of Memory.* But while Yates viewed the art of memory essentially as a tool for memorization, Mary Carruthers has shown in her recent *Book of Memory* and especially in *Craft of Composition* that it was much more than an aide for rote learning: mnemonics served as a tool for the creation of new texts. Similarly, Jocelyn Penny Small has contributed much to our understanding of the role memory played in oral composition in antiquity.[66] The memorization of old texts and the creation of new ones are closely intertwined; both use the same tools. The importance of this point cannot be overstated.

Quintilian has a special term for oral composition: *cogitatio.* He describes it as follows:

> Having dealt with writing, the next point which claims our attention is premeditation *(cogitatio),* which itself derives force from the practice of writing and forms an intermediate stage between the labors of the pen and the more precarious fortunes of improvisation; . . . For there are places and occasions where writing is impossible, while both are available in abundance for premeditation *(cogitatio).* . . . Again, this practice will not merely secure the proper arrangement of our matter without any recourse to writing, which in itself is no small

64. Kmetz, "Singing Texted Songs," and *Sixteenth-Century Basel Songbooks,* 222–24.
65. Ong, *Orality and Literacy,* 34. See also above, chap. 5.
66. Small, *Wax Tablets,* 181–85.

> achievement, but will also set the words which we are going to use in their proper order, and bring the general texture of our speech to such a stage of completion that nothing further is required beyond the finishing touches. And as a rule the memory is more retentive of thoughts when the attention has not been relaxed by the fancied security which results from committing them to writing.[67]

Authors not only planned the general outline of their written works, but worked out the entire composition word for word, so much so that they were able to dictate it fluently.[68] To us, who need to put everything into writing, it is hard to imagine how this could have been done. What tools did they use to work out compositions in the mind?

Throughout antiquity and the Middle Ages authors used architectural structures or diagrams to organize their thoughts. I have discussed in chapter 3 the basic principles of artificial memory described in Cicero's *De oratore,* the anonymous *Rhetorica ad Herennium,* and Quintilian's *Institutio oratoria.* The orator memorizes a background grid of places, say an architectural structure, places particularly striking images in these places, and then, when delivering the speech, visualizes each part of the grid with the image in it. Thus, the art of memory is a kind of imaginary writing.

Carruthers demonstrates in her *Craft of Thought* the importance of architectural structures for the process of *inventio* in early Christianity and the Middle Ages. She points out that Paul sees himself as a builder; the foundation of this edifice is Christ, and others build on this foundation.[69] Similarly, she interprets Malachy's vision from Bernard of Clairvaux's *Life of St. Malachi* as follows:

> When he has a vision, Malachy is in the location in which he plans to build. The plan and elevation of the building are projected in every detail, laid out with his mental line, in that particular location, and then, when every detail has been drawn in his mind's eye, the actual composition proceeds, rather in

67. "Proxima stilo cogitatio est, quae et ipsa vires ab hoc accipit, estque inter scribendi laborem extemporalemque fortunam media quaedam . . . Nam scribere non ubique nec semper possumus; cogitationi temporis ac loci plurimum est. . . . Neque vero rerum ordinem modo, quod ipsum satis erat, intra se ipsa disponit, sed verba etiam copulat totamque ita contexit orationem, ut ei nihil praeter manum desit. Nam memoriae quoque plerumque inhaerent fidelius, quae nulla scribendi securitate laxantur." Quintilian, *Institutio oratoria,* 10.6.1–2.

68. See in particular Bernardo Gui's testimony on Thomas Aquinas's habit of dictation, as quoted by Mary Carruthers: "he used to dictate in his cell to three secretaries, and even simultaneously so much various material without a special grace. Nor did he seem to be searching for things as yet unknown to him; he seemed simply to let his memory pour out its treasures . . . He never set himself to study or argue a point, or write or dictate without first having recourse inwardly—but with tears—to prayer for the understanding and the words required by the subject"; *Book of Memory,* 3.

69. Carruthers, *Craft of Thought,* 17.

> the manner that a literary composition is finally *scriptus* by pen or parchment. The actual building (or book) is only a "recollection" of the mental composition, itself composed or "gathered" from the inventory of the artist's memory. The building functions as a reminder, a cue, a machine for thought—but without the human beings who use it, it has neither value nor meaning.[70]

Numerous writers throughout the Middle Ages draw a comparison between the building of a structure and compositional process. Authors will always begin by drawing a mental picture before they start composing. Carruthers has written much about Noah's mystical ark, a huge mnemonic structure, where numbers and colors are used to help remember things. Also here the ark is used as an aid for composition. To quote Carruthers: "It is apparent, as one reads the complex description, that Hugh *saw* this building in his mind as he was composing: he 'walked' through it, and—especially given how often he returns to the Ark trope in his own compositions—he used it himself as he advised others to, as a universal cognitive machine."[71]

In the high Middle Ages, the architectural structures of the *Rhetorica ad Herennium* were reinterpreted by Albertus Magnus as monastic buildings.[72] Similarly, his slightly earlier contemporary Geoffrey of Vinsauf gives a description of compositional process around 1200 in his *Poetria nova:*

> If a man has a house to build, his hand does not rush, hasty, into the very doing: the work is first measured out with his heart's inward plumb line, and the inner man marks out a series of steps beforehand, according to a definite plan; his heart's hand shapes the whole body before his body's hand does so, and his building is a plan before it is an actuality. . . . Let the mind's inner compass circumscribe the whole area of the subject matter in advance. Let a definite plan predetermine the area in which the pen will make its way or where it will fix its Gibraltar. Ever circumspect, assemble the whole work in the stronghold of your mind, and let it be first in the mind before it is in words. When a plan has sorted out the subject in the secret places of your mind, then let Poetry come to clothe your material with words.[73]

70. Ibid., 225–26.

71. Ibid., 244; see also 243–46.

72. Ibid., 254–55. See also her translation of Albertus Magnus' *De ono,* Tractatus IV, Quaestio II, "De partibus prudentia," in *Book of Memory,* 267–80.

73. "Si quis habet fundare domum, non currit ad actum / Impetuosa manus: intrinseca linea cordis / Praemetitur opus, seriemque sub ordine certo / Interior praescribit homo, totamque figurat / Ante manus cordis quam corporis; et status ejus / Est prius archetypus quam sensilis. / . . . / Circinus interior mentis praecicinet omne / Materiae spatium. Certus praelimitet ordo / Unde praearripiat cursum stylus, aut ubi Gades / Figat. Opus totum prudens in pectoris arcem / Contrahe, sitque prius in pectore quam sit in ore. / Mentis in arcano cum rem digesserit ordo, / Materiam verbis veniat vestire poesis." Faral, *Les arts poétiques,* 198–99; trans. Kopp, 34–35; the whole treatise is on pp. 27–108.

Thomas Bradwardine's treatise *De memoria artificiali* was composed around 1333. He repeats the familiar rules about firm locations and images, which "are now inked on like letters and are then erased; and the locations are fundamental to the images, just as I earlier said of them. With regard to these locations, then, six matters are distinguished, that is size, configuration, characteristics, number, order, and distance-away."[74]

He goes on to list various requirements for the locations:

> Truly a location's configuration should be like a four-sided oblong. . . . that the places should not be formed in a crowded place, . . . that the places should be real rather than mostly imagined. . . . Fourthly, it is useful that contrasting locations be formed (as also might similarly be said in connection with the number of places). And so the first place might be like land unused and empty; the second like a green garden; the third like land having hay lying about or fruits as in time of harvest; the fourth as having stubble after gathering the fruits; the fifth like black ground after the stubble is completely burned. Then make for yourself another five places higher up, if you want, such as a large and high couch; then a cupboard; then a table; then a tomb; then an altar. Then if you want to climb more through another five places, first place the roof of a house made of wood, secondly of thatch, thirdly of stone, fourthly of red tile and fifthly *[lacuna* in the text]. Then if you want perhaps another five floors of upper-rooms, the first as though of earth, the second as though paved in green stone, the third as paved with tile, the fourth spread with grasses or straw, and the fifth furnished with carpets or cloths. These four times five backgrounds should suffice for all things to be remembered, or perhaps ten of them or somewhat fewer, unless a man should want to make unheard-of marvels.[75]

74. "[Y]magines vero nunc pinguntur ut littere, nunc delentur. Loca autem ymaginibus sunt priora; ideo de eis primitus est dicendum. Circa loca igitur sex notentur, scilicet quantitas, figura, qualitas, numerus, ordo, et distantia intercepta." Thomas Bradwardine, *De memoria artificiali adquirenda,* ed. Carruthers, 35.

75. "Figura vero sit sicut quadranguli oblongi. . . . Quod loca non ponantur nimis obscura, . . . quod loca non debent poni in loco frequentato, . . . quod loca sint vera quam tantum ymaginata vel ficta; . . . Quarto est utile quod ponantur dissimilia, quod et cum numero locorum, possit simile ostendi. Sit vero locus primus quasi terra inanis et vacua; secundus quasi viridarium; tertius quasi habens fenum dispersum vel fruges velud in tempore messis; quartus quasi habens stipulam post fruges collectas; quintus quasi terra nigra, stipula totaliter combusta. Deinde pone tibi alia quinque loca elevatiora, si velis, ut lectum magnum et altum, deinde archam, tunc mensam, tunc sepulcrum, tunc altare. Deinde si velis magis ascendere per alia quinque loca, pone primo tectum domus de ligno, secundo de stramine, tertio de lapidibus, quarto de tegula rubea, et quinto de plumbo. Deinde si velis quasi alios quinque fundos solarii: primum quasi terreum, secundum quasi viridi lapide pavatum, tertium tegulis pavatum, quartum stratum herbis vel stramine, et quintum paratum tapetis vel pannis. Hec autem quater quinque loco omnium memoratorum sufficiunt, ymmo decem istorum vel forsan pauciora, nisi homo voluerit facere mirabilia inaudita." Ibid., 35–36; trans. Carruthers, *Book of Memory,* 281–82.

Again this structure of four stories functions both as a depository of things that one remembers and as a place through which one wanders while composing. What is characteristic of these structures is that every room has a special quality that makes it memorable: straw, carpet, stone, etc.

All authors, starting with Aristotle, stress the importance of remembering the background places in order, so that one can wander through them backwards and forwards.[76] The author of *Ad Herennium* demands not only that the backgrounds be arranged in order,[77] but that the series be memorized before one puts images into the places. In memorizing it, he suggests, it helps to mark every fifth or tenth *locus*.[78] Quintilian also stresses in his *Institutio oratoria* the proper organization and arrangement (*dispositio*) of one's thoughts. He believes that "artistic construction" allows the author to dictate *verbatim* from memory.[79]

Similarly, Hugh of St. Victor fills his *archa* (chest) with knowledge: "Their orderly arrangement is clarity of knowledge. Dispose and separate each sin-

76. For Aristotle, see, for example, his *Poetics*, ed. Barnes, 1450^b34–1451^a7. See also his *Metaphysics*, where he talks about "the chief forms of beauty" as "order and symmetry and definiteness" (1078^b1).

77. "So with respect to the backgrounds. If these have been arranged in order, the result will be that, reminded by the images, we can repeat orally what we have committed to the backgrounds, proceeding in either direction from any background we please. That is why it also seems best to arrange the backgrounds in a series." ("[I]tem in locis ex ordine conlocatis eveniet ut in quamlibet partem quoque loco libebit, imaginibus commoniti, dicere possimus id quod locis mandaverimus. Quare placet et ex ordine locos conparare.") *Ad Herennium*, 3.17.30–31.

78. *Ad Herennium*, 3.18.31.

79. "But for the purpose of getting a real grasp of what we have written under the various heads, division and artistic structure will be found of great value, while, with the exception of practice, which is the most powerful aid of all, they are practically the only means of ensuring an accurate remembrance of what we have merely thought out. For correct division will be an absolute safeguard against error in the order of our speech, since there are certain points not merely in the distribution of the various questions in our speech, but also in their development (provided we speak as we ought), which naturally comes first, second, and third, and so on, while the connection will be so perfect that nothing can be omitted or inserted without the fact of the omission or insertion being obvious. . . . Again, if our structure be what it should, the artistic sequence will serve to guide the memory. For just as it is easier to learn verse than prose, so it is easier to learn prose when it is artistically constructed than when it has no such organisation. If these points receive attention, it will be possible to repeat *verbatim* even such passages as gave the impression of being delivered extempore." ("Nam qui recte diviserit, nunquam poterit in rerum ordine errare. Certa sunt enim non solum in digerendis questionibus, sed etiam in exsequendis, si modo recte dicimus, prima ac secunda deinceps; cohaeretque omnis rerum copulatio, ut ei nihil neque subtrahi sine manifesto intellectu neque inseri possit. . . . Etiam quae bene composita erunt, memoriam serie sua ducent. Nam sicut facilius versus ediscimus quam prosam orationem, ita prosae vincta quam dissoluta. Sic contingit, ut etiam quae ex tempore videbantur effusa, ad verbum repetita reddantur.") Quintilian, *Institutio oratoria*, trans. Butler, *On memory*, 11.2.36–39.

gle thing into its own place. . . . Confusion is the mother of ignorance and forgetfulness, but orderly arrangement illuminates the intelligence and firms up memory."[80] Likewise, Bradwardine echoes earlier writers when he states: "Truly order requires that the places have contiguity and direction, so that memory may with facility find all the inscribed images in their places easily, in forward order or backwards."[81] Bradwardine is typical of many writers throughout the Middle Ages in that he combines the correct order with the ability to manipulate the material, to recite single verses out of context or even backwards, an ability already ascribed to Seneca and Augustine's friend Simplicius.[82]

It is of central importance that the entire architectural structure used to compose and remember a text can be taken in at a single glance *(conspectus)*.[83] According to Carruthers, "each mnemonic background or scene is constituted by a sweep of one such mental gaze, and the individual mnemonic clues within each scene cannot be more in number and complexity than what one can distinguish clearly in one look of the memory."[84] And yet, the information or composition included in this one gaze need not be short. It is often abbreviated and the clue word or symbol will trigger additional words and sentences. Tables and tree diagrams fall into this category. In music they

80. "Dispositio ordinis illustratio est cognitionis. Dispone et distingue singula locis suis . . . Confusio ignoratiae et oblivionis mater est, discretio autem intelligentiam illuminat et memoriam confirmat." Hugh of St.Victor, *De tribus maximis circumstantiis gestorum,* ed. Green, 488; trans. Carruthers, *Book of Memory,* 261. See also Aquinas, *Summa theologica,* II-II 49,1 (1267/1273).

81. "Ordinem vero valet quod habeant continuum et directum, ut memoria possit de facili omnes locis inscriptas ymagines directe vel retrograde faciliter invenire." Bradwardine, *De memoria artificiali adquirenda,* 36; trans. Carruthers, *Book of Memory,* 282.

82. See Yates, *Art of Memory,* 16 and Carruthers, *Book of Memory,* 18–19.

83. There are numerous painters and architects who also believed in drawing entirely from memory. Michael Baxandall describes how the fifteenth-century humanist Rudolf Agricola was able to paint entirely from memory: "When he wanted to paint someone, it was his practice, surreptitiously in church—where he would have access to the person being unaware and more relaxed and could gaze at him more steadily—to fix his eyes and attention on him for no longer time than it took to celebrate Mass; and then afterwards at home he would draw with charcoal the entire lineaments of the man so marvellously and exactly, you would think you saw in those mute lineaments of the various features the living, breathing body." *Words for Pictures,* 69–70. I would like to thank Bonnie Blackburn for bringing this passage to my attention. This method was elaborated in great detail in the early 20th c. by the French drawing teacher Horace Lecoq de Boisbaudron in his *L'éducation de la mémoire pittoresque.* His students, among them Rodin and Fantin-Latour, would begin by drawing a straight line, then progress through various geometric shapes, all from memory, to various parts of human heads to entire heads. His students used memorized drawings, lithographs, and engravings as models. He would take his students on weekend trips where models were asked to dance around and students were asked to memorize particular gestures that were then drawn on paper the following Monday. See James Fenton's article "*Degas: Beyond Impressionism*"; he quotes Degas as saying that "training in art was training in memory" (p. 14).

84. Carruthers, *Craft of Thought,* 63.

might include the entire mensural system in summary form (see chap. 3 and Figure 12).[85]

In sum, we have seen that throughout antiquity and the Middle Ages architectural structures are used as aides for composers. While ancient writers preferred memorizing streets or houses, medieval structures are monastic or diagrammatic, such as with Bradwardine, who superimposes groups of five, or with Hugh, who uses every imaginable geometric shape. All stress the importance of structuring the texts in a specific order. Might we discover similar patterns of thinking in music theory and in isorhythmic motets?

Music Theory. Only a small number of music theorists discuss isorhythmic motets and what they have to say on this subject has been thoroughly analyzed.[86] Beginning with Ludwig, scholars have been puzzled by the fact that these theorists tell us very little about how composers went about composing such elaborate structures. All we find are general references to the tenor as the foundation of the composition and to the belief that the other parts have to follow the tenor; we also come across definitions of *color* and *talea.* Thus, if we look for evidence as to whether isorhythmic motets were composed in a way similar to verbal texts, all we can expect to find is indirect evidence. We would need to know specifically whether there are any references to the visualization of music, and whether the making of motets was discussed in a way similar to the making of verbal texts. In other words, were motets similarly structured and worked out in the mind before being written down?

The earliest reference to visualization I could discover is by Franco of Cologne, whose treatise *Ars cantus mensurabilis* dates from ca. 1280. Franco explains that one should first take the tenor and only next add a discant. Then, in the manuscript Paris, BNF lat. 16663, Franco uses the verb *respicere* twice, first in the following passage: "He who wishes to construct a triplum must have the tenor and discant in mind *(respiciendum est),* so that if the triplum be discordant with the tenor, it will not be discordant with the discant, and vice versa. And let him proceed further by concords, ascending or descending now with the tenor, now with the discant, so that his triplum is not always with either one alone."[87] A little later in the treatise, when he provides instructions as to

85. For more examples of tree diagrams, see Carruthers, *Book of Memory,* 209–19, 237–38, and also her *Craft of Thought,* 211–12. For a recent excellent discussion of such diagrams in the 16th c. see Bolzoni, *Gallery of Memory,* trans. Parzen, chap. 2.

86. See in particular Leech-Wilkinson, *Compositional Procedure*; and Bent, "Isorhythm."

87. Paris, BNF lat. 16663, fol. 82r, "Qui autem triplum uoluerit operari: respiciendum est tenorem et discantum: ita quod si discordat cum tenore non discordet cum discantu: uel econuerso. Et procedat alterius [ulterius corr. supra lin.] per concordancias nunc ascendendo cum tenore uel descendo: nunc cum discantu ita: quod non semper: cum altero tantum: ut in

how one should compose the quadruplum and quintuplum, there is an addition in the margin that suggests that one should keep in mind *(respiciat)* what has been composed earlier: "He who wishes to make the quadruplum and quintuplum should keep in mind what has been composed earlier. Since if it is discordant with one, it will not be discordant with the others."[88]

Jacques de Liège uses *respicere* in the same way in his *Speculum musicae,* bk. 7.[89] Note that the verb *respicere* derives from *spectare,* "to see," and means literally "to look back," an activity involving the use of memory. The verb is typically found in mnemonic treatises to describe a visual memorization, in contrast to *recordare* and *retinere,* which are more general.[90] Thus, we can conclude that the composer must have visualized the other parts (or perhaps the entire composition) on the staff when he composed. It seems unlikely that the theorists would have used *respicere* if one composed by ear alone.

As mentioned earlier, Franco uses the verb *imaginare,* which means "to imagine" or "visualize," in his *Compendium discantus:* "And note that when you want to ascend above the octave, you visualize that you are in unison with the tenor . . . "[91] I have already noted above the use of *ymaginare* in Power. Finally, the Dutch music theorist Johannes Boen says clearly that the visual sense is superior to the ears in recognizing *colores* (see the discussion below).

A number of theorists stress the importance of *divisio* in isorhythmic motets or liken motets to architectural structures. Johannes de Grocheio, whose treatise was written around 1300, talks about "composed music" *(musica composita),* under which he includes three kinds of pieces: *motetus, organum,* and *hoquetus.*[92] He compares the different parts of a composition to a house: "The tenor is that part on which the others are founded, as a foundation is for the parts of a house or building. The tenor rules them and gives them their quantities, as the bones do to the other parts of the body."[93] A little later he continues: "He who wants to put this together, first has to organize and put to-

---

exem [exemplo corr. in marg.] subsequenti apparet." Trans. Strunk, rev. McKinnon, in *Source Readings in Music History,* 241–42.

88. "Qui autem quadruplum uel quintuplum facere uoluerit, [accipiat uel respiciat m.sec. in marg.] [fol. 82v] prius factos. ut si cum uno discordat: cum aliis in concordanciis habeatur." Paris, BNF lat. 16663, fol. 82r–v.

89. "The singer of discant should keep in mind two or more [parts]" ("Discantus igitur cum magis proprie duos cantus respiciat quam plures"); ed. Bragard, chap. 3.

90. See also Carruthers, *Craft of Thought,* 174–75, for a discussion of the verb *spectare.*

91. "Et nota quando volueris ascendere supra diapason; ymaginabis te esse cum tenore in unisono . . . " Oxford, Bodleian Library, Bodley 842 (S.C. 2575), fols. 60r–62v; quotation on fol. 62v. Richard Crocker first called attention to this passage and related it to sights in his "Discant, Counterpoint, and Harmony," 8.

92. Facs., ed., and trans. Rohloff, 139.

93. "Tenor autem est illa pars, supra quam omnes aliae fundantur, quemadmodum partes domus vel aedificii super suum fundamentum. Est eas regulat et eis dat quantitatem, quemadmodum ossa partibus aliis." Ibid., 146–47.

gether the tenor and has to give it *modus* and measuring. Namely, the main part has to be formed first because afterwards through its help the others will be formed . . . I say organizing *(ordinare)* because in motets and organa the tenor is put together from an old and previously composed chant, but it is determined by the artist through *modus* and the correct measurement."[94]

Modus refers to one of the six Notre Dame rhythmic modes (see chap. 5). Even though Johannes does not make a direct association between memorization and strict organization, the first sentence quoted above suggests that composers may have conceived musical and architectural structures to be analogous. Such an understanding would enable them to work out structures in their minds and would permit singers to remember them accurately. Jacques de Liège draws a similar parallel between the tenor and the other parts in book 7, chapter 3 of his *Speculum musicae.*[95]

The Dutch priest and music theorist Johannes Boen has an intriguing discussion of isorhythmic motets in his *Ars (musicae)* from the middle of the fourteenth century. His presentation of the mensural system is sprinkled with examples from isorhythmic motets to explain notational complexities. In their discussion of isorhythm, fourteenth-century music theorists usually concentrate on two concepts: *color* and *talea.*[96] The former refers either to the succession of pitches, or to the segment that includes these pitches. Similarly, *talea* can refer both to the rhythmic pattern and to the segment of the tenor melody. Boen's discussion is a little different. Toward the end of the first part comes a discussion of *color* that is perhaps the most illuminating medieval treatment of the subject. I cite it in full:

> Since we have made mention of *color,* let us consider what *color* is, when it was invented, and how it has been used. Therefore *color,* as it is used in song, is the matching of some notes of some resemblance. *Color* was invented so that we might find the lost or carelessly placed note through its resemblance. And it is done in this way. First you look to see which shapes of notes you have to which you want to apply *color (colorare).* For instance, if there are thirty, you can divide this number in many ways. Divide the same, for instance, into five equal parts, and then each part will contain six notes, since six times five makes thirty. Then arrange the first part so that it will have six. Then you will arrange the six notes of the second part similarly to the six notes of the first part, so that the first note corresponds to the first and the second to the second. And

94. "Volens autem ista componere primo debet tenorem ordinare vel componere et ei modum et mensuram dare. Pars enim principalior debet formari primo, quoniam ea mediante postea formantur aliae, . . . Et dico *ordinare,* quoniam in motellis et organo tenor ex cantu antiquo est prius composito, sed ab artifice per modum et rectam mensuram amplius determinatur." Ibid.

95. Ed. Bragard, vol. 3, chap. 3.

96. For the best overview of *color* and *talea* in music theory, see Leech-Wilkinson, *Compositional Techniques,* 15–24.

as a result the music will be unified through this *color*. In this way *color* was made in the tenor *Virtutibus*.[97] For he first took a group of thirty notes and divided it into five parts, of which every part is similar to the other, because after six notes the seventh is similar to the first, in the same way after the twelfth begins the thirteenth as the first was similar to the seventh and so on. But since the tenor would be still too short if only thirty notes were used, he added another thirty that would make one-half of the length of the others and presented it in the same *color* as before. Thus, in the tenor *Flos virginum*[98] the composer, not content with the number thirty, doubled the same number to sixty notes. He divided the number sixty into three parts and made each part twenty notes. He arranged the first twenty so well that by an identical arrangement he preserved a beautiful *color* in the following two parts. However, since *color* is presented more to the sight than to the hearing, I therefore advise that not so much trouble or expense of intellect should be made concerning it in this matter [i.e. music], as a result of which [fussing over *color*] the melody would be impaired and the eye would have an occasion to rebuke the ear in respect of the sound.[99]

97. The motet Boen is discussing is *Impudenter circuivi / Virtutibus laudabilis* by Philippe de Vitry, which has a tenor consisting of thirty notes divided into five *taleae* of six notes each; then the *color* is repeated in diminution. *Complete Works*, ed. Schrade, no. 11.

98. The motet Boen has in mind is *Apta caro / Flos virginum / Alma redemptoris mater*, ed. Günther in *Motets of the Manuscripts Chantilly*, no. 3. This motet has a more complicated construction: the *color* consists of thirty notes, and is repeated, but the sixty notes are divided into three *taleae;* in other words, *color* and *talea* overlap.

99. "Quia de colore mentionem fecimus, ideo quid sit color, qualiter inventus fuit, et qualiter habet fieri, parum pertractemus. Est ergo color, prout in cantu utimur, aliquarum figurarum in aliqua similitudine comparabilitas. Fuit autem inventus color, ut figuram perditam vel negligenter positam per correspondentiam reperire valeamus. Et habet fieri hoc modo. Primo quidem inspicias quot corpora notarum habeas que colorare volueris. Sint verbi gratia triginta, hunc numerum multis modis dividere potes. Divide ipsum ergo, gratia exempli, in quinque partes equales, et tunc quelibet pars retinebit notas sex, nam sexies quinque triginta constituunt. Ordina ergo primam partem ut habeat sex. Sic ergo disposueris sex notas secunde partis ad similitudinem sex notarum in prima parte, ut prima nota correspondeat prime et secunda secunde. Et sic consequenter erit cantus ille colore iunctus. Isto modo fuit color factus in tenore Virtutibus. Cepit enim primo triginta corpora que divisit in partes quinque, quarum partium quelibet alteri similatur, quia post sex notas incipit septima que similis est note prime, item post duodecimam incipit tertiadecima que prime et septime similatur, et sic ulterius. Sed quia nimis brevis mansisset tenor si solis triginta corporibus fuisset usus, ergo adiunxit et alia triginta que medietatem faciunt aliorum et servatur in ipsis idem color qui prius. Sic in tenore Flos virginum actor non contentus numero tricenario, ipsum numerum duplicavit ad corpora sexaginta. Sexagenarium autem numerum secuit in partes tres, et obtinuit quelibet pars notas viginti. Primas ergo viginti bene sic disposuit, quod consimilis dispositionis pulchrum colorem in sequentibus duabus partibus [30] conservavit. Quia tamen color plus visui obicitur quam auditui, ideo non tantam curiositatem seu expensas intelligentium [should be *intellectus*] consulo circa ipsum fieri in hac materia, quo magis melodie derogetur et oculus occasionem habeat unde juxta sonum improperare possit auri." Johannes Boen, *Ars (musicae)*, ed. Gallo, 29. I would like to thank Leofranc Holford-Strevens for help with the translation of the last sentence.

Johannes uses the term *color* to describe what is most commonly considered *talea,*[100] and then asks why it was invented. The answer suggests that the "resemblance of lost or carelessly placed notes" would bring some badly needed order into the composition.[101] He also seems to imply that if a scribe made a mistake, singers would be able to correct it, once they saw how the pattern worked. In other words, *color* was invented to structure the notes in a composition. This means that composers (or performers) thought less in terms of separate note values, and more in terms of groups of notes; or, to use a term from psychology, they were "chunking." And "chunking" is done in order to memorize. His division of the thirty tenor pitches into 6 × 5 or 3 × 20 notes is reminiscent of what we read above in memory treatises. If one were to make a diagram of the isorhythmic structure described by Boen,[102] it would be very similar to the structures depicted by Bradwardine. Finally, he declares that the eye is able to see *color* (and, by implication, the *divisio* of the *color* into *taleae*) better than the ear can hear it.[103] Many memory treatises stress that the sense of sight is superior to that of hearing. What this implies is that the rhythmic organization and structure enable the composer to work out the piece and allow the performer to keep his place during the performance.[104] Boen's discussion leaves little doubt that the composer planned and visualized the composition before he wrote it down.

The mid-fourteenth-century theorist Egidius de Murino also stresses the importance of *divisio* in his *Tractatus cantus mensurabilis.*[105] He discusses di-

100. Prosdocimus uses the term in the same way in his *Tractatus practice* (CS 3:226a). For an explanation of these definitions, see Blackburn, Lowinsky, and Miller, *A Correspondence of Renaissance Musicians,* letter 28, paras. 11–18, pp. 384–91.

101. Note that Boen uses the noun *similitudo,* familiar from mnemonic treatises, to describe the resemblance between the place and the image, to explain the similarity between the *colores.* See, for example, Francesc Eiximeni, *On Two Kinds of Order that Aid Understanding and Memory,* trans. Rivers, 199 and 201.

102. For various diagrams of Vitry's and Machaut's motets, see Leech-Wilkinson, *Compositional Techniques,* vol. 2.

103. Daniel Leech-Wilkinson has made the intriguing suggestion that perhaps Boen uses the term *color* instead of *talea* because the former presupposes a stronger use of sight.

104. It might be of interest that Karol Berger was able to show that Boen also visualized the gamut only on the staff. When discussing double flats and double sharps, Berger observed that "for Boen, double flats or sharps were unthinkable, but a flat truly inflecting c or f and a sharp truly inflecting a, ♮, or e were possible. This suggests that Boen thought about these problems not so much in terms of solmization syllables (in which both a flattened step and c, for instance, are already fa and, consequently, cannot be additionally flattened) as in terms of the actual visual appearance of the staff notation (in which the note marking b is preceded by the round b, while the note marking c is not and, consequently, the latter can be additionally flattened, while the former cannot)." *Musica ficta,* 31.

105. CS 3:124–28. The best transcription with partial translation of the relevant passages is in Leech-Wilkinson, *Compositional Processes,* 18–23 and appendix 1.

vision in connection with textual underlay: "When the music is made and ordered, then take the words which are to be in the motet and divide them into four parts, and likewise divide the music into four parts, and compose the first part of the words above the first part of the music as well as you can, and thus proceed to the end."[106] Even though these descriptions of compositional process were intended for "the teaching of children,"[107] they make clear that composers worked out their pieces in sections.

There is no information in theoretical texts as to how the piece should be notated. And yet, Boen's discussion of 6 × 5 or 3 × 20 notes suggests that he thought about the entire piece. The manuscripts speak for themselves: like medieval mnemonic diagrams, an entire motet can be seen at once (Figures 19–20). The tenor is in the lowest left-page staff lines, the triplum on the top of the left page, the motetus on the facing right page. This layout is, of course, lost in modern transcriptions,[108] and it is one of the main reasons why many performers prefer to sing from the original manuscripts.

Motets. Let us look at a motet attributed to Philippe de Vitry by Gace de la Buigne,[109] *Douce playsence / Garison selon nature / Neuma quinti toni.*[110] The tenor is based on a neuma (see chap. 2) in the fifth mode consisting of twenty-eight tones (Example 39).[111] The *color* is presented twice, the second time in diminution. Each *color* is divided into four *taleae* and each *talea* consists of two sections, the first in perfect time, the second in imperfect time. The *taleae* present the same rhythmic pattern, but on different pitches. The tenor thus provides the structural and harmonic framework for the entire composition.[112]

The text of the triplum and motetus is given on page 229. The poetry scheme of the triplum is related to Dante's *terza rima.*[113] Both anticipate the end-rhyme of the new stanza and can be continued ad infinitum. But while with Dante the end-rhyme of the following stanza is in the middle line of the

106. "Postquam cantus est factus et ordinatus tunc accipe verba que debent esse in moteto et divide ea in quatuor partes, et sic divide cantum in quatuor partes, et prima pars verborum compone supra primam partem cantus, sicut melius potes." Ed. and trans. ibid., 19.

107. See ibid., 22.

108. Modern edition in *Motets of the Manuscripts Chantilly,* ed. Günther, 23–26.

109. See the Introduction by Edward Roesner in Philippe de Vitry, *Complete Works* (1984), iv.

110. For a modern edition, see Philippe de Vitry, *Works,* ed. Schrade, 1:72. For an excellent discussion of the motet and its relationship to Machaut's *Aucune gent / Qui plus aime / Fiat voluntas tua* see Leech-Wilkinson, *Compositional Techniques,* 88–104. See also Karl Kügle's discussion in *Manuscript Ivrea,* 109–13.

111. Sanders has pointed out the similarity of the neumas in two other Vitry motets: *Garrit gallus / In nova fert / Neuma* and *Floret / Florens / Neuma.*

112. This point has been stressed especially by Eggebrecht, "Machauts Motette Nr. 9."

113. On *terza rima,* see Freccero, "Significance of *Terza Rima.*"

Figure 19. *Alpha vibrans monumentum / Coetus venit heroicus / Amicum querit*, Chantilly, Musée Condé, MS 564, fol. 64v, reproduced by permission of the library. Digital imaging by the Digital Image Archive of Medieval Music (DIAMM)

preceding one (aba, bcb, cdc, etc.), in Vitry's poem the last cauda anticipates the new ending (aab bcc cdd, etc). Vitry's poem comprises ten stanzas, each consisting of two ten-syllable lines with a caesura after the fourth syllable (many of the syllables before the caesura also rhyme with the endings), followed by a four-syllable cauda. The first line is considered an extra line (it

Figure 20. Chantilly, Musée Condé, MS 564, fol. 65r

has twelve syllables), as are the last two, which lack the cauda. This poem must have been easy to memorize (the rhymes are in italics); the ending of the cauda would automatically trigger the rhyme, and hence imply the text of the next line.

The motetus text has the following rhyme scheme: abab, baba, and abba. This is also an aid to memorization. Both the triplum and motetus are almost entirely isorhythmic, particularly toward the beginnings and endings

Example 39. Tenor of *Douce playsence / Garison selon nature / Neuma quinti toni*

(a) *talea* 1

(b) in diminution

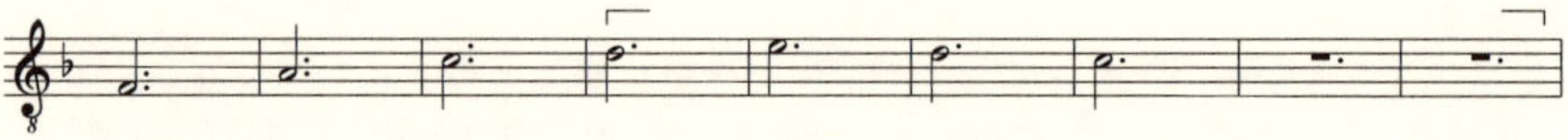

of the phrases (Example 40). When the isorhythmic pattern in the triplum is disturbed, it happens for the simple reason that there are more syllables to accommodate in the second half of the ten-syllable lines. This is important for our argument that isorhythmic structures assist the memory. The singer needs cues, particularly toward phrase ends.[114] It seems likely, as Leech-Wilkinson has suggested, that Vitry started out by making a grid of rhythmic patterns either mentally or in writing, and then he adjusted these patterns according to the amount of text that needed to be fitted.[115] Or, to put it differently, the composer/poet and performer will remember that the musical structure of this motet can be summarized as follows:

		PART I	PART II
A	Breves	4 × 12	4 × 12
	Semibreves	4 × 36	4 × 24
B	Breves	4 × 3	4 × 6
	Semibreves	4 × 9	4 × 12

Let us now look at the harmonic patterns. It is, perhaps, not surprising that the two *colores* are set with similar interval progressions (Table 3).[116] But note also that on the seventh pitch six out of eight *taleae* have an F-major triad; five of these, in turn, are preceded by a G-minor one. (I use anachronistic terminology here simply for brevity's sake: Vitry and his contemporaries thought in intervallic, not harmonic, terms.)

We can now imagine how a composer would have gone about creating

114. Note, though, that while the motetus lines always end two breves after the *talea*, the endings of the triplum stanzas are not related to the isorhythmic structure. Instead, the rests after the ending of a stanza (with the exception of the last one at "agre") occur at various points in the *talea*. Leech-Wilkinson has a graph of where the phrases end in *Compositional Techniques*, 2:14.

115. Ibid., 1:102.

116. I have numbered the pitches of the *taleae* in the top line. The capital letters indicate a major chord, lower case a minor.

TRIPLUM

Douce playsence	est d'amer loyalem*ent*
qar autrem*ent*	ne porroit bonem*ent*
amans suffrir	cele dolour ard*ant*
qui d'amors n*aist.*	
quant ces regars	par son soutil atr*ait*
en regardant	parmi soy mesmes tr*ait*
sans soy navr*er*	
l'impression	de ce qu'il veut am*er*
jusqu'à son cuer	lors estuet remenbr*er*
et souven*ir*	
du gentil cors	qu'il vit au depart*ir.*
puis le convient	trembler muer frem*ir*
entre sail*ant*	
et soupirer	cent fois en un ten*ant*
le dous soupirs	qui livrent au cuer n*ont*
par les cond*uis.*	
porquoy desirs	qui est accelle d*uis*
esprent et art	et croist en ardant: p*uis*
fayre le d*oit.*	
areu, hareu	cuers humains ne porr*oit*
cel mal soufrir	se playsance n'est*oit*
qui souvent l'*oint*	
mays on porroit	demander biau ap*oint*
comment lo mal	puet plaire qui si p*oint;*
et ie resp*ons;*	
en esperant	d'avoir bon guerred*on*
por en saisir	quant il leur sera b*on*
envret pluss*eurs*	
en traveylant	sans cesser nuit et i*our,*
donques doit	bien l'amoureuse dol*our*
Venir agr*e,*	
En attendant	la tres aute plant*e*
Dont bonament	a plusseurs saoul*e.*

MOTETUS

Garison selon nature
Desiree de sa doulor
Toute humaine creature.
Mais je qui ai d'un ardour
Naysant de loyal amour
Espris de garir n'ay cure.
Ains me plaist de iour en iour
Ades plus telle ardeure.
Ne pour quant elle est si dure
Que nuls hons n'auroyt vigour
Du soffrir sans la douchour
Qui vient de playsance pure

Example 40. Isorhythmic structure in *Douce playsence / Garison selon nature / Neuma quinti toni*

(a) triplum

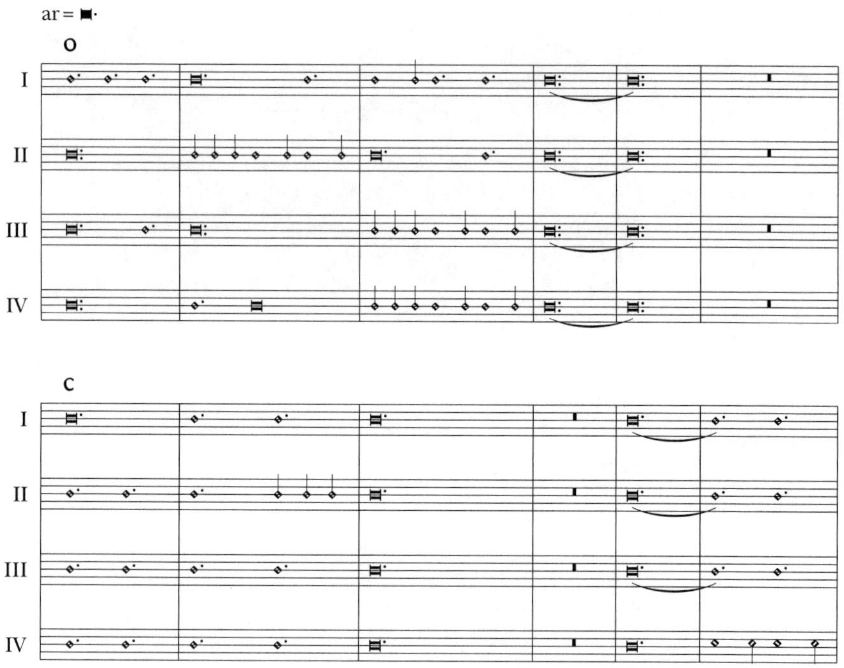

(b) motetus

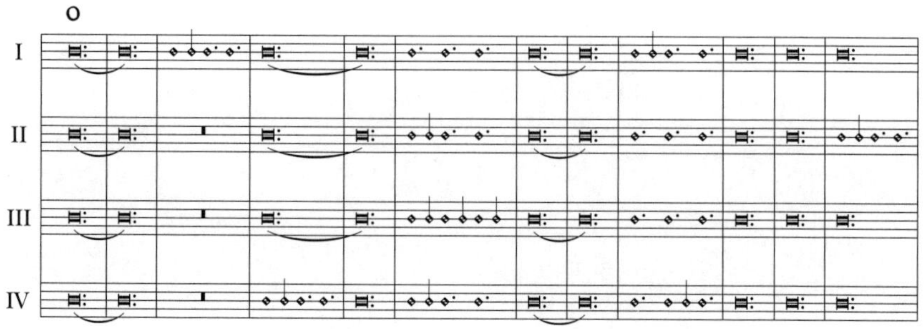

C

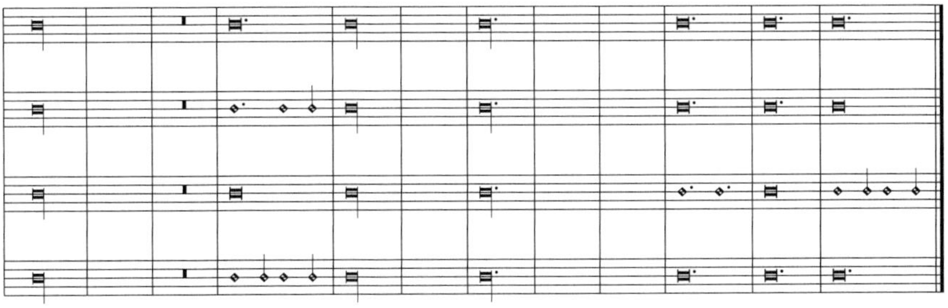

TABLE 3. Harmonic Structure of *Taleae* in Vitry, *Douce playsance / Garison selon nature / Neuma quinti toni*

						COLOR A								
Tenor pitch	*1*	*2*	*3*			*4*	*5*	*6*	*7*					
Talea I	F	a	C	d	‖	g	e/a	B♭	C	a	B♭	a	e/
Talea II	F	B♭	a	C d C/a	‖	g	a	g	F	C	d	C	B
Talea III	a	g	F	C d a/e	‖	B♭	d/a	g/e	F	d	c	d	g
Talea IV	g	a/F	g	d c d	‖	a	g	e	F	F	d	e	d/
						COLOR B								
Tenor pitch	*1*	*2*	*3*			*4*	*5*	*6*	*7*					
Talea 1	F	A	C		‖	B♭	a	B♭	C	B♭			
Talea 2	C	B♭	a		‖	g	a	g/e	F	F			
Talea 3	a	B♭	C		‖	b/g	a	g	F	F/e			
Talea 4	g	a	g		‖	a	g	g	F				

such a composition: he would take a tenor from his mental inventory, organize it, supply it with a harmonic framework, add rhythmic patterns for the upper parts, and create texts for them. Isorhythm could have helped to memorize the music. In the earlier motets, like our example by Vitry, it was applied only to the tenor and, in the upper voices, at phrase ends where it was most needed. In later increasingly complex motets it was used in all parts, perhaps again to aid the memory. The overall structure of the composition is strikingly similar to that of Bradwardine, who visualized different floors with new furnishings and patterns. I mentioned above that Bradwardine combined memorization of patterns and structures with manipulation of these patterns. Did composers apply similar games to motets? But before we turn to music, let us review how literary texts were manipulated.

Manipulation in Literary Texts

The use of puns and rebuses formed an important tool in committing texts to memory. According to Mary Carruthers and Jan Ziolkowski, "puns and rebuses abound in these [memory] texts, and words and images are often deliberately cut off from their ordinary contexts in order to provoke new thoughts and to put the mind 'in play.'"[117]

117. *Medieval Craft of Memory*, ed. Carruthers and Ziolkowski, 13.

As we have seen in chapter 2, medieval education was based on memorization of letters, syllables, words, phrases, and sentences. As a result, students did not necessarily consider sentences syntactic units, but rather as constructions made up of letters and syllables. A number of classicists have recently shown in fascinating detail the kind of word games employed by Lucretius, Ovid, and Prudentius, to name just a few.[118] For example, a letter, the smallest unit, was called an atom (Lucretius was the first to use this term), which can be permuted, changed, and mixed with other atoms. Poets delighted in wordplay of this sort. Martha Malamud gives an example from Lucretius where in the sentence *confiTEaRE Et RE Et sonitu distaRE sonanti* "the pairs TE and RE flip-flop through the line, changing both meaning and sound according to their new places."[119] Similarly, poets use syllables, words, and phrases as building blocks that are constantly recombined.

There can be little doubt that these poetry puzzles were a common pastime. For example, in a fourteenth-century manuscript from the Cathedral Chapter of Reims, where Machaut was a canon, there is a flyleaf in a copy of Petrus Comestor's *Historia scolastica* (a popular presentation of the biblical story) with the following poem:

Hodie Rex omnium parum venera-
Et pater per filium modicus ama-
Sosius *[sic]* per socium sepe defrauda-
Istud non est dubium, fides anula-

The poem is followed by the endings -tur, -re, -te, -num, -tem, -rum. It is obviously a play on word endings.[120]

A good example of the use of wordplay to aid memorization can be found in the fifteenth century in Jacobus Publicius of Florence's treatise *The Art of Memory,* a text based on *Ad Herennium.* According to Jacobus, memorizing happens "through long meditation and continual exercise, until we are able to retain, arrange, and reproduce [the places] from memory . . . "[121] A little later he says:

118. Snyder, *Puns and Poetry in Lucretius' "De Rerum Natura"*; Ahl, *Metaformations*; Levitan, "Dancing at the End of the Rope"; and Malamud, *Poetics of Transformation.*

119. Malamud, *Poetics of Transformation,* 30.

120. The poem is in Reims, Bibl. Municipale 1355 (14th-c. MS from the Cathedral chapter of Reims) on flyleaf E. Similarly, in another 14th-c. MS from the Cathedral chapter in Reims of Papias's *Elementarium* there is a metrical lexicon of ca. 2,100 words, each of which is accompanied by a verse taken from various poets (among them Alain de Lille, Bede, Boethius, Damasus, Fortunatus, Horace, Juvenal, Marcianus, Ovid, and Vergil) (Reims, Bibl. Municipale 1093, fol. 289). This also seems to have been used to create poetry. My warmest thanks to Anne Walters Robertson for telling me about this poem.

121. Trans. Henry Bayerle, in *Medieval Craft of Memory,* ed. Carruthers and Ziolkowski, 237–38.

> By the division of matters and the reversal of letters and of syllables, we will search out concealed figures: thus "things" *(rebus)* renders "cork" *(suber)*, "giraffe" *(nabo,* from *nabus)* renders "goods" *(bona)*, "praiseworthy" *(laudabilis)* is cut into "judgments of gall" *(lauda bilis)*, and "grove" *(nemus)* renders "teat" *(sumen)*. By the combination, addition and removal of letters and by the linking of one to another, memory will be stimulated. For example, from "that very woman" *(istam ipsam)* we will make *mipsam* by taking *m* away from the first word and joining it to the following one.[122]

Thus, an outcome of this pedagogy was that students learned how to juggle syllables, letters, and words. The examples given by Publicius show that the addition of a single letter totally changes the meaning of the word. Syllables and letters are combined and recombined with each other in ever new ways, and as a result new words or allusions are made. To quote Carruthers: "The result must have been to give the earliest education the aspect of a calculational game, in which pattern recognition was a key to success. Such calculative facility depends on a well-stocked memory 'disposed' in patterns that allow one readily to 'see where to put' new material, associating it with matters already in place."[123]

Manipulation in Musical Notes

Melodic Patterns. Obviously, the most important precompositional melodic patterns used by composers were tenors. Starting with Ludwig, a number of musicologists have pointed out that tenors were carefully chosen to complement the text of the upper voices.[124] To quote Erich Auerbach, these allusions offer infinite possibilities for mnemonic allusions, "with their unending abundance of combinations and allusions, intersections of motives and metaphors, which form the true foundation of Christian medieval poetry."[125]

There are many late thirteenth- and fourteenth-century motets that make extensive use of quotations from other pieces, sometimes the text, sometimes both text and music. The classic study on the topic is a 1972 ar-

122. Ibid., 243–44.

123. Carruthers, *Craft of Thought,* 137. Similarly, Jack Goody gives the example of the businessman Sonie from Ghana who, after he had mastered writing, started to devise number and word games. Goody, *Interface between the Written and the Oral,* 198.

124. I would again like to single out Eggebrecht's study "Machauts Motette Nr. 9" (pp. 286–93), where the tenor words "fera pessima" derive from a responsory based on Genesis 37:33–34, the story of Joseph, whose brothers sell him to slave traders, but the father is led to believe that he has been killed by a wild animal. The central topic of this motet is envy, and Eggebrecht points out numerous allusions between the tenor and the other voices that play with this topic.

125. "[M]it ihrer unendlichen Fülle von Kombinationen und Anspielungen, Motivkreuzungen und Metaphern, das eigentliche Lebenselement der christlich mittelalterlichen Dichtung bildet." Auerbach, *Typologische Motive,* 16–17.

ticle by Ursula Günther.[126] More recently, Anne Stone and Yolanda Plumley have succeeded in unraveling the reasons behind the quotations in a number of excellent studies. This is obviously an area that should be linked to the art of memory. Were the composers quoting from memory or from a manuscript? Stone, in particular, has related these citations to the transition from orally transmitted music to written compositions, pieces that were meant to be seen rather than heard.[127] Clearly, this is an important area that merits a book of its own. For now, all I can do is call attention to the fact that further investigation would prove fruitful.

Rhythmic Patterns. We have seen that throughout the Middle Ages it was not only the capacity to retain something in memory that was admired, but also the ability to manipulate the material in the mind (rather than in writing). Within a short time, composers began to delight in all kinds of games involving the tenor patterns: for example, tenors would undergo rhythmic manipulations; patterns would overlap, so that the *color* was longer (or shorter) than the *talea;* composers would extend the repetitions of these patterns to parts other than the tenor (these motets are called panisorhythmic); or the tenor could be presented in retrograde movement. I shall illustrate two of these techniques: rhythmic manipulations and retrograde movement.

Was the process of memorizing rhythmic formulas in treatises on mensural notation similar to the memorization of the counterpoint progressions discussed in chapter 4? Is there any evidence to support our reading of Boen that rhythmic patterns were seen as groups of notes, rather than individual notes? In other words, did musicians apply a process of "chunking" to mensural notation? Were these formulas or chunks manipulated in a way similar to memorized syllables, words, and sentences? If so, what kinds of games and puns did composers play with the notes, and what does the use of these note games tell us about written and oral transmission?

In the early fourteenth century two very important notational innovations took place that gave composers many more rhythmic options. First, every note could now be divided into three or two parts. The shape of a ternary note did not look different from a binary one, and the singer would only know from the mensuration sign or the context what the composer intended. As we will see below, this innovation allowed composers to play around with complex rhythmic manipulations, in particular the juxtaposition of ternary and binary mensurations. Second, four levels of mensuration became available: major mode, minor mode, tempus, and prolation. Major mode refers to the division of the longest note value, the maxima, into *longae;* it can be

126. "Zitate in französischen Liedsätzen."

127. Stone, "Music Writing and Poetic Voice." See also her "Singer at the Fountain." See also Yolanda Plumley, "Citation and Allusion"; "Intertextuality in the Fourteenth-Century Chanson"; and also "Ciconia's *Sus une fontayne.*"

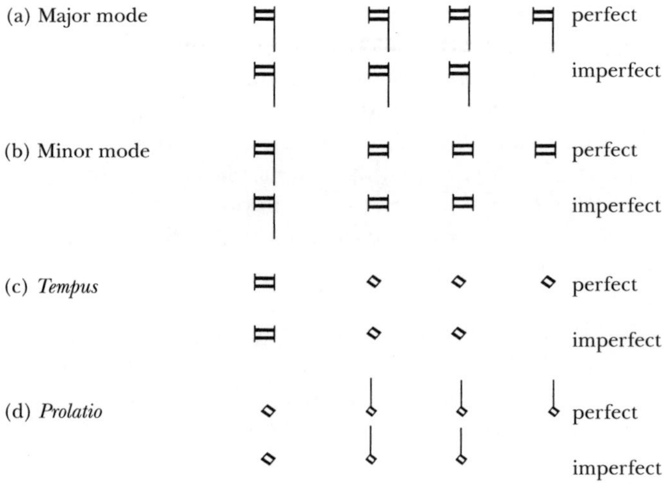

Figure 21. The mensural system

perfect (consisting of three *longae*) or imperfect (two *longae*). Minor mode refers to the division of the *longa* into *breves;* the *longa* again can be perfect (three *breves*), or imperfect (two *breves*). In *tempus perfectum* the *brevis* is divided into three *semibreves,* in *tempus imperfectum* into two. Finally, in major prolation the *semibrevis* includes three *minimae,* in minor prolation two (Figure 21). This means that composers could juxtapose very short and very long note values. Indeed, they had nine different basic note values available to choose from: perfect and imperfect maximas, longs, breves, and semibreves and an imperfect minim. In addition, these note values could be further imperfected (changed from perfect to imperfect) or altered (doubled in value, depending on their position). Thus, we can easily imagine that mensural notation of the Ars nova must have opened up exhilarating possibilities for the composer; but it must also have been a difficult subject to master, and music theorists therefore devoted many pages to explaining its intricacies.[128]

It is important to understand that a discussion of motets in these treatises *always* goes hand in hand with a discussion of mensural notation. In fact, I would go so far as to say that even those treatises on mensural notation that do not deal directly with motets were written in order to give students the technical tools to make them. Moreover, composers finally were able to make

128. For a more detailed discussion, see my *Mensuration and Proportion Signs,* in particular chap. 1. For a shorter summary, which also includes Ars antiqua notation, see my "Evolution of Rhythmic Notation."

use of a notational system where they could indicate note values clearly. Even though, say, the perfect semibreve looked exactly the same as the imperfect semibreve, it was possible to tell from the context or mensuration sign which of the two was intended. In short, for the first time composers had the notational tools to express a great variety of rhythms.

Philippe de Vitry, on whose teachings the treatise *Ars nova* is based,[129] is one of the first great composers of isorhythmic motets. Johannes de Muris, whose *Libellus cantus mensurabilis,* dating from ca. 1340,[130] was the most widely read treatise on mensural notation in the fourteenth and fifteenth centuries, provides the first discussion of isorhythm. Treatises on mensural notation make no less tedious reading than those on counterpoint. They are similarly repetitive and here too the music examples were meant to be memorized. Aegidius de Murino devoted almost half of his treatise to listing tenors that combine various mensurations.[131] Even more detailed is the late fourteenth-century treatise *Ars cantus mensurabilis mensurata per modos iuris,* published by Coussemaker as Anonymous V.[132] I have already mentioned the numerous tree diagrams in this text that aided the memorization of note shapes, alterations, and imperfections (see chap. 3). For the present purpose, the following eight chapters are of interest:[133]

Imperfections and the modes of the maxima (five conclusions)
Imperfection of the perfect maxima, of which all the parts are perfect (seventeen conclusions)
The modes of the long (five conclusions)
Imperfection of the perfect long itself, all parts of which are perfect (eight conclusions)
Perfect time (five conclusions)
The perfect breve, all parts of which are perfect (four conclusions)
Perfect or major prolation (four conclusions)
Imperfection of the perfect semibreve (two conclusions)

These chapters are followed by another four chapters that describe how to make the imperfect maxima, long, breve, and semibreve perfect. All of these rules are followed by examples. Again, we would want to know why theorists do this. Anyone who teaches mensural notation today will begin with a few basic rules and then start transcribing the music. We would certainly not dream of memorizing the many examples and "rules" given by Anonymous V.

129. Fuller, "Phantom Treatise."

130. *Libellus cantus mensurabilis secundum Johannes de Muris,* ed. Katz, 266–88; and CS 3:46–58.

131. *Tractatus cantus mensurabilis,* CS 3:125.

132. Trans. and ed. Balensuela. The treatise was published earlier in CS 3:379–98.

133. *Ars cantus mensurabilis,* 153–89.

I believe that the rhythmic formulas are analogous to the interval progressions we encountered in chapter 4. In both cases the theorists *could* have summarized everything in a few general rules; instead, they tediously list countless specific examples. Fourteenth-century theorists were simply not interested in schooling composers in originality. For them it was more important to have a well-stocked memory that included both intervallic progressions and rhythmic formulas. Thus, the student would have numerous rhythmic formulas characteristic of all mensurations in his mental inventory that he could apply either to help memorize a motet through chunking or to compose one himself. Leech-Wilkinson calls these formulas cells and has demonstrated that there are very few of them that are combined in ever new ways.[134]

And yet, as anybody who has analyzed isorhythmic motets knows, these pieces are anything but a mechanical application of rhythmic patterns. Rather, they seem to rejoice in juxtaposing as many rhythms as possible; they can best be described as a notational playground. They are music's equivalent of word games,[135] but they are also related to the art of memory.

Inter densas / Imbribus (Chantilly, Musée Condé 564, fols. 68v–69) is one of the most complex motets in the Chantilly Codex. It is possible that the composer felt that only an elaborate structure would do justice to the great Gaston Febus, "the man who solves mysteries beyond all others" (triplum, line 23).[136] The mensural transformations in the tenor certainly show that the composer had complete control over the new mensural system and the motet was undoubtedly made to demonstrate the composer's ability to handle all of the new mensurations. The triplum consists of eight four-line stanzas; each line has ten syllables, rhyming abba, with the exception of the first strophe, which rhymes abab (see p. 239).

The text sings extravagant praise of Febus. The motetus consists of fourteen hexameters and pentameters, each of which is divided into two parts. The motetus also makes numerous references to Febus' achievements (the towers he has built, the cow in his coat of arms; the last lines refer to his enemy, the Count of Armagnac). Ursula Günther has suggested that the text of the tenor, "Admirabile est nomen tuum" (added by a later scribe), similarly

134. Leech-Wilkinson, "Compositional Procedure in Machaut's 'Hoquetus David.'"

135. For two excellent studies of musical games that could not have come into existence without notation in the Ars subtilior, see Stone, "Singer at the Fountain"; and "Composer's Voice."

136. For more on Febus, see *Motets of the Manuscripts Chantilly*, ed. Günther, lxii–lxv. A modern edition of the motet is on pp. 66–70, as well as in *Motets of French Provenance*, ed. Harrison, 162–66.

TRIPLUM

Inter densas deserti meditans
silvas, pridem allectus ocio,
in sonore rivulus crepitans
invasit me sompni devocio.

"Ecce princeps occurit inclitus,
flava caput textum cesarie,
auro, gemmis desuper varie
per amictum solerter insitus.

Hunc circumdat caterva militum
et tironum non minor copia
nescientum quid sit inopia:
Reverentur hii omnes inclitum.

Is thesauri cumulos geminat,
quod invident cernentes emuli,
sed mirantur gaudentes populi
cum thesaurum hinc inde seminat.

Hic exhaurit orbis confinia
ut adamas, quod ferrum attrahit.
Quantum magnus se nullus retrahit
quin visitet potentis limina.

Hic vallatus rethorum gregibus
et auscultans prudentum dogmata
super omnes solvit enigmata:
Cunctos vincit libris et legibus.

Stupet orbis totus attonitus
conspiciens huius magnalia.
Deum hostium prosternit prelia,
terras omnes implevit sonitus."

Tunc exultans de tam miris rebus,
nomen querens huius magnifici
tam illustris, confestim didici
quod is erat potens ille Phebus.

MOTETUS

Imbribus irriguis et vivo fonte redundans,
plantis et arboribus vernoque tempore florens,
hortus odoriferis fragrans aromatibus, – umbris
otia querentes recreati plaudant amenis, –
turribus excelso protensis in ethere cinctus;
varia vestitum nutrit pictura pavonem.
Fertilis hic uberes fructus producit amenos,
prestat in occasum Phebo declinante recessus.
O quam spectandus! Colit hunc agricola tauro.
Mira res! Hunc genitrix tuetur cornibus hortum,
cavet ab ingressu merito temerarii manus
cornibus, o genitrix, saucia facta tuis.
Quisquis es invidens, ut frauds fructibus hortum,
huius ab agricola ne tenearis cave.

refers to Febus in comparing him to God as in Psalm 8: "Dominus noster, quam admirabile est nomen tuum in universa terra."[137] There is no known source of the tenor pitches.

The tenor consists of all six notes of the B-flat hexachord: B♭, c, d, e♭, f, g.[138] The idea behind the rhythm seems to be to employ all available note values, starting with the minim, officially the shortest note value, through the semibreve, breve, and long, and ending with the perfect maxima, the longest note value. In addition, the composer wants to demonstrate how these note values can be manipulated. The canon (the inscription instructing how to perform the tenor) reads as follows:

> The tenor is performed eight times, first in perfect mode and time of the greater [perfect and imperfect always apply to major mode and tempus, greater and lesser to minor mode and prolation], the second way in imperfect mode and time of the greater, third in perfect mode and time of the less, fourth in imperfect mode and time of the less, fifth in perfect mode of the greater and perfect time of the less, sixth in imperfect mode of the greater and imperfect time of the less, seventh in perfect mode of the less and perfect time of the greater, eighth in imperfect mode of the less and perfect time of the greater, choosing the [final] rests so that the mode may be perfect.[139]

The tenor is notated only once (Example 41), but appears in eight different rhythms: first in perfect major and minor mode, perfect time and major prolation (81 minims per maxima), second in imperfect major mode, perfect minor mode, imperfect time, and major prolation (36 minims), third in perfect major mode, imperfect minor mode, perfect time, and minor prolation (36 minims), fourth in imperfect major and minor mode, imperfect time, and minor prolation (16 minims), fifth in perfect major and minor mode, perfect time, and minor prolation (54 minims), sixth in imperfect major mode, perfect minor mode, imperfect time, and minor prolation (24 minims), seventh in perfect major mode, imperfect minor mode, perfect time, and major prolation (54 minims), and eighth in imperfect major and minor mode, perfect time, and major prolation (36 minims). Note that the composer did not use all available mensurations. For example, imperfect major and mi-

137. Ibid., lxiii.

138. Note that the hexachord is fictive, since the low B♭ is an addition to the gamut.

139. "Octies dicitur tenor: primo de modo et tempore maior[is] perfecto, 2° modo de modo et tempore maior[is] inperfecto, 3° de modo et tempore minoris perfecto, 4° de modo et tempore minoris inperfecto, 5° de modo maior[is] et tempore minoris perfecto, 6° de modo maior[is] et [tempore] minoris inperfecto, 7° de modo minoris et tempore maior[is] perfecto, 8° de modo minoris inperfecto et tempore maioris perfecto, elugendo [for eligendo] pausam ut modus sit perfectus." See *Motets of French Provenance*, ed. Harrison, 199. The motet is transcribed on pp. 162–66. See also the transcription by Günther in *Motets of the Manuscripts Chantilly*, lxiv.

Example 41. Tenor of *Inter densas / Imbribus,* Chantilly, Musée Condé 564, fols. 68v–69

nor mode, imperfect time, and major prolation is missing. But the student who had mastered this tenor would know how to handle alteration and imperfection on every mensural level.

The upper parts are not isorhythmic for the simple reason that the tenor appears in a new rhythmic guise each time it is repeated, and it would have been very difficult to construct repetitive patterns under such circumstances. And yet, the top parts would also not have been hard to memorize. First, the end of the *color* usually coincides with the end of a triplum stanza (mm. 25, 36, 50, 76), or with the end of a line (mm. 58, 83, 101). Similarly, the phrase- or hemistich-ends of the motetus text also fall together with the end of the *color.* More importantly, even though the triplum is not isorhythmic, it makes consistent use of rhythmic patterns that are either repeated note for note, or slightly varied. The triplum phrases include anywhere from five to sixteen perfections, but the vast majority (fourteen) measure five.[140] The rhythmic patterns in these phrases can be classified into two different groups (Table 4). The fifteen patterns of Group 1 appear twenty-one times in the triplum. Version (a) occurs four times (the measure numbers are indicated in the table), version (b) three times, and the remaining seven versions only once, except for (n), which occurs twice. The patterns of Group 2 start with longer note values and include seven phrases altogether. Note that within both groups the variations are minute.

Some of the rhythmic patterns also occur in the motetus: for example, pattern (a) from Group 1 appears in the second hemistich of line 13 (mm. 97–99), pattern (i) from Group 1 in the second hemistich of line 6 (mm. 46–48); others are indicated in the table. If the rhythmic pattern is not identical, but very similar, I have enclosed it in parentheses.

These patterns might not be easy to hear because the pitches vary. Yet, like the patterns of the rhythmic modes discussed in chapter 5, they would have made memorization easier.[141]

140. Lines 5, 18, 19, 20, 21, 22, 23, 24, 27, 28, 29, 30, 31, 32. Of the others, five include six perfections (lines 7, 8, 10, 17, 25), six seven (lines 6, 12, 13, 15, 16, 26); three eight (lines 9, 11, 14); one ten (line 4), one eleven (line 1), and one twelve (line 2). I have included rests in counting the perfections.

141. For a similar analysis of rhythmic cells, see Leech-Wilkinson, "Compositional Procedure in Machaut's 'Hocquetus David.'"

TABLE 4. Rhythmic Groups in *Inter densas deserti meditans / Imbribus irriguis*

Rhythm		*Triplum*	*Frequency*	*Motetu*
	GROUP 1			
(a)		31–33, 62–64, 79–81, 84–86	4	97–9
(b)		25–27, 59–61, 102–4	3	
(c)		34–36	1	
(d)		97–99	1	
(e)		69–71	1	
(f)		71–73	1	
(g)		99–101	1	
(h)		107–9	1	
(i)		34–40	1	46–4
(j)	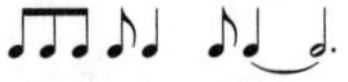	3–4	1	
(k)		81–83	1	
(l)		86–88	1	
(m)		41–43	1	
(n)		66–68, 104–6	2	(2–4), (104–6), (107–9
(o)		76–78	1	
	GROUP 2			
(a)	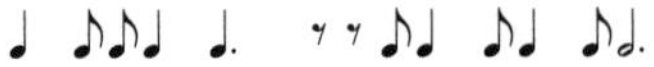	44–47	1	(84–85
(b)		93–96	1	(30–33
(c)	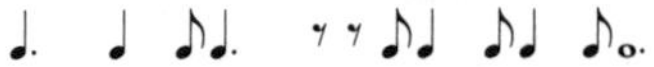	7–10	1	(100–2
(d)		13–17	1	
(e)		21–25	1	
(f)		27–30	1	
(g)		48–50	1	
(h)		89–92	1	

TABLE 5. Harmonic Rhythm in *Inter densas deserti meditans / Imbribus irriguis*

	TENOR PITCHES											
	g	e♭	f	B♭	d					c		
STATEMENT*												
1	c		d/B♭†	B♭	d/b♮	b♮	D	D	D	c	C	[G F Cg]‡
2	g	e♭/c	d	B♭	B♮/D	D				C		
3	g	e♭	d	B♭	d	B♮	D				C	[G F]
4	g	e♭	d	B♭	D	B♮					C	
5	g	e♭	d	B♭	B♭/d	d	d	d	D	D	C	
6	g/e♭	e♭	d	B♭	b♮						C	
7	G	c	B♭	B♭	b♮					D	C	
8	e♭	e♭	d/B♭	B♭			B♭/d				c	

*Capital letters signal a major chord, lower case letters a minor chord. Only chords at the beginning of the tenor note are given.

† A doubled note indicates a sixth chord.

‡ Bracketed notes represent the harmonies when the tenor is silent.

This motet also serves as an example of how composers could have planned the note-against-note framework. It is perhaps not surprising that, with a few exceptions, every time the *color* is repeated the chords are the same (Table 5). Note that the fourth note always has a B-flat chord, and the sixth note a C chord. The intervals are distributed differently, depending on the range. But if we look at the triplum and tenor for the first four tenor pitches in *taleae* 5, 6, and 7 (Example 42), where the triplum begins on the same tone, we notice that the interval progressions are virtually the same. Thus, the tenor would determine the harmonic and rhythmic outline of the entire piece.

Palindrome. The earliest known example of a retrograde statement goes back to the Notre Dame period. On fol. 150r–v of manuscript F the scribe notated a number of "Dominus" *clausulae,* followed by one entitled "Nusmido," which mirrors the three syllables of "dominus." The palindrome in the text is accompanied by a mirror of the tenor pitches (not the rhythm) that stretches over twenty notes. The fact that the mirror is so long suggests that it cannot have been conceived without writing or visualization.

Mirrors involving pitch and rhythm presuppose an unambiguous rhythmic notational system. Most early motet sources do not distinguish clearly between separate note values. Thus, it is often impossible to settle on one correct version of a piece. In the late thirteenth century many of the ambiguities characteristic of modal notation were gradually eliminated. Franco gives specific rules for the length of the notes in ligatures. He knew three

Example 42. Interval progressions in *Inter densas / Imbribus*

basic note values: the *longa,* the *brevis,* and the *semibrevis.* The *longa* could be divided into three *breves,* and the *brevis* into three *semibreves.* This system allowed for only limited rhythmic possibilities, which were covered by modal patterns.

It is, therefore, only in the fourteenth century that we encounter true palindromes of rhythmic patterns. Vitry's motet *Garrit gallus / In nova fert* has a tenor based on a neuma where the *talea* itself is a palindrome (Example 43).[142] Vitry begins his *talea* in the perfect minor mode with a ternary long and two breves. He then switches to imperfect minor mode, signaled through coloration. Next, the imperfect minor mode passage is given in mirror form, followed by the major mode section in mirror form. Virginia Newes has noticed that alteration of the second breve in the first ligature does not conform to Franco's rules.[143] Franco allows alteration of the second breve only when it is followed by a long. I am not convinced that Vitry is breaking Franco's rules of alteration, since in the example there is no doubt that the

142. Brackets indicate red notes. See also Margaret Bent's discussion of the motet in "Fauvel and Marigny."

143. Newes, "Writing, Reading, and Memorizing," 219–20.

Example 43. Palindrome in the *talea* of Vitry, *Garrit gallus / In nova fert*

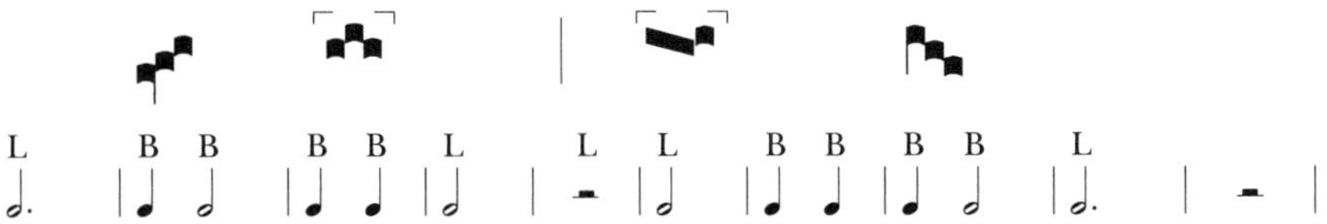

Example 44. Tenor pattern of *Alpha vibrans monumentum / Coetus venit heroicus / Amicum querit,* Chantilly, Musée Condé 564, fols. 64v–65

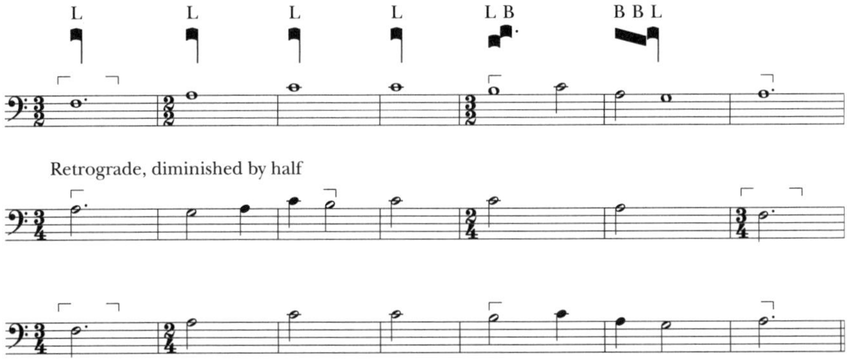

second breve comes at the end of a perfection because of the coloration. And this is probably what Franco had in mind when he stated that the second breve can only be altered before a long. But I think that Newes's suggestion is correct, that Vitry chose to notate this rhythm through a ternary ligature in order to mirror the ternary ligature at the end. Thus, the mirror is also presented graphically in mensural notation. The singer can see instantly that there is a palindrome. Note, though, that while the rhythm within each perfection is preserved, there is not a note-by-note palindrome. Just as a medieval scholar could demonstrate that he had really "learned" or "mastered" the text when he could recite it backwards, a medieval musician might be admired for applying mirrors to his tenors.

There is another such example in the isorhythmic motet *Alpha vibrans monumentum / Coetus venit heroicus / Amicum querit* from the Chantilly manuscript, discussed above. The tenor has one *color,* consisting of two nine-note *taleae* (Example 44; see Figures 19–20 above). The tenor has the following instruction: "The red [notes] are in perfect mode, the black in imperfect. And one must sing each division of the tune, before observing the rest, in diminution by half and in retrograde order, from the last note to the first; then one must sing the same division of tune, again in diminution by half, in normal order, from the first to the last."[144] Normally, coloration makes ternary notes binary, but here it makes binary notes ternary. The *color* comprises thirty-six notated notes, divided into four sections. In each section, after the tenor has been presented in its original note values, both the pitches and the note values are read in retrograde. In addition, all note values are diminished by one half. Then the segment is repeated again from the beginning, again in diminution.

The similarity of this procedure to the kind of word games described by Jacobus Publicius is obvious. The question is, how did musicians learn this tenor? Did they sing it from the manuscript or did they memorize it by listening to it? And how do these "note games" relate to the art of memory?

Virginia Newes has argued that the last ligature in the tenor, BBL, would not produce the desired alteration when read backwards. The second breve should be a long, which according to Franconian rules is not possible. She therefore concludes: "The tenor, once he had read through each nine-note melodic segment of his part, had to reproduce its realized durations from memory in reversed order and reduced by half; rereading the notational symbols backwards would not have produced the desired rhythmic sequence."[145] While Newes is probably right that singers sang the tenor by heart, I think they could have done so only when visualizing the pitches. Try to reverse a melody without visualizing it or writing it down, and you will soon see that it is impossible. Once it is seen or imagined as written, you will have no trouble singing it in retrograde, in inversion, or even retrograde inversion. We need some kind of visual reference in order to manipulate the tenors, but we do not in fact need to write them down. The important point is that it does not matter whether we visualize them on the staff or write them down. These are precisely the kind of word games Goody had in mind when he described the effects of writing.

But what about the retrograde version of the rhythm? While it is possible that the singer would remember to mirror it, we also have to consider the possibility that the problematic measure was sung breve–long. Jacobus Publicius reverses not only every single letter in a word (for example, *rebus* and *suber*) but also syllabic units (as in *nabo* and *bona*). If the composer of *Alpha vibrans* thought in terms of perfections (which are music's equivalent of syllables), he would have kept the original rhythm for every perfection, but mirrored the sequence of perfections.

The text of both the triplum and and the motetus consists of four stanzas with regular rhymes (see p. 247). The ending of the first stanza in the

144. "Rubee dicuntur modo perfecto, nigre imperfecto. Et in qualibet talia antequam pausetur retroeatur per semi ab ultima *ad primam* ipsius tallie notam. Et iterum eodem modo diminuendo a prima ad notam ultimam eiusdem tallie redicatur." Chantilly, Musée Condé 564, fol. 64v. Trans. from Harrison in *Motets of French Provenance,* 198, with some changes.

145. Newes, "Writing, Reading, and Memorizing," 224.

TRIPLUM

Alpha vibrans monumentum
alma vexit ad crementum.
Iubar fit Egipti portentum,
in lucem mox proditus;
onix fulgens in prerupta
intus gemma extra ducta,
altrinsecus non est rupta
sic puella incorrupta.

Achates apocalipsis
in scopulo discernitur.
Vates tunc matris felicis
in lectulo reperitur.
Thimus manta cum virore,
niveum ferens candorem
virgo mater cum pudore
utriusque tenens florem.

Novus partus novam prolem
prophitentem ipsum solem
destinat ad mundi molem
et vasta mundi spatia.
Frutex et flos pariunt fructum,
qui canit ante vultum.
Paranimphus et sodales
sistro ymno sunt equales.

A summis silicibus
prodeunt cives gloriosi,
perstrepentes laudibus
eunt heredes generosi.
Eya, pervigiles
inquiunt complices superni:
Accedite, humiles,
ad gaudium cordis interni.

MOTETUS

Coetus venit heroicus
nati vitam imitatus,
cuius princeps seraphicus
mirifice transformatus.
Hunc claustrales et regales
prosecuntur ad libitum
linquentes paternas lares
suum ferentes habitum.

Alter intrat vir etheus,
suffultus ut Heliseus
cui credit Philisteus,
prostratus ut Iebuseus,
alte sonans inclitus:
"Tua cupio comercia
ac necti volo penitus
michi tua consortia."

Amictusque floribus
clamat ex mentis letitia:
"Tuis accinctus funibus
letor et de inopia
certi", floresque relegavit.
Ex partu virgineo
novo flores adoptavit
conceptuque calcaneo.

Cygnus venit et columba,
rosa mundi, mens iocunda,
clara fit virgo iocunda,
Francisci timpanistria.
Amor traxit divinorum
rogatusque musicorum
biblicum insontem morum
nactus zelo contentorum.

Tenor: Amicum querit
[pristinum, qui spretum in]

top voices coincides with the end of the first *color* in the tenor (m. 30), the end of the second stanza with the end of the retrograde statement of the second part of this *color* (m. 63), and the end of the third stanza with end of the second *color* (m. 100). All four stanzas are followed by a hocket section. In other words, the poetry reinforces the tenor structure at all crucial points. Again, this would have helped memorization. In addition, the upper voices are strictly isorhythmic. The triplum *talea* consists of 172 notes. I have argued that all parts of an isorhythmic motet were sung by heart. How, then, would a performer have been able to commit a triplum of 172 notes to memory? Ursula Günther has noticed that the triplum alternates between perfect time with minor prolation and imperfect time with minor prolation. The triplum *talea* comprises sixty-seven breves, and of these, fifty-four are in imperfect time with minor prolation (I exclude mm. 24–29 because they are ambiguous). Table 6 summarizes the rhythmic cells according to their frequency: there are nine rhythmic motives, of which the first two are by far the most common (they occur twenty-one and eighteen times). These rhythmic cells are short and therefore similar to syllables that make up words, or numbers that become dates of important historical events. They are regarded as an entity, not as separate letters or numbers. It seems, then, that the performer would not remember that his *talea* consists of 172 notes; rather, he would remember the division of *talea* 1 into four stanzas, and within each stanza he would probably think in breve units, or do what psychologists call "chunking."

What can we conclude from this example? We should certainly not assume that because it is so complex it could not have been sung by heart. The rhythmic pattern of the tenor by itself is not difficult. All the singers needed to remember were nine notes and their transformations. Singing these transformations by heart would have required visualization and understanding of mensural notation. But a singer with a solid background in music theory would have had no problem in performing the entire motet without a manuscript. He could show that he had truly "mastered" the tenor and mensural notation just as an orator could show that he knew his text inside out when he could recite it backwards. Similarly, the singers of the other voices would easily be able to memorize the entire piece by following the isorhythmic structure and organization, consisting of a small number of rhythmic cells.

In this chapter I have suggested that composers would have applied mnemonic techniques to compose elaborate pieces in their mind, similar to the method orators and writers used in constructing their works. Composers of isorhythmic motets must have adapted a number of methods from composers of verbal texts. First, the text could either be written down or visualized. Only a written or imagined text could be recalled exactly. Second, a piece needed

TABLE 6. Rhythmic Cells in the Triplum of *Alpha vibrans monumentum / Coetus venit heroicus / Amicum querit*

Rhythm		*Frequency*
(a)	♩ ♩	21
(b)	♫ ♫	18
(c)	𝄾 ♪ ♩	4
(d)	𝅝	3
(e)	♪ ♩ ♪	2
(f)	𝄽 ♩	2
(g)	♩ 𝄽	1
(h)	♩ ♫	1
(i)	𝄼	1

to be structured well in order to be remembered. The structure could resemble a house, a monastic building, or a simple diagram. Evidence from music theory suggests that composers first structured the outline of the entire composition, then allocated the text, and finally worked out the isorhythmic *taleae* in sections, possibly in some kind of grid system. More specifically, the composer would use mnemonic techniques to organize both the larger structure of the motet and the filling-in of the different parts. He would begin by picking a tenor from his mental inventory of chant, organize it by repeating the pitch patterns *(colores),* and then divide it into shorter repetitive rhythmic units *(taleae).* The organization of the tenor would determine that of the other voices. We have seen that for every tenor progression there is only a limited number of interval progressions available. Then, when the larger outline was determined, the composer would not only visualize the larger structure but also the interval progressions on the staff as he composed or performed the piece. Reinhard Strohm has an astute description of compositional process in his *Rise of European Music:*

> The singer would know in advance that a total of twelve quavers was at his disposal for the whole passage. He would think in terms of larger units which he then filled with asymmetrical detail.
>
> Such a "hierarchical" procedure was quite comparable to the compositional structure of isorhythmic motets. It involved, whether in composition or in performance, first a "mapping out" of stretches of time and then a "filling them in." In motets, this kind of thinking separated the two parameters of "rhythm" *(talea)* and "pitch" *(color),* which were taken care of one at a time. The procedure was also analogous to that of a painter who first drew the lines and then coloured the spaces; it was analogous to that of the orator who first organized

> his material *(dispositio)* and then worked it out *(elocutio)*. The actual delivery of the speech followed *(actio, pronuntiatio)*, which could well be compared to a musical performance.[146]

Strohm is correct in drawing a parallel between the orator and the composer, the former mapping out his speech, the latter arranging the larger structure into *colores* and *taleae*, and then filling out each unit in turn. But I am taking Strohm's view a step further in that I believe that all these structures are related to the art of memory. Just as each "room" of Bradwardine's structure would have a characteristic quality that made it memorable, each *talea* would have a characteristic rhythmic pattern that would make it easy to remember. The composer would remember the mensurations, the particular pattern, and alterations of these patterns. In other words, he would no longer see separate note values, but instead would "chunk" them.

Friedrich Ludwig and Heinrich Besseler[147] have already commented extensively on the fact that isorhythm in all parts first appears in the hocket section. Precisely because the hockets appeared at phrase ends and had no text, they needed to follow rigid patterns in order to be memorable. Motets by the next generation of motet composers, such as our example from Chantilly, are usually isorhythmic in all parts. Here too, the rigid structures must have helped in the process of composition and performance.

Like the architectural structures described by Carruthers, the isorhythmic motet could be seen in a single gaze. The entire composition would fit onto an opening, and a glance at the tenor would tell the singer instantly how the piece was structured. This aspect of medieval notation is entirely lost in modern transcriptions, where a motet might take some six or seven pages and the singer has to look carefully for architectural structures.

Motets are the first musical genre that could be notated in an unambiguous notational system. Even someone who did not know the piece beforehand would be able to perform it if he had mastered mensural notation. The ability to control rhythm fully had an immediate effect on the musical repertory. Rhythmic notation led to a new way of composition. It led to what Jack Goody would call "visual perception of musical phenomena."[148] First, it was important to keep control of the bewildering rhythmic possibilities. This is why the musical notes were forced into *taleae* (see Johannes Boen above). But mensural notation did more than that: just as writing led to word games and crossword puzzles, notation led to notational games. A singer would not

146. Strohm, *Rise of European Music,* 46.

147. Besseler, "Studien zur Musik des Mittelalters II," 192 ff.

148. Goody, *Interface between the Written and the Oral,* 122. I have substituted "musical" for Goody's "linguistic."

be able to sing a melody retrograde without locating it on the staff or hand; he would not be able to apply the rhythmic manipulations we have observed in the tenor without notation. Thus, mensural notation ultimately resulted in what we would consider a modern artwork, a composition where the composer would determine the pitch and rhythm of every part, where he would develop a sense of ownership.

Conclusion

Throughout this book I have tried to determine how the oral and written transmission of music interacts with the art of memory; or, to put it differently, what effect mnemotechnics had on medieval performers, composers, and the music they produced. The single most important result of this study is that it allows us to see how oral and written transmission complement each other throughout the Middle Ages. This is particularly apparent in three areas:

First, we have seen that writing does not make memorization redundant; instead, it allows for new ways of committing musical material to memory. Throughout their lives, singers built up memorial archives consisting of chant, elementary music theory, and interval progressions. All of the memorized material, whether it was chant or counterpoint progressions, was organized in a systematic way according to abstract musical principles that helped in the process of memorization and retrieval. Thus, a singer who wanted to sing polyphony would take a chant melody from his mental inventory, organize it rhythmically, and then place a second or third part against it. This would be easy because he had all possible progressions of consonances at the tip of his tongue. Alternatively, he could choose to preserve his composition in writing.

Second, we have observed that a repertory preserved in writing tells us very little about its origin and transmission. The pieces transmitted in the Magnus liber organi, for example, long considered the first worked-out written compositions, were very likely transmitted orally and put together from memorized formulas in ever new ways. There is no such thing as one final correct version of these pieces; rather, the singers probably altered them whenever they sang them. While these pieces were written down, it seems that notation was not necessary to create and transmit them. They were sung by heart and most likely written down so that the whole repertory might be preserved, rather than to make it available for performance. Such a transmission goes hand in hand with an ambiguous notational system, which often allows for different rhythmic interpretations.

On the other hand, isorhythmic motets, which came into existence only about one hundred years later, could not have come about without writing. Their creation coincides with the development of Ars nova notation, which provided composers with a notational system that was more or less unambiguous and substantially increased the rhythmic possibilities. We now observe a distinct difference between composers and performers. Thus, it is not surprising that at this time pieces begin to be attributed to composers with increasing frequency. The composer takes pride in his creations, which need to be transmitted intact in order to make sense. A performer cannot suddenly decide to change pitches or note values or add a melisma without jeopardizing the intended structure. Very soon composers began to take delight in making use of rhythmic and melodic manipulations that would have been impossible without writing, such as diminution and retrograde motion.

And yet, these pieces were conceived in the mind and sung by heart. The art of memory played an important role in the transmission and composition of early polyphony and allows us to explain stylistic characteristics of the repertory. Notre Dame polyphony is written in modal notation, characterized by repetitive rhythmic patterns. A comparison with didactic poetry of the period shows that meters were regularly used to help memorize difficult material. Since music theorists draw a parallel between the rhythmic modes and poetic meters, it is likely that rhythmic modes helped singers to memorize the music. In fact, repetitive rhythmic patterns might have been used in the first place because they were memorable.

Similarly, the art of memory allows us to explain how composers could work out complicated three- and four-part structures like the isorhythmic motet in the mind and how singers could memorize these pieces. Orators and authors used architectural structures similar to those encountered in isorhythmic motets to work out entire speeches and books in the mind. Indeed, music theorists regularly draw a comparison between foundations of houses and tenors of motets. They also argue that isorhythm is useful to organize and plan compositions in the mind. There are numerous references to visualization. Thus, I suggest that composers of isorhythmic motets chose to organize their pieces in tightly organized structures because it allowed them to work out the pieces in their mind and make them memorable to performers. Ars nova notation allowed them to see the entire musical structure on an opening, an important condition for mnemonic structures.

In sum, this study should allow us to give up the naive picture of a written musical culture replacing an oral one with the more complicated picture of a culture in which orality and literacy interacted in many, often unexpected, ways.

BIBLIOGRAPHY

PRIMARY SOURCES

Aaron, Pietro. *Libri tres de institutione harmonica.* Bologna: Benedetto Ettore di Faellis, 1516. Repr. New York: Broude Bros., 1976.

———. *Thoscanello de la musica* (Venice: Vernardio and Matheo de Vitali, 1523). Revised edition with a supplement published as *Thoscanello in musica.* Venice: Bernardino and Matheo de Vitali, 1529. Repr. New York: Broude Bros., 1969.

Abbaco, Paolo dell', *Trattato d'aritmetica.* Edited by Gino Arrighi. Pisa: Domus Galilaeana, 1964.

Ad Herennium. Edited and translated by Harry Caplan. The Loeb Classical Library. Cambridge, MA: Harvard University Press, 1954.

Adam de la Halle. *Œuvres complètes.* Edited by Pierre-Yves Badel. Lettres gothiques. Paris: Le Livre de Poche, 1995.

Adam von Fulda. *Musica.* In GS 3:329–81. Translation by Peter John Slemon: "Adam von Fulda on musica plana and compositio de musica, Book II: A Translation and Commentary." Ph.D. diss., University of British Columbia, 1994.

Aegidius de Murino. *Tractatus cantus mensurabilis.* In CS 3:124–28.

Agobard of Lyon. *Agobardi Lugdunensis Opera omnia.* Edited by L. van Acker. Corpus Christianorum, Continuatio Medievalis, no. 52. Turnhout: Brepols, 1981.

Alain de Lille. *Textes inédits.* Edited by Marie-Therese d'Alverny. EPM 52. Paris: Librairie philosophique, 1965.

Alia musica: Édition critique commentée avec une introduction sur l'origine de la nomenclature modale pseudo-grecque au Moyen Age. Edited by Jacques Chailley. Paris: Centre de Documentation Universitaire, 1965. Translated by Edmund Heard: "'Alia Musica': A Chapter in the History of Medieval Music Theory." Ph.D. diss., University of Wisconsin, 1966.

Amerus. *Practica artis musicae.* Edited by Cesarino Ruini. CSM 25. Rome: American Institute of Musicology, 1977.

Anonymous IV. (CS I). *De mensuris et discantu.* Edited by Fritz Reckow, *Der Musiktratktat des Anon. IV.* Beihefte zum Archiv für Musikwissenschaft, nos. 4–5. Wiesbaden:

Franz Steiner, 1967. Translated by Jeremy Yudkin as *The New Music Treatise of Anonymous IV: A New Translation.* MSD 61. Neuhausen-Stuttgart: Hänssler-Verlag, 1975.

Anonymous V. (CS III). *Ars cantus mensurabilis mensurata per modos iuris.* Edited and translated by C. Matthew Balensuela. Lincoln: University of Nebraska Press, 1994.

Anonymous VII. (CS I). *De musica libellus,* in CS 1:378–83.

Anonymous XI. (CS III). *Tractatus de musica plana et mensurabili.* Edited and translated by Richard Joseph Wingell as "Anonymous XI (CS III): An Edition, Translation, and Commentary." Ph.D. diss., University of Southern California, 1973.

Anonymous of St. Emmeram. *De musica mensurata.* Edited by Heinrich Sowa in *Ein anonymer glossierter Mensuraltraktat, 1279.* Kassel: Bärenreiter, 1930. New edition and translation by Jeremy Yudkin: *De musica mensurata: The Anonymous of St. Emmeram.* Bloomington, IN: Indiana University Press, 1990.

Anonymus tractatus de contrapuncto et de musica mensurabili. Edited by Christian Meyer. CSM 40. Neuhausen-Stuttgart: Hänssler-Verlag, 1995.

Aquinas, Thomas. *Commentary on Aristotle's De anima.* Translated by Kenelm Foster and Silvester Humphries. London: Routledge, 1951.

———. *Summa theologica.* Blackfriars edition. New York: McGraw-Hill, 1964–81.

Aribo. *De musica.* Edited by Joseph Smits van Waesberghe. CSM 2. Rome: American Institute of Musicology, 1951.

Aristotle. *Metaphysics.* Edited by Richard McKeon in *The Basic Works of Aristotle,* 689–926. New York, 1941.

———. *On Memory.* Translated by Richard Sorabji. Providence, RI: Brown University Press, 1972.

———. *Poetics.* In *The Complete Works of Aristotle. The Revised Oxford Translation.* Edited by Jonathan Barnes. Bollingen series, no.71.2. Princeton: Princeton University Press, 1984.

Ars contrapuncti secundum Johannem de Muris. CS 3:59–68.

Augustine. *De musica.* Edited and translated by L. Schopp as "On Music." In *The Writings of Saint Augustine.* New York, 1947.

Aurelian of Réôme. *Musica disciplina.* Edited by Lawrence Gushee. CSM 21. N.p.: American Institute of Musicology, 1975. Translated by Joseph Ponte as *The Discipline of Music.* Colorado College Music Press, Translations, no. 3. Colorado Springs: Colorado College Music Press, 1968.

Barzizza, Gasparinus. *De imitatione.* Edited by G. W. Pigman in *Bibliothèque d'Humanisme et Renaissance* 44 (1982): 341–52.

Berno of Reichenau. *Epistola de tonis*; *Prologus in tonarium;* and *Bern Augiensis tonarius.* Edited by Alexander Rausch in *Die Musiktraktate des Abtes Bern von Reichenau: Edition und Interpretation.* Tutzing, 1999.

Boen, Johannes. *Ars (musicae).* Edited by F. Alberto Gallo. CSM 19. N.p.: American Institute of Musicology, 1972.

Bradwardine, Thomas. "De memoria artificiali adquirenda." Edited by Mary Carruthers in *Journal of Medieval Latin* 2 (1992): 25–43.

———. "De memoria artificiali." Translated by Mary Carruthers in *The Book of Memory: A Study in Medieval Culture,* 281–88. Cambridge, 1990.

Burchard, Udalrich. *Hortulus musices.* Leipzig: Melchior Lotter, 1514.

Burtius, Nicolaus. *Florum libellus.* Edited by Giuseppe Massera. Historiae Musicae Cultores Biblioteca 28. Florence: Olschki, 1975. Translated by Clement Miller. MSD 37. Neuhausen-Stuttgart: Hänssler-Verlag, 1983.

Calandri, Filippo. *Aritmetica.* Florence, Biblioteca Riccardiana, MS 2669. Facs. Florence: Cassa di risparmio di Firenze, 1969.

Cataneo, Pietro. *Le practiche delle due prime matematiche.* Venice: Giovanni Griffio, 1567.

Charland, T. M., ed. *Artes praedicandi.* Ottawa: Institut d'études médiévales, 1936.

Cicero. *De oratore.* Vol. 2. Edited and translated by W. Sutton and H. Rackham. Loeb Classical Library. London: Heinemann, 1942–48.

Cochlaeus, Johannes. *Musica activa.* 2nd ed. N.p., 1505. Second ed. edited by Hugo Riemann. "Anonymi Introductorium Musicae." *Monatshefte für Musikgeschichte* 29 (1897): 147–54 and 157–64, and 30 (1898): 1–8 and 11–19.

———. *Tetrachordum musices.* Nuremberg: Johann Weyssenburger, 1511. Repr. Hildesheim: Olms, 1971. Translated by Clement Miller. MSD 23. N.p., 1970.

Commemoratio brevis de tonis et psalmis modulandi. Edited and translated by Terence Bailey. Ottawa: The University of Ottawa Press, 1979.

Commentum super tonos. Edited by Joseph Smits van Waesberghe. Divitiae musicae artis A. I. Buren: Frits Knuf, 1975.

Compendium discantus. (Pseudo-Franco). Oxford, Bodleian Library, MS Bodley 842, fols. 60^r–62^v.

De contrapuncto quaedam regulae utiles. Attr. to Andrea Phillipotus in CS 3:116–18.

De discantu simplici. Edited by Jacques Handschin in "Aus der alten Musiktheorie, I–II." *Acta musicologica* 14 (1942): 22–27.

De modorum formulis et tonarius. Edited by Clyde Brockett. CSM 37. Neuhausen-Stuttgart: Hänssler-Verlag, 1997.

Della Porta, Giovanni Battista. *L'arte del ricordare.* Naples: Marco Antonio Passaro, 1566.

Dico che 'l contrapunto. Washington, DC, Library of Congress, ML 171. J6, fols. 81–94v. Edited by Pier Paolo Scattolin in "La regola del *grado* nella teoria medievale del contrappunto." *Rivista italiana di musicologia* 14 (1979): 52–74.

Dico che noi abbiamo nel contrapunto. Edited by Albert Seay in *Anonymous (15th-Century), Quatuor tractatuli italici de contrapuncto,* 25–39. Colorado College Music Press Critical Texts, no. 3. Colorado Springs: Colorado College Music Press, 1977.

Dietricus. *Regula super discantum.* Edited by Hans Muller in *Eine Abhandlung über Mensuralmusik in der Karlsruher Handschrift St. Peter pergamen. 29a.* Leipzig: B. G. Teubner, 1886.

Egidius de Murino. *Tractatus cantus mensurabilis.* CS 3:124–28.

Eiximenis, Francesc. *On Two Kinds of Order that Aid Understanding and Memory.* In *The Medieval Craft of Memory,* edited by Mary Carruthers and Jan Ziolkowski and trans. Kimberly Rivers, 189–204. Philadelphia: University of Pennsylvania Press, 2002.

Finck, Hermann. *Practica musica.* Wittenberg: Georg Rhau, 1556. Repr. Bologna: Forni, 1969.

Florilegium Treverense. Edited by F. Brunhölzl in *Mittellateinisches Jahrbuch* 1 (1964): 65–77 and 3 (1966): 129–217.

[*Fondamenti di teoria musicale*], *Con ciò sia cossa che l'arte practicha de la musica.* In MS Vercelli, Biblioteca Agnesiana, cod. 11, fols. 161^r–194^r. Edited by Anna Cornagliotti and Maria Caraci Vela in *Un inedito trattato musicale del medioevo.* Tavarnuzze, Impruneta, and Florence: Sismel, 1998.

Fortunatianus. *Artis rhetoricae libri III.* Edited by Carolus Halm in *Rhetores latini minores.* Leipzig: Teubner, 1863.

Franco of Cologne. *Ars cantus mensurabilis.* MS Paris, BNF lat. 16663, fols. 76^{v}–83. Edited by Gilbert Reaney and André Gilles. CSM 18. N.p.: American Institute of Musicology, 1974. Translated by Oliver Strunk, revised by James McKinnon in *Source Readings in Music History,* 226–45. Revised edition by Leo Treitler. New York: W. W. Norton, 1998.

Frosch, Johann. *Rerum musicarum opusculum rarum ac insigne, totius eius negotii rationem mira industria & brevitate complectens.* Strassburg: Peter Schöffer and Mathias Apiarius, 1535. Repr. New York: Broude Bros., 1967.

Frutolfus. *Breviarium de musica et tonarius.* Edited by P. Cölestin Vivell. Akademie der Wissenschaften in Wien, Philosophisch-historische Klasse, Sitzungsberichte, vol. 188, no. 2, 26–113. Vienna: Alfred Hölder, 1919.

Fux, Johann Joseph. *Steps to Parnassus: The Study of Counterpoint.* Edited and translated by Alfred Mann. New York: Norton, 1943.

Gaffurius, Franchinus. *Practica musicae.* Milan: Guillaume Le Signerre, 1496.

Geoffrey of Vinsauf. *Poetria nova.* In *Les arts poétiques du XIIe et du XIIIe siècle,* edited by Edmond Faral. Paris: Librairie Honoré Champion, 1971. Translation by Jane Baltzell Kopp as "The New Poetics," in *Three Medieval Rhetorical Arts,* edited by James J. Murphy, 27–108. Medieval and Renaissance Texts and Studies 228. Tempe, AZ: Arizona Center for Medieval and Renaissance Studies, 1971. Repr. 2001.

Goscalchus. *The Berkeley Manuscript.* Edited and translated by Oliver B. Ellsworth. Greek and Latin Music Theory, no. 2. Lincoln: University of Nebraska Press, 1984.

Guerson, Guillaume. *Utilissime musicales regule.* Paris: Michel de Toulouze, ca. 1500.

Guibert of Nogent. *Memoirs.* In *Self and Society in Medieval France: The Memoirs of Abbot Guibert of Nogent,* edited by John F. Benton. Toronto, 1984. Revised edition and translation by C. C. Swinton Bland. New York: Harper & Row, 1970.

Guido of Arezzo. *Guido d'Arezzo's Regule rithmice, Prologus in antiphonarium, and Epistola ad Michahelem: A Critical Text and Translation with an Introduction, Annotations, Indices, and New Manuscript Inventories.* Edited by Dolores Pesce. Ottawa: The Institute of Mediaeval Music, 1999.

———. *Micrologus.* Edited by Joseph Smits van Waesberghe as *Guido Aretini Micrologus.* CSM 4. Rome: American Institute of Musicology, 1955. Translated by W. Babb in *Hucbald, Guido, and John on Music,* 57–83.

———. *Prologus in Antiphonarium.* Edited by Joseph Smits van Waesberghe in *Tres tractatuli.* Divitiae Musicae Artis A 3. Buren: Frits Knuf, 1975.

———. *Regulae rhythmicae.* Edited by Joseph Smits van Waesberghe. Divitiae musicae artis A 4. Buren: Frits Knuf, 1985.

Guilielmus Monachus. *De preceptis artis musicae.* Edited by Albert Seay. CSM 11. N.p.: American Institute of Musicology, 1965.

Here follows a little treatise (Pseudo-Chilston). London, British Library, Lansdowne MS 763, fols. 113^{v}–116^{v}. Edited by Manfred F. Bukofzer in *Geschichte des englischen Diskants und des Fauxbourdons nach den theoretischen Quellen,* 53–56, 146–53. Strassburg, 1936. And by Thrasybulos Georgiades in *Englische Diskanttraktate aus der ersten Hälfte des 15. Jahrhunderts,* 23–27, 39–45. Munich: Musikwissenschaftliches Seminar der Universität München, 1937.

Hermannus Contractus. *Musica.* Edited by Leonard Ellinwood. Rochester: Eastman School of Music, University of Rochester, 1952.

Hieronymus de Moravia, *Tractatus de musica.* Edited by Simon Cserba. Regensburg: F. Pustet, 1935. Translated by Janet Knapp in "Two Thirteenth-Century Treatises on Modal Rhythm and Discant." *Journal of Music Theory* 6 (1962): 200–15.

Hothby, John. *De arte contrapuncti.* Edited by Gilbert Reaney. CSM 26. Neuhausen-Stuttgart: Hänssler-Verlag, 1977.

Hucbald. In *Hucbald, Guido, and John on Music,* 1–46.

Hucbald, Guido, and John on Music: Three Medieval Treatises. Translated by Warren Babb. Edited, with introductions, by Claude V. Palisca. New Haven: Yale University Press, 1978.

Hugh of St. Victor. "De tribus maximis circumstantiis gestorum." Edited by William M. Green in *Speculum* 18 (1943): 484–93.

Jacques de Liège. *Speculum musicae.* Edited by Roger Bragard. CSM 3. Rome: American Institute of Musicology, 1973.

Johannes Affligemensis. *De musica cum tonario.* Edited by Joseph Smits van Waesberghe. CSM 1. Rome: American Institute of Musicology, 1950. Translated by W. Babb in *Hucbald, Guido, and John on Music,* 87–190.

Johannes de Garlandia. *De mensurabili musica.* Edited by Erich Reimer in *Johannes de Garlandia: De mensurabili musica: Kritische Edition mit Kommentar und Interpretation der Notationslehre.* Beihefte zum Archiv für Musikwissenschaft, nos. 10–11. Wiesbaden: Franz Steiner, 1972.

Johannes de Grocheio. *De musica.* Edited by Ernst Rohloff in *Die Quellenhandschriften zum Musiktraktat des Johannes de Grocheio.* Leipzig: Deutscher Verlag für Musik, 1972.

Johannes de Muris. "Cum notum sit." CS 3:60–62.

———. *Libellus cantus mensurabilis secundum Johannes de Muris.* Edited by Daniel Katz in "The Earliest Sources for the 'Libellus cantus mensurabilis secundum Johannem de Muris.'" Ph.D. diss., Duke University, 1989.

———. "Quilibet affectans." CS 3:59–68.

Johannes Vetulus de Anagnia. *Liber de musica.* Edited by Frederick Hammond. CSM 27. Neuhausen-Stuttgart: Hänssler-Verlag, 1977.

John of Salisbury. *Policratus.* In *Ioannis Saresberiensis Policraticus.* Edited by K. S. B. Keats-Rohan. Corpus Christianorum Continuatio Mediaevalis, vol. 118. Turnhout: Brepols, 1993.

Lambertus. *Tractatus de musica.* CS 1:251–81.

Libellus tonarius. Edited by Heinrich Sowa in *Quellen zur Transformation der Antiphonen: Tonar- und Rhythmusstudien.* Kassel: Bärenreiter, 1935.

Liber argumentorum. Edited by Joseph Smits van Waesberghe. In *Expositiones in Micrologum Guidonis Aretini,* 19–58. Musicologica medii aevi, no. 1. Amsterdam: North-Holland Publishing Company, 1957.

Lipphardt, Walther. *Der karolingische Tonar von Metz.* Münster: Aschendorff, 1965.

Macrobius. *Saturnalia.* Edited by J. Willis. Leipzig: Teubner, 1963.

Metz tonary. Metz, Stadtbibliothek, MS 351. Edited by Walther Lipphardt in *Der Karolingische Tonar von Metz.* Münster, 1965.

Musica et scolica enchiriadis una cum aliquibus tractatulis adiunctis. Edited by Hans Schmid. Munich: Verlag der Bayerischen Akademie der Wissenschaften, 1981.

Translated by Raymond Erickson as *Musica Enchiriadis and Scolica Enchiriadis.* Edited by Claude V. Palisca. New Haven: Yale University Press, 1995.

Odington, Walter. *Summa de speculatione musicae.* Edited by Frederick F. Hammond. CSM 14. Rome, 1970. Part IV translated by Jay A. Huff. MSD 31. N.p., 1973.

Odo of Arezzo. *Tonarius.* GS 1:248–50.

Othlo. *Libellus proverbium.* Edited by W. C. Korfmacher. Chicago: Loyola University Press, 1936.

Perche dico il contrapunto richiede avere quatro cose. Florence, Biblioteca Medicea Laurenziana, MS Redi 71, fols. 24v–28v.

Person, Gobelinus. *Tractatus musicae scientiae.* Edited by Hermann Müller in "Der Tractatus musicae scientiae des Gobelinus Person (1358–1421)." *Kirchenmusikalisches Jahrbuch* 20 (1907): 180–96.

Peter of Ravenna. *Foenix domini Petri Raven[n]atis memoriae magistri.* Venice: Bernardino de Choris de Cremona, 1491. Translated by Robert Coplande as *The Art of Memory that Otherwyse Is Called Phenix.* London: Wyllyam Myddylton, 1548.

Petrarch. *Rerum memorandum libri.* Edited by Giuseppe Billanovich. Florence: Sansoni, 1945.

Petrus dictus Palma Ociosa. *Compendium de discantu mensurabili.* Edited by Johannes Wolf in "Ein Beitrag zur Diskantlehre des 14. Jahrhunderts." *Sammelbände der Internationalen Musikgesellschaft* 15 (1913–14): 505–34.

Post octavam quintam. CS 3:116–18. Florence, Biblioteca Medicea Laurenziana, Ashb. 1119, fols. 75v–77v. Florence, Biblioteca Medicea Laurenziana, Pl. XXIX.48, fols. 88v–89v. Milan, Biblioteca Ambrosiana, I.20 inf., fol. 36r–v. Einsiedeln, Stiftsbibliothek, MS 689, fol. 45v. Rio de Janeiro, Biblioteca Nacional, Cofre 18, fol. 619r–v. Chicago, Newberry Library, MS 54.1, fols. 6v–7r. Vercelli, Biblioteca Agnesiana, cod. 11, fols. 182v–183r.

Power, Lyonel. *This Tretis is contriuid upon the Gamme for hem.* London, BL Lansdowne MS 763, fols. 105v–113. Edited by Thrasybulos Georgiades in *Englische Diskanttraktate aus der ersten Hälfte des 15. Jahrhunderts,* 12–23. Munich: Musikwissenschaftliches Seminar der Universität München, 1937.

Prosdocimus de Beldemandis. *Contrapunctus.* Edited and translated by Jan Herlinger. Greek and Latin Music Theory, no. 1. Lincoln: University of Nebraska Press, 1984.

Pseudo-Odo of Cluny. *Dialogus in musica.* Edited by Michel Huglo in "Der Prolog des Odo zugeschriebenen 'Dialogus de Musica.'" *Archiv für Musikwissenschaft* 28 (1971): 138–39. Translated by Oliver Strunk and James McKinnon in *Strunk's Source Readings in Music History.* Revised edition by Leo Treitler, 198–210. New York: W. W. Norton, 1998.

Quatuor principalia musice. CS 4:200–98.

Quintilian. *Institutio oratoria.* Translated and edited by H. E. Butler. Loeb Classical Library. Cambridge, MA: Harvard University Press, 1968.

Ramis de Pareia, Bartolomeus. *Musica practica.* Bologna: Baltasar de Hiriberia, 1482. Edited by Johannes Wolf. Publikationen der Internationalen Musikgesellschaft, no. 2. Leipzig: Breitkopf & Härtel. Translated by Clement Miller, *Musica practica.* MSD 44. Neuhausen-Stuttgart: Hänssler-Verlag, 1993.

Ratio sequitus est ista. Edited by Jacques Handschin in "Aus der alten Musiktheorie, III-V." *Acta musicologica* 15 (1943): 2–15.

Regino. *Epistola de armonica institutione.* Edited by Michael Bernhard in *Clavis Ger-*

berti, eine Revision von Martin Gerberts Scriptores ecclesiastici de musica sacra potissimum (St. Blasien 1784). Munich: Bayerische Akademie der Wissenschaften, 1989.
———. *Tonarius*. Edited by Alexander Rausch in *Die Musiktraktate des Abtes Bern von Reichenau*, 202–24.Tutzing, 1999.
Reichenau Tonary. Bamberg, Staatsbibliothek, Ms. lit. 5, fols. 1–27.
Salomonis, Elias. *Scientia artis musicae*. GS 3:16–64.
Santa María, Tomás de. *Libro llamado arte de tañer fantasia*. Valladolid: Francisco Fernandez de Cordova, 1565. Repr. Geneva, 1973.
Sigebertus Gemblacensis (Sigebert of Gembloux). *Chronica*. PL 160:204.
———. *Liber de scriptoribus ecclesiasticis*. PL 160:579.
Spechtshart von Reutlingen, Hugo. *Flores musicae*. Edited by Karl-Werner Gümpel. Abhandlungen der Geistes- und Sozialwissenschaftlichen Klasse, Jahrgang 1958, 51–177. Wiesbaden: Akademie der Wissenschaften, 1958.
The Summa musice: A Thirteenth-Century Manual for Singers. Edited and translated by Christopher Page. Cambridge: Cambridge University Press, 1991.
Tinctoris, Johannes. *Expositio manus*. In *Opera theoretica*, 1:27–57. Edited by Albert Seay. CSM 22. Rome: American Institute of Musicology, 1975.
———. *Liber de arte contrapuncti*. In *Opera theoretica*, 2:11–157. Edited by Albert Seay. CSM 22. Rome: American Institute of Musicology, 1975. Translated by Albert Seay as *The Art of Counterpoint*. MSD 5. N.p., 1961.
———. *Proportionale musices*. In *Opera theoretica*, 2a. Edited by Albert Seay. CSM 22. Neuhausen-Stuttgart: Hänssler-Verlag.
Tractatus de cantu figurativo et de contrapuncto (ca. 1430–1520). Edited by Christian Meyer. CSM 41. Neuhausen-Stuttgart: Hänssler-Verlag, 1997.
Tractatus de contrapunto. Edited by Gilbert Reaney. CSM 39:44–58. Neuhausen-Stuttgart: Hänssler-Verlag, 1997.
Tractatus de discantu. Edited by Gilbert Reaney. CSM 36:37–45. Neuhausen-Stuttgart: Hänssler-Verlag, 1996.
Ugolino of Orvieto. *Declaratio musicae disciplinae*. Edited by Albert Seay. CSM 7. Rome: American Institute of Musicology, 1959–62.
Valla, Lorenzo. *L'arte della grammatica*. Edited by Paolo Casciano. N.p.: Fondazione Lorenzo Valla, Mondadori, 1990.
"The Vatican Organum Treatise—A Colour-Reproduction, Transcription, and Translation." Edited by Irving Godt and Benito Rivera in *Gordon Athol Anderson, in Memoriam*, edited by Irving Godt and Hans Tischler, 2:264–345. Ottawa and Henryville, PA: Institute of Mediaeval Music, 1984.
"Versus de musica anonymi Pragensis 'Iam post has normas.'" Michaelbeuern, Stiftsbibliothek, Cod. man. cart. 95, fols. 150–53. Edited by Renate Federhofer-Königs in "Ein anonymer Musiktraktat aus der 2. Hälfte des 14. Jahrhunderts in der Stiftsbibliothek Michaelsbeuern/Salzburg." *Kirchenmusikalisches Jahrbuch* 46 (1962): 49–54. Also edited by Alexander Rausch in "Mensuraltraktate des Spätmittelalters in österreichischen Bibliotheken." In *Quellen und Studien zur Musiktheorie des Mittelalters*, edited by Michael Bernhard, 3:273–92. Munich, 2001.
Wollick, Nicolaus. *Enchiridion musices*. Paris: Jehan Petit and François Regnault, 1512.
Zarlino, Gioseffo. *Le istitutioni harmoniche*. Venice, 1558. Repr. New York: Broude Bros., 1965. Part III translated by Guy A. Marco and Claude V. Palisca as *The Art of Counter-*

point, Part Three of Le Istitutioni harmoniche, *1558*. New Haven: Yale University Press, 1968.

Zweig, Stefan. *Schachnovelle*. Stockholm: Bermann-Fischer Verlag, 1943.

Music Manuscripts

Chantilly, Musée Condé, MS 564.

Florence, Biblioteca Medicea Laurenziana, Plut. 29.1. Facsimile by Luther Dittmer. New York, 1966–67.

Ivrea, Biblioteca Capitolare, MS 115.

Paris, Bibliothèque Nationale de France, MS lat. 1112.

Paris, Bibliothèque Nationale de France, MS fr. 1584, fols. ii^c ij.xv^v –vj^r.

Paris, Bibliothèque Nationale de France, MS fr. 22546, fols. 123v–124r.

Wolfenbüttel, Herzog August Bibliothek, MS 628 (W_1). Facsimile by Martin Staehelin. Wiesbaden: Otto Harrassowitz, 1995.

Wolfenbüttel, Herzog August Bibliothek, MS 1099 (W_2). Facsimile by Luther Dittmer. New York: Institute of Mediaeval Music, 1960.

Music Editions

Günther, Ursula, ed. *Motets of the Manuscripts Chantilly, Musée Condé, 564 (olim 1047) and Modena, Biblioteca estense, α. M. 5, 24 (olim lat. 568)*. N.p.: American Institute of Musicology, 1965.

H 159 Montpellier: Tonary of St Bénigne of Dijon. Edited by Finn Egeland Hansen. Copenhagen, 1974. Facsimile in *Paléographie musicale: les principaux manuscrits de chant,* vol. 8. Solesmes: Abbaye Saint-Pierre, 1901–5.

Harrison, Frank Ll., ed. *Motets of French Provenance.* Polyphonic Music of the Fourteenth Century, vol. 5. Monaco: Éditions de l'Oiseau-Lyre, 1968.

Husmann, Heinrich, ed. *Die drei- und vierstimmigen Notre-Dame-Organa.* Leipzig: Breitkopf & Härtel, 1940.

Machaut, Guillaume de. *Mass of Notre Dame.* Edited by Heinrich Besseler. In *Collected Works of Guillaume de Machaut,* vol. 4. Leipzig: Breitkopf & Härtel, 1954.

———. *Musikalische Werke.* Edited by Friedrich Ludwig. 3 vols. Publikationen älterer Musik. Leipzig: Breitkopf & Härtel, 1926–29.

Perotin. *The Works of Perotin.* Edited and with an introduction by Ethel Thurston. New York: Kalmus, 1970.

Roesner, Edward, ed. *Les quadrupla et tripla de Paris.* Vol. 1 of *Le magnus liber organi de Notre Dame de Paris.* Monaco: Éditions de l'Oiseau-Lyre, 1993.

Vitry, Philippe de. *The Works of Philippe de Vitry.* Edited by Leo Schrade. Polyphonic Music of the Fourteenth Century, nos. 2–3. Monaco: Éditions de l'Oiseau-Lyre, 1956. New edition, *The Complete Works of Philippe de Vitry,* by Edward Roesner, 1984.

SECONDARY LITERATURE

Ahl, Frederick M. *Metaformations: Soundplay and Wordplay in Ovid and Other Classical Poets.* Ithaca: Cornell University Press, 1985.

Amidzic, Ognjen, Hartmut Riehle, Thorsten Fehr, Christian Wienbruch, and Thomas

Elbert. "Pattern of Focal γ-bursts in Chess Players: Grandmasters Call on Regions of the Brain not Used so much by Less Skilled Amateurs." *Nature* 412 (August 9, 2001): 603.

Apel, Willi. *Gregorian Chant.* Bloomington, IN: Indiana University Press, 1966.

———. *The Notation of Polyphonic Music, 900–1600.* 5th ed. Cambridge, MA: The Medieval Academy of America, 1953.

Arlt, Wulf. "Denken in Tönen und Strukturen: Komponieren im Kontext Perotins." In *Perotinus Magnus,* edited by Jürg Stenzl, 53–100. *Musik-Konzepte,* no. 107. Munich: Edition Text + Kritik, 2000.

Atkinson, Charles M. "Modus." In *Handwörterbuch der musikalischen Terminologie,* edited by Hans Heinrich Eggebrecht. Wiesbaden: Franz Steiner, 1995.

———. "The Other *Modus:* On the Theory and Practice of the Intervals in the Eleventh and Twelfth Centuries." In *The Study of Medieval Chant: Paths and Bridges, East and West,* edited by Peter Jeffrey, 233–56. Woodbridge, Suffolk: Boydell Press, 2001.

Auerbach, Erich. *Typologische Motive in der mittelalterlichen Literatur.* Schriften und Vorträge des Petrarca-Instituts Köln, no. 2. Cologne: Krefeld, 1953.

Baddeley, Alan. *Working Memory.* Oxford: Clarendon Press, 1986.

Bailey, Terence. *The Intonation Formulas of Western Chant.* Toronto: Pontifical Institute of Mediaeval Studies, 1974.

Baltzer, Rebecca A. "Notre Dame Manuscripts and Their Owners: Lost and Found." *Journal of Musicology* 5 (1987): 380–99.

———. "Thirteenth-Century Illuminated Miniatures and the Date of the Florence Manuscript." *Journal of the American Musicological Society* 25 (1972): 1–18.

Bartels, Ulrich. "Musikwissenschaft zwischen den Kriegen, Friedrich Ludwig und seine Schule." In *Musik der zwanziger Jahre,* edited by Werner Keil, 86–107. Hildesheim: Olms, 1996.

Baxandall, Michael. *Words for Pictures: Seven Papers on Renaissance Art and Criticism.* New Haven: Yale University Press, 2003.

Beck, Jean. *Die modale Interpretation der mittelalterlichen Melodien.* Strassburg: Karl J. Trübner, 1908. Repr. New York, 1976.

Bellermann, Heinrich. *Contrapunkt.* 3rd ed. Berlin: J. Springer, 1887.

Benson, Larry D. "The Literary Character of Anglo-Saxon Formulaic Poetry." *Publications of the Modern Language Association* 81 (1966): 334–41.

Bent, Margaret. "Deception, Exegesis and Sounding Number in Machaut's Motet 15 'Amours qui a le pouoir/Faus samblant/Vidi dominum.'" *Early Music History* 10 (1991): 15–27.

———. "Fauvel and Marigny: Which Came First?" In *Fauvel Studies: Allegory, Chronicle and Image in Paris, Bibliothèque Nationale de France, MS français 146,* edited by M. Bent and A. Wathey, 35–52. Oxford: Clarendon Press, 1998.

———. "Isorhythm." *New Grove Online,* accessed October 5, 2003.

———. "Musica Recta and Musica Ficta." *Musica disciplina* 26 (1972): 73–100.

———. "Notation." *New Grove Online,* accessed October 5, 2003.

———. "*Resfacta* and *Cantare Super Librum.*" *Journal of the American Musicological Society* 36 (1983): 371–91.

Benton, John, F. *Self and Society in Medieval France: The Memoirs of Guibert of Nogent,* trans. by C. C. Swinton Bland, revised by the editor. New York: Harper & Row, 1970.

Berger, Anna Maria Busse. "Cut Signs in Fifteenth-Century Musical Practice." In *Music in Renaissance Cities and Courts: Studies in Honor of Lewis Lockwood,* edited by Jessie Ann Owens and Anthony M. Cummings, 101–12. Warren, MI: Harmonie Park Press, 1997.

———. "The Evolution of Rhythmic Notation." In *The Cambridge History of Western Music Theory,* edited by Thomas Christensen, 628–56. Cambridge: Cambridge University Press, 2002.

———. *Mensuration and Proportion Signs: Origins and Evolution.* Oxford: Clarendon Press, 1993.

———. "Mnemotechnics and Notre Dame Polyphony." *Journal of Musicology* 14 (1996): 263–98.

———. "Musical Proportions and Arithmetic in the Late Middle Ages and Renaissance." *Musica disciplina* 44 (1990): 89–118.

———. Review-essay of Jürg Stenzl, *Perotinus Magnus, Musik-Konzepte,* 107 (Munich: Edition Text + Kritik, 2000), in *Plainsong and Medieval Music* 11 (2002): 44–54.

———. "Die Rolle der Mündlichkeit in der Komposition der 'Notre Dame Polyphonie.'" *Das Mittelalter* 3 (1998): 127–43.

Berger, Karol. "The Guidonian Hand." In *The Medieval Craft of Memory: An Anthology of Texts and Pictures,* edited by Mary Carruthers and Jan Ziolkowski, 71–82. Philadelphia: University of Pennsylvania Press, 2002.

———. "The Hand and the Art of Memory." *Musica disciplina* 35 (1981): 87–120.

———. *Musica ficta: Theories of Accidental Inflections in Vocal Polyphony From Marchetto da Padova to Gioseffo Zarlino.* Cambridge: Cambridge University Press, 1987.

Bernhard, Michael. "Didaktische Verse zur Musiktheorie des Mittelalters." In *Cantus Planus: Papers Read at the the Third Meeting, Tihany, Hungary, 19–24 September 1988,* ed. László Dobszay *et al.*, 227–36. Budapest: Hungarian Academy of Sciences Institute for Musicology, 1990.

———. "Das musikalische Fachschrifttum im lateinischen Mittelalter." In *Geschichte der Musiktheorie,* vol. 3, edited by Frieder Zaminer, 37–103. Darmstadt: Wissenschaftliche Buchgesellschaft, 1990.

———. "Parallelüberlieferungen zu vier Cambridger Liedern." In *Tradition und Wertung: Festschrift für Franz Brunhölzl zum 65. Geburtstag,* edited by Günter Bernt, Fidel Rädle, and Gabriel Silagi, 141–45. Sigmaringen: Jan Thorbecke Verlag, 1989.

Bernstein, Lawrence F. "Ockeghem: The Mystic Interpretation of 1920." In *Johannes Ockeghem: Actes du XLe colloque international d'études humanistes,* Tours, 1997, edited by Philippe Vendrix, 811–41. Paris: Klincksieck, 1998.

Besseler, Heinrich. "Friedrich Ludwig." *Zeitschrift für Musikwissenschaft* 13 (1930–31): 83–91.

———. "Gustav Jacobsthal." *MGG* 6:1615–19.

———. "Musik des Mittelalters in der Hamburger Musikhalle, 1.-8. April, 1924." *Zeitschrift für Musikwissenschaft* 7 (1924–25): 42–54.

———. "Studien zur Musik des Mittelalters II: Die Motette von Franko von Köln bis Philipp von Vitry." *Archiv für Musikwissenschaft* 8 (1926): 137–258.

Blackburn, Bonnie J. "The Dispute about Harmony *c.* 1500 and the Creation of a New Style." In *Théorie et analyse musicales 1450–1650 / Music Theory and Analysis,* ed. Anne-Emmanuelle Ceulemans and Bonnie J. Blackburn, 1–37. Louvain-la-Neuve: Département d'histoire de l'art et d'archéologie, 2001.

———. "Hothby, John." *New Grove Online,* accessed October 5, 2003.
———. "On Compositional Process in the Fifteenth Century." *Journal of the American Musicological Society* 40 (1987): 210–84.
———. "Ugolino of Orvieto." *New Grove Online,* accessed October 5, 2003.
Blackburn, Bonnie J., Edward E. Lowinsky, and Clement Miller, eds. *A Correspondence of Renaissance Musicians.* Oxford, 1991.
Boisbaudron, Horace Lecoq de. *L'éducation de la mémoire pittoresque et la formation de l'artiste.* Paris: Laurens, 1920.
Bolgar, R. R. *The Classical Heritage and Its Beneficiaries.* Cambridge: Cambridge University Press, 1954.
Bolzoni, Lina. *La stanza della memoria.* Turin: Einaudi, 1995. Translated by Jeremy Parzen as *The Gallery of Memory: Literary and Iconographic Models in the Age of the Printing Press.* Toronto: University of Toronto Press, 2001.
Boncella, Paul Anthony Luke. "Regino Prumiensis and the Tones." In *Songs of the Dove and the Nightingale, Sacred and Secular Music c. 900–1600,* edited by Greta Mary Hair and Robyn E. Smith, 74–89. Sydney: Currency Press, 1994.
Bower, Calvin M., "Natural and Artificial Music: The Origins and Development of an Aesthetic Concept." *Musica disciplina* 25 (1971): 17–33.
Boynton, Susan. "The Sources and Significance of the Orpheus Myth." *Early Music History* 18 (1999: 47–74.
Brinkmann, Reinhold, "Schwierigkeiten mit dem Mittelalter." *Neue Zeitschrift für Musik* 134 (1973): 202–3.
Brinkmann, Reinhold, and Bernd Wiechert. "Grell, Eduard." *New Grove Online,* accessed October 5, 2003.
Brückner, Hans, and Christa Maria Rock, eds. *Judentum und Musik. Mit dem ABC jüdischer und nichtarischer Musikbeflissener.* 3rd ed. Munich: Hans Brückner Verlag, 1938.
Bukofzer, Manfred F. *Geschichte des englischen Diskants und des Fauxbourdons nach den theoretischen Quellen.* Sammlung musikwissenschaftlicher Abhandlungen, no. 21. Strassburg: Heitz, 1936. Repr. Baden-Baden: Valentin Koerner 1973.
Butterworth, Brian. "What Makes a Prodigy?" *Nature Neuroscience* 4 (January 2001): 11–12.
Carruthers, Mary. *The Book of Memory: A Study in Medieval Culture.* Cambridge: Cambridge University Press, 1990.
———. *The Craft of Thought: Meditation, Rhetoric, and the Making of Images, 400–1200.* Cambridge: Cambridge University Press, 1998.
Carruthers, Mary, and Jan Ziolkowski, eds. *The Medieval Craft of Memory: An Anthology of Texts and Pictures.* Philadelphia: University of Pennsylvania Press, 2002.
Clanchy, M. T. *From Memory to Written Record: England 1066–1307.* 2nd ed. Oxford: Blackwell, 1993.
Coleman, Janet. *Ancient and Medieval Memories: Studies in the Reconstruction of the Past.* Cambridge: Cambridge University Press, 1992.
Crocker, Richard. "Chants of the Roman Office." In *The Early Middle Ages to 1300. New Oxford History of Music,* vol. 2, edited by Richard Crocker and David Hiley, 111–46. Oxford: Oxford University Press, 1990.
———. "Discant, Counterpoint, and Harmony." *Journal of the American Musicological Society* 15 (1962): 1–21.

———. "Hermann's Major Sixth." *Journal of the American Musicological Society* 25 (1972): 19–37.

———. *An Introduction to Gregorian Chant.* New Haven: Yale University Press, 2000.

Curtius, Ernst Robert. "Gustav Gröber und die romanische Philologie." In *Gesammelte Aufsätze zur romanischen Philologie,* 428–55. Bern and Munich: Francke, 1960.

Dahlhaus, Carl. *Foundations of Music History.* Translated by J. B. Robinson. Cambridge: Cambridge University Press, 1983.

———. "Geschichte als Problem der Musiktheorie: Über einige Berliner Musiktheoretiker des 19. Jahrhunderts." In *Studien zur Musikgeschichte Berlins im frühen 19. Jahrhundert,* edited by Carl Dahlhaus, 405–13. Regensburg: Gustav Bosse, 1980.

Dalglish, William. "The Origin of the Hocket." *Journal of the American Musicological Society* 31 (1978): 3–20.

Daly, Lloyd W. *Contributions to a History of Alphabetization in Antiquity and the Middle Ages.* Collection Latomus, no. 90. Brussels: Latomus, 1967.

Daly, Lloyd W., and Betty A. Daly. "Some Techniques in Mediaeval Latin Lexicography." *Speculum* 39 (1964): 229–39.

D'Avray, D. L. *Medieval Marriage Sermons: Mass Communication in a Culture without Print.* Oxford: Oxford University Press, 2002.

———. *The Preaching of the Friars: Sermons Diffused from Paris before 1300.* Oxford: Clarendon Press, 1985.

Desmond, Karen. "*Sicut in grammatica:* Analogical Discourse in Chapter 15 of Guido's *Micrologus.*" *Journal of Musicology* 16 (1998): 467–93.

Dreyfus, Laurence. "Early Music Defended against Its Devotees: A Theory of Historical Performance in the Twentieth Century." *Musical Quarterly* 69 (1983): 297–322.

Dronke, Peter. *Verse with Prose from Petronius to Dante: The Art and Scope of the Mixed Form.* Cambridge, MA: Harvard University Press, 1994.

Eckhardt, Caroline D. "The Medieval Prosimetrum Genre (from Boethius to Boèce)." *Genre* 16 (1983): 21–38.

Eggebrecht, Hans Heinrich. "Machauts Motette Nr. 9." *Archiv für Musikwissenschaft* 25 (1968): 173–95.

Egmond, Warren van. "The Commercial Revolution and the Beginnings of Western Mathematics in Renaissance Florence, 1300–1500." Ph.D. diss., Indiana University, 1976.

Elo, A. E. *The Rating of Chess Players, Past and Present.* New York: Arco, 1978.

Emerson, John A. "Peter Wagner." *New Grove Online,* accessed October 5, 2003.

Everist, Mark. "Drying Rachel's Tears: The *Conductus cum caudis* as Mixed Form." Forthcoming.

———. "From Paris to St. Andrews: The Origins of W_1." *Journal of the American Musicological Society* 43 (1990): 1–42.

———. "Reception and Recomposition in the Polyphonic *Conductus cum cauda:* The Metz Fragment." *Journal of the Royal Musical Association* 125 (2000): 135–63.

Falconer, Keith. "The Modes before the Modes: Antiphon and Differentia in Western Chant." In *The Study of Medieval Chant: Paths and Bridges, East and West: In Honor of Kenneth Levy,* edited by Peter Jeffrey, 131–45. Woodbridge, Suffolk: Boydell, 2001.

Fallows, David. "Placement des paroles in Chansonnier de Jean de Montchenu." In *Chansonnier de Jean de Montchenu,* edited by Geneviève Thibault and David Fallows.

Paris: Publications de la Société Française de Musicologie, 1991. English Translation as "Texting in the Chansonnier of Jean de Montchenu." In David Fallows, *Songs and Musicians in the Fifteenth Century,* no. X, 1–13. Aldershot: Ashgate, 1996.

Faral, Edmond. *Les arts poétiques du XIIe et du XIIIe siècle.* Paris: Librairie Honoré Champion, 1971.

Fenton, James. "*Degas: Beyond Impressionism.* Exhibition at the National Gallery, London, and the Art Institute of Chicago, Catalog of the exhibition by Richard Kendall." Part 2. *The New York Review of Books,* vol. 43, no. 16 (October 1996): 14–18.

Ferand, Ernest T. "Guillaume Guerson's Rules of Improvised Counterpoint." In *Miscelánea en homenaje a monseñor Higinio Anglés,* 1:253–63. Barcelona: Consejo Superior de Investigaciones Científicas, 1958–61.

Finnegan, Ruth. *Oral Poetry: Its Nature, Significance, and Social Context.* Cambridge: Cambridge University Press, 1977. Repr. (with added material) Bloomington, IN: University of Indiana Press, 1992.

Flotzinger, Rudolf. *Der Discantussatz im Magnus Liber und seiner Nachfolge.* Vienna: Hermann Böhlau, 1969.

———. *Perotinus musicus: Wegbereiter abendländischen Komponierens.* Mainz: Schott, 2000.

———. "Zur Frage der Modalrhythmik als Antike-Rezeption." *Archiv für Musikwissenschaft* 29 (1972): 203–8.

Freccero, John. "The Significance of *Terza Rima.*" In *Dante, the Poetics of Conversion,* 258–71. Cambridge, MA: Harvard University Press, 1986.

Friis-Jensen, Karsten. *Saxo Grammaticus as Latin Poet.* Analecta Romana Instituti Danici, Suppl. 14. Rome: L'Erma di Bretschneider, 1987.

Fritsch, Theodor. *Handbuch der Judenfrage.* 39th ed. Leipzig: Hammerverlag, 1935.

Frobenius, Wolf. "Modus (Rhythmuslehre)." In *Handwörterbuch der musikalischen Terminologie,* edited by Hans Heinrich Eggebrecht. Wiesbaden: Franz Steiner, 1972–.

———. "Perfectio." In *Handwörterbuch der musikalischen Terminologie,* edited by Hans Heinrich Eggebrecht. Wiesbaden: Franz Steiner, 1972–.

Fuller, Sarah. "*Organum-discantus-contrapunctus* in the Middle Ages." In *The Cambridge History of Western Music,* edited by Thomas Christensen, 477–502. Cambridge: Cambridge University Press, 2002.

———. "A Phantom Treatise of the Fourteenth Century: The *Ars nova.*" *Journal of Musicology* 4 (1985–86): 23–50.

Gallo, F. Alberto. "Die Notationslehre im 14. und 15. Jahrhundert." In *Die mittelalterliche Lehre von der Mehrstimmigkeit,* edited by Frieder Zaminer, 257–356. Geschichte der Musiktheorie, vol. 5. Darmstadt: Wissenschaftliche Buchgesellschaft, 1984.

———. "La tradizione orale della teoria musicale nel medioevo." In *L'etnomusicologia in Italia,* edited by D. Carpitella, 161–66. Palermo: S. F. Flaccovio, 1975.

Garratt, James. *Palestrina and the Romantic Imagination.* Cambridge: Cambridge University Press, 2002.

Gennrich, Friedrich. *Die Straßburger Schule der Musikwissenschaft.* Würzburg: Triltsch, 1940.

———. "Wer ist der Initiator der 'Modaltheorie.'" In *Miscelánea en homenaje a monseñor Higinio Anglés,* 1:314–30. Barcelona: Consejo Superior de Investigaciones Científicas, 1958–61.

Georgiades, Thrasybulos. *Englische Diskanttraktate aus der ersten Hälfte des 15. Jahrhunderts.* Munich: Musikwissenschaftliches Seminar der Universität München, 1937.

Gevaert, François-Auguste. *La mélopée antique dans le chant de l'église latine.* Ghent: Librairie Générale de Ad. Hoste, 1895–96.

Ghellinck, J. de. *L'essor de la littérature latine.* Vol. 1. Brussels: L'Édition Universelle, 1946.

Gladwell, Malcolm. "A Reporter at Large: The Physical Genius: Why Are Some People the Best at What They Do?" *New Yorker* (August 2, 1999): 56–65.

Goody, Jack. "The Consequences of Literacy." *Comparative Studies in Society and History* 5 (1963): 304–45.

———. *The Interface between the Written and the Oral.* Cambridge: Cambridge University Press, 1987.

———. *The Logic of Writing and the Organization of Society.* Cambridge: Cambridge University Press, 1986.

Goody, Jack, and I. P. Watt. *Literacy in Traditional Societies.* Cambridge: Cambridge University Press, 1968.

Grendler, Paul F. *Schooling in Renaissance Italy: Literacy and Learning, 1300–1600.* Baltimore: Johns Hopkins University Press, 1989.

Grier, James. "Adémar de Chabannes, Carolingian Musical Practices, and *Nota* Romana." *Journal of the American Musicological Society* 56 (2003): 43–98.

Günther, Hans. *Johann Gottfried Herders Stellung zur Musik.* Leipzig: n.p., 1903.

Günther, Ursula. "Friedrich Ludwig in Göttingen." In *Musikwissenschaft und Musikpflege an der Georg-August-Universität Göttingen,* edited by Martin Staehelin, 152–75. Göttingen, 1987.

———. "Zitate in französischen Liedsätzen der Ars Nova und Ars Subtilior." *Musica disciplina* 26 (1972): 55–68.

Haar, James. "Lessons in Theory from a Sixteenth-Century Composer." In *Altro Polo: Essays on Italian Music in the Cinquecento,* edited by Richard Charteris, 51–81. Sydney, 1990.

Haas, Max. "Die Musiklehre im 13. Jahrhundert von Johannes de Garlandia bis Franco." In *Die mittelalterliche Lehre von der Mehrstimmigkeit,* 136–53. Geschichte der Musiktheorie, no. 5, edited by Frieder Zaminer. Darmstadt: Wissenschaftliche Buchgesellschaft, 1984.

———. "Organum." *MGG* 7:871 f.

Haines, John. "The Footnote Quarrels of the Modal Theory: A Remarkable Episode in the Reception of Medieval Music." *Early Music History* 20 (2001): 87–120.

Hajdu, Helga. *Das mnemotechnische Schrifttum des Mittelalters.* Vienna: Franz Leo, 1936.

Hammond, Frederick F. "Summa de speculatione musicae of Walter Odington: A Critical Edition and Commentary." Ph.D. diss., Yale University, 1965.

Handschin, Jacques. "Aus der alten Musiktheorie, III-V," *Acta musicologica* 15 (1943): 2–23.

———. "Conductus." *MGG* 2:1615–26.

———. "Die Modaltheorie und Carl Appels Ausgabe der Gesänge von Bernart de Ventadorn." *Medium Aevum* 4 (1935): 69–82.

———. "A Monument of English Medieval Polyphony." *Musical Times* 73 (1932): 510–13; 74 (1933): 697–704.

———. "Musicologie et musique." In International Musicological Society, Fourth Congress, Basle, June 29–July 3, 1949, 9–22. Kassel, 1949.

———. *Musikgeschichte im Überblick.* Lucerne: Räber, 1948.

———. "Der Organum Traktat von Montpellier." In *Studien zur Musikgeschichte, Festschrift für Guido Adler zum 75. Geburtstag,* 51–57. Vienna: Universal Edition, 1930.

———. "The Summer Canon and Its Background." *Musica disciplina* 3 (1949): 55–94.

———. *Der Toncharakter, eine Einführung in die Tonpsychologie.* Zürich: Atlantis Verlag, 1948.

———. "Über das Improvisieren." In *Gedenkschrift Jacques Handschin: Aufsätze und Bibliographie,* edited by Hans Oesch, 327–31. Bern: P. Haupt, 1957.

———. "Was brachte die Notre Dame-Schule Neues." *Zeitschrift für Musikwissenschaft* 6 (1924): 545–58.

———. "Eine wenig beachtete Stilrichtung innerhalb der mittelalterlichen Mehrstimmigkeit." *Schweizerisches Jahrbuch für Musikwissenschaft* 1 (1924): 56–75.

———. "Zur Biographie Hermanns des Lahmen." In *Gedenkschrift Jacques Handschin: Aufsätze und Bibliographie,* edited by Hans Oesch, 170–74. Bern: P. Haupt, 1957.

———. "Zur Frage der Conductus-Rhythmik." *Acta musicologica* 24 (1952): 113–30.

———. "Zur Frage der melodischen Paraphrasierung im Mittelalter." *Zeitschrift für Musikwissenschaft* 10 (1928): 513–19.

———. "Zur Geschichte von Notre Dame," *Acta musicologica* 4 (1932): 6–14.

———. "Zur Leonin-Perotin-Frage," *Zeitschrift für Musikwissenschaft* 14 (1932): 319–21.

Havelock, Eric A. *The Muse Learns to Write.* New Haven: Yale University Press, 1986.

———. *Preface to Plato.* Cambridge, MA: Harvard University Press, 1963.

Herder, Johann Gottfried. "Cäcilia." In vol. 16 of *Johann Gottfried Herder, Sämtliche Werke,* 253–72. Berlin: Weidmannsche Buchhandlung, 1887. Repr. Hildesheim, 1994.

Herlinger, Jan. "Prosdocimus de Beldemandis." *New Grove Online,* accessed October 5, 2003.

Higgins, Paula. "Tracing the Career of Late Medieval Composers: The Case of Philippe Basiron of Bourges." *Acta musicologica* 62 (1990): 1–28.

Hiley, David. *Western Plainchant: A Handbook.* Oxford: Clarendon Press, 1993.

Hoffman, E. T. A. "Old and New Church Music." In *E.T.A. Hoffmann's Musical Writings: "Kreisleriana," "The Poet and the Composer", Music Criticism.* Edited by David Charlton. Translated by Martyn Clarke. Cambridge: Cambridge University Press, 1989.

Holford-Strevens, Leofranc. "Tinctoris on the Great Composers." *Plainsong and Medieval Music* 5 (1996): 193–99.

Holsinger, Bruce. *Music, Body, and Desire in Medieval Literature and Culture, 1150–1400: Hildegard of Bingen to Chaucer.* Stanford: Stanford University Press, 2001.

Howe, Michael A. *Introduction to the Psychology of Memory.* New York: Harper & Row, 1983.

Hucke, Helmut. "Toward a New Historical View of Gregorian Chant." *Journal of the American Musicological Society* 33 (1982): 437–67.

Hughes, Andrew. "Pseudo-Chilston." *New Grove Online,* accessed October 5, 2003.

Hughes, David. "Evidence for the Traditional View of the Transmission of Gregorian Chant." *Journal of the American Musicological Society* 40 (1987): 377–404.

Huglo, Michel. "L'auteur du 'Dialogue sur la musique' attribué à Odon." *Revue de musicologie* 55 (1969): 119–71.

———. "Grundlagen und Ansätze der mittelalterlichen Musiktheorie von der Spätantike bis zur Ottonischen Zeit." In *Die Lehre vom einstimmigen Liturgischen Gesang,* edited by Thomas Ertelt and Frieder Zaminer, 17–102. Geschichte der Musiktheorie, no. 4. Darmstadt: Wissenschaftliche Buchgesellschaft, 2000.

———. *Les livres de chant liturgique.* Typologie des sources du Moyen Age occidental, no. 52. Turnhout: Brepols, 1988.

———. "La notation franconienne: antécédents et devenir." *Cahiers de civilisation médiévale* 3 (1988): 123–32.

———. *Les tonaires: Inventaire, analyse, comparaison.* Paris: Heugel, 1971.

———. "Tonary." In *New Grove Online,* accessed October 5, 2003.

———. "Tradition orale et tradition écrite dans la transmission des mélodies grégoriennes." In *Studien zur Tradition in der Musik: Kurt von Fischer zum 60. Geburtstag,* edited by Hans Heinrich Eggebrecht and Max Lütolf, 31–42. Munich: Katzenbichler, 1973.

Hunter, I. M. "Lengthy Verbatim Recall: The Role of Text." In *Progress in the Psychology of Language,* vol. 1, edited by A. Ellis, 207–35. London: Erlbaum Associates, 1985.

Husmann, Heinrich. "The Origin and Destination of the *Magnus liber organi.*" *Musical Quarterly* 59 (1963): 311–30.

Immel, Stephen. "The Vatican Organum Treatise Re-examined." *Early Music History* 20 (2001): 121–72.

Jacobsson, Ritva, and Leo Treitler. "Sketching Liturgical Archetypes: Hodie surrexit leo fortis." In *De musica et cantu: Studien zur Geschichte der Kirchenmusik und der Oper. Helmut Hucke zum 60. Geburtstag,* edited by Peter Cahn and Ann-Katrin Heimer, 157–202. Hildesheim: Georg Olms, 1993.

Jacobsthal, Gustav. *Die chromatische Alteration im liturgischen Gesang der abendländischen Kirche.* Berlin: Springer, 1897.

Jahandarie, Khosrow. *Spoken and Written Discourse: A Multi-disciplinary Perspective.* Stamford, CT: Ablex, 1999.

Jeffery, Peter. "The Earliest Oktoechoi: The Role of Jerusalem and Palestine in the Beginnings of Modal Ordering." In *The Study of Medieval Chant: Paths and Bridges, East and West,* edited by Peter Jeffery, 147–209. Woodbridge, Suffolk: Boydell, 2001.

Klopsch, Paul. *Einführung in die Dichtungslehren des lateinischen Mittelalters.* Darmstadt: Wissenschaftliche Buchgesellschaft, 1980.

Kmetz, John. "Singing Texted Songs from Untexted Songbooks: The Evidence of the Basler *Liederhandschriften.*" In *Le Concert des voix et des instruments à la Renaissance,* edited by Jean-Michel Vaccaro, 121–43. Paris: CNRS-Éditions, 1995.

———. *The Sixteenth-Century Basel Songbooks: Origins, Contents, Contexts.* Bern: Haupt, 1995.

Knapp, Janet. "Polyphony at Notre Dame of Paris." In *The Early Middle Ages to 1300,* edited by Richard Crocker, 557–635. *New Oxford History of Music,* vol. 2. Oxford: Oxford University Press, 1990.

Kniazeva, Janna. "Handschin, Jacques." *New Grove Online,* accessed October 5, 2003.

Korte, Werner. Review of Friedrich Gennrich, *Die Straßburger Schule für Musikwissenschaft. Ein Experiment oder ein Wegweiser? Anregung zur Klärung grundsätzlicher Fragen.* Kleine deutsche Musikbücherei, no. 3. Würzburg, 1940. In *Archiv für Musikforschung* 6 (1941): 121–22.

Kosslyn, Stephen M. *Ghosts in the Mind's Machine: Creating and Using Images in the Brain.* New York: Norton, 1983.

———. *Image and Brain: The Resolution of the Imagery Debate.* Cambridge, MA: MIT Press, 1994.
———. *Image and Mind.* Cambridge, MA: Harvard University Press, 1980.
———. "Visual Mental Imagery Activates Topographically Organized Visual Cortex: PET Investigations." *Journal of Cognitive Neuroscience* 5 (1993): 263–87.
Kügle, Karl. "Isorhythmie." *MGG²* 4:1219–29.
———. *The Manuscript Ivrea, Biblioteca Capitolare 115: Studies in the Transmission and Composition of Ars Nova Polyphony.* Ottawa: The Institute of Medieval Music, 1997.
Leclercq, Jean. *The Love of Learning and the Desire for God: A Study of Monastic Culture.* Translated by Catharine Misrahi. New York: Fordham University Press, 1961.
Leech-Wilkinson, Daniel. "Compositional Procedure in Machaut's 'Hoquetus David.'" *Royal Musical Association Research Chronicle* 16 (1980): 99–109.
———. *Compositional Techniques in the Four-Part Isorhythmic Motets of Philippe de Vitry and His Contemporaries.* New York: Garland, 1989.
———. *Machaut's Mass: An Introduction.* Oxford: Clarendon Press, 1990.
———. "Machaut's *Rose, Lis* and the Problem of Early Music Analysis." *Music Analysis* 3 (1984): 9–28.
———. "Petrus frater dictus Palma ociosa." *New Grove Online,* accessed October 5, 2003.
———. "*Le Voir Dit:* A Reconstruction and a Guide for Musicians." *Plainsong and Medieval Music* 2 (1993): 103–40.
———. "*Le Voir Dit* and *La Messe de Nostre Dame:* Aspects of Genre and Style in Late Works of Machaut." *Plainsong and Medieval Music* 2 (1993): 43–73.
———. "Written and Improvised Polyphony." In *Polyphonies de tradition orale, histoire et traditions vivantes,* edited by C. Meyer, 170–82. *Actes du colloque de Royaumont–1990.* Paris: Éditions Créaphis, 1993.
Levitan, William. "Dancing at the End of the Rope: Optatian and the Field of Roman Verse." *Transactions of the American Philosophical Association* 115 (1985): 245–69.
Levy, Kenneth. "Charlemagne's Archetype of Gregorian Chant." *Journal of the American Musicological Society* 40 (1987): 1–40.
———. *Gregorian Chant and the Carolingians.* Princeton: Princeton University Press, 1998.
Lord, Albert. *The Singer of Tales.* Cambridge, MA: Harvard University Press, 1960.
Lowinsky, Edward E. "Musical Genius—Evolution and Origins of a Concept." *Musical Quarterly* 50 (1964): 321–40, 476–95.
Ludwig, Friedrich. *Die älteren Musikwerke der von Gustav Jacobsthal begründeten Bibliothek des "Akademischen Gesang-Vereins" Strassburg.* Strassburg: Heitz, 1913.
———. *Die Aufgaben der Forschung auf dem Gebiet der mittelalterlichen Musikgeschichte = Beilage zur Allgemeinen Zeitung* (Munich), 12 (January 17, 1906): 97–99, and 14 (January 18, 1906): 107–9. Translated by John Haines, in "Friedrich Ludwig's 'Musicology of the Future': A Commentary and Translation." *Plainsong and Medieval Music* 12 (2003): 129–64.
———. "Beethovens Skizzen." *Göttinger Zeitung* (December 12, 1920).
———. *Die Erforschung der Musik des Mittelalters. Festrede im Namen der Georg-August-Universität am 4. Juni 1930.* Göttingen: Dieterichsche Universitäts-Buchdruckerei, W. Fr. Kaestner, 1930.

———. "Die 50 Beispiele Coussemakers aus der Handschrift von Montpellier." *Sammelbände der internationalen Musikgesellschaft* 5 (1903–4): 177–224.

———. "Die geistliche nichtliturgische/weltliche einstimmige und die mehrstimmige Musik des Mittelalters bis zum Anfang des 15. Jahrhunderts." In *Handbuch der Musikgeschichte,* edited by Guido Adler, 157–295. 2nd ed. Berlin: Keller, 1930. Repr. Tutzing: Schneider, 1961.

———. "Gustav Jacobsthal." *Zeitschrift der internationalen Musikgesellschaft* 3 (1912): 67–70.

———. "Die liturgischen Organa Leonins und Perotins." In *Riemann Festschrift: Gesammelte Studien. Hugo Riemann zum sechzigsten Geburtstag überreicht von Freunden und Schülern,* 200–13. Leipzig: Max Hesse Verlag, 1909.

———. "Die mehrstimmige Messe des 14. Jahrhunderts." *Archiv für Musikwissenschaft* 7 (1925): 417–35.

———. "Die mehrstimmige Musik des 14. Jahrhunderts." *Sammelbände der internationalen Musikgesellschaft* 4 (1902–3): 16–69.

———. "Ein mehrstimmiges St. Jakobs-Offizium des 12. Jahrhunderts." *Kirchenmusikalisches Jahrbuch* 19 (1905): 10–16.

———. "Musik des Mittelalters in der Badischen Kunsthalle Karlsruhe, 24.-26. September, 1922." *Zeitschrift für Musikwissenschaft* 5 (1922–23), 434–60.

———. "Perotinus Magnus." *Archiv für Musikwissenschaft* 3 (1921): 361–70.

———. "Die Quellen der Motetten ältesten Stils." *Archiv für Musikwissenschaft* 5 (1923): 184–222 and 273–315. Repr. in *Repertorium organorum recentioris et motetorum vetustissimi stili,* vol. 1, pt. 2, edited by Friedrich Gennrich. Summa musicae medii aevi, vol. 7. Langen bei Frankfurt, 1961.

———. *Repertorium organorum recentioris et motetorum vetustissimi stili,* vol. 1: *Catalogue raisonné der Quellen.* Pt. 1: *Handschriften in Quadrat-Notation.* Halle: M. Niemeyer, 1910. Repr., edited by Luther Dittmer. New York: Institute of Mediaeval Music, and Hildesheim: Georg Olms, 1964. Pt. 2: *Handschriften in Mensuralnotation,* edited by Friedrich Gennrich. Summa musicae medii aevi, vol. 7. Langen bei Frankfurt, 1961.

———. Review of Johannes Wolf, *Geschichte der Mensuralnotation von 1250–1460.* In *Sammelbände der internationalen Musikgesellschaft* 6 (1904–5): 597–641.

———. "Studien über die Geschichte der mehrstimmigen Musik im Mittelalter." *Sammelbände der internationalen Musikgesellschaft* 5 (1903–4): 177–224.

———. "Über den Entstehungsort der grossen 'Notre Dame-Handschriften.'" In *Festschrift für Guido Adler zum 75. Geburtstag,* 45–49. Vienna: Universal Edition, 1930.

———. "Über die Entstehung und die erste Entwicklung der lateinischen und französischen Motette in musikalischer Beziehung." *Sammelbände der internationalen Musikgesellschaft* 7 (1905–6): 514–28.

———. *Untersuchungen über die Reise- und Marschgeschwindigkeit im XII. und XIII. Jahrhundert.* Berlin: Mittler, 1897.

———. "Zur 'modalen Interpretation' von Melodien des 12. und 13. Jahrhunderts." *Zeitschrift der internationalen Musikgesellschaft* 11 (1910): 379–82.

Luria, A. R. *The Working Brain: An Introduction to Neuropsychology.* London: Allen Lane, 1973.

Lütteken, Laurenz. "Heinrich Besselers musikhistoriographischer Ansatz." In *Musikwissenschaft—eine verspätete Disziplin? Die akademische Musikforschung zwischen Fortschrittsglauben und Modernitätsverweigerung*, edited by Anselm Gerhard, 213–32. Stuttgart: J. B. Metzler, 2000.

Malamud, Martha A. *A Poetics of Transformation: Prudentius and Classical Mythology*. Ithaca: Cornell University Press, 1989.

Manitius, Max. *Geschichte der lateinischen Literatur des Mittelalters*. Vol. 3: *Vom Ausbruch des Kirchenstreites bis zum Ende des zwölften Jahrhunderts*. Handbuch der klassischen Altertumswissenschaft, edited by W. Otto. Munich: C. H. Beck, 1931.

Martin, Henri-Jean. *The History and Power of Writing*. Translated by Lydia G. Cochrane. Chicago: University of Chicago Press, 1994.

McGee, Timothy J. *The Sound of Medieval Song: Ornamentation and Vocal Style according to the Treatises*. Oxford: Clarendon Press, 1998.

Meier, Bernhard. "The Musica Reservata of Adrianus Petit Coclico and its Relationship to Josquin." *Musica disciplina* 10 (1956): 67–106.

Merkley, Paul. *Italian Tonaries*. Ottawa: The Institute of Mediaeval Music, 1988.

Messer, August. *Geschichte der Pädagogik. Erster Teil: Altertum und Mittelalter*. Breslau: Hirt, 1931.

Moll, Kevin. "Structural Determinants in Polyphony for the Mass Ordinary from French and Related Sources (ca. 1320–1410)." Ph.D. diss., Stanford University, 1994.

Möller, Hartmut. "Die Metzer Schola Cantorum, Amalar und das Offizium." In *Die Musik des Mittelalters*, edited by Hartmut Möller and Rudolf Stephan, 174–84. In *Neues Handbuch der Musikwissenschaft*, vol. 2. N.p., 1991.

Moss, Ann. *Printed Commonplace-Books*. Oxford: Clarendon Press, 1996.

Müller-Blattau, Joseph. *Nachruf auf Ludwig*. Kassel: Bärenreiter, 1930.

Munk Olsen, Birger. "Les classiques latins dans les florilèges médiévaux antérieurs au XIIIe siècle." *Revue d'histoire des textes* 9 (1979): 47–121; 10 (1980): 115–64.

———. *L'étude des auteurs classiques latins aux XIe et XIIe siècles*. Vol. 1: *Catalogue des manuscrits classiques latins copiés du IXe au XIIe siècle*. Paris: Éditions du Centre national de la recherche scientifique, 1982.

Newes, Virginia. "Writing, Reading, and Memorizing: The Transmission and Resolution of Retrograde Canons from the 14th and Early 15th Centuries." *Early Music* 18 (1990): 218–32.

Norberg, Dag. *An Introduction to the Study of Medieval Latin Versification*. Translated by Grant C. Roti and Jacqueline de la Chapelle Skubly. Washington, DC: The Catholic University Press of America, 2004.

Nowak, Adolf. "Johannes Eccards Ernennung zum preußischen Palestrina durch Obertribunalrat von Winterfeld." In *Studien zur Musikgeschichte Berlins im frühen 19. Jahrhundert*, edited by Carl Dahlhaus, 293–300. Regensburg: Gustav Bosse, 1980.

Oesch, Hans. *Berno und Hermann von Reichenau als Musiktheoretiker*. Bern: P. Haupt, 1961.

———. "Handschin, Jacques Samuel." *MGG* 5:1440–43.

———, ed. *Gedenkschrift Jacques Handschin: Aufsätze und Bibliographie*. Bern: P. Haupt, 1957.

Oesch, Hans, and Janna Kniazeva. "Handschin, Jacques." *New Grove Online,* accessed October 5, 2003.

Ong, Walter J. *Orality and Literacy: The Technologizing of the Word.* London: Methuen, 1982.

Opland, Jeff. *Xhosa Oral Poetry: Aspects of a Black South African Tradition.* Cambridge: Cambridge University Press, 1983.

Owens, Jessie Ann. *Composers at Work: The Craft of Musical Composition, 1450–1600.* New York and Oxford: Oxford University Press, 1997.

———. "The Milan Partbooks: Evidence of Cipriano de Rore's Compositional Process." *Journal of the American Musicological Society* 37 (1984): 270–98.

Pabst, Bernhard. *Prosimetrum: Tradition und Wandel einer Literaturform zwischen Spätantike und Spätmittelalter.* Ordo, vol. 4, nos. 1–2. Cologne: Böhlau, 1994.

Page, Christopher. *Discarding Images: Reflections on Music and Culture in Medieval France.* Oxford: Clarendon Press, 1993.

———. *Latin Poetry and Conductus Rhythm in Medieval France.* Royal Musical Association Monographs, no. 8. London: Royal Musical Association, 1997.

Palisca, Claude V. "Guido of Arezzo." *New Grove Online,* accessed October 5, 2003.

———. "Kontrapunkt." *MGG* 7:1521–55.

Parkes, Malcolm B. "The Influence of the Concepts of *Ordinatio* and *Compilatio* on the Development of the Book." In *Medieval Learning and Literature: Essays Presented to Richard William Hunt,* edited by J. J. G. Alexander and M. T. Gibson, 115–41. Oxford: Clarendon Press, 1976.

Parry, Adam. "Have We Homer's Iliad?" *Yale Classical Studies* 20 (1966): 177–216.

Payne, Thomas B. "Poetry, Politics, and Polyphony: Philip the Chancelor's Contribution to the Music of Notre Dame School." Ph.D. diss., University of Chicago, 1991.

Pesenti, Mauro, Lauro Zago, Fabrice Crivello, Emmanuel Mellet, Dana Samson, Bruno Duroux, Xavier Seron, Bernard Mazoyer, and Nathalie Tzourio-Mazoyer. "Mental Calculation." *Nature Neuroscience* 4 (2001): 103–7.

Pinegar, Sandra. "Exploring the Margins: A Second Source for Anonymous 7." *Journal of Musicological Research* 12 (1993): 213–43.

———. "A 'New Philology' for Medieval Theory." Paper presented at the American Musicological Society, Chicago, October 1991.

Plumley, Yolanda. "Ciconia's *Sus une fontayne* and the Legacy of Philipoctus de Caserta." In *Ciconia, musicien de la transition,* ed. Philippe Vendrix, 131–68. Turnhout: Brepols, 2003.

———. "Citation and Allusion in the Late *Ars nova:* The Case of *Esperance* and the *En attendant* Songs." *Early Music History* 18 (1999): 287–363.

———. "Intertextuality in the Fourteenth-Century Chanson." *Music & Letters* 84 (2003): 355–77.

Powers, Harold. "Language Models and Musical Analysis." *Ethnomusicology* 24 (1980): 1–60.

Powers, Harold, and Frans Wiering. "Mode." *New Grove Online,* accessed October 5, 2003).

Rausch, Alexander. *Die Musiktraktate des Abtes Bern von Reichenau.* Tutzing: Schneider, 1999.

Reaney, Gilbert. "A Postscript to Philippe de Vitry's *Ars Nova.*" *Musica disciplina* 14 (1960): 29–32.

Reckow, Fritz. "Diapason-diocto-octava." In *Handwörterbuch der musikalischen Terminologie,* edited by H. H. Eggebrecht. Wiesbaden: Steiner, 1979.
———. "Das Organum." In *Gattungen der Musik in Einzeldarstellungen: Gedenkschrift Leo Schrade,* edited by Wulf Arlt, 434–96. Bern: Francke, 1973.
Reichardt, Johann Friedrich. *Musikalisches Kunstmagazin* 2 (1791).
———. *Berlinische Musikzeitung* 1 (1805).
Reynolds, Christopher. *Papal Patronage and the Music of St. Peter's, 1380–1513.* Berkeley: University of California Press, 1995.
Reynolds, Suzanne. *Medieval Reading: Grammar, Rhetoric, and the Classical Text.* Cambridge: Cambridge University Press, 1996.
Riché, Pierre. "Apprendre à lire et à écrire dans le haut Moyen Age." *Bulletin de la Société Nationale des Antiquaires de France* (1978–79): 193–203.
———. *Education and Culture in the Barbarian West, Sixth through Eighth Centuries.* Translated by John J. Contreni. Columbia, SC: University of South Carolina Press, 1976.
———. "Le rôle de la mémoire dans l'enseignement médiéval." In *Jeux de mémoire: aspects de la mnémotechnique médiévale,* edited by Bruno Roy and Paul Zumthor, 133–48. Montreal: Presses de l'Université de Montréal, 1985.
Roesner, Edward H. "The Emergence of Musica mensurabilis." In *Studies in Musical Sources and Style: Festschrift for Jan LaRue,* edited by Edward H. Roesner, 41–74. Madison: A-R Editions, 1990.
———. "Johannes de Garlandia on *organum in speciali.*" *Early Music History* 2 (1982): 129–60.
———. "The Origins of W_1." *Journal of the American Musicological Society* 29 (1976): 337–80.
———. "The Problem of Chronology in the Transmission of Organum Duplum." In *Music in Medieval and Early Modern Europe,* edited by Iain Fenlon, 365–99. Cambridge: Cambridge University Press, 1981.
———. "Who 'Made' the *Magnus liber?*" *Early Music History* 20 (2001): 227–66.
Rossi, Paolo. *Clavis universalis: arti mnemoniche e logica combinatoria da Lullo a Leibnitz.* Milan: Ricciardi, 1960. Translated by Stephen Clucas as *Logic and the Art of Memory: The Quest for a Universal Language.* Chicago: University of Chicago Press, 2000.
Rouse, Richard Hunter, and Mary Ames Rouse. "The *Florilegium Angelicum:* Its Origin, Content, and Influence." In *Medieval Learning and Literature: Essays Presented to Richard William Hunt,* edited by J. J. G. Alexander and M. T. Gibson, 66–114. Oxford: Clarendon Press, 1976. Reprinted in Mary A. Rouse and Richard H. Rouse. *Authentic Witnesses: Approaches to Medieval Texts and Manuscripts,* 101–52. Notre Dame, IN: University of Notre Dame Press, 1991. (Page references are to the 1976 edition.)
———. "*Statim invenire:* Schools, Preachers, and New Attitudes to the Page." In *Renaissance and Renewal in the Twelfth Century,* edited by Robert L. Benson and Giles Constable, 201–25. Cambridge: Cambridge University Press, 1982. Reprinted in *Authentic Witnesses,* 191–219. (Page references are to the 1982 edition.)
Sachs, Klaus-Jürgen. "Arten improvisierter Mehrstimmigkeit nach Lehrtexten des 14. bis 16. Jahrhunderts." *Basler Jahrbuch für historische Musikpraxis* 7 (1983): 166–83.
———. *Der Contrapunctus im 14. und 15. Jahrhundert: Untersuchungen zum Terminus, zur Lehre und zu den Quellen.* Wiesbaden: Franz Steiner, 1974.
———. "Counterpoint." *New Grove Online,* accessed October 5, 2003.
Salmen, Walter. "Johann Friedrich Reichardt." *MGG* 11:151–61.

———. *Johann Friedrich Reichardt: Komponist, Schriftsteller, Kapellmeister und Verwaltungsbeamter der Goethezeit.* Freiburg: Atlantis Verlag, 1963.

Sanders, Ernest. "Conductus and Modal Rhythm." *Journal of the American Musicological Society* 38 (1985): 439–69.

———. "The Question of Perotin's Oeuvre and Dates." In *Festschrift für Walter Wiora zum 30. Dezember 1966,* edited by Ludwig Finscher and Christoph-Hellmut Mahling, 241–49. Kassel: Bärenreiter, 1967.

Sanders, Ernest, and Peter M. Lefferts. "Discant." *New Grove Online,* accessed October 5, 2003.

———. "Motet." *New Grove Online,* accessed October 5, 2003.

Sasse, Dietrich. "Bellermann, Heinrich." *MGG* 1:1608–10.

Scattolin, Pier Paolo. "La regola del *grado* nella teoria medievale del contrappunto." *Rivista italiana di musicologia* 14 (1979): 11–74.

Schick, Hartmut. "Musik wird zum Kunstwerk: Leonin und die Organa des Vatikanischen Organumtraktats." In *Studien zur Musikgeschichte: Eine Festschrift für Ludwig Finscher,* edited by Annegrit Laubenthal, 34–43. Kassel: Bärenreiter, 1995.

Schmidt, Helmut. "Zur Melodiebildung Leonins und Perotins." *Zeitschrift für Musikwissenschaft* 14 (1931–32): 129–34.

Schubert, Peter. "Counterpoint Pedagogy in the Renaissance." In *The Cambridge History of Western Music Theory,* edited by Thomas Christensen, 503–53. Cambridge: Cambridge University Press, 2002.

Schweitzer, Albert. *Out of My Life and Thought: An Autobiography.* Translated by C. T. Campion. New York: Henry Holt, 1933.

Scott, Ann Besser. "The Beginnings of Fauxbourdon: A New Interpretation." *Journal of the American Musicological Society* 24 (1971): 345–63.

Seebass, Tilman. *Musikdarstellung und Psalterillustration im früheren Mittelalter: Studien ausgehend von einer Ikonologie der Handschrift Paris Bibliothèque Nationale, fonds Latin 1118.* Bern: Francke Verlag, 1973.

Sherman, Claire Richter. *Writing on Hands: Memory and Knowledge in Early Modern Europe.* Dickinson College, Carlisle, PA: The Trout Gallery, 2000.

Small, Jocelyn Penny. *Wax Tablets of the Mind: Cognitive Studies of Memory and Literacy in Classical Antiquity.* London: Routledge, 1997.

Smith, Darwin. "Arnoul Greban." *MGG*² 7:1541–45.

Smith, D. E. *History of Mathematics.* 2 vols. Boston: Ginn, 1923–25. Repr. New York: Dover, 1951.

Smits van Waesberghe, Joseph. *De musico-paedagogico et theoretico Guidone Aretino eiusque vita et moribus.* Florence: L. S. Olschki, 1953.

———. "Einige Regeln der lateinischen rhythmischen Prosa in mittelalterlichen Traktaten." In *Musica scientiae collectanea: Festschrift Karl Gustav Fellerer zum siebzigsten Geburtstag,* edited by Heinrich Hüschen, 577–89. Cologne: Arno Volk Verlag, 1973.

———. *Musikerziehung: Lehre und Theorie der Musik im Mittelalter.* Musikgeschichte in Bildern, no. 3, pt. 3. Leipzig: Deutscher Verlag für Musik, 1969.

———. *School en muziek in de Middeleeuwen: De muziekdidactiek van de vroege Middeleeuwen.* Amsterdam: Uitgeversmaatschappij Holland, 1949.

Snyder, Jane. *Puns and Poetry in Lucretius' "De Rerum Natura."* Amsterdam: B. Gruner, 1980.

Sowa, Heinrich. *Quellen zur Transformation der Antiphonen: Tonar- und Rhythmusstudien.* Kassel: Bärenreiter, 1935.

Stengel, Theo, and Herbert Gerigk, eds. *Lexikon der Juden in der Musik.* Berlin: Bernhard Hahnefeld Verlag, 1941.

Stenzl, Jürg. "Perotinus Magnus. Und die Musikforschung erschuf den ersten Komponisten." In *Perotinus Magnus.* Musikkonzepte, no. 117. Edited by Jürg Stenzl, 19–52. Munich: Richard Boorberg, 2000.

Stone, Anne. "The Composer's Voice in the Late Fourteenth-Century Song: Four Case Studies." In *Ciconia, musicien de la transition,* edited by Philippe Vendrix, 169–94. Turnhout: Brepols, 2003.

———. "Music Writing and Poetic Voice in Machaut: Some Remarks on B12 and R14." In *Machaut's Music: New Interpretations,* edited by Elizabeth Eva Leach, 125–38. Woodbridge, Suffolk: Boydell Press, 2003.

———. "A Singer at the Fountain: Homage and Irony in Ciconia's 'Sus une fontayne.'" *Music & Letters* 83 (2001): 361–90.

Strohm, Reinhard. "The Close of the Middle Ages." In *Antiquity and the Middle Ages: From Ancient Greece to the 15th Century,* edited by James McKinnon, 269–312. Englewood Cliffs, NJ: Prentice Hall, 1990.

———. *Music in Late Medieval Bruges.* Oxford: Clarendon Press, 1985.

———. *The Rise of European Music, 1380–1500.* Cambridge: Cambridge University Press, 1993.

Strunk, Oliver, ed. *Source Readings in Music History.* Revised edition by Leo Treitler. New York: Norton, 1998.

Taruskin, Richard. "On Letting the Music Speak for Itself." *Journal of Musicology* 1 (1982): 338–49.

———. *Text and Act: Essays on Music and Performance.* New York: Oxford University Press, 1995.

Taylor, Barry. "Medieval Proverb Collections: The West European Tradition." *Journal of the Warburg and Courtauld Institutes* 55 (1992): 19–35.

Thibaut, Anton Friedrich Justus. *Über die Reinheit der Tonkunst.* 2nd ed. Edited by Raimund Heuler (includes 1st ed. [1824] and 2nd ed. [1826]). Paderborn: Ferdinand Schöningh, 1907.

Thompson, J. W., et al. *The Medieval Library.* University of Chicago Studies in Library Science. Chicago: University of Chicago Press, 1939.

Thorndike, Lynn. "*Unde versus.*" *Traditio: Studies in Ancient and Medieval History, Thought and Religion* 11 (1955): 163–93.

Tischler, Hans. "The Early Cantors of Notre Dame." *Journal of the American Musicological Society* 19 (1966): 85–87.

———. "The Evolution of the *Magnus liber organi.*" *Musical Quarterly* 70 (1984): 163–74.

———. "Perotinus Revisited." In *Aspects of Medieval and Renaissance Music: A Birthday Offering to Gustave Reese,* edited by Jan LaRue, 803–17. New York: Norton, 1966.

———. "The Structure of Notre-Dame Organa." *Acta musicologica* 49 (1977): 193–99.

Treitler, Leo. "Centonate Chant: *Übles Flickwerk* or *E pluribus unus.*" *Journal of the American Musicological Society* 28 (1975): 1–23.

———. "The Early History of Music Writing in the West." *Journal of the American Musicological Society* 35 (1982): 237–79.

———. "Homer and Gregory: The Transmission of Epic Poetry and Plainchant." *Musical Quarterly* 60 (1974): 333–72.

———. "Oral, Written, and Literate Process in the Transmission of Medieval Music." *Speculum* 56 (1981): 471–91.

———. "Regarding Meter and Rhythm in the *Ars antiqua*." *Musical Quarterly* 65 (1979): 524–58.

———. "The 'Unwritten' and 'Written Transmission' of Medieval Chant and the Start-up of Musical Notation." *Journal of Musicology* 10 (1992): 131–91.

———. "Der vatikanische Organumtraktat und das Organum von Notre Dame de Paris: Perspektiven der Entwicklung einer schriftlichen Musikkultur in Europa," *Basler Jahrbuch für historische Musikpraxis* 7 (1983): 23–31.

———. *With Voice and Pen: Coming to Know Medieval Song and How It Was Made.* Oxford and New York: Oxford University Press, 2003.

Tropfke, Johannes. *Geschichte der Elementarmathematik.* 4th ed. Berlin: Walter de Gruyter, 1980.

Trowell, Brian. "Faburden and Fauxbourdon." *Musica disciplina* 8 (1959): 43–78.

Urquhart, Peter. "Calculated to Please the Ear: Ockeghem's Canonic Legacy." *Tijdschrift van de Koninklijke Verenigung voor Nederlandse Muziekgeschiedenis* 47 (1997): 72–98.

Waite, William. *The Rhythm of Twelfth-Century Polyphony.* New Haven: Yale University Press, 1954.

Wegman, Rob C. "From Maker to Composer: Improvisation and Musical Authorship in the Low Countries." *Journal of the American Musicological Society* 49 (1996): 409–79.

Werf, Hendrik van der. "Anonymous IV as Chronicler." *Musicology Australia* 15 (1992): 3–13.

"Who Wants to be a Genius?" *The Economist* (January 13–19, 2001): 77–78.

Winterfeld, Carl von. *Der evangelische Kirchengesang.* Leipzig: Breitkopf und Härtel, 1843–47.

———. *Johannes Gabrieli und sein Zeitalter.* Berlin: Schlesinger, 1834.

———. *Johannes Pierluigi Palestrina.* Breslau: G. P. Anderholz, 1832.

Witzleben, Lawrence. *"Silk and Bamboo" Music in Shanghai: The Jiangnan Sizhu Instrumental Ensemble Tradition.* Kent, Ohio: Kent State University Press, 1995.

Wolf, Johannes. "Ein Beitrag zur Diskantlehre des 14. Jahrhunderts." *Sammelbände der Internationalen Musikgesellschaft* 15 (1913–14): 505–34.

———. "Florenz in der Musikgeschichte des 14. Jahrhunderts." *Sammelbände der internationalen Musikgesellschaft* 3 (1901–2): 599–646.

———. *Geschichte der Mensuralnotation von 1250 bis 1460.* 3 vols. Leipzig: Breitkopf & Härtel, 1904.

Wright, Craig. "Leoninus, Poet and Musician." *Journal of the American Musicological Society* 39 (1986): 1–35.

———. *Music and Ceremony at Notre Dame of Paris, 500–1550.* Cambridge: Cambridge University Press, 1989.

———. "Performance Practices at the Cathedral of Cambrai, 1475–1550." *Musical Quarterly* 64 (1978): 295–328.

Yates, Frances A. *The Art of Memory.* London: Routledge and Kegan Paul, 1966.

Yudkin, Jeremy. "The *Copula* according to Johannes de Garlandia." *Musica disciplina* 34 (1980): 67–84.

Zaminer, Frieder. *Der vatikanische Organum-Traktat (Ottob. lat. 3025).* Tutzing: Hans Schneider, 1959.

Ziolkowski, Jan. *Alan of Lille's Grammar of Sex: The Meaning of Grammar to a Twelfth-Century Intellectual.* Speculum Anniversary Monographs, no. 10. Cambridge, MA: The Medieval Academy, 1985.

———. "Cultural Diglossia and the Nature of Medieval Latin Literature." In *The Ballad and Oral Literature,* edited by Joseph Harris, 193–213. Harvard English Studies, no. 17. Cambridge, MA: Harvard University Press, 1991.

———. "Ernst Robert Curtius (1886–1956) and Medieval Latin Studies." *Journal of Medieval Latin* 7 (1997): 147–67.

———. "The Prosimetrum in the Classical Tradition." In *Prosimetrum: Cross-Cultural Perspectives on Narrative in Prose and Verse,* edited by Joseph Harris and Karl Reichl, 45–65. Cambridge: Brewer, 1997.

———. *Nota bene: Reading Classics and Writing Songs in the Early Middle Ages.* Forthcoming in Publications of the *Journal of Medieval Latin.* Turnhout: Brepols.

———, ed. and trans. *The Cambridge Songs, Carmina Cantabrigiensia.* New York: Garland, 1994.

INDEX

Compositor: Integrated Composition Systems
Indexer: Bonnie Blackburn
Music Engraver: Rolf W. Wulfsberg
Text: 10/12 Baskerville
Display: Baskerville
Printer/Binder: Edwards Brothers, Inc.